Linux®
FOR
DUMMIES®
7TH EDITION

Linux® FOR DUMMIES® 7TH EDITION

by Dee-Ann LeBlanc

Wiley Publishing, Inc.

Linux® For Dummies®, 7th Edition

Published by
Wiley Publishing, Inc.
111 River Street
Hoboken, NJ 07030-5774
www.wiley.com

For general information on our other products and services, please contact our Customer Care Department within the U.S. at 800-762-2974, outside the U.S. at 317-572-3993, or fax 317-572-4002.

For technical support, please visit www.wiley.com/techsupport.

Wiley also publishes its books in a variety of electronic formats. Some content that appears in print may not be available in electronic books.

Library of Congress Control Number: 2006920624

ISBN-13: 978-0-471-75282-0

ISBN-10: 0-471-75282-7

Manufactured in the United States of America

10 9 8 7 6 5 4 3 2 1

7B/QU/QV/QW/IN

WILEY

About the Author

Dee-Ann LeBlanc, RHCE (Red Hat Certified Engineer), is a writer, course developer, journalist, and trainer who specializes in Linux. While these various professions may sound scattered, they in fact reinforce one another by allowing her to see what people are doing with Linux in the real world and where they need help. She is the Linux Games editor for the *Linux Journal*, the Desktop editor for *LinuxToday.com,* and is the author of numerous books on Linux and other computer topics. Dee-Ann has also been a regular contributor to *Computer Power User* magazine for two years, writing this publication's Linux content.

When Dee-Ann isn't teaching, developing course materials, writing technical nonfiction or fantasy fiction, interviewing interesting people, chatting about Linux online or at conferences, or trying in one way or another to save the world, she hikes with her dogs and experiments on her husband Rob with new recipes. See the latest that Dee-Ann's up to and join her readers' mailing list at www.Dee-AnnLeBlanc.com and http://dee-ann.blog-city.com/. (Contact Dee-Ann at dee@renaissoft.com.)

Dedication

I continue to dedicate this book to my husband, who always has to listen to my stressed whining when I'm running behind, and my dogs, who really would like their mom to stop staring at the glowing box once in a while.

Author's Acknowledgments

I, as usual, have lots of people I'd like to thank. First off, thanks to the folks without whom the earlier editions of this book would have never existed. For one, there's John "maddog" Hall for giving me the opportunity to take over this book's evolution. He was too busy leading Compaq's UNIX Software Group, acting as Executive Director for Linux International, and sitting on the board of advisors for Sair Linux/GNU certification to continue handling this project. There's also the folks at LANWrights for all their hard work, along with Melanie Hoag and Evan Blomquist for their strong efforts. Finally, of course, to the editors and staff at Wiley Publishing, Inc. Without them and their guidance, this book would not exist or continue to improve over time.

Most of all, I'd like to thank the readers who contacted me with their questions, suggestions, and concerns. I apologize to anyone who got lost in the great deluges of e-mail and didn't get an answer, but please trust that, at the very least, when I dug your e-mail out from the pile three months later, I filed it away as one more thing to consider in the next edition. It's reader participation that keeps books like this improving over the years, and it's my goal to continue refining *Linux For Dummies* to keep it the best desktop Linux book available.

Publisher's Acknowledgments

We're proud of this book; please send us your comments through our online registration form located at www.dummies.com/register/.

Some of the people who helped bring this book to market include the following:

Acquisitions, Editorial, and Media Development

Project Editor: Blair J. Pottenger

Acquisitions Editors: Terri Varveris, Tiffany Ma

Senior Copy Editor: Barry Childs-Helton

Technical Editor: Bryan Hoff

Editorial Manager: Kevin Kirschner

Media Development Specialist: Kit Malone

Media Development Manager: Laura Carpenter VanWinkle

Media Development Supervisor: Laura Moss

Editorial Assistant: Amanda Foxworth

Cartoons: Rich Tennant (www.the5thwave.com)

Composition

Project Coordinator: Michael Kruzil

Layout and Graphics: Carl Byers, Andrea Dahl, Lauren Goddard, Denny Hager, Stephanie D. Jumper, Barbara Moore, Julie Trippetti

Proofreaders: Jessica Kramer, Techbooks

Indexer: Techbooks

Publishing and Editorial for Technology Dummies

Richard Swadley, Vice President and Executive Group Publisher

Andy Cummings, Vice President and Publisher

Mary Bednarek, Executive Acquisitions Director

Mary C. Corder, Editorial Director

Publishing for Consumer Dummies

Diane Graves Steele, Vice President and Publisher

Joyce Pepple, Acquisitions Director

Composition Services

Gerry Fahey, Vice President of Production Services

Debbie Stailey, Director of Composition Services

Contents at a Glance

Table of Contents

Introduction

*W*elcome to the fascinating world of open source software that is Linux. In this book, I introduce you to the wonders of the Linux operating system, originally created as a labor of love by Linus Torvalds in the early 1990s. My goal is to initiate you into the rapidly growing ranks of Linux users and enthusiasts busily rewriting the rules for the operating system marketplace.

If you've contemplated switching to Linux but find the prospect too forbidding, you can relax. If you can boil water or set your alarm clock, you, too, can become a Linux user. (No kidding!)

When this book appeared in its first edition, Linux was an emerging phenomenon that was neither terribly well known nor understood. In this edition — for a new generation of Linux users — so much material is available that I have steered this particular title toward what Linux is and how you can make the best use of it on your desktop. To that end, these pages contain various online resources, tips, and tricks, as well as more general instruction. If you're looking for material on servers, *Linux All-in-One Desk Reference For Dummies* (Wiley Publishing, Inc.) can serve your needs.

I keep the amount of technobabble to a minimum and stick with plain English as much as possible. Besides plain talk about Linux installation, boot-up, configuration, and software, I include many examples, plus lots of detailed instructions to help you set up and use your very own Linux machine with a minimum of stress or confusion.

I also include with this book a handy DVD-ROM that contains Fedora Core 5 and Knoppix, along with the CD-ROM *images* (the files you use to burn your own CDs) for Linspire, Mandriva, SuSE, and Xandros. (To find out what exactly is included on the DVD-ROM, see Appendix B.) Ubuntu is also covered, but there wasn't enough room on the DVD for it so instructions are included in Chapter 4 on how to download this distribution yourself. If you have no idea of what I'm talking about, don't worry. You'll know soon enough!

About This Book

Think of this book as a friendly, approachable guide to tackling terminology and the Linux collection of tools, utilities, and widgets. Although Linux isn't terribly hard to figure out, it does pack a boatload of details, parameters, and *administrivia* (administrative trivia, in Unixspeak). You need to wrestle those details into shape while you install, configure, manage, and troubleshoot a

Linux-based computer. Some sample topics you find in this book include the following:

- ✔ Understanding where Linux comes from and what it can do for you
- ✔ Installing the Linux operating system
- ✔ Working with a Linux system to manage files and add software
- ✔ Setting up Internet access and surfing the Web
- ✔ Customizing your Linux system
- ✔ Managing Linux system security and resources

Although it may seem, at first glance, that working with Linux requires years of hands-on experience, tons of trial and error, advanced computer science training, and intense dedication, take heart! It's not true! If you can tell somebody how to find your office, you can certainly build a Linux system that does what you want. The purpose of this book isn't to turn you into a full-blown Linux geek (that's the ultimate state of Linux enlightenment, of course); it's to show you the ins and outs that you need to master in order to build a smoothly functioning Linux system and to give you the know-how and confidence to use it.

How to Use This Book

This book tells you how to install, configure, and customize a Linux desktop system. Although you can do most things in Linux these days by pointing and clicking, you still may want to try using Linux at the command prompt — where you type detailed instructions to load or configure software, access files, and do other tasks. In this book, input appears in monospace type like this:

```
rmdir /etc/bin/devone
```

When you type Linux commands or other related information, be sure to copy the information exactly as you see it in the book, including uppercase and lowercase letters, because that's part of the magic that makes Linux behave properly.

A failure to follow instructions exactly can have all kinds of unfortunate, unseemly, or unexpected side effects.

The margins of a book don't give you the same amount of room as your computer screen; therefore, in this book some URLs and lengthy commands at the command prompt may appear wrapped to the next line. Remember that your computer sees these wrapped lines as a *single set of instructions,* or as a single URL — so if you're typing a hunk of text, keep it on a single line. Don't insert a hard return if you see one of these wrapped lines. I clue you in that it's supposed to be all one line by breaking the line at a slash mark or a natural word break (to imply "Wait — there's more!") and slightly indenting the over-age, as in the following silly example:

```
www.infocadabra.transylvania.com/nexus/plexus/lexus/
        praxis/okay/this/is/a/make-
        believe/URL/but/some/real/ones/
        are/SERIOUSLY/long.html
```

Note that as you dig your way into and through this book — and other sources of Linux wit, wisdom, and inspiration that you're likely to encounter — you may find some terms used interchangeably. For example, you may see the same piece of software called a *program*, a *command,* a *utility,* a *script,* an *application,* or a *tool,* depending on the source, the context, and the author of the information you're consulting. To a large extent, you can treat these terms as interchangeable, and when an important distinction needs to be made among them, I'm sure to point it out. Similarly, when you're working with various commands or configuration controls, you may also encounter terms such as *flag, switch, option,* or *parameter* used more or less interchangeably. In this case, all these terms refer to ways in which you can control, refine, or modify basic commands or programs to make them do what you want. Again, wherever distinctions and clarifications may be needed, I provide them.

Three Presumptuous Assumptions

They say that making assumptions makes a fool of the person who makes them and of the person about whom those assumptions are made. (And just who are *they,* anyway? I *assume* that I know, but — never mind.) Even so, practicality demands that I make a few assumptions about you, gentle reader:

- ✔ You can turn your computer on and off.
- ✔ You know how to use a mouse and a keyboard.
- ✔ You want to install, configure, and/or use a desktop Linux system because you're curious or interested or it's your job to do so.

You don't need to be a master logician or a wizard in the arcane art of programming to use this book, nor do you need a PhD in computer science. You don't even need a complete or perfect understanding of what's going on in your computer's innards.

If you have an active imagination and the ability to solve rudimentary problems, that's even better — you have already mastered the key ingredients necessary to making Linux work for you. The rest is mere details and a bit of patience. I can help you with the details, but the patience is up to you!

How This Book Is Organized

This book contains six major parts, arranged in an order to take you from Linux installation and configuration through keeping a Linux desktop system up and running, if not purring like a cat in the sun! Most parts contain three or more chapters or appendixes, and each chapter or appendix contains modular sections. Whenever you need help or information, pick up this book and start anywhere you like, or use the Table of Contents and the Index to locate specific topics or key words.

Following is a breakdown of the book's six parts and what you find in each one.

Part I: Getting Your Feet Wet

This part sets the stage and includes an overview of and introduction to the terms, techniques, and software components that make Linux the raging software tiger that's so ready, willing, and able to do its thing. To be a little more specific, I start out with a Linux overview that explains what Linux is, where it came from, and how it works. Next, I tackle the various tasks and activities involved in preparing for and installing Linux on a PC. If you're not a diehard Fedora Core fan, I also cover what's involved in installing Linspire, Mandriva, SuSE, Ubuntu, and Xandros, but in a little less detail (or this book would be the size of a set of encyclopedias!). After that, I tell you how to give Linux the boot — not to get rid of it by any means, but rather, to fire up your brand-new system to reach the heights of computing ecstasy (at least, I hope it's as good for you as it usually is for me). Finally, I help you explore standard Linux tools and interfaces, work with accounts, and get the skinny on various aspects of distribution-related Linux tools.

If you don't want to install but do want to try Linux, I also give you the option of using what's called a *LiveCD*, or *bootable* distribution. Knoppix is probably the most popular of these, so it's covered here as well.

Part II: Internet Now!

In this part, you explore the issues involved in connecting a Linux system to the Internet, including configuring a modem, managing a dialup connection to an Internet Service Provider (or ISP), and configuring the various Internet protocols involved to make your Internet connection work. You also go through the details involved in configuring and using a Web browser and setting up and using an e-mail client.

Part III: Getting Up to Speed with Linux

Linux includes a great many facilities and capabilities, so after you get past the initial installation and configuration, you probably want to use your system to *do* something. Here's where the doing begins! In this part of the book, you can read about the Linux file system and how to work with files, directories, and related access rights — called *permissions* in Linuxspeak. You discover how to move in, out, and around GNOME and KDE, the two major graphical interfaces (GUIs) in Linux. In addition, I include an in-depth exploration of the Linux command-prompt environments, also known as *shells.* Part III also contains important security information, along with how to add software to your system and keep it updated.

Part IV: Getting Things Done

In this part of the book, you discover how to use a variety of software available in Linux. Everything from plain text editors to full office suites is addressed, as well as whiz-bang multimedia tools and Microsoft Windows-based file formats and media. Even better, did you know that you can run many Windows programs under Linux? I show you how in this part.

Part V: The Part of Tens

In this book's grand climax, I sum up and distill the essence of what you now know about Linux and its inner workings. Here, you have a chance to revisit some key troubleshooting tips and tricks for Linux systems, along with learning two cool uses for Knoppix.

Part VI: Appendixes

This book ends with a set of appendixes designed to sum up and further expand on this book's contents. Appendix A delivers groups of Linux commands, complete with syntax and explanations, arranged according to their function. Appendix B lists details about what's on the *Linux For Dummies,* 7th Edition, DVD. As I note in this appendix, the materials on the DVD include the Fedora Core 5 distribution.

Icons Used in This Book

Within each chapter, I use icons to highlight particularly important or useful information. You find the following icons in this book:

The Tip icon flags useful information that makes living with your Linux system even less complicated than you feared that it might be.

I sometimes use this icon to point out information you just shouldn't pass by — don't overlook these gentle reminders. (The life, sanity, or page you save may be your own.)

Be cautious when you see this icon — it warns you of things you shouldn't do. This icon is meant to emphasize that the consequences of ignoring these bits of wisdom can be severe.

This icon signals technical details that are informative and interesting but not critical to understanding and using Linux. Skip these paragraphs if you want (but please come back and read them later).

Where to Go from Here

This is where you pick a direction and hit the road! *Linux For Dummies,* 7th Edition, is much like *1001 Nights* because it almost doesn't matter where you start out. You look at lots of different scenes and stories as you prepare yourself to build your own Linux system. Although each story has its own distinctive characters and plot, the whole is surely something to marvel at. Don't worry — you can handle it. Who cares whether anybody else thinks that you're just goofing around? I know that you're getting ready to have the time of your life.

Enjoy!

Part I

Getting Your Feet Wet

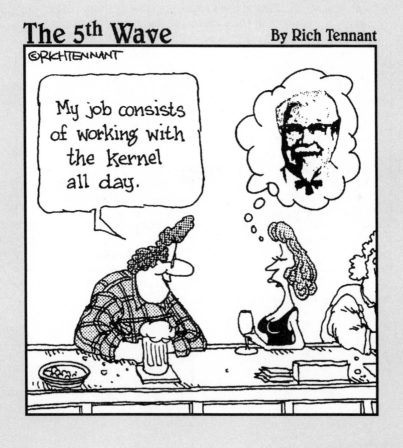

In this part . . .

This part includes an introduction to the development and capabilities of the Linux operating system. I also cover the terms and tools that make Linux what it is, along with detailed step-by-step instructions about what it takes to prepare your computer for Linux and to install Linux on your very own PC. For those interested in Linux distributions other than Fedora Core 5, which is included with this book, I also cover what's involved in installing four other popular distributions — namely, Linspire, Mandriva, SuSE, Ubuntu, and Xandros. I even explain how to configure this marvelous operating system to do what you want it to do and how to boot your brand-spanking-new system into a computing colossus — not to mention how to shut it off properly so that you don't lose any data. After that, you find out what's involved in working with standard Linux tools, the point-yand-click GUI, accounts, and printers, as well as get a quick tour of your distribution-related Linux tools.

Chapter 1

Getting Acquainted with Linux

• •

• •

Ford, you're turning into a penguin. Stop it!

— Arthur Dent

*W*elcome to the world of Linux, the operating system developed by over a thousand people around the world! In this chapter, you find out about Linux itself — what it is, where it comes from, and why it gets so much attention in the news these days. Prepare to have your assumptions about how software *must* be developed and sold challenged, and your mind opened to new possibilities.

Is Free Really Free?

Understanding Linux requires a radical shift of thought regarding the way that you acquire and use computer software. (***Note:*** By *radical,* I mean getting to the root of the matter, rather than putting on beads and camping out in the administration building.) Your first step toward shifting your mind-set is to alter your general connotation of the word *free* to represent *freedom,* rather than *free lunch.* That's right; you can sell "free" software for a fee . . . and you're encouraged to do so, as long as you relay the same freedom to each recipient of the software.

Don't scratch your head too hard; these concepts are tough to grasp initially, especially when you consider the conditioning you've received from the marketing departments of the commercial software industry. Perhaps you don't know that when you purchase most proprietary, shrink-wrapped software, you don't actually *own* the software; rather, you're granted permission to use the software within the bounds dictated by the licensor.

Linux also has a license, but the motives and purpose of the license are much different from those of most commercial software. Rather than use the license to protect ownership of the software, the GNU General Public License (GPL) that Linux is licensed under ensures that the software will always be open to anyone. No company can ever own or dictate the way in which you use or modify Linux — though they can have their own individual copyrights and trademarks on their various brands of it, like Red Hat. In essence, you already own Linux, and you can use it for anything you like, as long as you propagate the GPL freedoms to any further recipients of the software.

Linux: Revolution or Just Another Operating System?

> *Contrary to popular belief, penguins are not the salvation of modern technology. Neither do they throw parties for the urban proletariat.*
>
> — Anonymous

> ***Author note:*** *Cute quote . . . obviously Anonymous has never been to a Linux convention!*

Before going any farther into Linux, I need to get some terminology out of the way.

Tux is the formal name of the mascot penguin that represents Linux. Rumor has it that Linux's creator, Linus Torvalds, is rather fond of these well-dressed inhabitants of the Antarctic.

An *operating system* is the software that runs your computer, handling all interactions between you and the hardware. Whether you're writing a letter, calculating a budget, or managing your recipes on your computer, the operating system provides the essential air that your computer breathes. Furthermore, an operating system isn't just one program; it consists of hundreds of smaller programs and utilities that allow us humans to use a computer to do something useful. You then run other programs (such as your word processor) on top of the operating system to get everything done.

In recent technological history, Linux has evolved from water-cooler techie chatter to a rock-solid solution for the business enterprise. The same software that was once dismissed as rogue is now being adopted and promoted by industry leaders such as IBM, Hewlett-Packard, Motorola, and Intel. Each of these computer manufacturers has, in some way, determined that Linux provides value for their customers (as well as for their own operations). Of these companies, the only one that has publicly denounced Linux is Microsoft. Note that one doesn't have to look very far to conclude that Microsoft is merely running scared from the threat that Linux poses to its waning monopoly on personal-computer operating systems.

Linux has been accused of being "just another operating system." On the surface, it may appear so, but if you look deeper, you can see that this isn't so. The Linux project is a flagship leading the current trend toward open source and free (as in freedom, not free beer) software within the computing industry. A rock-solid operating system because of the model under which it was (and continues to be) developed, Linux represents much that is good and pure in software development.

Two fundamental distinctions separate Linux from the rest of the operating-system pack:

✔ Linux is licensed under the unique and ingenuous *GNU General Public License,* which you can read about in the next section.

✔ Linux is developed and maintained by a worldwide team of volunteer programmers, working together over the Internet.

Linux is great for many reasons, including the fact that the folks who built it from the ground up wanted it to be

✔ **Multiuser:** More than one user can be logged in to a single computer at one time.

✔ **Multiprocess:** True *preemptive multitasking* enables the operating system core to efficiently juggle several programs running at once. This is important for providing multiple services on one computer.

✔ **Multiplatform:** Linux currently runs on 24 *platforms* (hardware types), including Intel-based PCs, Digital/Compaq Alpha, PowerPC-based Apple Macintosh, Sun SPARC, Amiga, and StrongARM-based computers.

✔ **Interoperable:** Linux plays nice with most network protocols (languages) and operating systems, allowing you to interact with users and computers running Microsoft Windows, Unix, Novell, both Mac OS 9 and the generation beginning with OS X, and other, more niche groups.

✔ **Scalable:** As your computing needs grow, you can rely on Linux to grow with you. The same Linux operating system can run on a desktop computer or a very large, industrial strength server system.

✔ **Portable:** Linux is mostly written in the C programming language. *C* is a language created specifically for writing operating system-level software and can be readily *ported* (translated) to run on new computer hardware.

- **Flexible:** You can configure the Linux operating system as a network host, router, graphical workstation, office productivity PC, home entertainment computer, file server, Web server, cluster, or just about any other computing appliance that you can think of.

- **Stable:** The Linux *kernel* (the operating system) has achieved a level of maturity that makes most software developers envious. It's not uncommon to hear reports of Linux servers running for years without crashing.

- **Efficient:** The modular design of Linux enables you to include only the components needed to run your desired services. Even older Pentium computers can utilize Linux and become useful again.

- **Free!:** To most people, the most intriguing aspect of Linux is the fact that it's often available free of charge. How (the capitalists murmur) can anyone build a better mousetrap with no incentive of direct monetary return?

In this chapter, I intend to answer that last question for you. I also hope to paint a picture of the open source software development model that created Linux.

So where did Linux come from?

The quickest way to understand Linux is to take a peek at its rich heritage. Although programming of the Linux core started in 1991, the design concepts were based on the time-tested *Unix* operating system.

Unix was developed at Bell Telephone Laboratories in the late 1960s. The original architects of Unix created it back when there were few operating systems, with the desire to have one that shared data, programs, and resources both efficiently and securely — something that wasn't available then (and is still sought after now). From there, Unix evolved into many different versions; its current family tree is so complicated that it looks like a kudzu infestation!

In 1991, Linus Torvalds was a computer science student at the University of Helsinki in Finland. He wanted an operating system that was like the Unix system that he'd grown fond of at the university, but both Unix and the hardware it ran

on were prohibitively expensive. A Unix version called Minix was available for free, but it didn't quite meet his needs. So, as a computer science student, Torvalds studied Minix and then set out to write a new version himself. In his own words (recorded for posterity on the Internet, since this was in an early version of an online chat room), his work was "just a hobby, won't be big and professional like GNU."

Writing an operating system is no small task. Even after six months of hard work, Torvalds had made very little progress toward the general utility of the system. He posted what he had to the Internet — and found that many people shared his interest and curiosity. Before long, some of the brightest minds around the world were contributing to Linus's project by adding enhancements or fixing bugs (errors in the code).

Anatomy of an Open Source Software Project

Linux isn't a product. Linux is an organic part of a software ecosystem.

— Michael Robinson, *Netrinsics*

To the casual observer (and some corporate IT decision-makers), Linux appears to be a freak mutation — a rogue creature randomly generated by anarchy. How, after all, can something so complex and discipline-dependent as a computer operating system be developed by a loosely knit band of volunteer computer geeks from around the world?

Just as science is constantly attempting to classify and explain everything in existence, technology commentators are still trying to understand how the open source approach can create superior software, especially in cases where this is no charge. Often the reasons have much to do with the usual human desire to fill a need with a solution. When a programmer in the Linux world wants a tool, the programmer simply writes one — or bands together with other people who want a similar package, and they write it together.

GNU who?

Imagine — software created out of need rather than projected profit. Even though Unix ultimately became expensive proprietary software, the ideas and motives for its creation were originally based on practical needs. What people usually refer to (in the singular) as *the Linux operating system* is actually a collection of software tools that were created with the express purpose of solving specific computing problems.

Linux also wouldn't be possible without the vision of a man whom Steven Levy (author of the book *Hackers*) refers to as "The Last of the Great MIT AI-LAB Hackers" — in the original sense of the word *hacker,* (someone who plays with code), not the current popular meaning that implies criminal intent. This pioneer and advocate of *freedom* software is Richard Stallman.

The Massachusetts Institute of Technology (MIT) has long held a reputation for nurturing the greatest minds in the technological disciplines. In 1984, Stallman, a gifted student and brilliant programmer at MIT, was faced with a dilemma — sell his talent to a company for a tidy sum of money or donate his gifts to the world. He did what we'd all do . . . right?

Stallman set out on a journey to create a completely free operating system that he would donate to the world. He understands — and continues to live — the original hacker ethic, which declares that information wants to be free. This concept wasn't new in his time. In the early days of the computing industry, many advancements were made by freely sharing ideas and programming code. Manufacturer-sponsored user groups brought the best minds together to solve complicated problems. This ethic, Stallman felt, was lost when companies began to hoard software as their own intellectual property with the single purpose of profit.

As you may or may not have gathered by this point, widespread and accessible source code is paramount to successful software development. *Source code* is the term for the human-readable text (as opposed to the unreadable cyber-hieroglyphics in an "executable" file) that a programmer types to communicate instructions to the computer.

Writing computer programs in binary is an extremely arduous task. Modern computer software is usually written in a human-friendly language and then *compiled,* or translated, into the computer's native instruction set. To make changes to this software, a programmer needs access to a program's source code. Most proprietary software comes only as a precompiled product; the software developer keeps the source code for those programs under lock and key.

After determining that his operating system would be built around the conceptual framework of Unix, Stallman wanted the project name to distinguish his system from Unix. So, he chose the recursive acronym *GNU* (pronounced ga-*new*), which means GNU's Not Unix.

To finance the GNU project, Stallman organized the Free Software Foundation (FSF), which sold free (open source) software to help feed the programmers who worked on its continuing development. (Remember, we're talking *free* as in *free speech*, not *free beer*.) Although this organization and goal of creating a complete operating system was necessary and important, a much more important piece of the puzzle had to be put into place to protect this new software from big-business pirates — a concern still all too relevant today as a former Linux company tries to hijack ownership of decades of volunteer work from thousands of people around the world.

The *GNU General Public License* (GPL) is a unique and creative software license that uses copyright law to protect the freedom of the software user, which is usually the opposite of how a copyright works. Generally, a copyright is an enforceable designation of ownership and restriction from duplication by anyone but the copyright holder. When software is licensed under the GPL, recipients are bound by copyright law to respect the freedom of anyone else to use the software in any way they choose. Software licensed with the GPL is also known as copy*left* software (the reverse of right, get it?). Another way to remember the GPL is through its ultimate result: Guaranteed Public for Life.

Who's in charge of Linux anyway?

As an open source project evolves, various people emerge as leaders. This leader is often known as the project's *benevolent dictator*. A person who becomes benevolent dictator has probably spent more time than anyone else on a particular problem and often has some unique insight. Normally, the words *democratic* and *dictator* are never paired in the same sentence, but the open source model is a very democratic process that endorses the reign of a benevolent dictator.

Linus Torvalds is still considered the benevolent dictator of the Linux *kernel* (the operating system's core). He ultimately determines what features are added to the kernel and what features aren't. The community trusts his vision and discretion. In the event that he loses interest in the project, or the community decides that he has gone senile, a new leader will emerge from amongst the very competent people working with him.

Einstein was a volunteer

Someone who is a volunteer or donates time to a project isn't necessarily providing a second-rate effort (or only working on weekends and holidays). In fact, any human resources expert will tell you that people who choose to do a job of their own free will produce the highest quality products.

The volunteers who contribute to open source projects are often leaders in their fields who depend on community collaboration to get useful work done. The open source concept is no stranger to the scientific community. The impartial peer-review process that open source projects foster is critical in validating some new feature or capability as being technically correct.

Those who paint the open source community as copyright violators and thieves often misunderstand — or outright ignore — these vital issues. Open source programmers are very proud of their work *and* are also very concerned about their own copyrights, not wanting their work to be stolen by others — hence licenses such as the GPL. This concern creates an atmosphere with the greatest respect for copyright. Bandits who claim that they're "just being open source" when they steal other people's hard work are grossly misusing the term to soothe their own consciences.

Many have also pointed out that if copyright is violated in open source, it's easy to tell. Watch the news and notice how often large software corporations are convicted of stealing other people's code and incorporating it into their own work. If the final product is open source, it's easy for anyone to look and make sure nothing stolen is in it. As you might imagine, tracking down such copyright violations is much more difficult in a closed source scheme.

Packaging Linux: The Distribution

What people call a *Linux distribution* is actually the culmination of the GNU project's tools, the Linux kernel, and any number of other open source (and closed source) software projects that sprang up along the way.

Robert Young, cofounder and current chairman of Red Hat, has coined an analogy comparing Linux to ketchup. Essentially, the operating system called Linux — including the GNU tools, Linux kernel, and other software — is a freely available commodity that, like ketchup, different distributors can package and label in different containers. Anyone is encouraged to package and market the stuff, even though the ingredients are fundamentally the same.

Linux is a complex, malleable operating system, and thus it can take on many appearances. The greatest Linux advancement in recent years has been making it easier to install. After all, the tools that today enable the casual PC user to install Linux weren't originally available. Companies such as Red Hat saw this as an opportunity to add value to an existing product, and the concept took off like gangbusters.

To draw again on the ketchup analogy, various distributions of Linux have a slightly different *flavor* or texture; your distribution preference may be spicy, mild, thick and gooey, or runny. However, you can rest assured that any of the following distributions have the same Linux and GNU heart and soul. Each short description in this list includes a Web address where you can find more information about each project:

- **Debian GNU/Linux:** This distribution — one of the oldest — is a recognized favorite among advanced technical circles. Historically, it's relatively difficult to install. The Debian team works closely with the GNU project; Debian is considered the most "open" of the Linux distributions. Easier to install (and use) distributions with Debian underneath are Ubuntu, Xandros, and Linspire (formerly known as Lindows).

  ```
  www.debian.org
  www.xandros.com
  www.ubuntulinux.org
  www.linspire.com
  ```

- **Mandriva:** This distribution demonstrates the power of the GPL by allowing this competing company to stand on the shoulders of giants. Mandriva (formerly known as Mandrake) was originally based on Red Hat Linux (something that simply could not happen in a closed source environment), but has since become an excellent solution in its own right.

  ```
  www.mandrivalinux.com
  ```

✔ **Red Hat and Fedora:** Red Hat claims the prize for successfully mass-marketing the Linux operating system. Red Hat has validated Linux by packaging the GNU and Linux tools in a familiar method of distribution (shrink-wrapped) and has included value-added features to its product, such as telephone support, training, and consulting services.

```
www.redhat.com
http://fedora.redhat.com/
```

✔ **Slackware:** Of all the more widely recognized surviving Linux distributions, Slackware has been around the longest (in fact, its installation interface remained unchanged until about a year ago). Slackware has a very loyal following, but isn't well known. Like Debian in terms of spirit, the Slackware crowd is as respected in Linux circles as the weathered old-timers who share stories of carrying around a shoebox full of diskettes.

```
www.slackware.com
```

✔ **SuSE:** (Pronounced *soo*-za) This distribution hails originally from Germany, where it has a very loyal following, and was purchased by Novell, Inc., as part of the company's new focus on Linux. SuSE, like Red Hat, is a commercial distribution. Following in Red Hat's footsteps, Novell has also created openSuSE, an effort similar effort to that of Fedora.

```
www.opensuse.org
www.novell.com/linux/suse/
```

As you can see, many paths (in the form of distributions) lead to Linux. It's important to note that regardless of which distribution you choose, you're using the same basic ingredients: the GNU tools and the Linux kernel. The major differences you'll encounter among distributions are

✔ **Installation programs:** Each distribution has developed its own installation program to help you achieve a running computer system. Some installation programs are designed for the casual computer user (hiding the technical details); others are designed with the seasoned system administrator in mind. Some of the simpler ones offer an "expert mode" for those who want to have more control right from the beginning.

✔ **Software versions:** Different distributions may use different versions of the *kernel* (the core of the operating system) and other supporting software packages — which makes for a plethora of versions. Open source projects are dynamic and release new versions regularly, as opposed to the often-sluggish development cycle of traditional commercial software.

✔ **Package managers:** Even though one Linux program should be able to run on any distribution, tools called *package managers* keep track of the software on your system and ensure that you have all the required supporting software as well. Distributions are usually dependent on one particular package manager. More recent in the grand scheme of things, package management has also come to involve adding easy-to-use update routines, as well as an easy way to add software without the need of a computer science degree. Chapter 12 provides more information about package management.

It would be impossible to account for *every* possible installation of every Linux distribution. Okay, maybe not literally impossible, but you'd need a forklift to bring your *Linux For Dummies* book home from the bookstore if I did. Consequently, I try to summarize the concepts needed to install any Linux distribution into this one book with enough detail to get you through the process. (As you can imagine, that's a bit of a challenge!)

I chose **Fedora Core** as the sample distribution because Red Hat has become a recognized Linux standard, and its Fedora Core project is specifically aimed at home and small business users who cannot afford (or have no need) to purchase higher-level products. Even better, if you do use Red Hat Enterprise Linux (RHEL) in your office or organization, Fedora Core is a proving ground for the technologies that will make their way into RHEL.

In addition to Red Hat coverage, I also include information about other popular distributions with beginners: Linspire, Mandriva, SuSE, Ubuntu, and Xandros. I certainly don't wish to discount Slackware and Debian because these are very powerful distributions. I just feel that they are more advanced than the others and best left for your post-*Linux For Dummies* endeavors. Included also is Knoppix, a *Live CD* that you can use to boot your computer into a full desktop without having to install a thing! See Chapter 4 for more information on Live CDs.

In fact, the DVD that comes with this book contains more than just Fedora. Check out Appendix B for a list of the goodies you can find on the DVD.

Chapter 2

Prepping Your Computer for Linux

• •

In This Chapter

▶ Taking basic preinstallation steps

▶ Using Linux and Windows on the same computer

▶ Customizing disk partitions before installation

▶ Knowing (and finding) your hardware information

▶ Preparing for CD or floppy disk installation

• •

Most current Linux distributions detect your hardware automatically and guide you through the installation process. In fact, some people just dive right in and start installing. However, if you're setting up a machine that will run both Windows and Linux (although not at the same time), don't leap in without at least reading the section "Preparing to Use Linux and Microsoft Windows Together," later in this chapter. Make sure you have the hard-drive space to install Linux — and that you don't accidentally wipe out your Windows installation.

Other people like to start with a bit more caution. You can save yourself potential headaches — or make it easier to troubleshoot technical problems — by becoming familiar with your computer's hardware.

You should watch out for several issues when preparing to install Linux. In this chapter, I address the tasks that prepare you for the Linux installation process, such as setting up your system to install Linux — whether directly from the DVD or CD, or with an installation floppy disk (should you end up needing one).

Installation Considerations

> You got to be careful if you don't know where you are going, because you might not get there.
>
> — Yogi Berra

If you have a spare machine that's only going to run Linux and nothing else, you're in luck! You can skip all of the "Preparing to Use Linux and Microsoft

Windows Together" section. In fact, if you're feeling brave, you may want to skip right to Chapter 3 or 4 (depending on which distribution you're using) and start your installation. There's troubleshooting information in Chapter 20 as well.

If you plan to run both Linux and Microsoft Windows on the same computer — a scenario called *dual booting* — *DO NOT PROCEED TO CHAPTER 3* without reading the next section, "Preparing to Use Linux and Microsoft Windows Together." Sorry for yelling, but you can wipe out your whole Windows installation if you don't take some precautions!

Preparing to Use Linux and Microsoft Windows Together

If you're planning to run Linux and Microsoft Windows on the same machine, the odds are that you already have Windows installed and have been using it for some time. Because I hate to hear screams of anguish all the way up here in western Canada, take a moment to assess what you have and what you need to do.

On the off chance that you actually don't have Windows installed yet and still want that dual-boot capability, you'll want to install Windows *before* you install Linux. Otherwise, during installation, Windows will overwrite the part of your hard drive that Linux uses to store its boot menu. (This can create a bit of a mess later when you want to boot back into Linux!) Those of you who are installing Windows first should skip down to the section "Working with Disk Partitions" to find out how to set up your Windows installation so it causes the least fuss when it's time to add Linux.

The majority of you, however, want to dual-boot because you've got one machine and it's already running Windows. If you have a brand new hard drive to work from that has nothing on it already, skip down to the section I just mentioned ("Working with Disk Partitions"). No need to do anything funny with the hard drive that Windows is using. However, if you need Linux and Windows to share the same hard drive and you already have Windows installed, you do have a bit of extra work to do if you're using Fedora Core (the default choice in this book), Linspire, Ubuntu, or some versions of Xandros: SuSE, Mandriva, and the Xandros Deluxe and Business Editions can resize things for you, and you don't have to install Knoppix so you don't need to make room for it. The rest of this section focuses on getting you through all this hassle.

If you're using SuSE, Mandriva, Xandros Deluxe Edition, or Xandros Business Edition, your Linux distribution can resize the Windows partition for you. Even so, you'll want to work through the appropriate "Peeking at your partitions in Windows" section (later in this chapter) for your version of Windows so you can decide how big to make your Linux partition when the installer asks you.

When you install Linux on a system that has Windows already installed, you can run only one operating system at a time. In other words, if you're using Windows and you want to run Linux, you have to shut down Windows, allow the computer to reboot, and then start Linux. Note, however, that with the use of some additional software, you can run Linux on a Windows system at the same time Windows is running. You can also run Windows software within Linux itself! (See Chapter 19 for more information.)

Partitioning from scratch for a dual boot

If you plan to take a fresh hard drive and install both Windows and Linux on it, *be sure to install Windows first.* While you're going through the Windows installation, you will be asked to partition your drives. Your hard drive can have three *primary* partitions and one *extended* partition. Inside that extended partition, you can have up to 12 *logical* partitions.

No matter what type of partition (primary, extended, or logical) you use for Linux, make sure to leave at least 10GB open for it. Typically, you'll want even more, because you may like to download big files like multimedia stuff.

Make a note of the partition you leave open, specifying the drive it's on (the first, second, third, and so on) and the partition number it is on the disk (again, first, second, and so on). You'll need this information later, when you start actually resizing your partitions.

If you're not installing on a fresh hard drive, you may have to make some changes to your current installation. Proceed to the next section to find out how.

Peeking at your partitions from Windows

Before I get into actually changing anything, it's important to collect some information about your current setup. You need to know two major types of data about your hard drives before you get started adding Linux. The first is to know whether you have any unpartitioned space left on your hard drive(s) — and, if so, how much space you have. If you have at least 10GB of unpartitioned space, then you can skip straight to the "Double-Checking Hardware Compatibility" section later in this chapter.

If you want a *really* minimal installation of Linux without even any graphical interface, you don't need nearly 10GB. If you don't have any unpartitioned space — or you have too little unpartitioned space available (for example, if you like to rip a lot of CDs, you'll want more than 10GB of space) — the appropriate "Peeking at your partitions" section can help you prepare to resize your existing partitions.

Peeking at your partitions in Windows 2000 and Windows XP

Windows 2000 and XP operating systems use accounts to control and secure the files and folders; to get information about the computer's disk-space usage, first you have to be logged on to the system as the Administrator (or use an account that has administrative permissions). After you log on, you use the Computer Management application in the Administrative Tools collection to find the details of the computer's hard-drive usage. Follow these steps:

1. **Open the Control Panel by choosing Start⇨Settings⇨Control Panel.**

2. **Open the Administrative Tools folder and double-click the Computer Management icon.**

3. **In the left pane of the Computer Management application, click the Disk Management folder icon.**

   Within a few seconds, the right pane displays the current status of the storage devices on your computer, such as the hard drive(s), CD drive(s), DVD/CD drive(s), and so on. Figure 2-1 is an example of the Windows XP Disk Management display, and Windows 2000 users will see a nearly identical view.

Figure 2-1 reflects a computer that has two hard drives and one CD drive. The important thing to look for here is the word *Unallocated* in the Disk listing — an example is shown in this figure. Unallocated partitions are not assigned to any operating system and are free to use for your Linux installation.

If you do find an unallocated partition (refer to Figure 2-1), you're all set — provided it's 10GB or larger (see the previous section). Make a note of which partition this is (what disk is it on and what numbered partition it is on that disk) and skip ahead to the section "Making space." For example, in Figure 2-1, the partition is on disk 1, and it's partition 2.

If you don't have any (or enough) unallocated space, keep this window open and see the section "Making space," later in this chapter, for more about how to proceed.

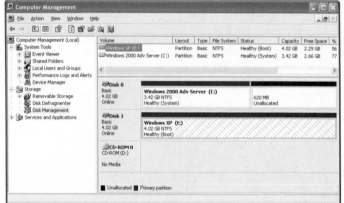

Figure 2-1:
Disk Man-
agement
information
within the
Windows XP
Computer
Manage-
ment tool.

Peeking at your partitions in Windows 98

If you absolutely must have Windows and Linux share the same hard drive, I'd like you to do some detective work before you move on. Here's the scoop: Windows 98 does not provide a graphical tool like Computer Management. Instead it uses FDISK, a command-line tool that indicates the partitions on your hard drive. To find out the details about a computer's hard drive in Windows 98, follow these steps:

Be careful in FDISK, you can wipe out your data if you make any changes with it. When you are exiting the program, be sure not to save any changes if it offers to do so.

1. **Open an MS-DOS prompt window by choosing Start⇨Programs⇨ MS-DOS Prompt.**

2. **Type** FDISK **and press Enter.**

   In Windows 98, you can enter FDISK in uppercase, lowercase, or any mixed case you like as long as you spell FDISK correctly!

   You will very likely be prompted to display large "disk" (drive) information — "large" is relative to what was a big hard drive in the time of Windows 98, which means a drive larger than 512MB. If you don't see the prompt, skip to Step 4, and the FDISK menu options will be similar to Figure 2-2.

3. **If you see the large disk prompt, choose Y at this prompt and then press Enter.**

   The FDISK menu options appear.

Figure 2-2:
FDISK
menu
options.

4. **Display the current drive-partition information.**

If you have more than one hard drive in your computer, FDISK displays a fifth menu choice so you can change between disks.

Here's how to use the fifth menu choice to change to another disk:

a. **Type 5 and press Enter.**

The FDISK screen displays all the hard drives in your system.

b. **Type the number of the disk you want and then press Enter.**

The top of the FDISK menu screen displays the number of the drive that FDISK is working with.

5. **To display partition information for the disk number displayed, type** 4 **and press Enter.**

Figure 2-3 shows an example of the Display Partition Information screen within FDISK.

Figure 2-3 indicates that no free, unallocated disk space is on the drive. If the disk had unpartitioned space, FDISK would display the amount of space available.

However, in Figure 2-3, you see that a portion of the disk space is configured as an *extended partition* EXT DOS. Extended partitions can contain what are called *logical partitions,* so it's possible that there might be free space available *inside* the extended partition that you could use to install another operating system such as Linux, or even another type of Windows.

Think of primary partitions as empty boxes that you put data into. Extended partitions are those annoying boxes that have a collection of smaller boxes stacked next to each other inside. You only put data into the smaller boxes with an extended partition. These smaller boxes are the logical partitions.

Figure 2-3:
Partition
information
in FDISK.

Unfortunately, FDISK doesn't tell you anything about what's inside this
extended partition. You have to dig deeper.

**6. To view the logical partitions within the extended partition, select the
EXT DOS entry and press Enter.**

Figure 2-4 is an example of a logical-partition setup. In this case, all
space within the extended partition is currently assigned. You can tell
whether there's free space by totaling the Usage percentages for the
drive. That total determines what you do next:

- If the total is 100 percent, then no space is available. If this is the
  case (or if you have less than 10GB available), leave this tool open
  and go to the next section, "Making space."

- If you have 10GB or more available, skip to the next section,
  "Making space."

Figure 2-4:
Logical
drive
information
in FDISK.

Making space

You may have unallocated space — but less than 10GB of it — or you may have none at all. Either way, you have to rearrange the data on your hard drive(s) to make room for Linux, unless you decide to add a second hard drive to the machine. If you're installing SuSE or Mandriva, these distributions can handle the resizing for you, so users of these Linux versions are welcome to skip ahead to the section "Double-Checking Hardware Compatibility." Everyone else is encouraged to stay right where you are and keep reading.

Keep in mind that you may actually want *more* than 10GB of space. For example, if you download lots of multimedia, you'll eat up that space fast! In that case, 10GB might be a better amount to shoot for — *at minimum*.

If it turns out that you have free/unallocated space in more than one spot on your hard drive (maybe between various partitions), add this space up and see how much the total is. You can move things around if you have to; it's a matter of resizing the partitions.

If you don't have any free/unallocated space, then you'll definitely have to resize your partitions. The key to doing this is (first) to determine how much of your drive space you're really using.

- ✔ In Windows XP and 2000, you can figure out how much of your Windows partitions are actually empty by looking at the Capacity, Free Space, and % columns in the Computer Management tool.

- ✔ If you're bringing a venerable Windows 98 and 95 machine back to dual-boot life, use the Computer Management tool this way:

    1. **Double-click My Computer to open the Computer Management tool.**

    2. **Choose View⇨Web Page.**

    3. **Highlight your first drive.**

        You see something like what is shown in Figure 2-5.

Determining how much space is enough for your Windows setup — you don't want to shrink it so much that you run out of space in Windows! — also involves taking a look at how you use your machine. Again, if you download and save a lot of multimedia stuff, it's wise to keep enough room around to accommodate your downloading habit.

If you find that your Windows drives are all too full (or you download and save too many audio, video, or graphics files), it may be time to burn some of your files off onto CDs so you can delete them from your hard drive.

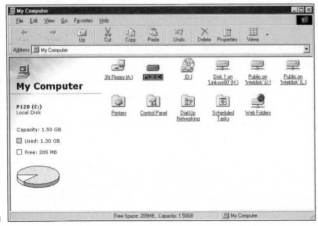

Figure 2-5:
How much
disk space
is available
on this
Windows 98
user's C:
drive.

When you've decided which partition you want to resize, make a note of which hard drive it's on and which partition it is (first, third, second, and so on). You'll need this information when it comes time to tell the installer where to put Linux.

Commercial tools, such as Partition Magic, provide an easy way to resize and work with the partitions on your hard drives. You can find information about Partition Magic from the company's Web site at www.powerquest.com. In the next section, "Working with Disk Partitions," you also find out how to get and use a free alternative, qtparted.

Working with Disk Partitions

In the section "Preparing to Use Linux and Microsoft Windows Together" (at the beginning of this chapter), I discuss why you might need to set aside disk space for Linux on a computer that's already running Windows. The techniques I cover here assume you've found free space that you can give to Linux after you resize your partitions. If you're installing on a fresh, additional hard drive, are wiping out a whole hard drive to give it over to Linux, or already have a chunk of unallocated/free space bigger than 10GB, skip ahead to the section "Double-Checking Hardware Compatibility," later in this chapter.

If the thought of changing anything on your Windows drive makes you queasy, a cheap, additional hard drive can be worth its weight in gold.

Choosing a partitioning tool

Perhaps the easiest way to adjust your existing partitions is through the use of a commercial program such as Partition Magic. Partition Magic enables you to view the partition information for your hard drive(s). You can also use this utility to resize, move, and add partitions. If all you want to do is resize, however, you don't have to go out and buy software just to get that done. Instead, you can download a free tool to do the job for you (see the next section for how to do so).

No tool is perfect. Before going any farther, make a backup of anything you don't want to lose off your Windows installation! Things can go wrong during the various steps of partitioning, even when using Windows tools on Windows.

If you create an open partition by using Partition Magic (after resizing your Windows partition), make a note of which drive and partition it is (first, second, and so on). You'll need this information when you're telling the installer where to put Linux.

Getting and resizing partitions with qtparted

A free resizing program you can use is called qtparted. This utility can work with both VFAT and NTFS partitions, so it can handle both of the file systems you may have used when you set up your machine in Windows. The program comes with Knoppix, which is a *Live CD* — another term is *bootable distribution* — meaning that you can put this CD into your CD-ROM drive, boot your computer with it, and it brings you into a full version of Linux that you don't have to install. Knoppix is handy for showing people Linux, but more important (for my purposes), it's useful for rescuing machines that can't boot and resize partitions.

Knoppix comes on the DVD included with this book, which is pretty handy. If you can't use the DVD for whatever reason, see Chapter 4 for how to get Knoppix on CD. Before proceeding, double-check that you have backed up all your important data before you proceed. Then, pull out any notes you may have made in the section "Preparing to Use Linux and Microsoft Windows Together" earlier in this chapter — specifically, which partition(s) you want to change — and then do the following:

1. **Put your Knoppix CD or DVD, or the DVD that came with this book, into the CD- or DVD-ROM drive and reboot your computer.**

   If you're using the book's DVD, a menu appears, asking whether you want to use Fedora or Knoppix. Select Knoppix, and you're taken to the Knoppix welcome screen. If you're using a plain Knoppix CD or DVD, your computer boots directly to the Knoppix welcome screen.

2. At the `boot:` **prompt, press Enter.**

Lots of text scrolls by as Knoppix figures out all the hardware on your system. It takes perhaps a minute for Knoppix to fully launch on many machines: it runs entirely from CD- or DVD-ROM. After it's up and running, you see the Knoppix desktop (see Figure 2-6).

If anything goes wrong during the Knoppix startup process, press Ctrl+Alt+Del or the Reset button your computer to reboot. When you reach the `boot:` prompt, press F2 and F3 to see the boot options you can add to try to get Knoppix to work.

3. From the K (main) menu, choose System⇨QTParted.

The QTParted tool opens (see Figure 2-7).

4. On the left, select the drive you want to work with.

If necessary, refer to your notes (see the section "Preparing to Use Linux and Microsoft Windows Together," earlier in this chapter) to see whether it's the first, second, third, or so on of your hard drives. If you have both IDE and SCSI hard drives — most home users have IDE drives, you usually have to go out of your way to get SCSI, which are more expensive — you can tell the difference between them in the list by the "hd" starting IDE names and the "sd" starting SCSI names. The order they're installed on the machine is indicated alphabetically. For example, hda is the first IDE hard drive, hdb is the second, and so on. (It's the same for SCSI, sda and sdb.)

After you make your selection, the drive's partitions and other information appear in the bottom and right portions of the window (see Figure 2-8).

Figure 2-6:
The initial
Knoppix
desktop
with the
help
browser
closed.

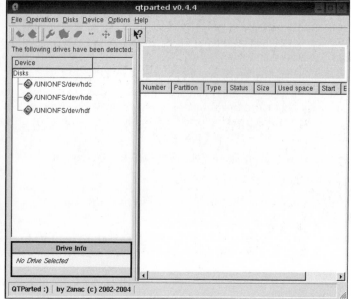

Figure 2-7:
The initial
QTParted
partition-
editor
screen.

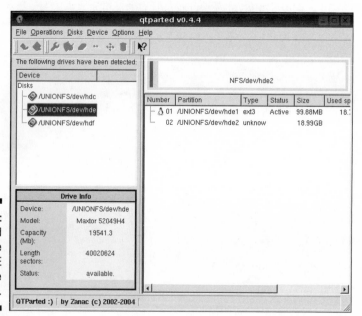

Figure 2-8:
QTParted
with the
second IDE
hard drive
selected.

5. **On the right, select the partition you want to resize.**

   If you see the penguin icons in your own window as are shown in Figure 2-8, these are Linux partitions. You won't see these if you have never installed Linux on this machine.

   Again, refer to your notes from the section "Preparing to Use Linux and Microsoft Windows Together," earlier in this chapter, to see which partition you want to change.

6. **Choose Operations⇨&Resize to open the Resize Partition dialog (see Figure 2-9).**

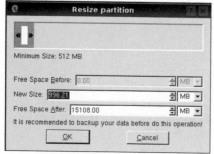

Figure 2-9:
QTParted's
Resize
Partition
dialog box.

7. **Make your sizing changes.**

   Note that you have multiple options here. You can choose Free Space Before to resize the partition and leave the specified amount of empty space in front of it, New Size to specify an exact new size for the partition, or Free Space After to resize the partition such that there is the specified amount of empty space after it. If you have smaller pieces of blank space scattered through your drive between partitions, you can start by absorbing them into the other partitions. Do so by changing the Free Space Before or After entry for each partition to zero, thus squeezing things together more efficiently (by moving all your free space to the end of the drive). This concept is perhaps better illustrated with an image, so see Figure 2-10.

8. **Click OK to save the changes for that partition.**

   Your hard drive isn't permanently changed just yet.

9. **Return to Step 5 if you have more partitions you want to change. Otherwise, proceed to Step 10.**

10. **Choose File⇨Commit to put the changes into effect.**

   Now is when your hard drive is actually changed!

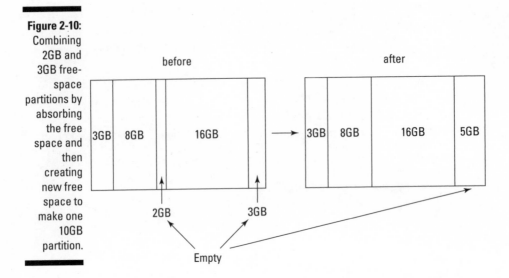

Figure 2-10:
Combining
2GB and
3GB free-
space
partitions by
absorbing
the free
space and
then
creating
new free
space to
make one
10GB
partition.

11. **Double-check that you have given yourself at least 10GB, if not more, of free space to install Linux in.**

    If not, resize things further.

12. **Choose File⇨Quit to close QTparted.**

    You're now finished with your repartitioning.

13. **From the Knoppix main menu, choose Log Out.**

14. **From the End Session for Knoppix dialog box, choose Restart Computer.**

15. **Click OK to reboot the machine.**

    The computer may speak as it shuts down; this is normal, and fortunately this is only the default Knoppix behavior at shutdown time. When the shutdown process is complete, you're told (politely, of course) to remove the CD, close the CD-ROM drive, and press Return/Enter. Follow the instructions and just let the machine boot back into Windows so you can make sure nothing went wrong. If something did, use your Windows system-recovery disc (such as your XP CD) to try to repair the damage. Fortunately, such damage is very rare!

After you've finished your repartitioning, proceed to the next section to continue gathering the remaining information needed for the installation.

Double-Checking Hardware Compatibility

Most hardware these days works just fine with Linux. Okay, sometimes the *very* latest whiz-bang video card or other fancy new electronic widget may run into some trouble; if you're an early-adopter sort of person, check your distribution's hardware-compatibility list and make sure you're covered. If you like to be organized and check out hardware ahead of time anyway (or if you run into problems and want to do some research to see what's wrong), check out the following:

✔ **Your Linux distribution's Web site:**

- **Fedora:** There's no official Fedora hardware list as yet. In the meantime, you can use the Red Hat listings at `http://hardware.redhat.com/hcl/`. Keep in mind that this list focuses on business equipment instead of home stuff and doesn't entirely apply to Fedora users.

- **Linspire:** Check out `www.linspire.com/lindows_hwsw_compatibility.php`.

- **Mandriva:** Go to `wwwnew.mandriva.com/en/hardware`.

- **SuSE:** The place to start is `www.suse.com/us/private/support/online_help/`. From here, click the Hardware Database link to search.

- **Ubuntu:** Go to `https://wiki.ubuntu.com/HardwareSupport`.

- **Xandros:** Check out `http://support.xandros.com/hcl.php`.

Don't worry about items being *Certified* (heavily tested to make sure they work properly) or not. *Supported* (drivers are included and the hardware is known to work) will do just fine most of the time. These definitions are there for enterprise users who need such information.

If you're new to computers or aren't all that familiar with hardware definitions and details, and are drowning in technical jargon, you can find a lot of information about hardware on the Internet. (One good Web site is `www.tomshardware.com`.) If your hardware isn't listed, don't panic.

✔ **Other Linux-oriented Web sites:** You can also check the generic Linux hardware list at `www.tldp.org/HOWTO/Hardware-HOWTO/`.

✔ **Web sites discussing your specific hardware:** If you still can't find the hardware listed, point your Web browser to `www.google.com/linux` and do a Web search on the make and model of the hardware, plus the word **Linux**. For example, you can search on Innovision DX700T Linux to find out how other people are faring with this particular brand and model of hardware. (No endorsement of any hardware mentioned as examples is implied here, of course.)

✔ **Vendor Web sites:** Many hardware vendors offer information about their level of support of Linux on their sites. However, many don't mention Linux at all even though the hardware works fine on Linux. You also may find drivers you can download on vendor sites. Only do this if there is no other way to get the driver for your distribution. This will be the most awkward way to get the driver.

If worst comes to worst, you might not find support listed for a piece of hardware. Try it anyway; it might work fine with a few minor caveats. For example, you might not be able to use the very latest features of your latest-generation video card, but you'll be able to use it as a generic SVGA at the very least. Also, sometimes older hardware is left off the lists but is still supported.

✔ **The dreaded manuals:** When possible, keep your computer manuals (especially those for your video card and monitor) handy, just in case you need them in order to answer a question asked by the installer — most people won't have to deal with this at all, but some will.

If the installer can't detect your particular video card, then you'll need to know exactly what it is, and what its specifications are — or just choose the Generic option. (I get to how to do this when you install Linux in Chapter 3 or 4, depending on your distribution.) If you're determined to know what exactly is in your machine — or want to find out because you have to do some extra research — you have the following options:

✔ **Use an existing operating system to document your hardware.** If your computer is already running Windows, you can collect a lot of information from the Windows environment. Use one of the following methods, depending on your system:

- **In Windows 98:** (Yes, some folks are still running it.) Choose Start⇨ Settings⇨Control Panel⇨System⇨Device Manager to access the dialog box shown in Figure 2-11.

- **In Windows 2000:** Choose Start⇨Control Panel⇨System⇨ Hardware⇨Device Manager to access the list of hardware installed on your machine, as shown in Figure 2-12.

- **In Windows XP:** Choose Start⇨Control Panel⇨Printers And Other Hardware. Here you can select one of the items from the dialog box under "or Pick a Control Panel Icon," or you can look to the "See Also" section and select System. If you choose System, from there you choose Hardware⇨Device Manager to access the list of hardware installed on your machine (as shown in Figure 2-13).

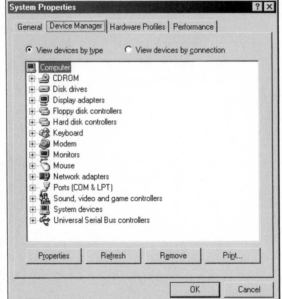

Figure 2-11:
In Windows 98, the Device Manager gives you information on what hardware you have installed.

Figure 2-12:
The Windows 2000 Device Manager.

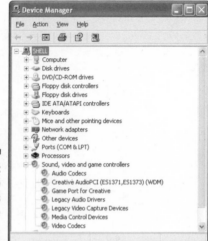

Figure 2-13:
The
Windows
XP Device
Manager.

You can double-click each item within the Device Manager to display the corresponding details.

✔ **Download a PC hardware-detect tool.** If you don't have any diagnostic tools and you have a relatively current version of DOS, you can download various PC hardware detect tools, such as PC-CONFIG, from the Internet. The PC-CONFIG tool contains several screens of information and menus to choose hardware areas and options. This tool is shareware, and the usage and fee information is available from the Holin Datentechnik Web site (www.holin.com).

✔ **Gather information by reading the screen when the computer starts.** If your system doesn't contain any operating systems and you don't have any of your system's documentation, you can resort to reading the screen as your computer starts. On some systems, the video information is displayed as the computer boots. You may have to reboot several times to read the information if it goes by too fast. Also, some systems display the PCI components and their settings as the system is starting up. Again, you may have to reboot several times to gather all the information.

You can try pressing the Pause-Break key on your computer (it should be near the Scroll Lock key) to get it to freeze during boot. You can then unfreeze it by pressing any key when you have finished reading.

✔ **Access the Basic Input/Output System (BIOS) information.** Stored in a small area of memory and retained by a battery, this is sometimes referred to as CMOS (Complementary Metal-Oxide Semiconductor), which indicates the type of computer chip that can store and retain information. The amount of information stored in the BIOS can range from very little to quite a lot. Some newer systems may display several screens of information about the computer's hardware.

If you choose to access the BIOS, make sure you do so before *any* operating systems load. Most manufacturers indicate the keyboard key (or key sequence) that gets you into the BIOS (or Setup) on-screen when the system is starting up — for example, `Press Del to enter Setup`. If you can't find the keyboard sequence, check the manufacturer's Web site. After you've entered the BIOS, you typically navigate around with the arrow keys, Tab key, or Enter key. Some BIOS environments also use the function keys; look for a list of function-key options at the top or bottom of the screen.

Be especially leery of labels on hardware boxes and Web sites that include the term *Win* (as in *Windows*). These components, such as *WinModems* rely on Microsoft Windows to be able to function — even worse, the packaging may show nothing that suggests this limitation. Only a very slight chance exists that you can find a Linux driver for *Win* hardware. If you do find one, copy it to a floppy *before* you install Linux. If you can't find a driver and you need to use a modem, put down a little cash and get a modem that is supported properly. (For more information about WinModems in particular, see Chapter 8.)

Finally, Finally, Before You Get Started

The bootable first CD or DVD is the last thing you will need before proceeding to install Linux. Fedora comes on the bootable DVD that comes with this book. If your computer doesn't have a DVD-ROM drive, use the coupon included in the back of this book to get the CDs — if you do, the first CD is bootable.

Laptop considerations

The current distributions of Linux do very well on relatively new notebooks and laptops. (See `www.linux-laptop.net` for an excellent research site on how Linux gets along with various makes and models.) If your laptop is a common brand, you shouldn't encounter any problems installing Linux. However, laptops often contain WinModems. (Hardware labeled with the *Win* prefix is only for Windows, and can't figure out what to do with Linux.)

If you plan to purchase a laptop for Linux, check out its modem and other hardware (such as network cards) to make sure they're not Win-branded. If the built-in or default hardware for the laptop is Win-labeled (or you discover while researching the machine that it contains a Win product, even if it isn't properly labeled), you might be able to switch the offending hardware for a PC (or PCMCIA) card. Most current laptops contain at least one PC Card slot to give you a place to slip in a PC card modem, network card, or combo modem-network card. As long as you stick with a common brand of PC card, it should work well with Linux.

If you have to make changes in your BIOS, be sure you save them before you exit! It's easy to forget and end up wondering why the machine isn't doing what you told it to do.

Now, before you go any farther, there's one more thing I want you to do: Locate your Linux distribution's documentation. These manuals can help you get past installation roadblocks and contain lots of useful information for after the installation is finished. If you purchased your distribution, it probably came with printed manuals. Otherwise, for the included distributions, you can find their various help forums and interfaces at:

- ✔ **Fedora:** The Fedora Documentation Project (`http://fedora.redhat.com/docs`) is still quite new, but its collection should grow over time. In addition, there's the Fedora Forum (`www.fedoraforum.org`), Fedora News (`www.fedoranews.org`), and the Unofficial Fedora FAQ (`www.fedorafaq.org`).

- ✔ **Linspire:** The official Linspire support page is `http://support.linspire.com`. Be sure to examine all the links because they contain lots and lots of help pointers.

- ✔ **Mandriva:** The official Mandriva documentation page is `www.Mandrivalinux.com/en/fdoc.php3`, and you can visit an additional help site at MandrivaExpert.com.

- ✔ **SuSE:** The official SuSE support page is `www.suse.com/us/private/support/` and the page for OpenSuSE is `www.opensuse.org/Documentation`.

- ✔ **Ubuntu:** The Ubuntu support page is available at `www.ubuntu.com/support`.

- ✔ **Xandros:** The official Xandros support page is `http://support.xandros.com/`.

As you surf the Web, don't be surprised if you keep seeing the term *wiki*. A wiki is a Web page (or collection of Web pages) maintained collectively, where anyone can make changes (or a group of designated people can, depending on how the wiki is set up). Wikis are growing popular for generating community-based support sites because anyone with the desire to contribute can pitch in with a minimum of hassle. Another popular place to go for help is `linuxquestions.org`. If you're ready to install, proceed to Chapter 3 for Fedora and Chapter 4 for Linspire, Mandriva, SuSE, Ubuntu, Xandros, and more.

Chapter 3

Installing Fedora Core

• •

In This Chapter

▶ Considering some last-minute issues before installation

▶ Installing Fedora as a personal desktop

▶ Booting Fedora for the first time

• •

Do, or do not. There is no "try."

— Yoda, *The Empire Strikes Back*

*N*o longer are arcane glyphs and complex sorcerer's spells required to
install Linux. The graphical installation is now quite easy to perform
and will be familiar to users coming from another graphical operating system,
such as Microsoft Windows. This chapter provides the details.

If you're installing Linspire, Mandriva, SuSE, Ubuntu, or Xandros, proceed to
Chapter 4 — do the same if you want to use Knoppix without having to install
anything. Even if you're not using Fedora, you can still discover plenty in this
chapter — all Linux distributions share common elements.

Things to Consider Before You Begin Installation

You can install Fedora Core by

✔ Booting with the DVD-ROM included in this book and choosing Fedora
from the initial menu.

✔ Booting with the Fedora Core installation CD, which is CD number 1 if
you ordered the CD set by using the included coupons at the back of this
book, or from a third-party vendor such as those listed on the Fedora
Project's vendors page at

```
http://fedora.redhat.com/download/vendors.html
```

To begin the installation from the DVD-ROM or CD-ROM, you must first change your system to start, or *boot,* from a DVD-ROM or CD-ROM. In Chapter 2, I cover how to configure a computer to boot from these devices.

I concentrate on Fedora Core 5 and its installation for two main reasons:

- ✔ Fedora Core 5 is included on the DVD with this book, and on the CDs you can order with your coupon.
- ✔ Covering the installation of every Linux distribution in existence would make this book into a set of encyclopedias.

I am assuming that you want to install a desktop. There are plenty of books out there that focus on servers, so my goal is that Linux for Dummies focus entirely on those who want to use Linux as their actual desktop machine. Also, it is just not possible to cover both desktop and server functions in a book of this size to a satisfying depth.

Please note that if you're installing Red Hat Enterprise Linux, some other version of Fedora Core, or a different distribution of Linux, your screens *will* look different from what is shown in this book (for Linspire, Mandriva, SuSE, Ubuntu, and Xandros, see Chapter 4). Each Linux distribution's installation routine covers the same basic tasks, but the specific actions may be presented in a different order, or be customized to look different on-screen. For example, one distribution may present account creation before network configuration, and another may have those two topics reversed.

With Fedora, up until you reach the About To Install (GUI install) screen, you can back out of the installation without changing anything on your system. None of the configuration options you make *before* you get to the About To Install screen are saved to your disks. After you continue beyond the About To Install screen, data is written to disk, and your system is changed.

The Installation Process

In this section, I follow the graphical installation. If you can't use the graphical installer for some reason (if Linux doesn't support your video card, for example), follow the text-based installation instead. The steps are the same, it's just not as pretty, and you don't quite get all the options that you have available in the point-and-click version.

Since the DVD that came with this book has multiple distributions on it, the boot screen is different from the default one that you will find if you were installing Fedora Core 5 directly from its own DVD or CDs. If for some reason you are using a DVD or CDs that only contain Fedora Core 5, then follow the same instructions but just press Enter when you reach the boot prompt. Those who are using the DVD that came with this book should do the following:

1. **If you want to boot and install from the Fedora DVD-ROM that comes with this book, place the DVD in your DVD-ROM drive, reboot your system, type** linux, **and press Enter.**

   There are a number of boot options, as shown in Figure 3-1, which are each described in the following list:

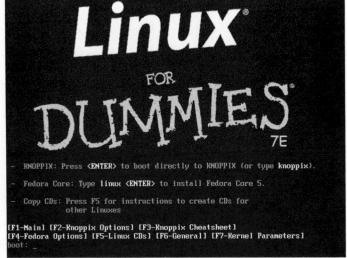

Figure 3-1:
The initial
Linux for
Dummies
installation
screen.

- KNOPPIX: Press <ENTER> to boot directly to KNOPPIX (or type **knoppix**).

- Fedora Core: Type **linux** <ENTER> to install Fedora Core 5.

- Copy CDs: Press F5 for instructions to create CDs for
              other Linuxes

[F1-Main] [F2-Knoppix Options] [F3-Knoppix Cheatsheet]
[F4-Fedora Options] [F5-Linux CDs] [F6-General] [F7-Kernel Parameters]
boot: _

- **Install Or Upgrade In Graphical Mode:** The first option in the graphical interface is for installing Fedora Core for the first time or for upgrading an existing version of Fedora Linux. This installation probes to detect your system's hardware. The graphical interface is designed to work with a mouse to select options. If you don't have a mouse, you can use the keyboard to navigate around the screens. In most places, the Tab key or the arrow keys advance you to the next option; the spacebar toggles options off and on; and the Enter key accepts the choices and moves to the next screen. In most screens, if you want to change a previous setting, a Back button is available to navigate to earlier selection screens. The graphical installation screens also include help in the left panel. The content changes to reflect information about the current configuration screen.

- **Install Or Upgrade In Text Mode:** The second option enables you to install or upgrade Fedora Core by using a text-menu interface. All the options show up on-screen in text menus, and you use the arrow keys or Tab key to move to the selection you want. In some areas, you use the spacebar to turn options off and on. To install by using the text interface, type linux text at the boot: prompt and press Enter.

- **Use The Function Keys:** The last item listed points out the function keys displayed at the bottom of the initial installation screen.

  The F1 function key presents the initial installation splash screen, which offers general instructions, the boot prompt, and pointers to the function keys labeled F2 through F5.

  The F2 function key includes options related to booting the Knoppix Live CD included on the DVD. See Chapter 4 for more information on Knoppix and live distributions.

  The F3 function key offers more options for Knoppix.

  The F4 function key offers Fedora options for disabling hardware detection during installation (you must know the details of your hardware before proceeding); enabling rescue mode; using a driver disk, CD, or DVD that isn't included with the Linux installation media; and testing your system's memory. Type the specialized options to use them.

  The F5 function key explains what else is available on the DVD.

If you don't choose any options and just press Enter, the Knoppix distribution loads. If you type linux and press Enter, the Fedora graphical installation process starts. I will assume you did the latter.

2. **Press Enter to start the graphical installation.**

   The default installation mode for Fedora (and most versions of Linux) is graphical. When you press Enter, many lines of information scroll past as the installer launches.

   If you downloaded the full version of Fedora Core and burned it onto CDs or a DVD yourself, the CD Found (media-check) screen appears. This screen allows you to check the integrity of the media that you're using to install Linux. If this is the case, I recommend taking the time to perform this test on all the CDs or the DVD you downloaded personally. It's best to know now whether one of them is damaged or incomplete.

Dealing with damaged CDs or DVDs

If your CD or DVD appears to have a problem, what you do next depends on where you got the DVD or CDs. If the DVD came with this book, contact Wiley Customer Care at 800-762-2974 to get the disc replaced. Do not contact Red Hat's technical support to have the DVD replaced in this case.

On the other hand, if you burned your own CDs or DVD, you may be experiencing one of two different problems. Try burning the disc again at a slower speed. If the newly burned disc also fails the media check, download the images again (they may have been corrupted during the file transfer, though that's unlikely).

WARNING!

Because the DVD that accompanies this book contains not only a full edition of Fedora Core 5 (minus the source code; see Appendix B), but files for a number of other distributions, I don't recommend trying a media check on this device, so choose Skip for this DVD. It will most likely fail even if the DVD is fine.

Whether you check your media or not, the initial Fedora Core installer screen eventually appears. If you want, click the Release Notes button to open the file containing information about this version. It might be a bit geeky but you might find something interesting or useful.

3. **When you're ready to proceed, click Next.**

   The initial screen disappears and is replaced by the language-selection screen, as shown in Figure 3-2. Linux supports many different languages.

Figure 3-2:
The
language-
selection
screen.

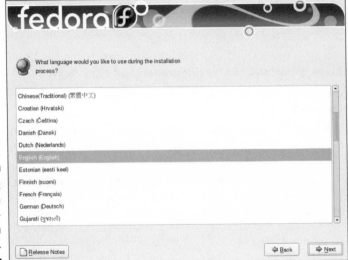

4. **Use the mouse or the ↑ or ↓ keys to select your language and click Next.**

   The keyboard-configuration screen appears, as shown in Figure 3-3.

   Different languages arrange the keys differently on keyboards; you may want to choose the matching language for your keyboard. (The default is U.S. English.)

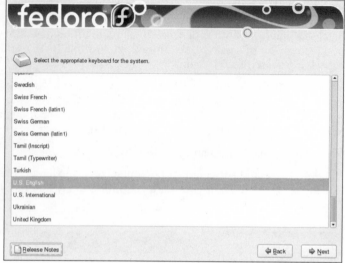

Select the appropriate keyboard for the system.

Spanish

Swedish

Swiss French

Swiss French (latin1)

Swiss German

Swiss German (latin1)

Tamil (Inscript)

Tamil (Typewriter)

Turkish

U.S. English

U.S. International

Ukrainian

United Kingdom

Release Notes   ◆ Back   ◆ Next

Figure 3-3:
The
keyboard-
configuration
screen.

5. **Choose your keyboard configuration and click Next.**

   The partitioning screen appears, as shown in Figure 3-4. You're given
   four options:

   - **Remove all partitions on selected drives and create default
     layout:** Wipe everything off the hard drives you select in the check
     boxes below this option.

   - **Remove Linux partitions on selected drives and create default
     layout:** If you already installed a version of Linux on the hard
     drives marked with the check boxes shown below this option, the
     installer will find the previous instance and install over it, wiping
     the old one out.

   - **Use free space on selected drives and create default layout:** Find
     available free space and install there.

   - **Create custom layout:** Manually define where to install. If you go
     this route, see the nearby sidebar "Defining partitions manually."

   As a hint for choosing the proper drives, the first hard drive in your
   computer is typically `hda`, the second is `hdb`, and the third is `hdc`. (With
   some kinds of hard drive technology, the first drive will be `hde`, the
   second `hdf`, and so on — just count from the lowest to the highest.) If
   you have SCSI drives, you see `sda`, `sdb`, and `sdc` instead.

   If you're both nervous *and* technical enough to understand hard-drive
   lingo, click the `Review and modify partitioning layout` check
   box first. If you do that, a layout screen appears. Those who choose to
   delete existing partitions will be asked if they really want to do this.
   Refer back to your notes to double-check before you actually make anything go away.

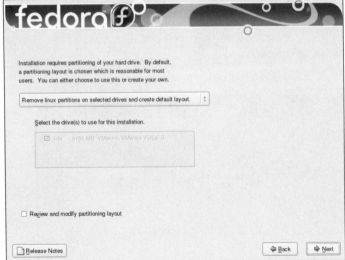

Figure 3-4:
The
partitioning
screen.

Be careful — you lose *all* data in existing partitions when you choose to remove partitions. They won't be immediately changed, however — not until the final installation screen.

Defining partitions manually

If you choose to define partitions manually, you'll be using Red Hat's Disk Druid. Disk Druid enables you to delete existing partitions and add new partitions. If you don't know how to use Disk Druid, I recommend that you *don't proceed any farther*. Click Back to return to the Automatic Partitioning screen, and then choose to review the automatic setup that the Disk Druid suggests instead of starting from scratch.

If you choose to Review and decide to change things, here are some terms you'll want to know: The *mount point* is where a *device* (maybe the first partition on your first IDE hard drive, which would be /dev/hda1) attaches within your *filesystem* (your directory hierarchy). The start

for your filesystem is the *root directory*, which is shown as /. You need to have a partition mounted as /, and you want it to be as large as possible if you're not making many partitions. You also want a partition mounted as /boot, but that one can be small, around 150MB. Finally, you want a partition that's about twice as big as the amount of memory in your computer. (There's no mount point shown for the swap partition, just a file-system type of swap that you have to choose. Otherwise, when it comes to Fedora, you'll be sticking with ext3 as your file-system type because it's the default. (I get more into these kinds of things in Chapter 10.)

6. **Choose the appropriate option and make sure the correct drives are selected; then click Next.**

   After you click Next, the network-configuration screen appears, as shown in Figure 3-5.

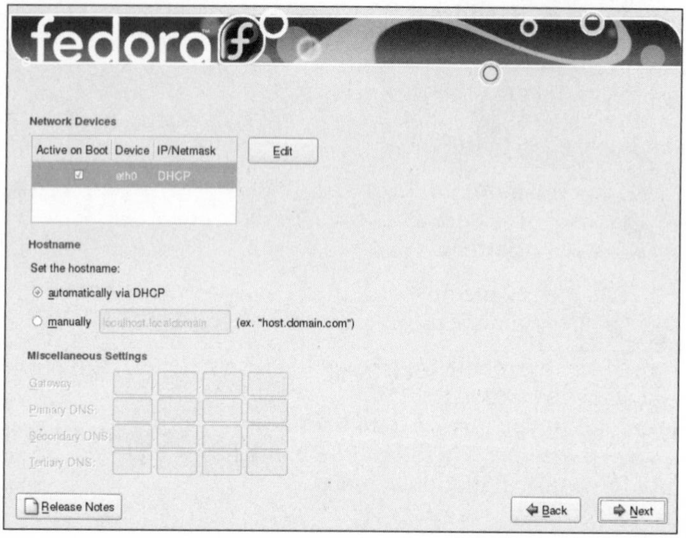

Figure 3-5:
The network-configuration screen.

If you're using a modem and don't have an Ethernet card in this system, you won't see this screen at all, so skip to Step 8. If you do see this screen, go ahead with Step 7.

7. **Configure your network. If your ISP or network administrator told you to use the Dynamic Host Configuration Protocol (DHCP) to let the computer automatically get its network settings, then most of the job is done for you. Otherwise, you will need to set the information manually.**

   If your networking is being set through DHCP, then the only item you may want to change in this screen is the *hostname*, which gives a name to your computer on the network. You can choose to override this name and set your Linux system's hostname manually (instead of letting the DHCP server pick one for you). To do so, follow these steps:

   a. **Rather than Automatically Via DHCP, select the Manually radio button.**

      The hostname text box becomes active.

   b. **Change the value in the text box by typing in a hostname.**

   If you are not using DHCP, but instead are using *static* networking — which means you have to feed in specific values manually — then do the following:

a. **Click the Edit button next to the Network Devices box.**

   The Edit Interface eth0 dialog box appears.

b. **Click the Configure Using DHCP check box to uncheck it.**

   The text boxes below the check boxes become available.

c. **Take the IP address that your network administrator gave you, and type it into the IP Address text boxes.**

   For example, if your IP address was 192.168.1.46, you would type the 192 in the first box, the 168 in the second, the 1 in the third, and the 46 in the fourth.

d. **Type the *netmask* (network "mask," or address) given to you by your network administrator into the Netmask boxes, following the same pattern as you did for the IP address.**

   The Miscellaneous Settings section will be available, and so will the hostname text box.

e. **In the hostname text box, enter the hostname your administrator asked you to use.**

f. **In the main screen, enter the values in the** Gateway **and** DNS **fields that your network administrator gave you.**

   If your network has more than one DNS server, you can enter up to three DNS server addresses — a DNS server helps your computer find other machines on the Internet.

8. **After you've set your configuration, click Next.**

   The time zone selection screen appears, as shown in Figure 3-6.

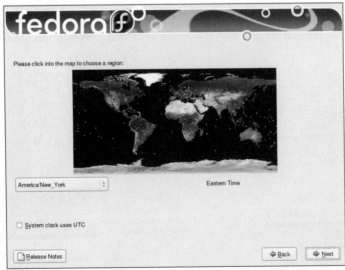

Figure 3-6:
The time-
zone
screen.

9. **Choose the region of the world in which your Linux system resides.**

   If you travel, set this to where you are now. You can change this setting whenever you need to later.

10. **Choose your city, or if you don't find it in the listing, choose another city in the same time zone that supports the same options (such as daylight-savings time).**

11. **If necessary, click System Clock Uses UTC (Universal Time, Coordinated) — most people don't need this option.**

   If it turns out that your computer is (or isn't) using UTC and you chose the wrong way, you can change this value after you've installed the computer, so don't sweat this setting too much.

12. **Click Next to proceed to the next step in your installation.**

   The root-password screen appears.

13. **In the root password screen, type the root (administrator) account password into the Root Password field and then type the same password in the Confirm field.**

   You don't see the password when you type it — just an asterisk for each character. (The asterisks prevent unauthorized individuals from seeing the password.) If you mistype something in one of the boxes, you're warned when you try to move on to the next step of the installation and have a chance to reenter the values.

   Don't forget your root password! You need it to do any administrative task on your Linux box.

14. **After you've entered your root password twice, click Next.**

   The application types screen appears, as shown in Figure 3-7.

Figure 3-7: The application types screen.

15. **Add or remove types of packages to customize your system.**

To add a type, there needs to be a check in its checkbox. To remove one, the box needs to be empty. You can add and remove checks by clicking in the box.

The groups available are:

- **Office and Productivity:** I assume you are setting up a desktop system, so you will want to make sure this one is selected.

- **Software Development:** If you are a programmer, you will want to add this group. Otherwise, you can do without it.

- **Web server:** If you want to run a Web server on this system or just experiment with the Apache Web server, add this one. Otherwise, you don't need it.

Keep in mind that the last three options are beyond the scope of this book.

16. **At the bottom of the screen, select Customize Now, and then click Next to proceed.**

The package selection screen appears, as shown in Figure 3-8.

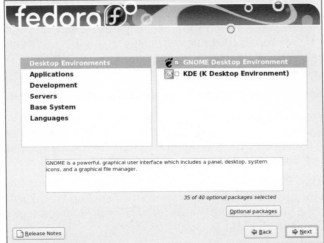

Figure 3-8:
The package selection screen.

17. **Click KDE (K Desktop Environment) if you want to have both of the major graphical interfaces installed on your system.**

I cover these interfaces in detail in Chapter 6 and 15.

18. **Click Applications.**

The types of packages available in this category appear on the right. You can really start anywhere you want, but I thought this section might be a good example.

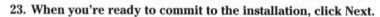

19. **Scroll through the list on the right. Make sure the check boxes are checked for the groups you want, and aren't checked for the groups you don't want.**

    You can click the name of the group to see a description of it below.

20. **If you want to look through the optional packages (programs) for this group, then while it is selected, click the Optional Packages button.**

    This action opens the Packages dialog box for that group. Read descriptions and add/remove checks from check boxes until you are satisfied with your choices, and then click Close to close the dialog box. This button will not be available if the group isn't already marked for installation.

21. **When you have finished choosing optional packages for each group, choose the next category on the left (for example, Base Systems) and then return to Step 19.**

22. **When you have finished going through all the possibilities — you can change what is installed later — click Next.**

    First, a dialog box appears and tells you that the installer is looking over your list of selected software. If it discovers that you've left out programs that the software you chose depends on, it offers you the chance to add those too. (Say yes!) When all that's done, the install screen appears.

    If you want to stop your installation of Linux, the install screen is the *last* place where you can stop without changing anything on your hard drive(s). To stop the installation, press Ctrl+Alt+Del and your system reboots. If you do that, be sure to pull out the DVD or first CD if you don't intend to restart your installation.

23. **When you're ready to commit to the installation, click Next.**

    The Required Install Media dialog box may appear if you're installing from CDs, telling you exactly what CDs you need for the installation. If you're using CDs, you may not need all four of them, depending on the software you requested.

    After this, the package-installation screen appears. The system first prepares for the installation and then starts installing. As the system is installing, you see progress bars for each individual package being installed, as well as for the total installation.

    After the package installation has finished, you reach the final installation screen, which has text beginning with "Congratulations, the installation is complete." The CD or DVD is automatically ejected (if not, eject it manually); if you used a floppy disk, remove that as well. After you've removed all the installation media, click Reboot to restart your machine and proceed to the next section of this chapter, "Your First Boot."

Your First Boot

The first time your Fedora Core system boots, you have your first chance to see your new boot menu fly by. It's the blue screen that offers you three seconds before proceeding to boot into your default choice. If you set Windows as your default, press a key (such as the spacebar) to enter the menu, select the Linux entry, and press Enter — if Linux is the default — or the only — operating system installed, just sit back and let the machine boot on its own. If, for any reason, your computer fails to boot at this point, see Chapter 5.

The first time your computer boots, you see the first boot Welcome screen. Do the following to complete your machine's initial setup:

1. **Click Forward to proceed to the setup routine.**

   The License Agreement screen appears.

2. **Read through this text, select Yes, I Agree To The License Agreement and then click Forward.**

   The Firewall screen appears, as shown in Figure 3-9.

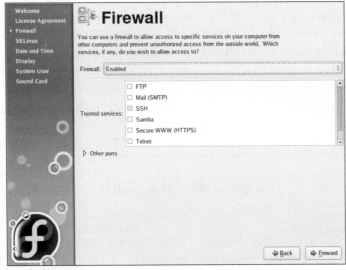

Figure 3-9:
The Fedora
Core
Firewall
screen.

Firewalls protect your system from unauthorized access and discovery. When you're connected to the Internet at high speed, your computer becomes one of hundreds of thousands. I wish that I could tell you that there *aren't* tons of nasty people and programs trying to break into your computer, but I can't; unfortunately, there's a horde of them. A firewall is your first (but not only) protective barrier against cyber-hoodlums, viruses, worms, and a host of other items that might try to skulk in through doors that should have been kept closed; see the sidebar "Firewalls and you" for more information.

3. **Unless you are *100 percent sure* that this computer is safe from both the Internet and other machines you may have on your home or office network, leave Enabled as your firewall setting.**

It's worth keeping in mind that before viruses and worms, most business computer break-ins happened from *inside* rather than outside. If you are absolutely determined to have your firewall off, select Disabled. I wish you luck!

4. **Determine which of the available services you want to let through your firewall.**

I recommend leaving SSH enabled so you can access this computer remotely, using the techniques discussed in Chapter 12. While I don't cover running your own Web server, you can run one on this computer — if so, you'll also want to enable the WWW (HTTP) and Secure WWW (HTTPS) entries (no need to enable these if you just want to browse the Web). The same goes for FTP (which can be handy for moving files around) and Mail (SMTP) — if you intend to run an FTP server or a mail server (SMTP), then you'll need to enable these services.

5. **Next to each item you want to enable, click in the box so it has a check mark in it; click Forward when you are ready to proceed.**

For my desktop machines, I tend to check the SSH and FTP entries. For how to use an FTP client to get files off this machine later, see Chapter 8. When you click Forward, a Warning dialog box may appear.

Firewalls and you

Anyone connected to the Internet, especially using *broadband* (see Chapter 7 for more on the different types of connections available; broadband tends to be DSL and Cable), really should have a firewall of some sort. You can purchase a firewall *appliance* (a special little box that you use to connect to the Internet and then hook up to your other computer[s]) or have a Linux box doing your firewalling for just itself — or even for your whole home or business network. Although this is quite an extensive topic that can easily take up an entire book of its own, I cover some basics in Chapter 7. In the meantime, protect at least this machine with a firewall of its own.

6. **If you see the Warning dialog box, click Yes to set the firewall configuration to what you have selected.**

   The SELinux screen appears.

7. **Select Permissive unless you are positive that you want to experiment with SELinux (otherwise known as Security-Enhanced Linux).**

   SELinux is explained in great geekly terms at

   ```
   http://fedora.redhat.com/docs/selinux-faq/
   ```

   This extra layer of security is quite an advanced topic, far beyond the scope of this book. In fact, it's new enough that even seasoned Linux administrators are still trying to figure it out.

8. **Click Forward to proceed to the next stage of your post-install configuration.**

   The Date And Time screen appears.

9. **If you're on a computer network that is currently connected to the Internet, and is usually connected to the Internet (or your network administrator told you to use a time server), click the Network Time Protocol tab. Otherwise, skip to Step 12.**

   Letting a *time server* control your date and time makes sure that your computer gets regular input on what time and day it really is. Otherwise, over time, your computer's clock actually drifts.

10. **Click the Enable Network Time Protocol check box to enable this feature.**

11. **If your network administrator told you to add a specific time server, click Add and then enter the address for this server. Otherwise skip to Step 14.**

12. **If you intend to control the date and time on the machine manually, verify that the date and time are accurate; if they're not correct, fix those settings now.**

13. **After you've finished adjusting the date and/or network time server, click Forward to proceed.**

    If you told the system to use the Network Time Protocol (NTP), it may take a moment for the system to contact the server you selected. After a few seconds, the Display dialog box appears, as shown in Figure 3-10.

14. **Look to the left of the Configure button. If you don't see your monitor correctly listed, click the Configure button, select the appropriate monitor in the Monitor dialog box, and then click OK to close the dialog box. Otherwise proceed to Step 15.**

    If you cannot find your monitor in the list, choose the most appropriate Generic option toward the top.

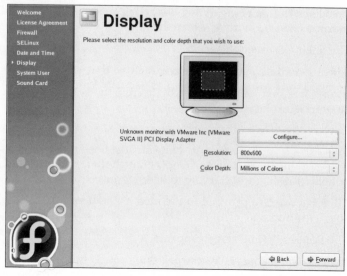

Figure 3-10:
The Fedora
Core Display
first-boot
screen.

15. **In the Resolution drop-down list box, select the video resolution you want to use.**

    You're offered only the resolutions that the installer thinks your monitor and video card can support. If you find that you aren't offered a full range, go ahead and select the best you can get; you can change your video settings later. (A popular setting is 1024 x 768.)

16. **In the Color Depth drop-down list box, select the number of colors you want to be able to use.**

    Again, you're offered what the installer thinks your system supports. You'll probably want Millions Of Colors.

17. **Click Forward to continue your first-boot machine setup.**

    The System User screen appears.

18. **Type the name you want for your personal account into the Username text box, and then your name into the Full Name text box.**

    For example, zorro in Username and Zorro the Dog in Full Name.

19. **Enter your account password both in the Password and Confirm Password text boxes.**

    This password is the one for your personal account and has nothing to do with your root (administrator) account. Feel free to use a different password than you did for root. In fact, it's a good idea to do so. If you accidentally don't type the password the same both times, you're warned in Step 20 and returned to this step.

20. **Click the Forward button to proceed.**

    The Sound Card screen appears.

21. **Make sure that your speakers or headphones are on and click the Play arrow button.**

    You should hear a sound from the right channel, the left, and then both at the same time. If you want to play it again but louder or softer, use the volume slider to make the change and then click the Play arrow again.

22. **When asked whether you heard the sound properly, click Yes if you heard all three sounds and No if you did not.**

    If you didn't hear the sounds properly, see Chapter 18 for help with getting your sound working later. Those who are sound hardware geeks might want to alter the optional entries toward the bottom. Otherwise, leave them at their defaults.

23. **Click Finish to launch your new installation.**

    That's it! You've just survived the second Linux gauntlet! Your computer now brings you to a graphical login prompt. See Chapter 5 for instructions on how to proceed.

Chapter 4

Installing Other Linux Distributions

A quick read in any of the chapters in this book should give you the picture that Linux is more than just some newfangled computer program. Linux is a fully equipped workshop of software tools and building materials that you can use to construct any of a wide spectrum of computing solutions. Developing the killer Linux distribution has been the Holy Grail of the Linux community. This ultimate Linux distribution would provide all the support and capability that the preschooler, the rocket scientist, the housewife, and the crotchety old computer science professor would need to harness the power available with Linux.

However, it's just about impossible to make something that makes absolutely everyone happy. In this chapter, I survey five more of the most popular (and easiest-to-install) distributions. Some of these are commercial products, so if you're considering getting one of them, my hope is that this chapter helps you decide which one (if not Fedora) meets your needs. I don't cover every aspect of the commercial items (such as how much support you get); for more information, see the distributions' respective Web sites.

Occasionally in this chapter, I mention burning an "ISO image" onto a CD-ROM or DVD-ROM — an ISO image is a file whose name ends in `.iso` and which holds the contents of a CD or a DVD. When this subject comes up, refer to the sidebar "Burning your ISOs" for tips.

Jump-Starting Linux with Knoppix

In Chapter 2, I explain that Knoppix is included on the DVD-ROM that comes with this book. You can boot with the book's DVD-ROM and just press Enter at the boot prompt, skipping any need to install anything on your computer (Linux runs directly from the DVD). If you're concerned about messing up something on your computer with an installation, give Knoppix a try.

If you can't use the DVD-ROM included with this book, you can download the CD-ROM ISO image to burn onto your own CD by going to `www.knoppix.net/get.php`. If you want to burn a larger version, you can get an image that fits onto a DVD by choosing the DVD version, but keep in mind it will take much longer to download than the CD image because it is a much larger file. Your download client will tell you how long the download will take for your connection.

Living Large with Linspire

Linspire (`www.linspire.com`) — formerly known as Lindows — is especially designed for people coming over from the Windows world to Linux. This commercial distribution offers additional subscription services available that I describe in the "Recognizing some special Linspire features" and "About the various Linspire versions" sections later in this chapter. Linspire is designed for ease of installation and ease of adding new software, and it contains many tutorials to help people get used to the system. Yet, Linspire isn't designed in particular for the aspiring Linux geek.

Linspire is built as a friendlier version of the more advanced, but popular, Debian (`www.debian.org`) distribution.

If you're curious about Linspire, you're in luck — an ISO file to create your own CD-ROM of the full version of Linspire is included on the DVD-ROM that comes with this book! In Chapter 12 you find out how to sign up for your free trial of the Click And Run Warehouse for getting and installing software, so you can decide for yourself whether it's worth paying for membership after that.

If you decide to purchase Linspire, you have a number of options:

- ✔ Purchase it online and download it immediately from the Linspire Web site.
- ✔ Purchase it online and have a physical box shipped.
- ✔ Purchase a boxed set in a store (`www.linspire.com/lindows_feature_reseller.php`).
- ✔ Purchase a computer with Linspire preinstalled (`www.linspire.com/lindows_feature_preinstall.php`).

Burning your ISOs

If you end up having to use the ISO files on the DVD-ROM or that you download in order to create distribution CD-ROMs or DVD-ROMs, I have some handy tips that can make this process easier for you.

Get some good CD-burning software, such as the popular Nero program (www.nero.com/en). Another good program that's free is BurnCDCC from www.terabyteunlimited.com/utilities.html. When you have a CD-burning tool ready, look at the file size of the ISO you want to burn. While most ISOs can be burned onto a standard 650MB/74-minute CD-R or CD-RW, some are large enough that you need 700MB (80-minute) discs instead. Knoppix is one Linux distribution that needs the larger CD-Rs. Another is Mandriva.

When possible, use CD-RWs, because they're rewriteable and you can download and burn other distributions (or newer versions) onto them later. Note, however, that your burning hardware has to actually *support* rewriteable functions. Look on its front to see whether it says CD-R (it can't rewrite), or CD-RW (it can rewrite).

As you prepare to burn your CD or DVD, make sure your software understands that you want to burn an ISO (look in the menus for image) and not just a file. If you burn your CD or DVD, put it into the drive, open it up, and then see only one file, you have burned it incorrectly. An ISO should be unpacked onto the CD or DVD as a bunch of files and directories.

Finally, it's a good idea to burn these types of CDs and DVDs at a speed of four or lower. You reduce your chance of introducing errors that way.

Linspire offers a nice FAQ on burning the CD at http://info.linspire.com/installhelp/. The info is helpful whether you're burning it from the DVD-ROM that comes with this book, or one you acquired from Linspire directly.

Installing Linspire

Linspire is primarily a commercial distribution, and you have access to this through the ISO image included on the DVD-ROM that comes with this book. I cover this full Linspire Five-0 release. Differences between this and other versions are addressed in the "About the various Linspire versions" section later in this chapter.

To install Linspire Five-0:

1. **Place the CD into your CD-ROM drive.**

2. **Boot the machine.**

   If the machine ignores your CD-ROM and tries to boot normally, see Chapter 2 on how to make the necessary changes to your BIOS.

3. **At the initial screen, choose INSTALL or UPDATE Linspire on this computer's hard drive and press Enter.**

   Linspire starts doing all the standard preinstallation tasks, such as scanning your computer's hardware and starting the installer. A progress bar shows you how far along it's gotten. After the bar is full, your screen turns black. (Don't panic! It's supposed to!) Eventually you reach the Welcome screen. If you want to use Linspire as a Live CD instead of installing it at the moment, select RUN Linspire Directly From The CD Without Installing (LinspireLive!).

4. **On the Welcome screen, click Next.**

   The Keyboard Layout screen appears, as shown in Figure 4-1.

5. **If you are using a Dvorak keyboard layout (or one of the supported languages other than English), select the language your keyboard should be laid out for.**

6. **Click Next.**

   The Install or Update screen appears, as shown in Figure 4-2. You may or may not see the statement that a previous installation has been detected, depending on whether you already have Linspire installed.

7. **Select Install unless you already have Linspire on your system and want to update to version Five-0, and then click Next.**

   The Installation Method screen appears, as shown in Figure 4-3.

Figure 4-1:
The Linspire
Keyboard
Layout
screen.

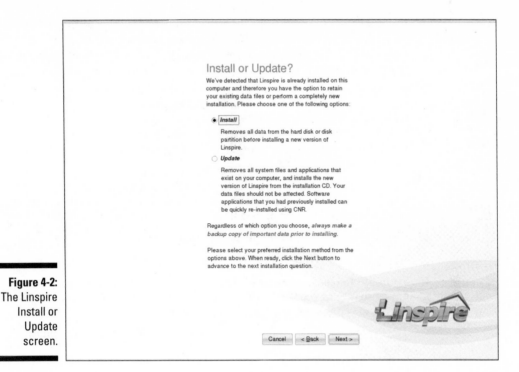

Figure 4-2:
The Linspire
Install or
Update
screen.

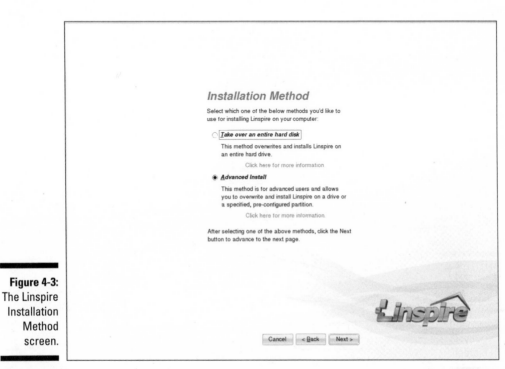

Figure 4-3:
The Linspire
Installation
Method
screen.

8. **If you're installing Linspire on a computer by itself or letting it have an entire hard drive, select Take Over An Entire Hard Disk. Otherwise, if Linspire has to share a hard drive with another operating system, select Advanced Install.**

Because the second option is more complex, I cover that one. If you choose the first option, the next step asks you which hard drive you want Linspire to use. Use the order that Windows sees them in, so the first drive is C:, the second is D:, and so on. If you have to, you can look in the BIOS at the sizes and other information to try to figure out which is first, second, or third.

If you choose Advanced Install, better check your system's existing free space before proceeding; otherwise the installer won't let you get to the partition-selection screen. See Chapter 2 for how to free up space.

9. **When you've made your selection, click Next to proceed.**

The Advanced Install dialog box appears, as shown in Figure 4-4.

10. **From the list, select the hard drive (if you want to install onto an entire drive) or partition (if you want to install in a particular emptied partition) you want to install Linspire onto, and then click Next.**

The Computer Name And Password dialog box appears, as shown in Figure 4-5.

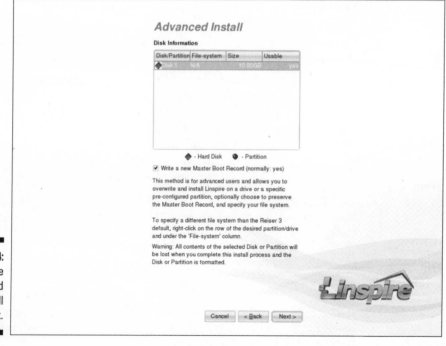

Figure 4-4:
The Linspire
Advanced
Install
dialog box.

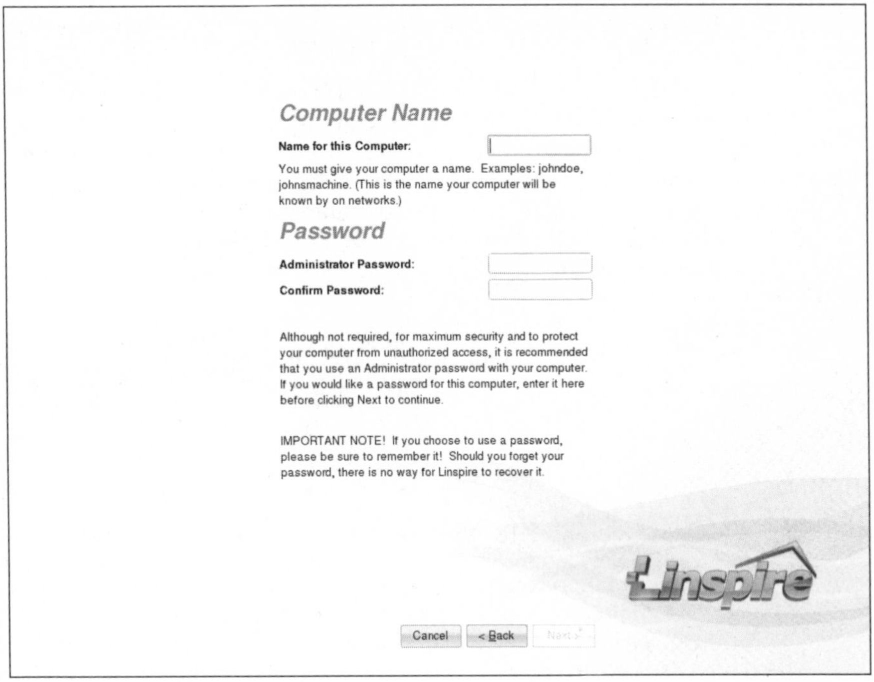

Computer Name

Name for this Computer: [   ]

You must give your computer a name. Examples: johndoe,
johnsmachine. (This is the name your computer will be
known by on networks.)

Password

Administrator Password: [   ]

Confirm Password: [   ]

Although not required, for maximum security and to protect
your computer from unauthorized access, it is recommended
that you use an Administrator password with your computer.
If you would like a password for this computer, enter it here
before clicking Next to continue.

IMPORTANT NOTE! If you choose to use a password,
please be sure to remember it! Should you forget your
password, there is no way for Linspire to recover it.

Linspire

[Cancel] [< Back] [Next >]

Figure 4-5:
The Linspire
Computer
Name And
Password
dialog box.

11. **Type the name you want this computer to have into the Computer Name text box.**

    For example, maybe you want to name your computer Fred. Your network administrator may ask you to use a certain name.

12. **Type your administrative password into both of the Password text boxes and then click Next.**

    You will not be able to proceed until the red Passwords Do Not Match text is replaced by the black Passwords Match statement. When you click Next, the Setup Confirmation dialog box appears.

13. **Read the values specified in the dialog box and then click Finish when you're ready to start the install.**

    Yes, that's it! Your installation now begins. You may be asked to verify that you want to take over a hard drive or partition; if so, double-check the information it shows you and answer appropriately.

14. **When the installation finishes, click OK.**

    The screen goes black, you see a progress bar, and then your CD-ROM ejects.

15. **Remove the CD from the drive and then press Enter to reboot the machine; to boot it, select Linspire from the options and press Enter (or just let it do so on its own).**

Recognizing some special Linspire features

One of the most-talked-about special features of Linspire is its CNR (Click and Run) Warehouse. This online store allows you to surf through more than a thousand software programs and purchase, download, and install them with just a few clicks. Even better, if you subscribe to the CNR service, a lot of the items in the Warehouse are free. (No need to keep your CNR membership up-to-date if you want to keep using the software you downloaded; after you've got it, it's yours.) I cover how to add software by using this service in Chapter 11.

Another cool aspect of some versions of Linspire is their audio/visual tutorials. After your installation is complete, the tutorials launch immediately and start walking you through how to use the system. You can stop them and come back to them at any time.

About the various Linspire versions

The folks at Linspire are pretty creative about putting together packaging options. In the section "Living Large with Linspire" (earlier in this chapter), I address various ways you can purchase this distribution. In this section, I look at the various ways Linspire is packaged for boxed sets and downloads. I'm not going to go into all the add-ons. (If I did that for every distribution, this book would end up an encyclopedia!) Instead, I look at the main versions available at the time of this writing:

- ✔ **Linspire Five-0:** The main Linspire product. This version has lots of software included, along with support.

- ✔ **Linspire Five-0 CNR:** This version is the same as the previous one, except it comes with a year's subscription to CNR (see Chapter 12) already bundled in — and offers additional support.

Both versions of Linspire can be booted into a live version instead of actually installing the system. See the section "Using LiveCDs and LiveDVDs," later in this chapter, to find out about live distributions

Maxin' Out the Fun with Mandriva

Mandriva (www.mandrivalinux.com) — formerly Mandrake — has a huge, enthusiastic fan base. This distribution, designed in 1998 with the goal of creating an easy and intuitive installation for everyone, specializes in ease of use — for both server and home/office installations. To accomplish this objective, the creators of Mandriva focused on making an easy transition so you can move your Microsoft Windows or Mac skills to Linux.

8. Click Next.

The Partitioning screen appears. You can choose existing partitions by clicking the partitions in the graphical listing. Each has a suggested mount point (see Chapter 3 for more on mount points) already attached. You can delete or resize a particular partition by clicking the appropriate button below the partition graphics. If you already have a bunch of free, unallocated space, you can click the Auto Allocate button to have Mandriva suggest a set of new partitions for you. To create a new one, click the empty space and then click Create. You can see an example layout in Figure 4-7.

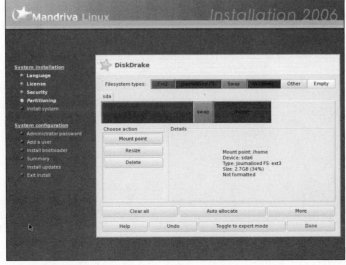

Figure 4-7: The Mandriva 2006 Custom Partitioning dialog box with an example disk layout.

9. After you're finished laying out your partitions, click Done.

As the warning that appears says, the changes are made to your hard drive when you click Done — when you click this button, the changes will be made immediately and you won't be able to return to your disk as it was before. After the formatting is complete, the installer scans through its list of software. Then the installation-media screen appears.

10. Beneath the list of installation CDs or DVDs, if you have plenty of room above the minimum hard-drive requirements, click the Copy Whole CDs check box to place a check in the box, and then click Next.

Doing so copies all the available software from the CDs or DVD to your computer so you don't have to fuss with the CDs, the DVD, or online packaging later — your installation will also take longer if you select this option. The Supplementary installation-media screen appears.

11. **Click OK unless you have specific places online or extra CDs that you want to use.**

    If you chose to copy what's on the media, the copying begins. You're asked to insert the appropriate CDs or DVDs when the time comes. For each of these, put in the requested media and then click OK.

    The Package Group Selection screen appears (see Figure 4-8).

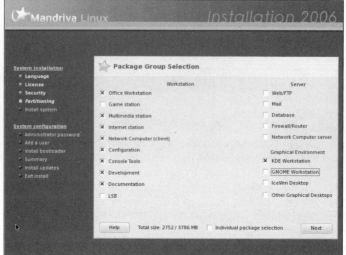

Figure 4-8:
The
Mandriva
2006
Package
Group
Selection
dialog box.

12. **Choose the groups of packages that you want to install.**

    For a desktop (for example), you might include each of the items in the Workstation section, plus both KDE and GNOME in the Graphical environments if you have the room. These items give you lots of software to play with.

13. **Select the Individual Package Selection box if you want to look inside each group and choose what you want.**

    I assume that you clicked this option.

14. **Click Next.**

    The Choose The Packages You Want To Install dialog box appears.

15. **Select and remove packages according to your needs.**

    - In the left column, you can click a right-facing arrow to expand a category and see all the groups beneath it, or you can click a down-facing arrow to compress the category and clean up the list. A check mark next to a group means you selected that group; a check mark next to a category means you selected the whole category.

- You also find arrows next to groups. Expand a group, and you can see (at left) all the software that will and won't be installed — you won't get *everything* from the group by default. You can then click any package in the list to see a description on the right.

If you find that a package you want isn't being installed, click the empty box next to its name to check it. If you don't want to install something that's checked, click the check mark to deselect it.

16. **After you make your selections, click Install.**

The installation begins. You may be asked whether you really want to install this or that software — read the description and choose Yes or No as appropriate; you can always change the software you have installed later as well. You're given a projection of how much time it will take. Keep in mind that if you have to swap CDs (which you won't if you copied the contents to the hard drive in Step 10), you won't know until it asks you for the next one, so don't just walk away and ignore the system expecting it to be finished when you get back. You can click the Details button to see the progress for each individual package.

As with most mainstream Linux distributions, Mandriva has some tasks to take care of after the main installation, before you start using the system. Here's a bird's-eye view:

1. After the main files are placed onto your system (but before rebooting), you're asked to do things like enter your *root* (administrative) *password*. Chapter 3 explains how to select a strong root (administrative) password — and why you want to do so.

2. After you choose your root password, you're asked to create a regular user account. When you do so, click the icon image and have fun selecting a picture to go with your user account.

Speaking of users, do *not* configure the computer to automatically log in any account unless no one else could possibly have access to the machine. Automatic login isn't a secure practice, and it's a great way to set yourself up for some annoying practical jokes.

3. When you reach the Summary screen — which isn't entirely a Summary because it lets you configure things that you haven't looked at yet — make sure that everything is set properly.

In particular, the graphical user interface entry refers to your monitor and video card. If these devices aren't configured, then you'll definitely want to change that. In the Security section, click Configuration next to Firewall, uncheck the Everything check box, and add checks only next to the services you'll run on this computer. For example, you may want to check SSH, FTP, and Echo (ping).

4. Finally, when you're given the chance to download updated packages, select Yes if you are already on a network that's connected to the Internet. Otherwise you can do it later.

After you finish this part of the configuration process, you're asked to reboot. You may, at this point, be offered a chance to do some final configuration tasks.

About the various Mandriva versions

Mandriva offers both server and desktop solutions, but I focus on the desktop here — which is considered by many to be Mandriva's real strength. You can see Mandriva's full range of commercial products by going to `www.mandriva.com/products/`, and you can see the full range of download options by following the instructions available in the earlier section of this chapter, "Maxin' Out the Fun with Mandriva." (As usual, I focus only on items that include the desktop itself instead of covering add-ons.)

At the time of this writing, you can purchase and/or download Mandriva for the desktop in the following versions:

✔ **MandrivaMove:** The *LiveCD* version of Mandriva, which allows you to pop the CD-ROM into any PC, boot the PC with this CD-ROM, and find yourself in a fully functional Mandriva environment without having to install anything.

✔ **Mandriva Discovery/Lx:** A commercial package for people brand new to Linux, aimed at beginners. This package includes MandrivaMove.

✔ **Mandriva 2006 PowerPack:** The commercial desktop power user package.

✔ **Mandriva 10.1 PowerPack+:** The commercial offering containing both desktop (all of PowerPack) and additional server offerings.

Mandriva also has commercial and/or free versions available for a number of other hardware architectures, such as AMD64, PowerPC, and SPARC. In addition to this, if you're a bleeding-edge kind of person (which is how geeks refer to the "very latest and greatest that most people haven't started using"), you may enjoy downloading the Mandriva Cooker at `www.mandrivalinux.com/en/cookerdevel.php3`

It's the development (or *beta*) version. Most people are better off sticking with the main version of Mandriva; betas, in general, are more likely to be full of bugs — hence the term *beta test* (the prodding and tweaking that finds — and, with any luck, fixes — software bugs).

Starting Off with SuSE

The SuSE ("SOO-za," www.suse.com) company and Linux distribution were founded in 1992 and were purchased by Novell (www.novell.com) in 2004. The distribution is named after a German acronym for *Software und Systementwicklung* (Software and System Development). One SuSE claim to fame is its international support. Most major distributions provide some level of support for users around the globe, but some are better at language integration for particular groups than for others; SuSE — understandably — excels in the German and western European space.

In this section, I focus on installing the free version, OpenSuSE 10. However, instead of including the five ISO files required to install this distribution, the DVD-ROM that comes with this book contains a LiveDVD image containing SuSE 10. No installation is required, so you can just burn the ISO onto a DVD-ROM, put that DVD into your drive, and boot your machine to experience this version of SuSE Linux — see Appendix B for where to find these files. You can also download this distribution for free (from www.opensuse.org/Download) if you can't use the DVD-ROM, or you can purchase a boxed set with manuals and more from the Novell (www.novell.com/linux/suse).

 Throughout the book, since GNOME is the new default desktop environment in SuSE, I assume that you are using GNOME. However, the LiveDVD by default gives you KDE, which can be confusing. You can switch to GNOME by logging out of the LiveDVD, and in the login screen, select Session Type⇨GNOME.

Installing SuSE

Those who are using the version of SuSE included on the DVD-ROM in this book can skip this section. Instead, it is aimed at those who choose to download and install OpenSuSE 10 — however, the installation routine discussed here is identical to that of the commercial SuSE product. In Chapter 2, I mention that SuSE can resize your existing Windows partitions. OpenSuSE can as well.

To install this distribution, follow these steps:

1. **Put either CD 1 or DVD 1 (the one on the left) in your CD-ROM or DVD-ROM drive.**

2. **Reboot your machine.**

   The Welcome screen appears, followed by the installer's menu.

3. **Choose Installation from the menu and press Enter.**

   The installer begins to look at what kind of hardware you're using. (This process can be a bit slow, so be patient.) Finally the Welcome To YaST2 (the system's installer and administration program) screen appears.

4. **Select the primary language you want to use on this computer and then click Next to proceed.**

   The Media Check screen may appear if you obtained your version of SuSE by downloading ISO files and burning your own CDs or DVDs. If so, you may want to use this feature — click Start Check to check the disks — though you likely don't need it if you downloaded the images through BitTorrent, which verifies the files automatically. Skip or proceed past this screen after checking your media by clicking Next.

   The License Agreement screen appears after — or rather than — the Media Check screen.

5. **Read the license agreement and click** Yes, I Agree to the License Agreement **when you are finished, and then click Next.**

   Your computer is scanned, and then the Installation Mode screen appears.

6. **Choose New Installation and click Next.**

   The Clock and Time Zone screen appears.

7. **If your time zone is not set correctly, make the appropriate changes and click Next.**

   Choose your region on the left and then the time zone on the right. The Desktop Selection screen appears.

8. **Select either GNOME or KDE for your default desktop, and click Next.**

   If you're not sure which one you want, choose GNOME for now. (This is the desktop I'll be assuming you're using for SuSE.) Next, the Installation Settings screen appears (see Figure 4-9). It can take a minute or so for the system to complete its auto-detection routine, and a few more minutes to fill out all the entries.

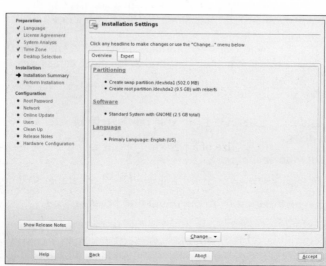

Figure 4-9:
The
OpenSuSE
10 Instal-
lation
Settings
screen.

9. **In the Partitioning section, if you aren't happy with what you're being offered, click the Partitioning link. Otherwise skip to Step 14.**

   Clicking the link brings you to the Suggested Partitioning screen.

10. **If you want to just make some adjustments, click the Base Partition Setup on this Proposal radio button. If you want to completely change the recommended partitioning setup, select the Create Custom Partition Setup radio button.**

    Because the last option is really for more advanced users, I assume that you've chosen Base Partition Setup on this Proposal, to adjust what you were already assigned.

11. **Click Next to make your changes.**

    The Expert Partitioner screen opens (see Figure 4-10).

Expert Partitioner

Device	Size	F	Type	Mount	Start	End	Used By	Label
/dev/sda	10.0 GB		VMware,-VMware Virtual S		0	1304		
/dev/sda1	502.0 MB	F	Linux swap	swap	0	63		
/dev/sda2	9.5 GB	F	Linux native (Reiser)	/	64	1304		

Create   Edit   Delete   Resize

LVM...   RAID... ▾   Crypt File... ▾   Expert. ▾

Figure 4-10:
The
OpenSuSE
10 Expert
Partitioner
screen.

12. **Make your changes.**

    You can change the size of a partition by clicking it in the list (ignore the whole drive entry, such as /dev/hda; focus instead on the partitions, such as /dev/hda1) and then clicking the Edit button to open the Edit Existing Partition dialog box. If you want to resize one of your NTFS or FAT32 partitions, then click that partition in the list and click the Resize button to get the job done.

13. **When you're finished with your changes, click Finish to return to the Installation Settings dialog box.**

14. Click the Software link.

You probably do want to pick and choose what programs to install! This action brings you to the Software Selection screen (see Figure 4-11).

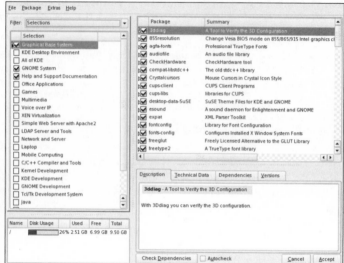

Figure 4-11:
The
OpenSuSE
10 Individual
Software
Selection
screen.

15. Spend as much time here as you want, surfing through the options and selecting items to add.

- Here's a recommended technique for working through this dialog box as a first timer. Start by looking to the left, under Selection, and picking the big groups you want to use. As a desktop user, you may want to add the KDE Desktop Environment, All Of KDE, and GNOME system so you can have both environments available (one should already be selected from Step 8), Games, Office Applications, Multimedia, Java, and Voice over IP. Choosing these groups adds big chunks of programs to your list. You can look in the lower left to see how much of your disk all your selections take up.

- If there are certain types of software you want to make sure you have, click the Filter drop-down list box and select Package Groups. This action changes the listing on the left to software types. You can click the plus signs to expand lists and the minus signs to shrink them. Then on the right, you can look at the individual programs in the group selected on the left and then check them to add them to your installation list or uncheck them to remove them.

16. Click Accept when you're happy with your software selections.

You may be told that extra packages have been added to fix dependencies. Click Continue if this happens.

17. **If you want your default language to be something other than U.S.-flavored English, click the Language entry and make your changes.**

18. **If you're a more advanced user (or just adventurous), click the Expert tab and investigate the other possible settings; otherwise click Accept to proceed.**

    At this point, you may be asked to accept licenses for packages such as the Macromedia Flash Player. Read these licenses and (if you want the packages) click I Agree to proceed. The Confirm Installation dialog box appears when it is time to move on to the actual installation.

19. **If you're sure you want to keep going, click Install. If you've changed your mind, click No to go back to the Installation Settings dialog box.**

    If you clicked Install, let the installation begin! The SuSE installer shows you which discs it needs, how much material it needs from them, and a progress bar for each as it goes through the installation. Note, however, that it reboots right in the middle of that process. You can just let it go and let it choose its defaults as it comes back up, and it will return to the installation routine — if you walk away, all of this will happen automatically. However, you will need to be there to swap CDs if you're using them, so don't walk too far away.

After the installation is finished, SuSE continues with its post-installation setup routine.

Because I don't have infinite space in this book, from here I give you some quick notes on how to walk through this initial boot-and-setup routine. (Keep in mind that you can change the configuration for any of these items later if you want to.) Here's the drill:

1. **Choose a solid password for the root (administrative) user.**

   See Chapter 3 for pointers.

2. **In the Network Configuration section, first check to see that your Internet hookup is properly detected.**

   To review the types of hookups you might have, see Chapter 8. If yours is detected, you see the make and model of the card underneath the appropriate section. If not, you see Not Detected. You can change these settings later.

3. **If your Internet hookup is not detected, click the link for that section to go to its configuration.**

   To do so, click Add, walk through the settings (using Chapter 8 as a guide), and click Finish when you're done.

   • You may need information from your ISP or hardware documentation in order to do so. If the process gets overwhelming, just click Back until you return to the main Network Configuration section and select the Skip Configuration radio button and use Chapter 8 to set things up later.

TIP

- I also suggest that you look to the Firewall section in Network Configuration — in particular, the line starting with SSH — and then click the word *disabled*. This will change the word to *enabled*. You can find out more about SSH in Chapter 13.

4. **When you reach Test Internet Connection, if you're online and have immediate access to the Internet, select Yes. Then click Next.**

   If your attempt fails, don't be discouraged if you have to give up for now and move on. You can try again later.

5. **When asked whether you want to get online updates, choose Yes (if you're able to access the Internet right now).**

   This way you'll be starting with a fully up-to-date system. In the Installation Source drop-down list box, select the site that's geographically closest to you.

6. **Click the Manually Select Patches box so it's empty.**

   That tells SuSE to update everything automatically and to refrain from asking you annoying questions every few seconds. This automatic update can take a while, and even then it pauses sometimes to ask questions. If it says it's running into an error getting a patch, keep telling it to try again for a bit. Usually, the error corrects itself within five attempts or so. If you've tried ten times or more and it still doesn't go through, tell it to skip that fix. You can update again later, using Chapter 12. (If the *kernel*, the operating system's core, is updated, the system will reboot again before you proceed.)

7. **In User Authentication Method (login) screen, leave this setting as Stand-Alone (Local (etc/password)) machine unless you know for a fact that your machine is part of an NIS, LDAP, or Samba network.**

8. **In the Add A New Local User screen, the User Login box (Username), define the name of your login account.**

   Your *login account* is the one you'll use most of the time you're logged in, instead of the root account (see Chapter 3 for the rationale).

   - The User's Full Name is where you put your full name so that it appears right in your e-mail From headers and all that fun stuff.

   - If the account you're creating now is your login account, select the Receive System Mail box to put an X in it. This way, you get all the system warnings and whatnot right here — and don't have to log in as `root` to see them.

   - I don't recommend leaving Auto Login checked. You should have to actually log in to the machine, or it's too easy for people to use your account.

The Release Notes can be worth reading just to see what little things crop up that might apply to you, and what tips you might find useful for dealing with your personal setup needs.

9. **Configure your hardware.**

The Hardware Configuration section works just like the others. If you want to fuss with something, click the appropriate link, and you can always just leave it as is and look at it later. I deal with sound (see Chapter 18) and printing (see Chapter 7) later, in particular.

After you're finished setting up things, you're brought to a login screen. Go ahead and start exploring! Just make sure, at this point, that your installation discs are out of the drive so they're not in the way if you reboot later.

About the various SuSE versions

SuSE has a broad range of server and desktop products, from the home user to the enterprise. As usual, I focus on the desktop. You can examine the full range of SuSe offerings at its Web site: `www.novell.com/products/suselinux/`.

The desktop versions available from SuSE include these:

✔ **SuSE Linux LiveEval**: The SuSE LiveDVD, whose image is included on the DVD-ROM that comes with this book. If necessary, you can download this version from `www.novell.com/products/suselinux/downloads/suse_linux/`.

Then just burn it to DVD and boot right into a SuSE environment without having to install anything.

✔ **OpenSuSE:** This free download version of SuSE Linux is available from `www.opensuse.org`.

It's five CDs-worth of material, and the download can take hours even if you have a high-speed connection.

✔ **SuSE Linux 10**: This is a boxed set you can purchase; it includes many extra pieces of software that can't be included with OpenSuSE (for licensing reasons), along with a set of thick manuals.

Utilizing Ubuntu

Ubuntu Linux (`www.ubuntulinux.org`) is the new kid on the block compared to the other distributions discussed in this book. Most new distributions take quite a lot of time to gain a broad base of support, but Ubuntu has skyrocketed in popularity among the Linux community. This is yet another Debian-based distribution, although its installation is not as specialized for beginners as the others.

Unfortunately, we ran into a space problem with the DVD that came with this book, and had to drop Ubuntu off of the DVD. However, one reason Ubuntu was chosen was that you can:

- ✔ **Download it off the Web site.** To do so, click the Download link off the main page, and find the section labeled Download Sites. Under there, click the location geographically closest to you and you will be offered the file for download. This distribution is just one CD so it is one of the easier ones to get online by going to the site, clicking Download, and following the instructions.

- ✔ **Request to have a free set of CDs mailed to you free of charge when the next version is released.** To do so, click the Shipit - Free CDs link on the main page. Click Create A New Account, create your account, log in, and then walk through the rest of the disk request process.

Installing Ubuntu

There are two versions of Ubuntu, the LiveCD (which doesn't require installation) and the Install CD (which does). The installation version is the one included on the DVD-ROM that comes with this book, and I focus on installing this version here. I want to reiterate that this is probably the most difficult installation of all the distributions covered in this book. If you are uncomfortable with issues such as dual booting, I highly recommend placing this distribution on a computer it can have all to itself.

To install Ubuntu, follow these steps:

1. **Place the CD-ROM into your CD-ROM drive.**

2. **Reboot your computer.**

   If your computer ignores the CD, then you have to change your BIOS so it checks the CD-ROM drive *before* it looks at your hard drive(s). (See Chapters 2 and 3 for more information.) The Ubuntu installation screen appears.

3. **Press Enter to begin the installation.**

   Text flashes past and then the Choose Language screen appears.

4. **If you don't want to use English, select a language. When ready, press Enter.**

   The Choose Your Location screen will appear.

5. **If you are not in the United States, choose the appropriate country and press Enter.**

   The Select A Keyboard Layout screen appears.

6. **If you have more than one option, choose the most appropriate. Press Enter when you're ready to proceed.**

   The installer locates your CD-ROM drives — if it appears to freeze while scanning, wait a minute or so, it will probably pick up again — and then auto-detects more hardware. The Configure the Network screen finally appears.

7. **Type in a name for your machine if one isn't already there, and press Enter.**

   If one's already filled in, leave it alone. Your ISP or network administrator may have told you to use a particular name, so use that if the line is blank. (If you have no idea, you can leave it blank or make something up.) After you press Enter, more auto-detection goes on, and eventually the Partition Disks screen appears (see Figure 4-12).

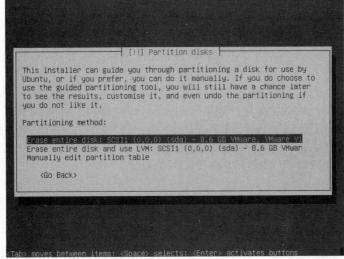

Figure 4-12:
The Ubuntu
5.10
Partition
Disks
screen.

8. **Referring to your notes from Chapter 2, select the partitioning option that you want to use, and then press Enter.**

   The three main options are Erase Entire Disk, Erase Entire Disk and Use LVM, and Manually Edit Partition Table. I recommend the LVM option when possible if you're erasing an entire disk. Since you might actually have to edit the partition table yourself, I will assume you've chosen the Manually Edit Partition Table option because it's the most difficult. If you choose this option, the second Partition Disks screen appears. If you chose one of the Erase Entire Disk options, then you can skip ahead to Step 26.

9. **If you need to clear some space, select a partition you want to get rid of and then press Enter. (If you have enough free space already, skip to Step 11.)**

The editing Partition Disks screen appears. You can spot empty space on your drive by the words FREE SPACE toward the right in the listings.

10. **Select Delete The Partition and press Enter.**

You are returned to the Partition Disks screen. If you have another partition to remove, return to Step 9.

11. **Use your up- and down-arrow keys to select the FREE SPACE section you want to use, and then press Enter.**

The free-space-use Partition Disks screen appears.

12. **If you want to use this selected free space to hold your entire Ubuntu installation, use your up- and down-arrow keys to select Automatically Partition The Free Space, and then press Enter. Otherwise select Create A New Partition and press Enter.**

Choose the automatic option if you only have one chunk of free space you're working with. There is also a Show Cylinder/Head/Sector Information option if you specifically want to look at that information; this option is likely to be of interest to advanced users. Because creating a new partition is the more complex task — choose this one if you're using more than one piece of free space to make your partitions (I cover how to do so in the remaining steps). If you're letting the installer partition things for you, walk through that process and proceed to Step 26 when you're finished.

13. **Specify how large you want this partition in the New Partition Size text box.**

The size already in the box is the maximum size you can make this partition. If you want to use that, just proceed to the next step. You'll need two partitions, one for *swap space* and one for your files. The swap one is a special kind of virtual memory for when your computer's real memory is full. Make the swap partition 2GB — type exactly that, **2GB** — if you aren't sure of how much RAM you have. If you do know, make your swap space twice the size of your RAM. For the other partition, make it as big as possible.

14. **After you have entered the swap-file value, use the Tab key to move to Continue, and then press Enter.**

The partition-type Partition Disks screen appears.

15. **Use the up and down arrows to select whether this is a Primary or Logical partition, and then press Enter.**

If you are unsure of what to choose here, choose Logical. It's a safe option. When you press Enter, the location Partition Disks screen appears.

16. Select either Beginning or End and press Enter.

It doesn't really matter which you choose. When you press Enter, the partition-settings Partition Disks screen appears.

17. If you are creating a swap partition, use the up and down arrows to go to the Use As line and press Enter. Otherwise skip to Step 20.

The how-touse Partition Disks screen appears.

18. Select Swap Area and press Enter.

You are returned to the partition-settings Partition Disks screen.

19. Use the up and down arrows to select Done Setting Up The Partition and press Enter.

You are returned to the overview Partition Disks screen with your new swap partition shown.

20. Use the up and down arrows to select the free space you want to use to contain the rest of your filesystem, and then press Enter.

The how-to-use Partition Disks screen appears.

21. Select Create A New Partition and press Enter.

The sizing Partition Disks screen appears.

22. You probably want to use all the available space, so just press Enter. If you don't want to use all the available space, change the value listed, and then press Enter.

The type Partition Disks screen appears.

23. Choose the partition type by using the up and down arrows, and then press Enter.

If this is the last partition you want to make, it's safe to choose either type. Again, if you aren't sure, choose Logical. When you press Enter, the editing Partition Disks screen appears.

24. Choose Done Setting Up The Partition and press Enter.

You are returned to the overview Partition Disks screen.

25. Choose Finish Partitioning and Write Changes To Disk and press Enter.

A warning screen appears.

26. Double-check your selections and choose Yes if you are satisfied, or No if you want to go back and make changes. Then press Enter.

The system sets up the partitions, installs Linux, and then takes you to the Time Zone Configuration screen.

27. Choose your location and press Enter.

The Set Up Users And Passwords screen appears.

28. **Type the real name or nickname you want your main account to have (*not* the administrator's account) and then press Enter.**

    The username Set Up Users And Passwords screen appears.

29. **Type the account login you want to use and then press Enter.**

    The password Set Up Users And Passwords screen appears.

30. **Type in your login's password, press Enter, and then repeat the process in the second screen.**

    See Chapter 3 for how to create solid passwords. After you press Enter both times, the installer sets up some more things behind the scenes and then ejects the CD.

31. **Remove the CD-ROM from the drive and press Enter, allowing the installer to reboot the machine.**

    After the machine reboots, it installs as much software as it can. If you are hooked up to the Internet, it will download and add things. When this process finishes, you see the Ubuntu login screen. Log in with the account you created during the installation process.

About the various Ubuntu versions

There are three versions of Ubuntu:

- ✔ **The installation version:** The version covered in this book can be installed on your machine.

- ✔ **The LiveCD version:** See the section "Using LiveCDs and LiveDVDs" (later in this chapter) for more on what these are and how to use them.

- ✔ **Combination DVDs:** The DVDs are really for those who want to install Ubuntu on many different types of hardware. If you just want to install it on a PC, you don't need a DVD.

Zapping Frustration with Xandros

Xandros (www.xandros.com) is another commercial distribution especially designed for people coming over from the Windows world to Linux; in particular, it's designed to integrate well with existing Windows networks in the workplace. It's another Debian-based distribution that is not meant for those who want to become full-fledged Linux geeks. Instead, it focuses on people who just want to get their work done.

Xandros is also particularly designed to make the transition from Windows to Linux as simple as possible. As such, it offers a layout and features that are similar to those in Windows XP. One handy item Xandros has introduced is the Xandros Networks tool, which is accessible from the desktop as an icon you can double-click. Xandros Networks lets you see the latest news from Xandros and browse through an online store for software (some of which is free to registered users). Downloading and installation through Xandros Networks require just a few clicks.

The version of Xandros included on the DVD-ROM that comes with this book is the Open Circulation Edition. You can burn this disk image to CD-ROM and then install it by using the instructions in the next section.

If you decide to purchase Xandros, you have a number of options:

- ✔ Purchase it online and have a physical box shipped to you.
- ✔ Purchase a boxed set in a store. You can find a list of places that carry Xandros by going to www.xandros.com/partners/channel partners.html.
- ✔ Purchase a computer with Xandros preinstalled (www.xandros.com/ partners/oempcs.html).

Installing Xandros

To install the Open Circulation edition of Xandros 3, follow these steps:

1. **Place the Installation Disk into your CD-ROM drive.**

2. **Reboot your computer.**

   If your computer ignores the CD, then you have to change your BIOS so it looks at the CD-ROM drive before it checks your hard drive(s). (See Chapters 2 and 3 for more information.) Expect it to take three minutes or so for the installer to launch.

3. **When you reach the Welcome dialog box, click Next.**

   The End User License Agreement appears.

4. **Read the agreement, click I Accept This Agreement and then click Next.**

   The Installation Selection screen appears.

5. **Choose either Express or Custom Install and then click Next.**

   I assume you've chosen Custom, because it's the more complex option. If so, then when you click Next, the Software Selection screen appears (see Figure 4-13).

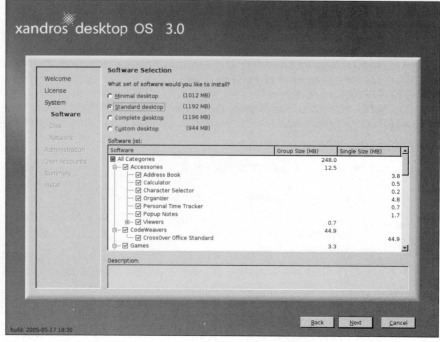

6. Select the software group you want to install.

Unless you're short on space, you might enjoy choosing the Complete Desktop because it gives you all the software. If you want to go that route, choose Complete to start with and then start removing items by clicking their check marks. Or you can choose Custom and then start adding things. When you click an item in the lower list, you see a description at the bottom of the screen.

If you do choose Complete, look in the Servers section and remove Apache (the Web server) from the list, along with FTP Server — unless you know for a fact that you intend to use an FTP server to let people get files.

7. After you finish choosing your software, click Next.

The Disk Configuration screen appears.

8. Select the disk configuration option that best represents what you want to do.

Handily, you can resize Windows partitions — even NTFS ones. Just to be different from the other sections in this chapter, I assume that you have an available hard drive (with enough free space) that you want to use for Linux — and that you selected Take Over Disk Or Partition.

9. When you're ready to proceed, click Next.

The Disk Configuration dialog box appears, as shown in Figure 4-14.

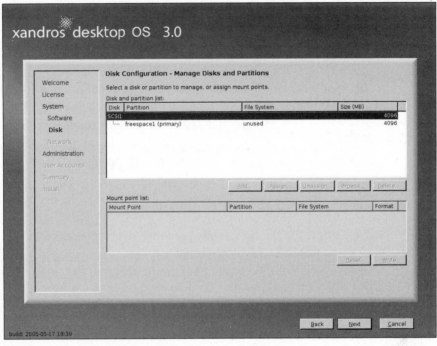

xandros desktop OS   3.0

Disk Configuration - Manage Disks and Partitions

Select a disk or partition to manage. or assign mount points.

Welcome
License
System
  Software
  Disk
  Network
Administration
User Accounts
Summary
Install

Disk and partition list:

Disk	Partition	File System	Size (MB)
SCSI1			4096
	freespace1 (primary)	unused	4096

Add   Assign   Unassign   Browse   Delete

Mount point list:

Mount Point	Partition	File System	Format

Reset   Write

Back   Next   Cancel

build: 2005-05-17 18:39

Figure 4-14:
The
Xandros 3
Disk Con-
figuration
dialog box.

10. **If you want to give a partition over to Xandros, then click that partition in the listing.**

    For an entire hard drive, you see them listed as IDE2, IDE3, and so on (or SCSI1, SCSI2, and so on).

11. **Click Next to proceed.**

    The Disk Configuration Summary dialog box appears.

12. **Examine the summary and click Back if something's wrong, or Next if you're ready to move on.**

    The Network Connection Configuration dialog box appears.

13. **Select the network device you want to use.**

    Typically, a desktop machine has only an Ethernet card, modem, or wireless card.

14. **If you're supposed to use DHCP, just click Next and skip to Step 18. Otherwise click Edit.**

    The Edit Interface dialog box opens.

15. **If you're using a dialup modem, select Do Not Configure Network Interface, click OK, and skip to Step 17. Otherwise select Static Address if you were told an IP address to use.**

    Modem setup is covered in Chapter 8.

16. **Fill in the IP Address and Subnet Mask fields as they were given to you by your ISP, and then click OK.**

17. **Click Next to continue your installation.**

    The Administration Configuration dialog box appears.

18. **Type your Administrator (root) password in both of the password text boxes.**

    See Chapter 3 for a discussion on safe use of the root account.

19. **If your computer has to integrate with a Windows network, enter its network name in the Computer Name text box.**

    What you're typing here is the NETBIOS name (if you're familiar with those). Follow the rules specified in that part of the dialog box. Traditionally, a NETBIOS name is in all-capital letters.

20. **Click the Make User Home Folders Private check box.**

    This feature not only makes it easier for each user to keep data private, but also helps the layout conform to what Red Hat uses in Fedora, making it easier for this book to make sense for you.

21. **Click Next to proceed.**

    The User Account Configuration screen appears.

22. **Click the Add button to create a normal user's account.**

    The Add/Edit User Account dialog box appears (see Figure 4-15). Because you want to avoid the Administrator (root) account as much as possible (see Chapter 3), this regular account is the one you use most of the time.

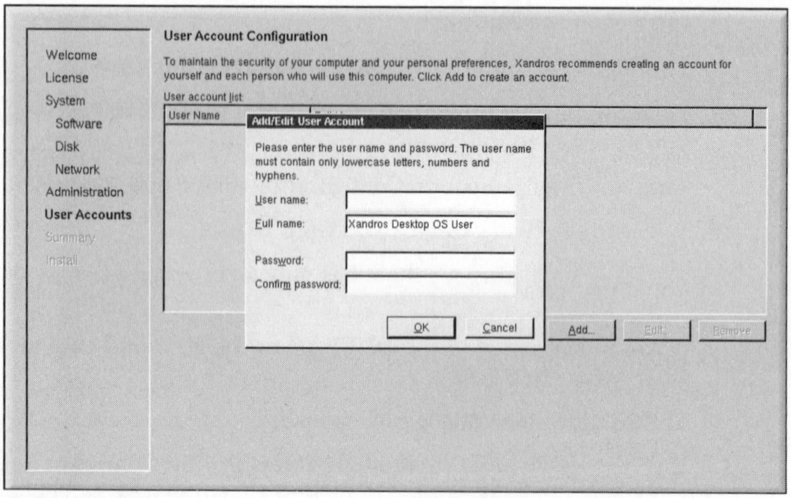

Figure 4-15:
The
Xandros 3
Add/Edit
User
Account
dialog box.

23. **Enter your login name in the User Name text box.**

    Your login name might be something like bob.

24. **Enter your full name in the Full Name text box.**

    This name has lots of uses in your system; it will, for example, appear as the Full Name field in your e-mail.

25. **Enter your password in both password text boxes and click OK to create the account.**

26. **Click Next to proceed.**

    The Installation Summary dialog box appears.

27. **Inspect the summary. If everything is as it should be, click Finish. Otherwise, click Back as much as you have to in order to fix things — and then work forward to this step once again.**

    Up until this point, nothing has been changed on your computer. When you click Finish, your installation actually begins. After it's done, the Installation Complete dialog box appears.

28. **Click Exit when you're ready to reboot the computer into Xandros.**

29. **Eject the CD when prompted and press Enter to reboot.**

    When the Xandros boot screen appears, you can either select the Xandros option and press Enter, or wait until it starts up on its own.

As with some other distributions covered in this book, Xandros has post-installation setup tasks for you to walk through. When you reach the login prompt, use your regular user account, which should automatically be selected. Type your password and click Login (or press Enter) to log in to the account and start the First Run Wizard. Here are some notes for walking through this process:

✔ Under Regional Settings, Locale is just for your language issues. It doesn't have anything to do with your time zone and whatnot. Also, unless you know for a fact that you want a particular item in Character set, just stick with what you're assigned. It's chosen based on your language, because a character set is literally the characters you have available to type. It's the same with keyboard layout.

✔ You don't have to set up your printers right now, but if you want to, you can — in the Printers dialog box. (I look closer at printers in Chapter 7.)

✔ Under System Behavior, you're choosing a combination of look-and-feel elements: Will it look like Microsoft Windows, MacOS, Linux (referred to as KDE here rather than Linux, you find out more about KDE in Chapter 6), or UNIX (Linux's ancestors)? And how will the system actually behave? (My coverage of Xandros in this book sticks to the default Xandros setting unless otherwise stated, but feel free to play with yours!)

✔ Under Registration, it's up to you whether you want to register immediately. You can always register later; you do have to register to get technical support, so here's a word to the wise: Register *before* you run into trouble. Registration also lets you download some of the programs available in Xandros Networks for free!

✔ When you reach the Finish screen, if you're on a network that's already connected to the Internet, click the Xandros Networks icon to update your system. This action makes sure that you've got all the latest security and bug fixes. The updater is automatic.

About the various Xandros versions

Xandros focuses on the desktop and has offerings for both home and business users. The free and commercial versions from Xandros include (at the time of this writing):

✔ **Xandros 3 Open Circulation Edition:** A free version, slightly different from the main commercial version. This is the version of Xandros included with this book. If you need to download this version for some reason, see the Xandros Web site at `www.xandros.com/products/home/desktopoc/dsk_oc_download.html`.

✔ **Xandros Desktop OS Version 3 Standard Edition**: The primary home use version of the Xandros desktop.

✔ **Xandros Desktop OS Version 3 Deluxe Edition:** Includes additional software for interoperating with Windows and Windows software, along with a larger manual than the one you get with the Standard Edition.

✔ **Xandros SurfSide Linux Edition:** For those who are big on using the Internet, including a USB headset for free Skype-to-Skype calling.

✔ **Xandros Desktop Version 3 Business Edition:** Includes extra software on top of what you would get with the Deluxe Edition, which allows Xandros to integrate better as a desktop on a Windows network, along with Sun's StarOffice, the commercial product behind the `OpenOffice.org` suite covered in Chapter 17.

Using LiveCDs and LiveDVDs

As I mention throughout this chapter (and book), *LiveCDs* and *LiveDVDs* (also called *bootable distributions*) are versions of Linux that you can launch directly — without having to install Linux — by rebooting a computer, using a Live CD-ROM (or DVD-ROM). The beauty of these versions, from a Linux newbie's point of view, is that you can try something out without having to actually install anything on your system. Old-timers love LiveCDs, too. If a system is broken into, rebooting it with a LiveCD is a way of giving yourself a "known good" (undamaged) system to work from while repairing the damage on the computer itself. Also, many bootable distributions offer highly specialized environments for particular tasks . . . but I'm getting ahead of myself.

LiveCDs and LiveDVDs tend to be slower than a traditionally installed system. That's because everything has to run directly from the CD or DVD-ROM.

Make sure, too, that you can save things if you have to. Many popular LiveCDs include a way to access your existing disks. You also can usually access your real hard drive space from a bootable distribution, though whether it supports NTFS or not depends on the version. Knoppix does support NTFS, though it's best to use it as read-only.

If I do actual work by using a live distribution and need to "save" it but can't access a hard drive for some reason, — or I won't be in that same location the next day — I quickly configure the distribution's mail client and just e-mail the work as attachments to myself. That's how I got those NTFS resizing images (see Chapter 2) from Knoppix over to my Fedora machine while writing this book!

Another popular option with LiveCDs and LiveDVDs is to use portable storage devices such as USB keychains. That way, you can carry around your keychain *and* your bootable distribution — and have access to both your preferred environment *and* your data at the same time. The important thing to know about USB storage is that Linux sees these items as SCSI drives, so if you have to access them manually (see Chapter 11), you'll access them as SCSI partitions. For example, if you've got your USB keychain plugged into the first SCSI slot, it would probably be `/dev/sda1`.

Finally, not all LiveCDs work with all PCs — but if one doesn't work for you, you just shrug and download another!

If you're using one of the LiveCDs or DVDs included with this book and it asks for a login password, what it's really asking you to do is to assign a password for this session. Just enter whatever password you want to use.

Finding Even More Linux

More than 300 different Linux distributions are available today, with new ones being created every year (while others fade from existence as the initial enthusiasm or funding behind them dwindles away). Many of these distributions are general purpose, or at least similar purpose (full desktop, full server, and so on), and so provide similar base software and surrounding tools to one another with different configurations, documentation, GUI trappings, installation procedures, and other bells and whistles. Even then, some general-purpose distributions serve some markets better than others. For example, TurboLinux is popular in Japan, Red Flag Linux is the official choice in China, and Conectiva is popular in Spanish-speaking countries. More special-purpose distributions exist as well. LiveCDs fall under this category, but even they fall into subcategories, with some of them (like Knoppix) serving the general-purpose segment, while others are fine-tuned as multi-media centers, system-rescue environments, and other cool specialist toys. To dig through the many full distributions available, check out DistroWatch (www.distrowatch.org) and let your mouse do the walking through more than 300 distributions. If you can't find enough to choose from here, go to this site's Related Links section, and you can find plenty more. If you're looking for LiveCDs, go instead to www.frozentech.com/content/livecd.php.

If you don't want to download and burn all this stuff — and don't happen to know any helpful Linux geeks — you may want to look up a local Linux Users Group (LUG). You can find a list of LUGs worldwide, listed by geographic region, on the GLUE (Groups of Linux Users Everywhere) Web site: www.ssc.com:8080/glue/groups. These folks are always happy to help the techno-logically challenged. These user groups also regularly sponsor events, called *demo days* or *install-fests,* where you can bring your computer and get all the help you need. These events are usually lots of fun for computer enthusiasts — hot- and cold-running caffeine and enough know-how to do just about any-thing with a computer.

Chapter 5

Booting and Stopping Linux

I like work; it fascinates me. I can sit back and look at it for hours.

— Jerome K. Jerome

*I*f you came here from Chapter 3 or 4, you likely just survived the first gauntlet of the Linux world: installing the operating system. I hope that booting for the first time worked well. If it did, and you decide that most of this chapter isn't for you, at least skip to the section near the end of this chapter, "Don't Just Turn Off the Machine!" Otherwise, if you're interested in finding out about what your machine does as it boots (this chapter can get pretty geeky!), read on.

Your Linux installation failing to boot properly is not necessarily an emergency. Much of this chapter is designed to help you deal with any problems you might run into. Before you curse Linux, remember that installing an operating system is no small task — and that, because many technical variables are associated with such an installation, many computer manufacturers insist on performing the task at the factory. (When's the last time you installed Windows yourself?) Companies such as Hewlett-Packard, Dell, and Wal-Mart (believe it or not) have been offering Linux preinstalled, so if you're too discouraged at this point, or are reading ahead and are too nervous to give it a shot, you can either use Knoppix (see Chapter 4 for how to use Knoppix without having to install it) or purchase a preinstalled machine from a vendor or a local computer builder.

To unravel the mystery of a Linux system that won't boot requires a bit of understanding of how your computer starts up. At the very least, being able to tell a repair person where the problem seems to be can make you feel a little less intimidated — and can even save you some money, because it speeds up their troubleshooting.

Giving Linux the Boot

Let's face it: As enjoyable as the experience is of staring at a dormant computer, the real fun starts when you turn on the computer. As with any electronic device, opening the electron floodgate is the first step to fun. A computer, however, has much more stuff to do than your toaster oven. Rather than warm up a simple heating element, your computer has to check all those gizmos that you (or the manufacturer) plugged into your computer's motherboard. After the initial power-up, the computer performs some simple hardware tests (called the POST, or Power-Up Self-Test) to determine whether those various components are working properly.

Checking all your hardware is just the beginning. Between the time you turn the computer on and the moment the glowing phosphor on your monitor prompts you for a login name, the computer is building itself an empire. If you listen and watch carefully, your computer and monitor show you signs of the boot process through bleeps, buzzes, whirring motors, clicks, messages on the monitor, and blinking lights.

Although you have heard the cliché "Rome wasn't built in a day," the boot process goes fairly quickly. This is pretty amazing, considering that the architecture of an operating system makes Rome's look like a stack of cardboard boxes; each time you power up your computer, it must build its whole operating system in memory. (Remember that an *operating system* is the core software that makes your computer work.) This process can be broken into four main steps, which I discuss in the following sections.

Step 1: Power-On Self-Test (POST) leads to BIOS

The POST process really has nothing to do with the operating system. Your computer performs this step whether you're running Linux or another operating system, such as Windows XP.

Some symptoms of a failed POST include these:

- ✔ An unusual series of long and short beeps

- ✔ Nothing displayed on the monitor

- ✔ No apparent activity other than the whirring fan on the power supply

- ✔ A puff of smoke or the pungent smell of burning electrical components from your computer case

- ✔ An error message, displayed on the monitor, indicating a hardware failure

If you encounter any of these problems, you have hardware troubles that need to be resolved before you can proceed. If your computer was running properly before you began your Linux installation, your computer *should* be getting through the POST just fine — POST problems don't tend to be caused by installing a new operating system; they're far more fundamental to the computer itself.

For all but the last of these errors, it's time to question your nephew Mortimer, who was last seen lurking around your computer with a screwdriver. (Or take your computer into a computer repair shop!) If you see an error message indicating a hardware failure, you might have a shot at fixing the problem in the BIOS. As the POST does its thing and finishes up, it briefly displays (usually at the bottom of the screen) instructions on how to enter "setup." Typically, these instructions mention pressing the DEL key or a function key such as F1. When you press this key (provided all goes well), you usually see a blue screen with black-and-white text. From here, if you're familiar with your hardware, you can try to figure out and fix the problem. However, many people would rather have a root canal with no anesthesia than mess with this stuff, so you may want to grab the nearest teenager or computer-repair-shop wizard and entreat him or her to take a look.

The good news is that if you can get to the BIOS at all, the problem *may* be easier to fix than one where the computer fails before you reach the BIOS.

Step 2: The BIOS passes the baton to the boot loader

After the BIOS gives the okey-dokey with a successful POST, the BIOS locates the first hard drive in your system and reads the first *sector* of that disk, which is often referred to as the MBR (Master Boot Record). On that first chunk of disk is a small program called a *boot loader.* The boot loader doesn't know much about anything, except how to start loading your operating system.

Two boot-loader programs understand how to load a Linux operating system: LILO (LInux LOader) and GRUB (GRand Unified Boot loader). LILO has been a tried-and-true boot loader for as long as Linux has been a gleam in a geek's eyeball; GRUB is newer — and much more sophisticated. Many distributions allow you to choose your boot loader. Typically, most people just stick with the defaults, which are as follows for six of the distributions I discuss in this book (Knoppix is not included because it boots directly from the CD-ROM or DVD-ROM drive):

Distribution	*Default Boot Loader*
Fedora Core	GRUB
Linspire	GRUB, with its own special routines on top of it
Mandriva	LILO
SuSE	GRUB
Xandros	LILO, with its own special routines on top
Ubuntu	GRUB

Sometimes "bad things" can happen to your boot loader. One common symptom of boot loader problems is a message saying that the operating system could not be found. Another hint that the problem is your boot loader is if you never see your *boot menu,* which is a screen that comes up during the boot process that lets you choose what operating system and version to boot.

The boot menu will look different from distribution to distribution.

If you suspect a boot-loader problem, see the section "Entering Rescue Mode," later in this chapter.

Step 3: The boot loader (LILO or GRUB) loads the system kernel into memory

Every computer (and electronic device) requires an operating system to run. The technical term for this operating system, or at least the core of it, is the *kernel.* If the kernel is your maestro, orchestrating all the components of your computer and delegating resources in a logical and cooperative manner, the boot loader is the red carpet on which the maestro arrives.

Many Linux distributions today actually put up a graphical progress screen during the kernel loading and *system initialization* phase (after the kernel finishes loading, when it finishes up the boot process). If you want to see what happens, typically you can click an icon or press a key. Just look for instructions on how to "see details." (Not all distributions offer this feature, so if you don't find a way to do this, don't panic.)

If available, watch the scrolling text for one of the symptoms below:

- ✔ The system freezes.
- ✔ A few dots appear across the top of the monitor, and then the system freezes.
- ✔ A few messages appear on the screen, and the final message reads `kernel panic`.
- ✔ The system reboots automatically.

The boot loader passes control over to the kernel. You know when the kernel is loading because you start to see crazy text like this:

```
Uncompressing Linux... Ok, booting the kernel.
audit(1092566112,337:0): initialized
```

Recovering from a kernel-loading failure (aside from the dread `operating system not found` situation described in the previous section) is one of the more challenging issues in Linux. This task is, unfortunately, not for the faint of heart. On the other hand, the failed kernel may be an updated one; if you have more than one Linux option in your boot menu, look at the version numbers for each of the options and choose the *second newest*. Doing so lets you boot into the last working kernel and have (at least) a working system. Then you can open up www.google.com and search on the specific error messages, or wait until the next kernel update comes out and ignore the bad one for now.

If it's your original installation that doesn't start properly, you unfortunately don't have a fallback kernel option. If this is your problem, I recommend either contacting your distribution's support address (if you purchased a commercial product) or joining the installation or beginner's help discussion list if you downloaded a free product. See Chapter 2 to find out where to locate help for each distribution discussed in this book. Or you could just reinstall; that's easier to do when it's a fresh installation. Sometimes things go a bit strange during the initial installation and reinstalling fixes the problem.

Step 4: Control is handed over to init

After the kernel's finished loading, it passes off the system initialization process to a program named init. The init program is responsible for starting all services and programs. You can see these processes starting as they scroll up the screen with [OK] or [FAILED] on the right side of the monitor. If you see these lines, you know that your kernel has finished loading.

The main problems you may encounter with init are *services* (programs that run in the background) that fail to start properly, as indicated by the [FAILED] status shown during the boot process. Services usually fail because of misconfigurations or unsupported hardware drivers. Sometimes a problematic service takes a long time to start up, so you may need some patience while you wait it out.

With many of these services, failure to start doesn't keep you from logging in and using your system. After the machine boots, you can use the techniques described in Chapter 13 to shut off a problematic service if it's being a pain. If the machine can't boot because of this service, you'll need to access your distribution's rescue mode to shut off the service — and rescue mode is covered in the next section.

Entering Rescue Mode

Heavy-duty system repair tends to happen in *rescue mode* — a special boot selection that simulates your hard disk by setting up what is called a *RAM disk,* holding the files entirely in memory. The benefit of this option is that you can perform necessary system surgery even if your installed system is hopelessly broken. The drawback is that this is a purely command-line interface — you really have to know your stuff to find your way around.

Appendix A contains a list of Linux commands to try to help you out. Chapter 20 addresses, among other things, how to fix your boot loaders from here (if your problem is with the boot loader), and how to track down the error messages your kernel might have left behind. You may also be able to find helpful tips by reviewing your distribution's documentation and online help forums.

Knoppix is quite popular to use for system rescues because it's a whole distribution on a CD or DVD. (For more on Knoppix and live CDs and DVDs, see Chapter 4.) See Chapter 21 for two ways you can use Knoppix for system repairs.

Just about every Linux distribution includes a rescue mode. Fedora's is the only rescue mode I have room to cover in step-by-step detail (a little farther along in this chapter), but at the very least, here's a quick reference to how to find the rescue mode in the distributions covered in this book:

Getting into rescue mode (a quick guide)

- ✔ **Linspire:** The CD contains a rescue mode and there's also one available at the boot loader menu if you can get that far. For the CD, when the installer starts, use your arrow keys to select ADVANCED OPTIONS, press Enter, and then navigate with the arrow keys to RUN Diagnostics, pressing Enter to proceed. If you can get into the boot-loader menu, select Diagnostics by using the arrow keys and then press Enter.

- ✔ **Fedora:** The DVD that came with this book, the DVD that you down-loaded, or the first installation CD, contains a rescue mode that you can enter by typing `linux rescue` at the installer's boot prompt.

- ✔ **Mandriva:** The first CD or DVD contains a rescue mode. When the installer starts, press F1 to access the command prompt, type `rescue`, and then press Enter.

- ✔ **SuSE:** If you obtained OpenSuSE or purchased the full version, the DVD, or the first installation CD, contains a Rescue System menu option. Use your arrow keys to highlight this option and then press Enter.

- ✔ **Ubuntu:** The CD contains a rescue mode. When the installer starts, press F1 to access the command prompt, type `rescue`, and then press Enter.

- ✔ **Xandros:** The CD contains a rescue mode. When the installer starts, press the Shift key. This action opens a list of menu options. Use the arrow keys to select Rescue Console, and then press Enter.

Using Fedora Code rescue mode (step by step)

To enter rescue mode in Fedora Core, place the DVD or your first CD into your DVD-ROM or CD-ROM drive and boot the machine. Then follow these steps:

1. **When the disk first loads, type `linux rescue` at the boot prompt.**

   This action begins booting the system into maintenance mode.

2. **Select your language and press Enter.**

3. **Select your keyboard type and press Enter.**

   The rescue system does its thing for a while, perhaps a minute or two on a slow system.

4. **When asked whether you want to start the network interfaces, answer No unless you know you need to download something.**

5. **At the Rescue screen, select one of the three options offered, and then press Enter.**

   Your three options are

   - **Continue:** The rescue interface tracks down your installed Fedora Core system for you.

     If you select this option (or the next) and it fails, you may need to reboot and restart the rescue system. After restarting, choose Skip.

   - **Read-Only:** The same as Continue, but you can't make any changes to your hard-drive installation.

   - **Skip:** If you choose this one, it's like saying *Don't bother trying to locate the filesystem, just give me a prompt!*

   I assume that you chose Continue. If so, a *shell prompt* (the rescue command-line interface) appears, and you now have access to the rescue interface.

6. **If the rescue process was able to load your Fedora installation, type** `chroot /mnt/sysimage`.

   Doing so enables you to use your system without having to type `/mnt/sysimage` in front of everything.

7. **When you're finished, keep typing `exit` until the machine reboots, and then eject the CD or DVD as the reboot happens.**

Don't Just Turn Off the Machine!

Even when you're not tapping the keyboard or clicking buttons, Linux is still running along in the background, doing lots of housekeeping chores. Some of these chores may involve swapping *cached data* to and from the fixed disk — a geeky way of saying that it's actually jotting down things onto your hard drive that before it had just been making sure to remember in RAM. When you shut off the power out of the blue, anything the computer was remembering but hadn't written is lost (kind of like when you or I fall asleep before making a to-do list for the next day).

If you're used to Windows 98, you need to recondition yourself: Don't just shut off the power when you're finished. For one thing, many Linux users leave their computers on when they're not using them — they just log out of their accounts so no one can mess with their stuff — and (oh yeah) shut off the monitor because monitors draw a lot of power.

When you do decide to turn off your Linux machine, for whatever reason, you must shut down the computer in an orderly manner. You can use one of these methods to shut down Linux properly:

> ✔ If you're in the GUI, log out of your account by using the main menu's Log Out option — Fedora Core users will find it under System⇨Shut Down — and then click the dialog box option that says (strangely enough) Shut Down.

> ✔ If you have a command prompt open, type the **halt** command at the shell prompt (#) followed by the root password; then when you press Enter, Linux shuts itself down and tells you when it's all right to turn off the machine.

> ✔ If you have a command prompt open, type the **reboot** command; then when you press Enter, Linux goes through the motions of shutting itself down, and then immediately reboots the machine.

> ✔ If you have a command prompt open, typing **shutdown -f now** (and then pressing Enter) is the most traditionally accepted method. The shutdown command optionally allows you to send messages to logged-in users and determine how long until the shutdown takes place. Another method is to use the poweroff command, which is just an alias to the previously mentioned halt command.

If you do accidentally cut the power to your Linux box, take heart; all is not lost. More often than not, you can reboot your computer and pick up where you left off. However, you may have to pay for your error by waiting during a quick filesystem check while the machine makes sure that nothing was damaged. This process is similar to the one Windows uses when somebody powers off incorrectly: The operating system may need to scan its hard drives to make sure that everything is okay.

If you're plagued with brief power outages or spikes that cause your computer to reboot, look into getting a UPS (Uninterruptible Power Supply) for your computer. These heavy, rechargeable batteries are designed not only to protect your computer from damage (read the box to see what features a particular UPS offers) but also to provide an extra five minutes or more of power so you have a chance to close your files properly and shut down your machine when the power goes out. Better yet, for those really brief spikes, the only inconvenience you'll have to deal with if you have a UPS in place is listening to it complain with beeps. The spike won't affect your computer at all!

Removing Linux from Your System

Although I'd hate to see you exit the Linux universe, I'd also hate to see you get trapped in Linux if you don't want to use it! How to most easily get rid of Linux depends on what you want to do:

- ✔ If you want to replace Linux with Windows, just install Windows on the machine. It will overwrite all of Linux, including the boot menu.

- ✔ If you want to remove Linux from a dual-boot setup, then boot into Windows, access a command prompt, and type **fdisk /mbr**. This action removes the Linux boot loader. It doesn't erase Linux, but you can then format the Linux drive(s) or partition(s) for Windows.

Windows XP and Xandros users have a special command they can use to remove this distribution. Boot your machine by placing your Windows XP CD-ROM into the Recovery Console. Change to the Windows directory, type fixmbr at the command prompt, and (oh yeah) press Enter.

Chapter 6

Checking Out Those Desktops

● ●

● ●

> *A bus station is where a bus stops.*
>
> *A train station is where a train stops.*
>
> *On my desk, I have a workstation . . .*
>
> — Steven Wright

A lot of people like to characterize Linux as a DOS-like environment, where all you can do is operate in this antique-feeling world where you have to type a lot of cryptic stuff without any pretty pictures. However, the Linux desktop offers you quite a nice working environment, as you see throughout this chapter. The cool thing is that most of it is configurable. Those who like to customize their systems can have way too much fun changing things around.

Deciding Which Interface to Use

Linux has two interface types: the *command-line interface (CLI)* and the *graphical user interface (GUI)*. If you use other computer systems, such as Windows or the Macintosh, you're already familiar with a GUI, with its pictures to look at and icons to click. Most Linux distributions include different versions of one of the two main GUIs available in the Linux world (GNOME and KDE).

If you've been using computers for a long time, you may also be familiar with the command-line interface, which usually consists of a black screen showing nothing but parallel lines of white text. The initial release and early development of Linux was all command-line oriented; GUIs then grew as the icing on the Linux cake, making it a lot more colorful to use and easier for people who would rather point and click than type.

In choosing between the command line and the GUI, you need to consider a number of factors. For a lot of people, this decision is pretty much a no-brainer issue. They have no intention of leaving GUIs behind. That's fine, but at the very least, you may want to become familiar with what's under the hood. Some day, your GUI might break and leave you at the ever-dreaded login prompt!

Speed is one important factor to consider when choosing between the command-line interface and a GUI. Keep in mind that if you're a programmer who needs to compile programs (or a scientist who needs to run software that does heavy number crunching), the GUI slows down your system. Also, typically, you have to shut off the GUI when using Linux as a server, because all those pictures are mostly a waste of RAM and processing speed — after all, more often than not, a server just does its thing with no one sitting there watching over it.

Readability can also be a big issue when you're choosing between the GUI and the command prompt. If you have a hard time reading text in those small command-prompt windows from within the GUI (Chapters 14 and 20 cover various ways to switch around), you can either make the windows and the font bigger, or work directly with the command prompt outside of the GUI. However, on a desktop that you want to use for word processing or editing images, you'll want a point-and-click environment. (This setup is the type I focus on, but I clue you in to the command line anyway, just in case!)

You also can choose from two major GUI versions: GNOME and KDE. Some people prefer one, and some the other; I'm not here to tell you which to use. If you stuck with the defaults for your distribution, then here's what you're using:

- **Fedora:** GNOME
- **Knoppix:** KDE
- **Linspire:** KDE
- **Mandriva:** KDE
- **SuSE:** GNOME
- **Ubuntu:** GNOME
- **Xandros:** KDE

Most distributions come with both KDE and GNOME, so most users simply choose their preferred desktop — Linspire, Knoppix, Ubuntu, and Xandros only come with their default GUI. Both GNOME and KDE are excellent desktops with strong fan bases. It's a personal preference, so I encourage you to install and experiment with both — and see which you like better. When you ask people why they chose one over another, often they really can't give you much of a good answer aside from, "That's what I've always used." Keep this in mind when people try to convince you that one or the other is the best thing since sliced bread!

The cool thing is that you can run most KDE programs under GNOME and vice versa. This ability is vital when it comes to making it easier on developers (and users) in the Linux community.

I cover how to switch between KDE and GNOME later in this chapter, in the section "Switching between GNOME and KDE."

Making the Best of the Command Line

The Linux command-line interface provides a quick, efficient way of entering commands and executing actions. Even if you're mostly a "GUI person," after you get the hang of using the command line, you discover that it's faster to perform some tasks at the command line than with a mouse in the GUI environment. However, if you prefer to use a GUI interface as your working environment, you can easily open a *terminal window,* which is a command-prompt window, to perform your command-driven tasks without having to completely leave the point-and-click environment (see Chapter 14).

There are some interesting things that you might find useful to know about using the command-line interface. One difference between the Linux command line and other interface command lines, such as the Windows MS-DOS prompt, Linux commands are case sensitive. Typing LS is completely different from typing ls, and, in fact, gives you an error because there is an ls command but there is no LS command. The Linux command line also has an *autocompletion* feature. If you know the first few characters of a command or filename, type part of it and press Tab to complete the rest automatically. For example, if you're trying to use the less command to view the contents of the file /home/bob/grocery_list, you can type less /home/bob/gro and press Tab to try and complete the filename. However, if you also have the subdirectory (folder) /home/bob/group_projects, you hear a beep. You can press the Tab key again, like double-clicking a mouse, to see the output:

```
grocery_list     group_projects
```

The cool thing here is that the command prompt beneath these items still has the text less gro so you don't have to retype it! You can then see that typing a c makes it clear that you're referring to grocery and not to group, so you just add a c to make less groc and press Tab again to finish the autocompletion. This technique can save you a ton of typing, especially with really long filenames!

Most Linux distributions also keep a running *history* of commands most recently used. To use this list, press the up-arrow key on your keyboard. This action pulls up the last command you typed. As you continue to press the up-arrow key, you step through the most recently entered commands from the most to least recent. If you accidentally pass what you're looking for, use the down-arrow key to go back. When the command you want appears at the command prompt, press Enter to execute the command, or edit it and then press Enter.

In Chapter 14, I cover the command-line environment in more detail.

When you installed Linux, you added a graphical login by default. (This addition is true for all versions discussed in this book.) Some versions of Linux give you the option of choosing a graphical or command-line login, which can cause a lot of confusion for folks who accidentally choose the command-line option. If you did so (or think you did) and find yourself lost after the machine boots up, see Chapter 20.

GNOME Basics

GNOME stands for the GNU Network Object Model Environment — not that this expansion tells you much! Suffice it to say that GNOME is a full graphical environment. Fedora, SuSE, and Ubuntu all use a similar version of GNOME, so I will focus on Fedora but try to point out where things differ. Mandriva is the only other distribution included with this book that also includes GNOME, but its version is similar as well. Figure 6-1 shows you what you see after you log in to your Fedora Core system.

To find out more about GNOME, visit the main GNOME site at www.gnome.org.

Keep in mind that the programs you have depend on the type of installation you chose and what customizations you made; if what you have is different from what you see in descriptions or the figures, don't panic!

The GNOME desktop environment is divided into four parts:

- ✔ The menus
- ✔ The menu-and-icon panel at the top of the screen
- ✔ The desktop panel on the bottom of the screen
- ✔ The icons on your desktop

Figure 6-1:
The default
GNOME
desktop
in Fedora
Core 5.

The menus

GNOME has three primary menus, all of them visible on the upper panel. From left to right, they are

- ✔ **Applications:** All the programs available through the GUI. (See Table 6-1 for Fedora and Ubuntu.)

- ✔ **Places:** Shortcuts to various locations on your hard drive. (See Table 6-2 for Fedora, SuSE, and Ubuntu.) Chapters 10 and 11 address this menu and its uses in far more detail.

- ✔ **System or Desktop:** Personal and system settings, along with more general overall system commands. The name can be either System or Desktop. (See Table 6-3 for Fedora.)

Menu items that have an arrow to the right offer submenus, which you can open by holding your mouse on that menu choice. Often the submenus have their own submenus within, offering even more programs.

SuSE and Ubuntu's menus contain slightly different lists of options, but mostly they offer the same content.

Table 6-1   Fedora and Ubuntu: Applications Menu Contents, Listed in the Order That They Appear

Menu Choice	What You Find
Accessories	Small, specific-function GNOME and X programs. Contains a calculator, character map, dictionary, PalmPilot tool, text editor, and more
Games	A collection of games
Graphics	A variety of graphics programs, including The GIMP
Internet	A few Internet tools, such as Evolution (e-mail and calendar program), Gaim (instant messenger), and Firefox (Web browser)
Office	The OpenOffice.org suite of applications (word processing, drawing, and more)
Sound & Video	Programs, such as a CD player and sound recorder, for working with your computer's multimedia hardware
System Tools	Many tools for managing, monitoring, and updating your system, such as a file browser and a software updater
Add/Remove Software or Add Applications	(Fedora and Ubuntu only.) Opens the application installation and removal utility

Table 6-2   Fedora, SuSE, and Ubuntu: Places Menu Contents, Listed in the Order They Appear

Menu Choice	What You Find
Home Folder	The contents of your user's home directory, as discussed in Chapters 10 and 11.
Desktop	The contents of your user's Desktop directory, which contains files and folders that should appear on your desktop.
Computer	The hard drives and temporary media available on your system.
Floppy	(SuSE only) A shortcut for floppy disks when inserted in the computer's floppy drive.
CD/DVD Creator	(Fedora only) A GNOME special folder for pulling together files that you want to burn onto a CD or DVD.

Menu Choice	*What You Find*
Network Servers	The computers and hard drives available on your network.
Connect To Server	A tool for connecting to many different types of servers.
Search	A filesystem search tool.
Recent Documents	Documents you have worked with lately.

Table 6-3	**Fedora: System Menu Contents, Listed in the Order They Appear**
Menu Choice	*What You Find*
Preferences	Your individual user settings.
System Settings or Administration	System-wide settings.
Help	The GNOME help tool.
About GNOME	Information about GNOME.
About Fedora	Information about Fedora Core.
Lock Screen	The capability to set your machine so no one can use your GNOME login without entering your password.
Log Out *user*	(Fedora only, in other distributions this menu option may be instead more like the Shut Down selection below.) Leave your current login session.
Shut Down	Suspend (put into sleep/hibernation mode), Restart (reboot), or Shut Down (shut off) the machine.

The Lock Screen tool

If you have your screen saver turned on and choose the Lock Screen option from the main menu, your screen saver appears or fades to black. Then if anyone moves the mouse or uses your keyboard, a dialog box appears with your login name in it and a password field. You can get back to work by entering your password. Until then, you're safe in knowing that no one else can mosey up to your computer and send off a joke e-mail to your boss while pretending to be you. Note that if you're logged in as the root user, the Lock Screen option doesn't work.

This feature is on by default in Fedora. To change it or its behavior in the distributions, using GNOME by default:

- ✔ **Fedora:** Choose System⇨Preferences⇨Screensaver.
- ✔ **SuSE:** Choose Desktop⇨GNOME Control Center⇨Screensaver.
- ✔ **Ubuntu:** Choose System⇨Preferences⇨Screensaver.

Going to the same menu will let you shut this feature off, or change how long it waits before automatically locking your screen.

I'm referring to just the GUI here, not the whole machine. Folks who know how to sidestep out of GNOME (something I discuss in Chapter 14) can start a virtual terminal session and do whatever they want. If you left yourself logged in to one of the virtual terminals, you can then do something there without trouble. But don't think of this feature as something that completely secures your computer! Your best bet, if you're walking away, is to check all the virtual terminals and make sure you're not logged in to *any* of them. Then you can either log out of your GUI or just use the Lock Screen option.

The Log Out tool

Depending on which distribution you're using, selecting Log Out either brings you to a dialog box that lets you log out, reboot, or shut the machine off, or it brings you to a dialog box where you can confirm that you want to log out of your current session. This section addresses the first option as the second is explained in Table 6-3.

In SuSE and Ubuntu, after you choose the Log Out option from the System menu, the screen darkens and the Are You Sure You Want To Log Out dialog box opens. To use this dialog box, follow these steps:

1. **If you want GNOME to remember which items you have open and return you to its current state after you log back in, make sure that you select the Save Current Setup check box.**

   This feature doesn't work with all programs, just some (mostly the ones that are part of GNOME).

2. **Click Log Out, Shut Down, or Restart The Computer to set the appropriate action into motion, or click Cancel if you don't want to do any of them.**

These options do the following:

- **Log Out:** Closes GNOME and returns to a login prompt.

- **Shut Down:** Shuts the machine down and then off.

- **Restart The Computer:** Shuts down the machine and then brings it back up.

Sometimes you will have a Suspend/Hibernate The Computer option if you want a computer to go into sleep mode.

3. **Click OK to go through with your choice or Cancel if you change your mind.**

The panels

Along the top and bottom of your GNOME desktop lives a pair of panels. Since these bars are neatly divided into sections, take a look at what's in each section from left to right, starting with the top panel. On the far left side of the top panel are the three menus discussed in "The menus" section earlier in this chapter.

As you continue your journey to the right, you run into a group of icons (refer to Figure 6-1). You can reach all these items through the main menu, but they're on the Panel to make them easy to find. In Fedora, these icons are

- **Firefox:** The Worldplanet-with-a-mouse pointer icon opens the Firefox Web browser. (See Chapter 9 for more.)

- **Evolution:** Just to the right of the Web browser button; launches an e-mail and calendar program. (See Chapter 9 for more.)

- **OpenOffice.org Writer:** Resembles two pieces of paper (and a pen) and opens the OpenOffice.org Writer word-processing program. (See Chapter 17 for more.)

- **OpenOffice.org Impress:** Opens the OpenOffice.org Impress presentation creation program. (See Chapter 17 for more.)

- **OpenOffice.org Calc:** Opens the OpenOffice.org spreadsheet program. (See Chapter 17 for more.)

Then you see a large blank space where you can add new icons. After the blank space in Fedora, here's what you find, from left to right — though your particular installation may have extra options displayed:

✔ **Date and Time applet:** Here you can see the day and time, depending on how this applet is configured.

✔ **Master Volume Control applet:** Click this to open the master volume control.

Now for the bottom panel. From left to right, you find on this panel in Fedora and Ubuntu:

✔ **Hide/Restore Desktop Applications:** This button lets you minimize all of your running programs immediately and then reopen them again with just one click.

✔ **Taskbar:** In this large space, you find entries for each program running on your desktop. You can change a program's status by using the boxes as indicated:

• If a program is minimized, you can open its window by clicking its panel task box.

• If a program is maximized but buried under another program, click its task box on the panel to bring it to the front.

• If a program is maximized and on top, you can minimize it by clicking its panel task box.

✔ **Workplace Switcher:** Allows you to work in four different desktop environments during a single login session. Each desktop environment has the same menus, panels, and background, but you can run different programs in each of the environments. It's an easy way to remain organized while you're working in multiple programs. Try it out. It's like having four monitors in one!

✔ **Trash Can:** A shortcut to your desktop trash can.

SuSE and Ubuntu have very similar layouts, though they offer slightly different icons.

Want to move a program from one workplace window to another? Click the little arrow or icon in the program's upper-left corner and select one of the following options:

✔ **Always On Visible Workplace:** Makes the window show up on all four.

✔ **Move To Workplace Right:** Slides the window horizontally to the right, into the "next door" workplace.

✔ **Move To Another Workplace:** Gives you the option of specifying Workplace 1 (far left), 2 (second in from the left), 3 (third in from the left), or 4 (far right).

You can see which workplace an open window is in by looking at the Workplace Switcher and spotting the little windows that match how your desktop is laid out.

Changing your panels

It's time to take a look at how to change the look and feel of your panels. You can customize your upper and lower panels individually through the Panel menu. You open this menu by finding free space on the panel you want to work with, and then right-clicking to pull up the Panel's context menu. (For a list of what this menu's items offer, see Table 6-4.)

If you have so many programs open that you're using the whole width of the lower panel, you may not have any free space to right-click in. Try being very precise with your mouse to find somewhere. If you can't, you may need to close a program or two to clear space.

Table 6-4	GNOME Panel Menu Contents
Menu Choice	*What You Find*
Add To Panel	The dialog box that lets you add applets, menus, and other objects to your main panel
Properties	The options for setting this panel's behavior
Delete This Panel	The capability to delete a secondary panel but not the main icon panel
New Panel	The options for creating new panels that sit on different parts of the screen
Help	The Help browser for GNOME
About Panels	A dialog box with some basic Panel information

The Add to Panel dialog box

The Add To Panel dialog box (see Figure 6-2) is accessible from the Panel menu (see the previous section). This dialog box contains a list of *applets* — small, specialized programs you can use to add particular functionality to a panel. To add one of these applets to your panel, open the dialog box, select the applet you want to use, and then click Add. The applet now appears on your panel. If you right-click the applet and choose Move, you can then slide the applet along your panel until you have it where you want it, and then click to release it.

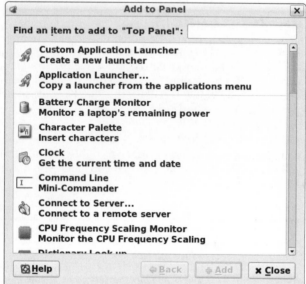

Figure 6-2:
The GNOME
Add to Top
Panel dialog
box in
Fedora.

Playing with GNOME desktop icons

Your initial desktop icons form a vertical line along the top left of your screen (refer to Figure 6-1), except in Ubuntu where there are none by default. In order, here's what you see from top to bottom in Fedora and SuSE:

- ✔ **Computer:** Opens the Nautilus file manager (see Chapter 10) with a list of your CD-ROM drive(s), hard drive(s), and more.

- ✔ **Home:** Opens the Nautilus browser (Chapter 10) with your home directory's contents displayed.

- ✔ **Floppy:** (SuSE only) Opens the contents of a floppy disk if you have one inserted.

- ✔ **Network Servers:** (SuSE only) Opens the Nautilus file manager (Chapter 10) with a list of the computers you can access over your local network.

- ✔ **Trash:** A GNOME shortcut that opens the Nautilus file manager to the Trash folder, which contains files that you dragged into it because you weren't sure if you wanted to delete them or not.

To use the trash can, drag into it any files you want to delete. Later, if you're sure that you want to be rid of them, you can empty the trash in one of three ways:

✔ Empty the entire contents by right-clicking the trash can icon and choosing Empty Trash from the context menu. When asked for confirmation, click Empty.

✔ Open the trash can by double-clicking the icon. Then delete the entire contents of the trash can by choosing File➪Empty Trash.

✔ Open the trash can by double-clicking the icon. To delete an individual item from the Trash, right-click it to pull up the Trash context menu, and choose Delete From Trash from the pop-up menu. When asked whether you're sure, click the Delete button to finish the job.

You can select more than one item by holding the Ctrl key to individually select them even if they're not next to each other; holding the Shift key to select a range of items; or left-clicking and then dragging to collect all the items that are in a box together.

✔ Another way to remove items from the trash can is to delete them manually from ~/.Trash.

KDE Basics

KDE, the *K Desktop Environment*, is the default in Knoppix, Linspire, Mandriva, and Xandros. Fedora and SuSE also include it and their KDE layouts are similar to that of the others. Because you can boot your system with Knoppix directly from the DVD that comes with this book, the KDE section focuses on Knoppix and points out where things are different in the other distributions.

To find out more about KDE, visit the main KDE Web site at www.kde.org.

The KDE desktop environment is essentially broken into three separate parts:

✔ The menus

✔ The menu and icon panel at the bottom of the screen

✔ The icons on your desktop

The menus

There is one primary menu in KDE, and you will find it on the left of the lower panel (Figure 6-3). In the four KDE-based distributions this menu is labeled:

✔ **Knoppix:** The letter K with a blue background

✔ **Linspire:** Launch

✔ **Mandriva:** A yellow star

✔ **Xandros:** Launch

Figure 6-3:
The Knoppix
4.0 KDE
desktop.

Menu items that have an arrow at the right offer *submenus,* which you can open by holding your mouse on that menu choice. Often, the submenus have their own submenus within, offering even more programs.

The main menus for each of the KDE-based distributions are quite different from one another, but their contents should ultimately be similar. Often KDE menus are broken up by horizontal bars dividing various types of entries. This section focuses on the Knoppix layout. The top portion of the Knoppix menu is All Applications and includes

- ✔ **Development:** Software-development tools
- ✔ **Editors:** Various text editors
- ✔ **Education:** Educational programs that are not games (DVD only)
- ✔ **Edutainment:** Educational games
- ✔ **Emulators:** Software used to emulate other platforms
- ✔ **Games:** Lots of games
- ✔ **Graphics:** Image editors

- ✔ **Help:** The help menu

- ✔ **Internet:** Internet-related software

- ✔ **KANOTIX:** Some configuration tools

- ✔ **Knoppix:** Knoppix-specific menus

- ✔ **Multimedia:** Sound, video, and other multimedia software

- ✔ **Office:** Various office productivity programs

- ✔ **Settings:** Various system settings

- ✔ **System:** System and administration tools

- ✔ **Toys:** Silly but fun stuff

- ✔ **Utilities:** More interesting tools

- ✔ **Lost & Found:** Additional tool. (DVD only)

- ✔ **Control Center:** The KDE control center for desktop configuration

- ✔ **Find Files:** The search program

- ✔ **Help:** The help interface

- ✔ **Home:** The Konqueror file manager open to your home directory

The second section of the Knoppix main menu is Actions, which contains

- ✔ **Bookmarks:** Bookmarks you've set in your Web browser(s)

- ✔ **Quick Browser:** Quick way to open various points in your filesystem in Konqueror (see Chapter 11)

- ✔ **Run Command:** An interface for starting programs by hand

- ✔ **Switch User:** Change to a different user login

- ✔ **Lock Session:** The same as the Lock Screen application in Table 6-3 (See the section "The Lock Screen tool" earlier in this chapter for more)

- ✔ **Logout:** Log out of your account, reboot the machine, or shut it down (See the section "The Log Out tool" earlier in this chapter for more)

The panel

Along the bottom of your KDE desktop lives a panel. Since this bar is neatly divided into sections, take a look at what's in each section from left to right. On the far left is the main menu, as discussed in the section "The Menus" earlier in the KDE portion of this chapter.

As you continue your journey to the right, you run into a group of icons (refer to Figure 6-3). You can reach all these items through the main menu, but they're placed on the Panel so you can find them quickly and easily. In Knoppix, from left to right these icons are

- **Knoppix Penguin Menu:** Configuration options.
- **Window List:** Here you can open and minimize program windows.
- **Desktop:** This button lets you minimize all your running programs immediately and then reopen them with just one click.
- **Home:** A shortcut to open your user files.
- **Konsole:** A program that gives you a terminal in a window.
- **Konqueror:** A Web browser.
- **Firefox:** The Worldplanet icon opens the Firefox Web browser. (See Chapter 9 for more.)
- **OpenOffice.org:** A general interface to the OpenOffice.org office suite, discussed in Chapter 17.

Next on the Knoppix panel is the **Workplace Switcher,** as discussed in the Panel section in the GNOME portion of this chapter. To its right is blank space where the taskbar appears. Here you find entries for each program running on your desktop. You can change a program's status by using the boxes as indicated:

- If a program is minimized, you can open its window by clicking its panel task box.
- If a program is maximized but buried under another program, click its task box on the panel to bring this program to the front.
- If a program is maximized and on top, you can minimize it by clicking its panel task box.

Continuing to the right of the Workplace Switcher on the Knoppix desktop, here's what you find:

- **Language Switcher:** The flag icon can be clicked to cycle through the supported languages, or you can right-click it to directly access the menu of options.
- **Screen Size and Rotate:** You click (or right-click) this icon to alter your screen resolution and other display settings.
- **Volume Control:** Set your volume for sound applications.
- **Time and Date:** View the time and date or click to open a calendar.

Changing your panel

You can customize your panel through the Panel menu. Open this menu by finding free space in the taskbar, and then right-clicking to pull up the Panel's context menu. This menu offers

- ✔ **Add to Panel:** Items you can add to this panel
- ✔ **Remove from Panel:** Options for removing items from the panel
- ✔ **Configure Panel:** Change the panel's current settings
- ✔ **Help:** Open the help files regarding KDE's panels

If you have so many icons on your panel that you're using the whole width of the upper panel, you may not have any free space to right-click in. You may need to remove an icon or two to clear space.

The KDE Add To Panel menu contains the following sections:

- ✔ **Applet:** Various applets (mini-programs) you can attach to your panel
- ✔ **Application:** Launchers for applications already in your main menu
- ✔ **Panel:** Create new panels
- ✔ **Special Button:** Add specialty buttons

Playing with KDE desktop icons

Your initial desktop icons form a vertical line along the top left of your screen (refer to Figure 6-3). Knoppix has a different layout than most in that its top icons are for each of the CD-ROM and DVD-ROM drives on the system, and then below these are icons for each of the hard drive partitions on your system, and then there is the floppy drive icon, and then an icon for help on Knoppix, and then the Trash can. Most distributions have a more standard layout similar to what you saw in the "Playing with GNOME desktop icons" earlier in this chapter.

To use the trash can, drag into it any files you want to delete. Later, if you're sure that you want to be rid of them, empty the entire contents by right-clicking the Trash can icon and choosing Empty Trash Bin from the context menu. You can put the contents back where they were originally by clicking the Trash can, right-clicking the file you want to place back, and selecting Restore.

Switching between GNOME and KDE

When a distribution offers you a choice between desktops, and you have installed both desktops, you can typically select which one to use when you log in. In Fedora, Mandriva, and SuSE you have this option in your login screen:

- ✔ **Fedora Core:** Click the Session icon on the lower part of your login screen to bring up a dialog box where you can choose which GUI you want to use.

- ✔ **Mandriva:** Click the Session Type icon and choose the GUI you want to use from the Session Type context menu.

- ✔ **SuSE:** Click the Session icon and choose the GUI you want to use from the dialog box that appears. When you have selected your choice, click OK.

Chapter 7

Configuring Linux

. . . .

. . . .

The doctor can bury his mistakes but an architect can only advise his client to plant vines.

— Frank Lloyd Wright (1869–1959)

*U*nlike both the architect and the doctor, the computer user isn't stuck with configuration mistakes. You can tweak and change things until you're happy with them! Because the first thing a lot of people like to do with a new system is get it set up just right, I thought I'd spend this chapter sharing some of the core bits of knowledge that can help you do just that. You start by finding out more about user accounts and why I am so insistent (in Chapters 3 and 4) that you create a special one for your own personal use. Then you find out how to set up your machine to talk to your printer. I also show you where the cool configuration tools are for your distribution so that you can get down to some serious customization.

Accounts Great and Small

Linux is a *multiuser* operating system. It allows every user to have a unique account and allows more than one user to log in at the same time. Typically, even if you're the only user on a system, you need an account of your own that *isn't* the root user's. (I explain why in the next section.) In addition, having multiple accounts is especially fun for experimenting with different user setups. That way you can create a main account to be more careful with and a goofing around account to completely mess around with.

Avoiding root

The *root user,* also known as the *superuser* or just *root,* has access to anything and everything on your machine. There is no blocking root from a directory, file, command, or device — so many Linux beginners figure they may as well use the root account all the time because it's so convenient.

In a word, don't. For lots of good reasons, you shouldn't use the root account for everyday use:

- ✔ **Overkill.** You don't always need root-level access for mundane tasks.
- ✔ **Root-level access is as much a curse as it is a blessing.** If you mess up as a regular user, you mess up only the stuff in your account. If you mess up as the root user, you can wipe out everything — *all the files on your entire Linux system!*

 Don't think that you really would wipe out everything? Many experienced Linux administrators tell horror stories about the day they made a fatal typo or weren't paying attention to what they were doing and completely destroyed an installation.

- ✔ **Root can make you look like a clueless braggart.** If you send e-mail or news posts as root for anything other than serious administrative business, people think that you don't know what you're doing or that you're showing off.
- ✔ **Root comes with too much temptation.** The superuser can read other people's e-mail messages and files, which introduces a few "tiny" ethical issues.

Linspire has a slightly different philosophy. By default, you have only one account when you're using Linspire — you can create more later, which I highly recommend doing. In the next section, I show you how to create new accounts in each of the distributions covered in this book so you don't have to use root for everyday work. Or, worse, let someone who's borrowing your computer for a moment browse the Web under root (bad idea, trust me)!

Creating user accounts

Most Linux distributions include a graphical interface application for creating and managing user accounts. Here's how you can find this application for your distribution:

✔ **Fedora Core:** Choose System⇨Administration⇨Users And Groups to open the User Manager.

✔ **Knoppix:** From theMain Menu, choose⇨System⇨KUser to open the KDE User Manager. However, if you're not leaving Knoppix running for the long term, there's often no need. By default you use it as the user `knoppix`.

✔ **Linspire:** Choose Launch⇨Settings⇨Additional Options⇨User Manager to open the KDE User Manager. After you've done this, you can select a different user to log in as at the graphical login prompt. By default, Linspire has you running as the root user.

✔ **Mandriva:** From the Main Menu, choose System⇨Configuration⇨Other⇨ User Administration to open the Userdrake tool.

✔ **SuSE:** Choose Desktop⇨YaST to open YaST. (See the upcoming section "SuSE tools" for more on YaST.) On the left, choose Security and Users. Then on the right, choose User Management to open the User And Group Administration dialog.

✔ **Ubuntu:** Choose System⇨Administration⇨Users and Groups to open the User Manager.

✔ **Xandros:** Choose Launch⇨Control Center to open up the Xandros Contol Center. From here, click the plus next to System Administration to expand this menu and then click User Manager to open the User Manager tool.

While these tools aren't exactly identical from distribution to distribution, they're all quite similar — and work in essentially the same way. After all, each application has pretty standard steps for creating user accounts. I walk you through how to create user accounts in Fedora Core, and most of the same steps apply elsewhere.

To create a new user account in Fedora, follow these steps:

1. **Choose System⇨Administration⇨Users And Groups.**

   Because you're (hopefully) using a regular user account, the Password for root dialog box appears.

2. **Enter the root password and click OK.**

   The User Manager window opens, as shown in Figure 7-1. When the application opens, the user account you created during installation already appears.

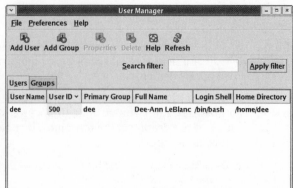

Figure 7-1:
The User
Manager
application,
in Fedora
Core 5.

3. **Click the Add User button.**

   The Create New User dialog box opens, as shown in Figure 7-2.

Figure 7-2:
The Create
New User
dialog box in
the User
Manager
application,
in Fedora
Core 5.

4. **Enter a name for your new user in the User Name field.**

   In Linux, the case of the user account is important, so note the case as you type the information. Typically people use all lowercase so they don't have to keep track.

5. **Fill in the user's full name (as you want it to appear in an e-mail From header, for example) or nickname in the Full Name field.**

Creating good passwords

Good passwords consist of the following:

✔ A combination of numbers, letters, and even punctuation marks

✔ Uppercase *and* lowercase characters

✔ No dictionary words

✔ Six or more characters

✔ No family or pet names, friends' names, birthdays, anniversaries, or other items that someone can easily guess about you.

6. **Enter the password in both Password fields.**

   The remaining items are more advanced, so you can ignore them for now.

7. **Click OK to save the new account.**

8. **If you want to create another account, repeat Steps 3 through 7; if you're finished, choose File⇨Quit to close the user creation program.**

Printing with Linux

Unless you live in a paperless environment, you most likely need to print something (such as a letter, a picture from your digital camera, or an invoice) from time to time. Therefore your Linux system has to be able to print; here's where you set it up to do that job. It can be helpful to know, before you continue, the make and model of your printer, as well as how it's connected to your computer:

✔ Is it a *local printer,* meaning that it's connected directly to your computer through a parallel, serial, or USB port?

✔ Is it a *network printer,* meaning that it doesn't have to be connected to any single computer and sits on the network as its own (usually shared) machine?

✔ Is it a *remote printer* but not a *network printer,* meaning that it's connected to another computer on your network? If so, is this a Windows, Linux, or OS X computer?

You can find your printer-configuration tool this way:

✔ **Fedora:** Choose System⇨Administration⇨Printing to open the Printer Configuration tool.

- **Knoppix:** From the Main Menu, choose Knoppix⇨Configure⇨Configure Printer(s) to open the Configure Printers tool.

- **Linspire:** Double-click the Printers desktop icon to open the Configure - Printers tool and then click the Add⇨Add Printer/Class button to open the Add Printer Wizard.

- **Mandriva:** From the Main Menu, choose System⇨Configuration⇨ Configure Your Computer to open the Mandriva Linux Control Center. Within this dialog box, click Hardware and then Set Up The Printer(s) to start Printerdrake.

- **SuSE:** Choose Desktop⇨YaST to open the YaST tool discussed later in this chapter, in the section "SuSE tools." From here, select Hardware on the left, and then Printer on the right, to open the Printer Configuration tool.

- **Ubuntu:** Choose System⇨Administration⇨Printing to open the Printers dialog box, and then choose Printer⇨Add Printer.

- **Xandros:** You had the option to add a printer with the First Run Wizard the first time your system booted — though, of course, you can skip this with no problem. If you skipped printer setup, choose Launch⇨Control Center to open the Xandros Control Center. Click the plus sign next to Peripheral Devices to expand this menu, and then choose Printers. Choose Add to open the Add Printer Wizard dialog box.

In this section, I describe how to set up a printer — though only in Fedora, due to space restrictions. Although each application is different, they all involve the same basic steps for configuration, even though these steps may be in different orders or worded a little bit differently. Follow these steps for Fedora (or if you're using another distribution, read through here and use what you find out to set up your printing through the appropriate tool):

1. **To access the printing setup tool, choose System⇨Administration⇨ Printing.**

   The Printer Configuration window appears, as shown in Figure 7-3. If you're not logged in as root, you're prompted to enter the root password.

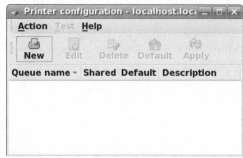

Figure 7-3: The opening window of the Printer Configuration tool.

2. **To begin setting up your printer, click the New button.**

   The Add A New Print Queue window appears. Click the Forward button to advance to the next step.

3. **In the Queue Name window, type the name you want to assign to this particular printer.**

   If you have multiple printers, add something in the Short Description text box to help you tell them apart later.

4. **When finished, click the Forward button to advance to the next step.**

   The Queue Type dialog box appears, as shown in Figure 7-4.

Figure 7-4:
The Queue Type dialog box in the Printer Configuration tool.

5. **Using the drop-down list, select the type of queue you need.**

   The queue type corresponds to how the printer is connected:

   - If the printer is directly attached to your Linux system, choose the Local Printer option (Locally-Connected).

   - If yours is a networked printer that understands the Internet Printing Protocol (IPP), or is attached across your network to another Unix (including Linux and OS X) machine, select Networked CUPS (IPP).

   - If yours is a printer connected to another Unix machine that's using LPD, choose Networked UNIX (LPD).

   - If the printer is attached to a Windows machine on your network, select Networked Windows (SMB).

   - If the printer is attached to a Novell Netware machine on your network, select Networked Novell (NCP).

   - If the printer has HP JetDirect networking technology, then choose Networked JetDirect.

The dialog box changes format depending on which of these items you selected.

 6. **Enter the additional information required for your particular choice.**

    For example, if you chose Networked CUPS (IPP), you need to fill in the print server's name (or IP address). You can ignore the Path text box and keep the defaults. Each of these options explains what information it needs from you. Click the Help button if necessary.

 7. **After you've entered the information, click Forward.**

    The Printer Model dialog box appears.

 8. **Click the Generic bar to open the list box that allows you to select your printer's manufacturer and then scroll to the appropriate option.**

    The selection of models changes, according to your manufacturer's list.

    Choosing the correct make and model of your printer is important because Linux loads and associates a specific print driver (software that talks to the printer) that corresponds to the information you supplied. If the wrong printer make and model are specified, the system tries to use the wrong print driver. The result of this mismatch is usually garbled characters and symbols when you attempt to print to your printer.

 9. **Select your printer model and then click Forward.**

    The Finish And Create New Print Queue dialog box appears.

10. **In the Finish And Create The New Print Queue dialog box, click Finish to enable your new printer.**

    You're offered the opportunity to print a test page.

11. **Click Yes to print a test page.**

    If this page doesn't print properly, make sure that you set the proper make and model for your printer. Some manufacturers assign similar model numbers to very different printers, and it's easy to get them confused.

12. **If the test page comes out great, click Yes when you're asked whether it looks okay; if it doesn't come out at all or it looks garbled, click No.**

    If your answer was No, you're shown a copy of all the data that went to the log file when you tried to print. Scroll down to the last few lines to find hints to what your problem is. (This situation happened to me once, and it turned out to be a problem with my networking, not with my printer!) If you're having problems, return to the beginning of this process and make sure that all your selections are correct.

    If your test page is okay and you clicked Yes, the main Printer Configuration window appears, and your new printer is listed in the tool.

13. **Choose Action⇨Quit⇨Save to close the printer configuration tool.**

Zen and the Art of Linux Configuration

One of the items that makes each distribution stand apart from the others is its collection of configuration tools. The friendlier the tools, the more likely that folks new to Linux will flock to that distribution. Mind you, old-timers don't mind having easy tools around either, especially when they're moving from one distribution to another. It saves them from having to re-learn where each distribution keeps its configuration files.

In this section, I look at the configuration tools available in each version of Linux covered in this book. An important thing to note is that the Control Panels in each of the KDE-default distributions (Knoppix, Mandriva, Linspire, and Xandros) all look (and work) in very similar manners because they're all based on the main KDE Control Panel.

Fedora Core and Red Hat tools

Red Hat's Fedora Core community project comes with a number of tools developed by Red Hat for its commercial products, as well as a variety of tools built by the community, such as the GNOME Project's tools. When it comes to customizing your desktop, you can find most of what you're looking for by choosing System⇨Preferences. Instead of having a large control center, GNOME has opted to keep the configuration tools broken into smaller, individual programs. You find this layout in other GNOME installations as well.

Keeping with the theme of smaller, more specialized tools, your various system-wide configuration options are available by choosing System⇨ Administration.

Knoppix tools

Knoppix comes with so many tools that it's easy to get lost as you stagger around the menus, overwhelmed. The main place to find configuration tools in this distribution is by choosing Knoppix from the Main Menu (the letter K in the bottom left corner). Inside this menu is a set of submenus, some of which offer configuration options:

- **Configure:** Options for setting up your computer's sound card, printers, a real home directory that sticks around between the times you boot with this distribution (persistent Knoppix disk image), and more.

- **Network/Internet:** Internet connection (see Chapter 8) programs for everything from modems to ISDN.

✔ **Services:** Options for starting various servers useful on the desktop, such as SSH (see Chapter 13), Samba for offering Linux files to your Windows machines over your network, and a firewall.

In addition to this location, you also find some configuration programs by choosing Settings from the Main Menu:

✔ **Configure The Panel:** This program lets you customize your panel — moving it elsewhere, hiding it, changing its appearance, and so on.

✔ **Desktop Settings Wizard:** This option opens the KDE setup wizard.

✔ **Menu Editor:** This option opens the KDE Menu Editor, where you can customize your Main Menu's contents.

✔ **Menu Updating Tool:** This option searches your system for particular programs and adds them to your menus if they're not there.

✔ **Printing Manager:** This program (see Figure 7-5) opens a handy print manager that can help you do things like printing to PDFs, sending to fax machines, and so on.

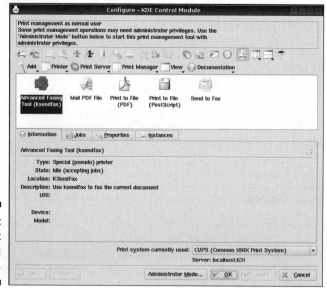

Figure 7-5:
The Knoppix
3.6 Printing
Manager.

Linspire tools

The first time you run Linspire, the First Time Setup dialog box appears, and it will keep appearing until you check the I Agree To License check box. In this tool, you have the option of walking through a system configuration process, setting values like your time zone, date, time, resetting your main password, changing your screen's resolution, creating new user accounts, and renaming the machine. Clicking Finish closes the tool and launches the Linspire Audio Assist Tutorials. Feel free to listen to (and watch) these as long as you like before moving on!

If you want to bail out immediately from the Audio Assist Tutorials, click the X in the upper-right corner to close the tutorials.

To find the remaining configuration tools, choose Launch⇨Settings and then choose one of the following:

- ✔ **Additional Options⇨Change Password:** Change the password for the account you're currently using.

- ✔ **Additional Options⇨Programs To Autostart:** Contains shortcuts for the programs you want to start automatically when you log in. To add items to this folder (when it's open):

    1. **Open the Main Menu.**

    2. **Browse to the program you want to launch when Linspire starts.**

    3. **Drag the program into the Autostart window.**

    4. **When the context menu pops up, select Copy Here.**

        Your new Autostart shortcut appears.

- ✔ **Additional Options⇨Rename Computer:** Change the name you assigned to this computer.

- ✔ **Additional Options⇨User Manager:** Create and remove user accounts.

- ✔ **Control Center:** The Linspire Control Center (see Figure 7-6) is the central point for configuring this distribution for everything except adding and updating your software. You find out how to do work with this panel in Chapter 12.

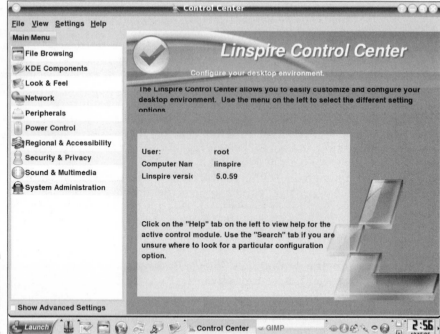

Figure 7-6:
The Linspire
5 Control
Panel.

Mandriva tools

Mandriva includes many configuration tools, though actually some of them are duplicates — often you have the option of running either a large tool or just a small component of that tool. You can find most of the Mandriva tools by going to the Main Menu and choosing System⇨Configuration. This sub-menu contains the following options:

- ✔ **Configure Your Desktop:** The KDE Control Center contains many, many options for tweaking your desktop settings. All users on your system can change things to fit their own preferences.

- ✔ **KDE:** Each individual option here maps to one of the choices in the KDE Control Center. It's a handy way to avoid having to open up the whole tool just to make one change.

- ✔ **Hardware:** A number of the hardware-related settings from the Mandriva Control Center are available here, eliminating the need to always open that tool.

✔ **Packaging:** This may be one of your more popular options as you use Mandriva over time. Here's where you find many of the Mandriva Control Center options for managing your software. (See Chapter 12 to find out more about these options.)

✔ **Printing:** This option leads you to printer-related programs and utilities.

✔ **Other:** A smattering of tools— some available in the Mandriva Control Center and some just plain handy by themselves.

✔ **Configure Your Computer:** The Mandriva Control Center (see Figure 7-7) is usable only by the system administrator (root account), who can alter system-wide settings here.

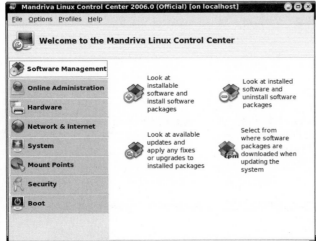

Figure 7-7:
The
Mandriva
Control
Center in
Mandriva
2006.

SuSE tools

SuSE offers two primary places to configure your system. One of them is the GNOME Control Center, which is available by choosing Desktop⇨GNOME Control Center. The other is YaST, which you will hear a lot about throughout this book. You can access this tool through Desktop⇨YaST (see Figure 7-8).

You can use many of the tools discussed in this chapter at the command prompt, though not all of them. YaST actually has a full command-line version in case you're not using a GUI!

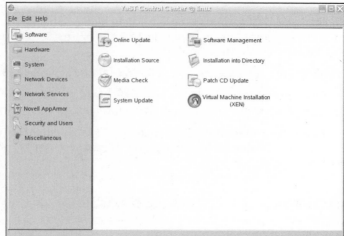

Figure 7-8:
The YaST
interface in
SuSE 10.

Xandros tools

Xandros offers a customized version of the KDE Control Center called the Xandros Control Center, available by choosing Launch⇨Control Center (see Figure 7-9). Both your system-wide and your individual look-and-feel settings are available in this tool.

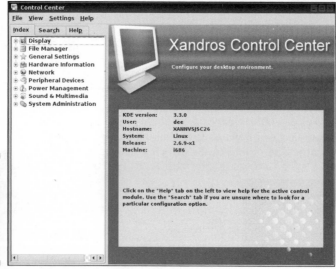

Figure 7-9:
The
Xandros
Control
Center in
Xandros 3.

Ubuntu tools

Ubuntu is probably the least fancy of the distributions included in this book. One reason is that Ubuntu is the newest; its developers haven't had the time to create as many tools. Another reason, however, is that Ubuntu is more of a "raw GNOME" distribution than the others that include GNOME (Fedora, Mandriva, and SuSE).

You will find most of Ubuntu's settings under the System menu, in both System⇨Preferences and System⇨Administration.

As you can see, the cool thing about learning one Linux distribution is that you're mastering useful things to help you survive *another* version of Linux. Remember that all these distributions are relatives, like cousins. Now get out there and have some fun tweaking your system!

Part II
Internet Now!

The 5th Wave   By Rich Tennant

"It's just until we get back up on the Internet."

In this part . . .

In this part, you make the necessary mental and physical connections to hook up your Linux machine to the Internet, including configuring telephone dial-up to an Internet Service Provider (ISP). You also discover how to do some basic network troubleshooting, just in case things don't go perfectly. Next, you set up your Web browser, e-mail client, and instant messaging software so that you can surf the Web, send and receive e-mail, and access newsgroups. Armed with the utilities you install in this part, you enable yourself to extend and customize your Linux system to your heart's content. You also find out how to travel on the electronic highways and byways of the Internet to get things done!

Chapter 8

Connecting to the Internet

● ●

In This Chapter

▶ Understanding common Internet connection methods

▶ Setting up your Internet connection

▶ Connecting to your Internet Service Provider (ISP)

▶ Understanding enough TCP/IP to be dangerous

● ●

> *Every improvement in communication makes the bore more terrible.*
>
> — Frank Moore Colby

*Y*ou may already be connected to the Internet if you're on a machine that's connected to a LAN and you've configured the networking during installation. To test whether you have a connection, open up a Web browser and try to go to an outside Web site (like www.gnu.org). If it works, you're up! No need for this chapter. Otherwise, read on.

Internet Connectivity 101

A few words regarding the broadband options (DSL and cable) are in order before I begin. The word *broadband* has a technical definition, but I just use it to mean high-speed Internet access. Although a dialup modem can typically transmit information at speeds up to 56 *kilobits* (thousand bits) per second, broadband connections can reach 50 times that speed. Nowadays, the Web contains lots of images and multimedia elements, and enjoying these features through a 56 Kbps dialup modem is similar to drinking a cold glass of water with an eyedropper when you're dying of thirst.

Don't let high-speed providers discourage you from using Linux with their services. Just because they don't support Linux directly doesn't mean that the technology doesn't work with Linux. TCP/IP (the set of traffic rules for the Internet) was developed for the Unix operating system, from which Linux descends.

If you are dual-booting to Windows, your ISP can help you install your broadband connection, and then you can tinker with getting Linux connected as you have the time and inclination. In the list below, I point you to some sites that can help you configure your broadband connection as you look at the types available:

- **Cable modems:** Many cable television companies have expanded their product lines to include Internet access over their cable infrastructure. When you subscribe to a cable Internet service, the installation technician often can provide you with a special device, called a *cable modem,* along with a standard network adapter (like an *Ethernet card*). The technician then installs the network adapter into your computer and connects the cable modem to it. As far as speed goes, to get the exact speeds available, you need to talk to your cable provider. The following Web page provides a document that contains helpful information about various cable providers and Linux:

   `www.tldp.org/HOWTO/Cable-Modem`

- **Digital Subscriber Line (DSL):** DSL carries data to your telephone jack in a digital format. DSL is popular because it provides a faster connection with lower installation and service costs than ISDN, and it utilizes the existing copper telephone wiring provided by your telephone company. You can even use the same phone line as a regular phone line! A DSL connection requires additional communication hardware, which your Internet Service Provider (ISP) should provide.

   Note that several variants of DSL exist:

   - ISDN (Integrated Services Digital Network) Digital Subscriber Line (IDSL) — see later in this section for a definition of ISDN

   - Symmetric Digital Subscriber Line (SDSL)

   - Asymmetric Digital Subscriber Line (ADSL)

   - Generic DSL (XDSL)

   You can find out from your ISP how fast your DSL connection would be, because it varies. For an overview of DSL and Linux, visit the following Web page:

   `www.tldp.org/HOWTO/DSL-HOWTO/`

- **Satellite modems:** Those who live in particularly remote or low-infrastructure areas might go the route of satellite modems (`www.tldp.org/HOWTO/Sat-HOWTO.html`). You can consider this service equivalent in many ways to cable, in that you get it typically through the same providers that you get your satellite television signals.

However, satellite has some drawbacks. If your satellite television service is unreliable, your Internet service suffers the same fate. The upload and download speeds can also vary dramatically.

✔ **Dialup modems:** The dialup modem is still widely used in areas where broadband is either not available or not affordable. It translates the *digital* signal from the computer into an *analog* signal required for transmission from the wall jack to the telephone company. Because the modem utilizes existing voice telephone service, you don't need any special setup beyond subscribing to an ISP. However, you can't use the same phone line for both dialup and a phone conversation at the same time. See the sidebar "Beware of devices posing as modems" for additional concerns if you're going the dialup route.

✔ **Wireless:** The realm of wireless networking is where Linux today may give you the most trouble, depending on what kind of wireless you're using. Four major types of wireless exist, and they're often referred to as a group as *WiFi* (802.11a, 802.11b, and 802.11g, or just A, B, and G, and Bluetooth). A and B are also the best supported in Linux so far, because again, they've been around the longest. G's security is what you should aim for, but it also adds levels of complexity that require more cooperation from the manufacturers of the cards. Many wireless cards today are, in fact, capable of doing more than one of these types, so if you don't own one, get one that supports both B and G.

The best advice I can give here is to do a Web search on the make and model of your wireless card (or the one you're thinking of buying), plus the word Linux, and see what you find — and, of course, you can check the hardware compatibility pages for the distributions as well. Because this area is one where technology is quickly advancing, always check the dates on the resources you find and make sure that they're recent. Even being six months old can mean you're getting out-of-date information. Some useful links (some are more advanced than others) for this topic include the following:

- A posting on my blog for Fedora users, apologies for the long URL: `http://dee-ann.blog-city.com/wireless_setup_on_an_emachines_m5310_notebook.htm`

- The Linux Wireless Networking Quick HOWTO: `www.linuxhomenetworking.com/linux-hn/wmp11-linux.htm`

- Wireless LAN resources for Linux: `www.hpl.hp.com/personal/Jean_Tourrilhes/Linux/`

- A method for using Windows wireless drivers in Linux: `www.linuxant.com/driverloader`

- Network Topology Guide: `www.homenethelp.com/network`

✔ **Integrated Services Digital Network (ISDN):** Not too long ago, ISDN was one of the only residential high-speed options. It appeared when 28 Kbps (half the speed of today's regular dialup modems) was about all that you could milk from the copper strands that connected your telephone to the telephone company. ISDN is still available in some areas and promises a steady 128 Kbps — as long as you're within 3.4 miles of the telephone company's central office. You need two special devices to use ISDN: an ISDN modem (typically provided by the ISDN ISP) and a network adapter (sometimes an Ethernet card). Because ISDN is used so little these days, not many specific sites are devoted to it. The overall modem HOWTO (`www.tldp.org/HOWTO/Modem-HOWTO.html`) does contain pointers to the latest ISDN information, as well as just being plain interesting to read.

Beware of devices posing as modems

I try to save you from some frustration — and your computer from your ball-peen hammer. Many Linux newbies have become irritated by not being able to communicate with their internal modems. "After all," the newbie reasons, "the same hardware works when I was running Microsoft Windows."

Well, here's the story: Years ago, hardware manufacturers developed a device, called a *software modem,* in an effort to reduce hardware costs. The idea was to trim some responsibility from the modem and relegate these tasks to the operating system. The result was an inexpensive modem that routed signals to proprietary software that operated only under Microsoft Windows. In short, these so-called modems, also known as *WinModems,* aren't really modems at all, but, rather, are telephone cable interfaces to Windows.

The following list shows methods you can use to determine whether you have a software modem:

✔ The model number has a HCF-, HSP-, or HSF- in front of it.

✔ The packaging refers to the device as a WinModem or designates that it works with only Windows (though sometimes these labels can be misleading because some manufacturers just don't bother to list other operating systems even though their hardware will work with those operating systems).

✔ Windows recognizes your modem, but Linux doesn't.

In short, if you determine that you have a software modem, Linux simply doesn't work with it. For the adventurous out there, the LinModem project (`linmodems.org`) has successfully written Linux drivers to work with a few of these software modems. I encourage you to become involved in this type of project, if you're so moved. These explorers drive the wonderful world of *freedom* software, which Linux is a prominent part of.

The bummer in all this is that, although you probably saved a few bucks by buying a machine with a software modem, you most likely need a real modem to use with Linux (unless you are lucky enough to have a LinModem). Your best bet is to purchase an external modem so that you can leave the software modem in place and have the external one just for Linux (or any other computer you may want to move it to later).

Setting Up the Hardware

Before you get too comfortable in your chair, you must physically check some items. This may require you to do some low-level maneuvers (such as crawling under your desk):

✔ **Cable modem, DSL modem, or any other fancy contraption:** If you have one of these babies, you need to make sure that:

- An Ethernet cable (like a phone cable but the connector is wider) is plugged into your computer's Ethernet card and into the special cable, DSL, satellite, or ISDN modem your ISP installed.

- The fancy modem thing is powered on. (These contraptions often have their own power supplies.)

✔ **External modem:** If you have an external modem (one that's independent of your computer case), you need to verify that:

- A cable is securely connected from the modem to the proper port on the computer.

- The modem is powered on. (External modems have their own power supply.)

- One end of a telephone cable is plugged into the wall jack, and the opposite end is plugged into the modem.

✔ **Internal modem:** If you have an internal modem, you need to verify that:

- The modem is *not* a software modem. See the sidebar "Beware of devices posing as modems" if you're not sure what a software modem is or whether you have one.

- One end of a telephone cable is plugged into the wall jack, and the opposite end is plugged into the phone plug on the back of your computer.

✔ **Wireless cards:** If you have a wireless card, you also have to have a wireless *router* to collect and direct your wireless traffic between computers and/or *bridge* to let your wireless card talk to your Ethernet network. How far and through what (walls, floors, and so on) a wireless router or bridge can be from the card depends on the technology you're using. Some handy primers on wireless hardware and setup include

- How WiFi Works: `http://computer.howstuffworks.com/wireless-network.htm`

- Creating a Wireless Network: `www.wi-fi.org/OpenSection/design.asp?TID=2`

Okay, now you can climb back into your chair.

Selecting an Internet Service Provider (ISP)

Because of the meteoric rise in the popularity of Linux, many ISPs are training their support staff in the ways of Linux. If you already have a dialup service, give one of them a call to let them know of your Linux pursuits. Chances are, that person already has information pertinent to Linux subscribers and can provide you with that information. If you're shopping for a new ISP, this section offers some practical selection advice.

Some ISPs provide their own proprietary software that you must install on your PC to connect to the Internet. The software they provide is likely to run only on Windows. Several free dialup services don't work with Linux because of this fact. The proprietary software meddles with the operating system to ensure that banner advertising isn't hidden or that you stay dialed in for only a specified duration.

If you're shopping around for an ISP, consider these questions:

- ✔ **Can you get local dialup numbers across the country and around the world?** If you travel often and need Internet access from different cities, this service is a handy money (and headache) saver.

- ✔ **Does it provide technical support for Linux?** If you're planning on running Linux, this consideration is an important one. However, it doesn't have to be a deal breaker.

- ✔ **Can you get a recommendation?** Ask a friend. An ISP's best friend is an endorsement from a satisfied customer.

- ✔ **Will you have trouble dialing in?** Although a subscriber-to-line ratio of 7-to-1 (an average of seven or fewer subscribers per line) or better isn't an entirely accurate measure of how often you'll get busy signals, it's probably the easiest measure for consumers. This is primarily a concern for dialup users.

Getting Information You Need from Your ISP

Most reputable ISPs provide you with a customer information sheet after you sign up for its services. This sheet should include the following information at the minimum:

- ✔ Local telephone dial-in numbers for modem users
- ✔ User login name

✔ User login password

✔ E-mail address

✔ E-mail outbound host or Simple Mail Transport Protocol (SMTP) server

✔ E-mail inbound host or Post Office Protocol (POP) server

✔ News host

✔ Whether your computer address will be

- **Static:** You always have the same IP address. Static addresses are more common for servers than for desktops. If you're using static, your ISP needs to give you your nameserver IP addresses, your gateway address, the network address, and the netmask. This information should all be on the customer information sheet.

- **Dynamic:** Your IP address changes each time you connect, or at regular intervals. On most desktops, you just don't always need to have the same address, and it makes life easier on ISPs. It also makes life easier for computers like laptops, which get moved around often from network to network. If you're using dynamic addressing, you're told that you need to connect using DHCP.

With this information, you can establish an Internet connection by using your Linux system.

Hooking Up

Fortunately, the Linux vendors provide tools that reduce the complexity of hooking up with Linux. It's not that networking has changed, but rather that many of its details have been hidden so that you just have to click here and press a key there. Not long ago, configuring dialup networking (in particular) on a Linux machine was nothing short of debugging a defective Rube Goldberg contraption.

The Internet connection configuration tools available in the distributions covered within this book are

✔ **Knoppix:** Click the Penguin menu icon on the panel and select Network/Internet. This menu contains a variety of tools you can use to get online with Knoppix, depending on the type of hardware you're using.

✔ **Linspire:** Select Launch⇨Run Programs⇨Internet⇨Internet Connection Tools, and then choose the most appropriate tool for your ISP.

✔ **Fedora:** Choose System⇨Administration⇨Network to open the Network Configuration dialog box. Click New to start the Add New Device Type wizard.

✔ **Mandriva:** From the Main Menu, choose System⇨Configuration⇨ Configure Your Computer to open the Mandriva Control Center. Enter password. Choose Network & Internet⇨Set Up A New Network Interface (LAN, ISDN, ADSL) to access the Connection Creation wizard and choose the connection you want to configure.

✔ **SuSE:** From the Main Menu, choose Applications⇨System⇨YaST to open the YaST configuration tool. Enter password. On the left, select Network Devices. On the right, choose the type of hardware you have in order to start configuring your setup.

✔ **Ubuntu:** Choose System⇨Administration⇨Networking to open the Network Settings tool. Enter password. Select either Ethernet Connection or Modem Connection, and then Properties. To set up this connection, click Enable this Connection and then fill in the information.

✔ **Xandros:** Select Launch⇨Control Center to open the Xandros Control Center. Click the plus next to Network to expand that menu and then choose Internet Connection to open your connection listing — you might need to click the Administrator button to enter your root password. Click New to launch the Connection Wizard.

Sometimes the choice isn't as obvious as you think. For example, maybe you have DSL, but because the DSL connection is going through your Ethernet card, your system sees it as a LAN/Ethernet connection. So if you can't get your connection to work, play with these factors.

Again, because I have only so much space, I walk you through setup using Fedora. Many of the decisions and required pieces of information are the same from distribution to distribution, so if you're not using Fedora, read through this section and use what you find out here to work on your own computer.

Configuring Your Connection

With your ISP's information in hand and a glowing monitor in front of you, follow these steps to configure your dialup connection to the Internet in Fedora:

1. **From the GUI desktop, choose System⇨Administration⇨Network.**

2. **Enter your root password in the dialog box, if necessary.**

   If you're logged in as a regular user (not root), you're prompted to enter the root password.

   The Network Configuration dialog box opens (see Figure 8-1).

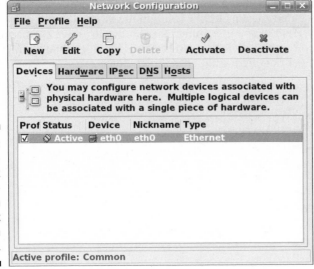

Figure 8-1:
The Net-
work
Con-
figuration
dialog box
in Fedora
Core 5.

3. **In the Network Configuration dialog box, click the New button.**

The Select Device Type dialog box appears, as shown in Figure 8-2. Because I can't cover all network connection types at once, and the dialup modem is the most complicated, I follow the dialup (Modem connection) option from here. Choose the right hardware type for yourself and proceed.

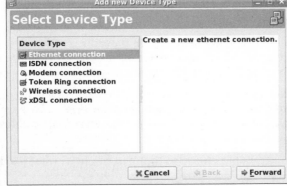

Figure 8-2:
The Select
Device Type
dialog box in
Fedora Core
5's Network
Configur-
ation tool.

4. **To set up a dialup modem, select Modem connection from the Device Type list box and then click the Forward button.**

After you click Forward, the tool probes for your modem. If your modem can't be found (again, I follow through the most difficult option), the Select Modem dialog box appears, as shown in Figure 8-3. I assume that you're staring this dialog box in the face. If it doesn't appear, proceed through your configuration until it matches these steps again.

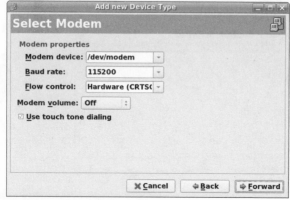

Figure 8-3:
The Select
Modem
dialog box in
the Network
Configura-
tion tool.

5. Select the proper device from the Modem Device drop-down list.

If you know your modem is on COM1 or COM2 in Windows, translating this techno-talk to Linux isn't hard: You just need to subtract 1. So, it's ttyS0 for COM1 and ttyS1 for COM2. If you're using a USB mouse (it has a flat, rectangular connector), your modem is probably on COM1. If you're not using a USB mouse, then your modem is probably on COM2.

6. Select your modem's speed from the Baud Rate drop-down list.

If you were told to use a specific speed, choose that speed here. Otherwise, choose the highest number available. The key is to try the highest setting and, if that doesn't work, start choosing slower and slower ones until you're able to properly make the connection.

Leave the Flow Control setting alone. Only change this setting if you're having a hard time getting your modem connection to work, or you're told by your ISP that you specifically need to select either Software Flow Control or No (None) Flow Control.

7. Turn on your modem volume so that you can hear what it's doing while testing it.

You'll want to come back later and shut off the volume. (Well, most people do; some like to leave it on. I think the 56.6 Kbps modems sound like an alien game of Pong while they're connecting.) It's up to you how loud you want to set the sound, as long as you can hear it.

Leave Touch Tone Dialing activated unless you live in an area that only supports rotary phones.

8. Click Forward to proceed.

The Select Provider dialog box appears, as shown in Figure 8-4.

Figure 8-4:
The Select
Provider
dialog box in
Fedora Core
5's Network
Configura-
tion tool.

```
┌──────────────────────────────────────────────────┐
│              Add new Device Type          _ □ X    │
│ Select Provider                                    │
│                                                    │
│                  Phone number                      │
│  Internet Provid   Prefix:      Area code:   Phone number: │
│  ⊞ ═ Austria      [_____]   [_____]  [_____]  │
│  ⊞ ▶ Czech Repu                                    │
│  ⊞ ▆ Germany                                       │
│  ⊞ ▆ Slovenia                                      │
│  ⊞ ▒ United King  Provider name: [_____]    │
│                      [  T-Online Account Setup  ]  │
│                   Login name:   [_____]     │
│                   Password:     [_____]     │
│                                                    │
│              [ ✗ Cancel ]  [ ⇦ Back ]  [ ⇨ Forward ] │
└──────────────────────────────────────────────────┘
```

9. Enter your ISP information and then click Forward.

The default list of countries that your ISP may be from is pretty limited. If you live in one of these regions, select your country, then the ISP — at which point the dialing entries are completed for you — and then skip to Step 16. Otherwise, proceed to the next step.

10. In the Prefix text box, enter any dialing prefix you have to dial before the actual phone number.

This prefix may be a long distance item, such as 1 for North American long distance calls, or a 9 to dial out of your building — or even 91 if you need to dial 9 to get out and you're dialing long distance. If you don't need a prefix, leave this box blank.

11. In the Area Code text box, enter the area code your modem needs to dial if it needs to dial one.

In some places, you have to dial the area code even if you're dialing a local number. If you don't have to use an area code, leave this box blank.

12. In the Phone Number text box, enter the phone number (minus prefix and area code) your modem needs to dial.

Dashes aren't necessary.

13. In the Provider Name text box, type the name of your ISP.

You just use this name as a description for this dialup entry.

14. **In the Login name text box, enter your dial-in account login name.**

15. **In the Password text box, enter your dial-in account login password.**

16. **Click Forward.**

    The IP Settings dialog box appears, as shown in Figure 8-5.

17. **In the IP Settings dialog box, select the appropriate radio button for whether your modem needs to obtain its IP addressing information from the ISP (*DHCP*, as discussed in the section "Getting Information You Need from Your ISP," earlier in this chapter) or whether you need to tell it what its IP data is (*static*).**

    Your ISP should have given you which of these you require. DHCP is the default. If you choose Static, the lower portion of the dialog box becomes available.

18. **If you selected DHCP, and your ISP told you to automatically get your nameserver settings from its equipment, leave the Automatically Obtain DNS Information From Provider box checked. Otherwise uncheck it.**

19. **If you selected static, then fill in the Address, Subnet Mask, and Default Gateway Address as given to you by your ISP.**

20. **Click Forward to proceed to the summary dialog box, and then click Apply to add the modem you have just set up to your main Network Configuration dialog box.**

    You now have a modem entry (look in the Type column) in your Network Configuration tool.

Connecting to (And Disconnecting from) the Internet

To connect to the Internet from the Fedora Core Network Configuration dialog box, highlight the modem entry you just created (see preceding section) and click the Activate button. With any luck, your modem springs to life with some beeps and then buzzes along with a dialog box indicating that a connection is being made. After a successful connection, the Network Configuration dialog box appears again; this time, the Status column of the modem device reads Active. Congratulations — you're now connected to the Internet!

To disconnect, click the Deactivate button in the Network Configuration dialog box. Your settings remain; the next time you want to connect, just open this dialog box and click Activate. If all is not well, skip to the next section, "It's All Fun and Games Until Something Doesn't Work," to find out how to get help.

Readers using other distributions should use that distribution's connection tool. You may find that just double-clicking your Web browser's icon and trying to go to a site activates your connection.

It's All Fun and Games Until Something Doesn't Work

In a perfect world, the dialup configuration steps in the preceding section would work 100 percent of the time. The Linux vendors have truly hidden all the mystery that has traditionally surrounded networking. Unfortunately, in many situations (mostly related to modems and hardware), a simplified configuration doesn't work. If you can't connect to the Internet after following these steps, an excellent site to find help is LinuxQuestions.org (`www.linux questions.org`). And yeah, I know — you'll have to use a computer that already has Internet access to get that help. (Catch-22, anyone?) It's simply impossible to anticipate the wide range of problems people can run into, and the Linux community is your best bet; this site is well known for its helpful community members.

Also, go to your favorite Web-search site and search on the error message you're getting from the system — or it doesn't hurt to add the network hardware's make and model and the name of your distribution as well if just the error message isn't working. When you're trying to figure out what's wrong with your network connection — or trying to gather information that can help someone else figure out what's wrong — you can use a cool tool: the handy command-line program, `ping`.

Some firewalls block the kind of traffic sent with `pings`, so these commands don't always work as expected, even with a good connection.

The `ping` command is akin to a submarine using sonar to detect other objects in the ocean. Sonar sends out a *ping* signal, which reflects off a hard surface. By measuring the amount of time between sending the ping and the ping's return, the submarine's engineer can determine whether an object is out there and how far from the submarine the object is.

The `ping` command in Linux provides information similar to what sonar provides — and it's so useful that you see it here as both a Linux command and a time-honored word. If you consider the Internet to be your ocean, you can determine, by *pinging*, what other network computers exist — and also how long it takes for your `ping` command to return. You use this command in the format `ping` *hostname* or `ping` *ipaddress,* such as `ping bob.` `example.com` or `ping 192.168.1.5`. If you can't ping another computer in your house or office (assuming that you have them all connected with Ethernet and not on separate dialup connections), then something is wrong with the machine you're pinging from. On the other hand, if you can ping another machine in your house or office but you can't ping a machine elsewhere on the Internet, then something may be wrong with your connection to your ISP.

Latency, or the amount of time it takes for a signal to travel on the Internet, has little to do with physical distance. Rather, factors such as network traffic, bandwidth, and network hardware all contribute to a slow latency. These factors determine whether a `ping` command to your neighbor's computer takes longer than pinging a host at the South Pole.

For example, try pinging Yahoo! by opening a command prompt (see Chapter 14) and typing the following command:

```
ping www.yahoo.com
```

Press Ctrl+C to stop the ping; otherwise your computer continues to `ping` the target.

The output, shown in Figure 8-6, provides information about what `ping` is doing. If the ping can't reach the host, you receive a message that the host is unreachable. If the ping can reach the host, you receive feedback that provides how long it takes — in milliseconds (ms) — for the signal from your computer to get to the destination computer and back again — the lower the numbers, the better. For computers connected through Ethernet, a `ping` time of 1 ms to 3 ms is an acceptable response time. For dialup connections, expect somewhere around 150 ms. When you start seeing `ping` times climbing to 900 ms or higher, the network is likely under heavy use (or you have something wrong with your cables).

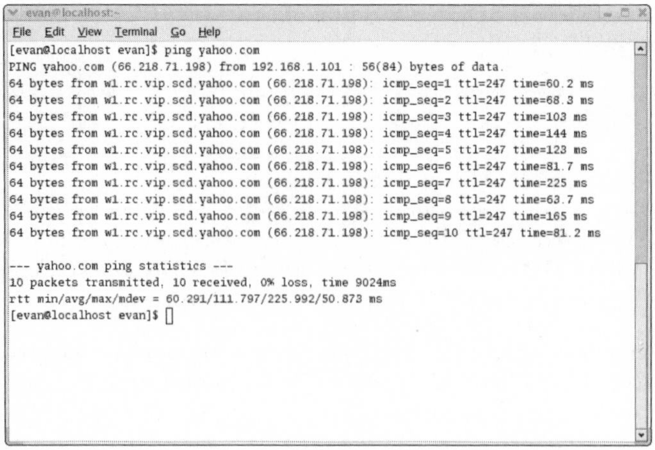

```
evan@localhost:~                                                        - □ X
File  Edit  View  Terminal  Go  Help
[evan@localhost evan]$ ping yahoo.com
PING yahoo.com (66.218.71.198) from 192.168.1.101 : 56(84) bytes of data.
64 bytes from w1.rc.vip.scd.yahoo.com (66.218.71.198): icmp_seq=1 ttl=247 time=60.2 ms
64 bytes from w1.rc.vip.scd.yahoo.com (66.218.71.198): icmp_seq=2 ttl=247 time=68.3 ms
64 bytes from w1.rc.vip.scd.yahoo.com (66.218.71.198): icmp_seq=3 ttl=247 time=103 ms
64 bytes from w1.rc.vip.scd.yahoo.com (66.218.71.198): icmp_seq=4 ttl=247 time=144 ms
64 bytes from w1.rc.vip.scd.yahoo.com (66.218.71.198): icmp_seq=5 ttl=247 time=123 ms
64 bytes from w1.rc.vip.scd.yahoo.com (66.218.71.198): icmp_seq=6 ttl=247 time=81.7 ms
64 bytes from w1.rc.vip.scd.yahoo.com (66.218.71.198): icmp_seq=7 ttl=247 time=225 ms
64 bytes from w1.rc.vip.scd.yahoo.com (66.218.71.198): icmp_seq=8 ttl=247 time=63.7 ms
64 bytes from w1.rc.vip.scd.yahoo.com (66.218.71.198): icmp_seq=9 ttl=247 time=165 ms
64 bytes from w1.rc.vip.scd.yahoo.com (66.218.71.198): icmp_seq=10 ttl=247 time=81.2 ms

--- yahoo.com ping statistics ---
10 packets transmitted, 10 received, 0% loss, time 9024ms
rtt min/avg/max/mdev = 60.291/111.797/225.992/50.873 ms
[evan@localhost evan]$ []
```

Figure 8-6:
Sample
results of
the ping
command.

After You're Connected

After you're connected, you'll probably want to leap straight to Chapter 9 for how to use the various Internet programs available to you. In the meantime, let me offer you a number of sites you might find useful when you need help, have questions, or otherwise want to explore the Linux world farther — some of these are pretty geeky, but you'll grow into them! You also may want to update your machine (see Chapter 12), add new software (also Chapter 12), and give extra thought to system security (see Chapter 13) to protect yourself from nasty people and programs.

Useful sites include

- ✔ www.linuxsecurity.com: A somewhat geeky (but useful) place where you can track what's going on in the world of Linux security.

- ✔ www.kerneltraffic.org: Everything you never wanted to know about what's happening with the Linux kernel but were afraid to ask. This place is great for tracking what new features are being added, if you're interested in things like bleeding-edge hardware or just like to be "in the know."

- ✔ www.linuxquestions.org: I mention this site elsewhere in the book, but it's worth mentioning again. It's a popular hangout for people who have questions to ask, and for those who like to help them find answers.

- ✔ http://linux-newbie.sunsite.dk/: The Linux Newbie Administrator Guide is a massive collection of information that you may find useful.

✔ www.tuxfiles.org: A collection of short help files on individual topics of interest.

✔ www.tldp.org: Contains lots of help documentation written for various user levels.

✔ www.tuxmagazine.com: A free digital magazine for Linux desktop users.

✔ www.slashdot.org: Uber-geek hangout (with a rather hostile culture, unfortunately) that features lots of pointers to interesting articles online. Best used to view the articles; skip the arguments in the comments section.

In addition to these recommendations, keep in mind that your favorite search site can also be very handy.

Chapter 9

Using the Internet

> *Give a man a fish and you feed him for a day; teach him to use the Net, and he won't bother you for weeks.*
>
> — Anonymous

*T*he *Internet* is a vast network of computers that spans the globe. Many different types of computers and operating systems work together to allow you access to information across the Internet. Linux, along with the other related Unix operating systems, has long supported and worked with the Internet. Practically all the different services available on the Internet are available from your Linux desktop.

When you install Linux (see Chapters 3 and 4), one or more Web browsers, mail programs, and instant messaging tools are placed onto your new system. In this chapter, I introduce you to some tools you can use to access different services on the Internet, such as accessing Web sites, using e-mail, investigating newsgroups, and utilizing FTP — assuming that your Internet connection is configured (see Chapter 8).

Browse the Web with Firefox

Many people attribute the explosive growth of the Internet to the graphical Web browser. The Internet has been around for much longer than the invention of the browser. It's just that most of the work done on the Internet was in plain old text, which held little attraction for those people who like pretty pictures. In the world of Linux, the most popular browser is arguably Firefox (`www.mozilla.org/products/firefox`), which is based off of Mozilla — essentially Firefox is just the Web browser portion of Mozilla, while Mozilla can also handle e-mail and news browsing. Another popular option is Konqueror (`www.konqueror.org`), whose file-browsing features you find out about in Chapter 10, but this tool can also be used as a Web browser.

Not all Linux distributions come with Firefox preinstalled. In some versions of Xandros, for example, you need to add the program by using the techniques covered in Chapter 12. You will find Firefox in Xandros Networks' New Applications⇨Internet folder. Linspire users also need to add Firefox, and can find it in the CNR section Internet⇨Browsers. Note that you will need to install one of the e-mail applications discussed in the section "Evolving into E-Mail," later in this chapter, if you choose Firefox over Mozilla.

Configuring Firefox

You can start surfing right now, if you want. You don't need to customize your browser. However, you may want to take a moment to tell Firefox your preferences, such as the default Web site to show when it starts up, what font sizes to use by default, what colors to use, and many other options.

The following steps introduce you to the Preferences window, where all the Firefox configuration parameters are stored:

1. **Start Firefox.**

   How you start Firefox depends on which distribution you're using. Typically it's either a shortcut on your panel (Fedora, Knoppix, Mandriva, SuSE, and Ubuntu and Xandros Business), a shortcut on your desktop (Xandros and Linspire after you have the software installed; its already there in Business), or it is available in the Internet portion of your Main Menu (all if you have the software installed). If you are asked if you want to import preferences, say no if this is a new installation and you haven't used any other browsers, or say yes if this is not a new installation and you've been using another browser such as Mozilla.

2. **Choose Edit⇨Preferences.**

   The Preferences window appears, as shown in Figure 9-1. This dialog box may look different from distribution to distribution and have slightly different options as not everyone offers the exact same version of Firefox, but for the most part the match should be complete.

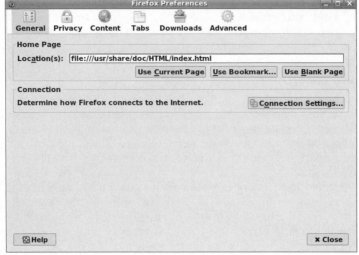

Figure 9-1:
The Firefox
Preferences
window
in Fedora
Core 5.

3. **Click the icons along the top of the Preferences window to access the various preferences categories.**

   Some categories are complex enough to offer tabs for various sub-categories. These tabs can be worth exploring as well.

4. **If you get tired of reading through menus, just click Close to close the Preferences dialog box and get back to surfing.**

General preferences

Selecting the General option — shown earlier in Figure 9-1 — allows you to determine how you want Firefox to look and act when it runs. This dialog box is governed by two separate sections:

✔ **Home Page:** This section allows you to choose what Firefox shows you immediately upon starting. You can type a URL directly into the Location(s) text box, or click one of the following buttons:

   • **Use Current Page:** Navigate to the page you want to use for your default Web page, and then click this button. The URL for this page appears in the Location(s) text box.

   • **Use Bookmark:** Click this button to open the Set Home Page dialog box, which contains all of your bookmarks. Select the bookmark you want to use and then click OK to add the URL for this page into the Location(s) text box.

   • **Use Blank Page:** Click this button to have Firefox open to just an empty window.

✔ **Connection:** Click the Connections Settings button to open the Connection Settings dialog box. You only need to do this if your network administrator told you that you have to use *proxy servers* to access online content.

Privacy preferences

Every time you send an e-mail or click a Web site, you're exchanging information across a network. Although you don't need to lose sleep over it, you should be conscious of every request you make on the Internet. Take a moment to examine the Privacy collection of tabs (see Figure 9-2) and determine if there's anything you want to change:

✔ **History:** The History tab lets you designate how many days you want your browser to remember where you've been. You can click the Clear Browsing History Now button to clear the history manually at any time (which is smart to do if you're in a library or another place where someone else may be using the browser after you). Click Settings to mark what information should be saved and what should be deleted when you clear out the browsing history — the Settings button remains visible no matter which tab you are in.

✔ **Saved Forms:** Firefox includes a helpful feature where it can remember what you typed into forms in the past and the names of the fields. Then when you're filling out these forms later, it will offer to fill in the same thing you used before. Firefox also remembers what you type into the search bar on the upper-right portion of the screen. If you want Firefox to stop saving, select this tab and click the Save Information I Enter In Forms And The Search Bar check box to uncheck it. You can also empty out the browser's form and search memory by clicking the Clear Saved Form Data Now button.

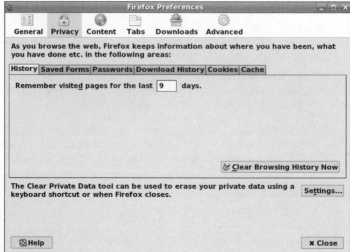

Figure 9-2:
The Firefox
Privacy
Preferences
window
in Fedora
Core 5.

✔ **Passwords:** When you enter a username and password to log into something over the Web, Firefox offers to save that information. If you want to shut that feature off, expand this section and click the Remember Passwords box to uncheck it. If you want to look through the passwords you have saved or the ones that you have told Firefox to never save, click the View Saved Passwords button to open the Password Manager window. In the Passwords Saved tab, you will see a list of sites and login names, and you can add the passwords to this list by clicking the Show Passwords button — don't do this when other people could be looking over your shoulder. In the Passwords Never Saved tab, you will see another list. In either tab, you can select an item and click Remove to have Firefox forget the entry, or you can click Remove All to forget everything in that category (or you can skip the dialog box completely and just click the Clear button). You can also click Master Password to make sure no one else can look in your list of passwords. Don't forget the Master Password if you set one!

✔ **Download History:** When you download files, Firefox keeps track of them in the Download Manager window. To empty it immediately, click the Clear button. You also can tell Firefox how to automatically handle things in the Remove Files From The Download Manager drop-down list box, by selecting:

- **Manually:** Only empty the list when you tell it to.

- **Upon Successful Download:** Remove an item from the list when you finish your download.

- **When Firefox Exits:** Clear the list whenever you close Firefox.

✔ **Cookies:** This is one of those buzzwords that sends some people into a frenzy. Cookies are bits of information a Web site stores on your machine so that this data can be accessed again when you return. Some people don't care how many cookies are created and some don't want any on their systems. To prevent cookies from being stored, click the Allow Sites To Set Cookies box to uncheck it. You can also only allow sites to set cookies for themselves, rather than for partner sites, by clicking the For The Originating Web Site only box to check it. To make this feature even smarter, you can check Unless I Have Removed Cookies Set By The Site so that Firefox will watch what you manually change and no longer trust certain sites. On the other hand, if there are sites that you want to let break the rules you just set, click the Exceptions button and enter their addresses in the text box. Allow for Session means allow it for now but not again, and Allow by itself means permanently.

You can view every cookie you currently have by clicking the View Cookies button, and can either remove them individually (select the cookie you want to remove and then click Remove Cookies) or permanently — or click the Remove All Cookies button to toss out all of your cookies immediately. For the Keep Cookies drop-down list box, choose how often you want Firefox to dump cookies:

- **Until they expire:** Most cookies have an automatic expiry date. If you want to let the cookies dictate when they will be deleted, choose this option.

- **Until I close Firefox:** If you are using a library computer or another machine that is shared, or just don't want the computer storing cookies past when you're done using the browser, choose this option.

- **Ask me every time:** If you want to be ultra-paranoid about cookies or to find how often they are actually used, choose this option.

✔ **Cache:** Firefox remembers the last few pages you stored so it can load them faster if you go back to them quickly. You can empty this cache by clicking the Clear Cache Now button. You can also change how much hard drive space is used to store this information by changing the value in the Use Up To text box.

Content preferences

Selecting Content brings you to the Content portion of the Firefox Preferences dialog box (Figure 9-3). This section lets you control how Firefox reacts to various types of content. The top portion refers to items to allow through or not — notice that each of these has a button to its right that offers additional control:

✔ **Block Popup Windows:** Tells Firefox to block new windows that you didn't ask for — this is a favorite feature and one reason that many people move to Firefox under Microsoft Windows. Some sites have functionality that require the ability to open, say, log-in windows, so you can click the Allowed Sites button to make exceptions for them. If you don't configure this feature, it still works. A yellow bar appears in the browser window whenever a pop-up is blocked, allowing you to access the settings at that point.

✔ **Warn me when web sites try to install extensions or themes:** Highly recommended that you leave this on. This setting prevents sites from automatically messing with your Firefox configuration. Again, there is an Exceptions button for sites you want to allow to do this.

✔ **Load Images:** Lets you block all images. Useful for those who are sight impaired or who are trying to speed up browsing by ignoring pictures. Selecting For The Originating Web Site Only is a way to block ads, because many ads are loaded from other sites and just appear on the one you're viewing, but it can also block legitimate graphics. The Exceptions button helps you manage what to see and what not to.

✔ **Enable Java:** If you have Java installed and this option enabled, Firefox will run Java code it finds.

✔ **Enable JavaScript:** Some people shut off this feature for security reasons. Many don't. Clicking the Advanced button opens the Advanced JavaScript Settings dialog box, which you can use to choose what you will allow this scripting language to do. If you find a site that does annoying things like resize your windows, go to this dialog box to disable that ability.

Figure 9-3:
The Firefox
Content
Preferences
window
in Fedora
Core 5.

The lower section is Fonts & Colors. These features include:

- **Default Font:** Click this drop-down list box to select the font you want to use.

- **Size:** Click this drop-down list box to choose the font size you want to use.

- **Advanced:** Click this button to open the Fonts dialog box, which lets you choose the default fonts and sizes to use for various font classes, along with other visual settings. Here you can also set that pages can use their own fonts rather than your overrides.

- **Colors:** Click this button to open the Colors dialog box and change the default colors assigned to text, the background, and links.

When browsing, if you are unhappy with a font's size you can hold down the Ctrl-+ keys to make the fonts bigger and the Ctrl– (minus) keys to make the fonts smaller. The + and - are the versions on your numberpad, not on the main keyboard.

Additional Preferences

There are still three more sections of settings:

- **Tabs:** Firefox offers "tabbed browsing," which opens new pages in tabs in the same window rather than in new windows — you can even use this feature to bookmark a whole group of tabbed pages at once. This section lets you configure this functionality.

- ✔ **Downloads:** Use this section to tell Firefox where to download files to by default, how the Download Manager window should behave, and how various file types should automatically be handled when downloaded.

- ✔ **Advanced:** This section offers three tabs: General, Update, and Security. The General tab lets you set up features for the movement impaired, extra browser control features, and the languages you can read in order of preference. The Update tab tells Firefox how to handle checking for updates for various things. Security determines your security settings; typically you'll want to just leave this last tab alone.

Them dad-gum browser plug-ins

Do you ever get irritated at those Web sites that insist that you download a *plug-in,* or additional piece of software, just to view the site? The difference between a plug-in and an external program is this: A plug-in displays the results in the browser, and an external program runs outside the browser. Although these plug-ins are annoying if you're just looking for some basic information, they can provide some pretty cool stuff, such as streaming video and music through your Web browser.

Chapter 12 explains how to add the popular plug-ins (like Macromedia's Flash plug-in) to your system for each of the distributions covered in this book. When you download a particular type of file, Firefox gives you the chance to tell it how to automatically handle those types of files later. Beware telling the browser to run things automatically, you could be opening yourself up for security problems.

Firefox also supports a concept called *extensions*, which refers to extra features that aren't included in the main browser because many people may not want to bother with them. Select Tools⇨Extensions to open the Extension dialog box (see Figure 9-4).

Figure 9-4:
The Firefox
Extensions
dialog box
in Fedora
Core 5.

Click the Get More Extensions link (if you are connected to the Internet) to open a Web page that lets you surf what extensions are available. If you find one you want to try, click the Install link underneath its description and then click Install Now if your version of Firefox falls in the listed range of versions supported (choose Help⇨About Mozilla Firefox to find out). Some extensions may give you an error and may be uninstallable because of it, unfortunately.

Surfing the Web

Firefox is your viewing window into the wonderful World Wide Web. Firefox's primary purpose is to fetch Web pages on your command, download all their graphics and related files into your computer's memory, and, finally, render the page for your interactive viewing pleasure.

If you're used to using Internet Explorer or Netscape, using Firefox should be a snap. It has all the familiar navigation tools, such as an address bar; Back, Forward, Reload, and Stop buttons; and a feature that stores links to your favorite Web sites (bookmarks).

Firefox, like Netscape, also has a History sidebar feature — press Ctrl-H to show or hide it (see Figure 9-5) — which you can use to access a Web page you recently visited.

Figure 9-5:
Firefox with the History Sidebar open, in Fedora Core 5.

Evolving into E-Mail

While most people think of the Web when they think of the Internet, e-mail may, in fact, be the most used and beloved of Internet applications. A multitude of e-mail programs is available for Linux users. The defaults in the various distributions discussed in this book are available in your distribution's Internet menu.

- **Knoppix:** KMail (`http://kmail.kde.org/`), although Mozilla Mail and Thunderbird (`www.mozilla.org/products/thunderbird`) are also included. You will find all of these in Main Menu⇨Internet.

- **Fedora:** Novell Evolution (`www.novell.com/products/evolution`), with KMail and Thunderbird available in yum, as discussed in Chapter 12.

- **Linspire:** Mozilla Mail, though you can add KMail, Thunderbird, and Evolution through CNR, as discussed in Chapter 12. The first two are available in Internet⇨Email and the third is in Internet⇨Communications.

- **Mandriva:** Kontact (`www.kontact.org`), with KMail and Evolution also installed.

- **SuSE:** Evolution with KMail also installed by default. Thunderbird is also available through YaST as discussed in Chapter 12.

- **Ubuntu:** Evolution, and you can install Thunderbird and Kmail, as discussed in Chapter 12.

- **Xandros:** Mozilla Mail, with KMail also included. You can also add Thunderbird and Evolution through Xandros Networks, as discussed in Chapter 12. Xandros Business Edition has Evolution installed by default.

Evolution and Kontact should both remind you very much of Outlook, so if you like being able to integrate your calendar, address book, task manager, and e-mail, you should like these programs. Mozilla Mail, Thunderbird, and KMail are more single purpose, although Thunderbird also supports news reading. Because Evolution is the default client in the default distribution included with this book (Fedora Core 5), I cover this program in the most detail in this chapter.

Setting up Evolution

The first time you open Evolution, the program walks you through the setup process, so be sure to have the following information on hand:

- Your assigned e-mail address, in the format `username@example.org`.

- The type of mail server used for incoming mail: for example, `POP`.

✔ The name of the mail server used for incoming mail, in the format `servername.example.org`.

✔ The type of mail server used for outgoing mail: for example, `SMTP`.

✔ The name of the mail server used for outgoing mail, in the format `servername.example.org`. This name may be the same as for the incoming mail server.

✔ Any special type of *authentication* required, for both mail coming in and going out. This authentication is typically just passwords for incoming mail and may be nothing for outgoing mail.

After you start Evolution for the first time, the Evolution Setup Assistant launches.

Click Forward to proceed past the Welcome screen, after which the Identity dialog box (see Figure 9-6) opens. To fill in this dialog box, complete the following steps:

1. Change the Full Name field, if you want.

Some people don't want to use their real name and opt to use a nickname. There may or may not be default values assigned, depending on what other programs you've configured on your machine.

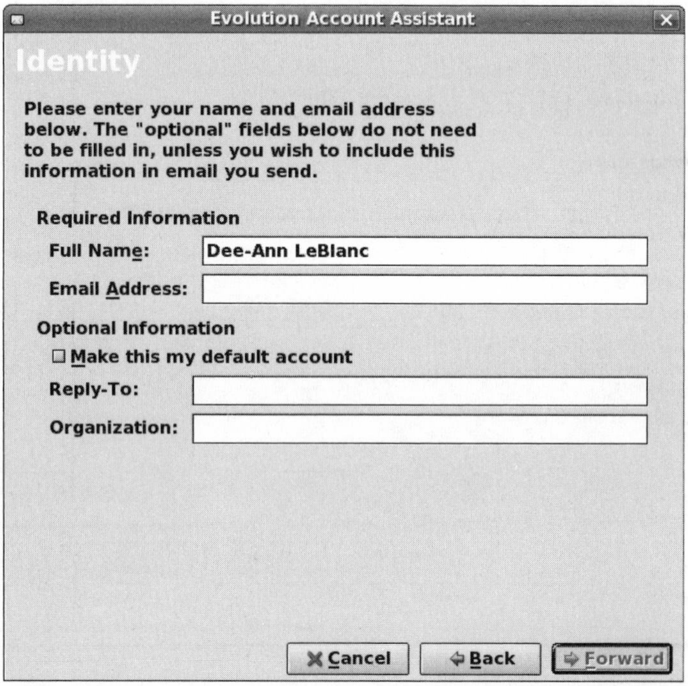

Figure 9-6:
The
Evolution
Identity
dialog box in
Fedora Core
5.

2. **Change the E-Mail Address field if it doesn't match the address your ISP gave you (it probably doesn't).**

3. **If you want this particular account to be your default mail account, make sure the Make This My Default Account check box is checked. Otherwise, make sure it is unchecked.**

4. **Click Forward to proceed.**

   The Receiving Mail dialog box opens.

5. **In the Server Type list box, select the type of incoming e-mail server your ISP uses.**

   Leave it as None if you don't want to receive e-mail on this computer — this setting is useful if you only want to be able to send or only want to use the calendar and task management features in Evolution. Depending on which item you choose, the dialog box changes to ask for the appropriate information. I assume that you're using a POP mail server to receive mail, so what you'll see when you select POP is shown in Figure 9-7. If you're not using POP, then complete the dialog box you do see and then proceed to Step 17.

Evolution Account Assistant

Receiving Email

Please select among the following options

Server **Type:**   POP

Description: **For connecting to and downloading mail from POP servers.**

Configuration

Server:

Username: dee

Security

Use Secure Connection: Never

Authentication Type

Password | **Check for Supported Types**

☐ Remember password

✗ Cancel   ⬆ Back   ➡ Forward

The latest versions of Evolution have support for Microsoft Exchange servers available. If you need this, it may or may not be already installed in your distribution. For Fedora, use the information in Chapter 12 to add the "evolution-connector" package to your system and then restart the Evolution setup process.

6. **Enter the full name for your POP mail server in the Server text box.**

   The name may be something like `pop.example.com`.

7. **Enter your login name for checking mail in the Username text box.**

   If your e-mail address is `jane@example.com`, your username is `jane`.

8. **If you were told to use SSL for security, in the Use Secure Connection (SSL) drop-down list box, select either Always or Whenever Possible, depending on what your ISP has specified.**

9. **Under Authentication Type, select the appropriate authentication option.**

   If you don't know what kinds of authentication your mail server uses, click the Check For Supported Types button. Typically, it's just Password.

10. **Check the Remember This Password check box so that you don't have to enter your e-mail password every time you check mail.**

    If you're going to walk away from your computer and someone else may possibly access it, protect yourself from outgoing prank e-mails by going to the Main Menu and selecting Lock Screen. Doing so makes sure that no one can use your GUI until you type in your login password.

    You have to have your screen saver turned on for this feature to work. Screen savers are on by default.

11. **Click Forward to proceed to the secondary Receiving Options dialog box (see Figure 9-8).**

    Whether or not this dialog box exists is determined by which type of incoming mail server you're using. If you're not using POP and you get a secondary dialog box, it may not match the one shown here, although it does share some of the options shown.

12. **If you want to check for new e-mail automatically, check the Automatically Check For New Mail check box.**

    If you don't have a permanent connection to the Internet, you may prefer to check mail manually. If so, leave the box unchecked and skip to Step 14.

13. **In the Minutes text box, set how often you want to automatically check for new e-mail.**

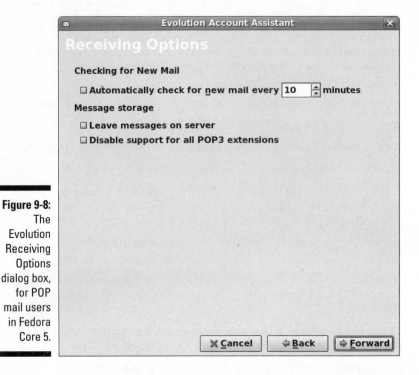

Figure 9-8:
The
Evolution
Receiving
Options
dialog box,
for POP
mail users
in Fedora
Core 5.

14. **If you check mail from multiple computers, you may want to check the Leave Messages On Server check box so that you can access the same messages from all your machines.**

    If you select this option, you'll end up with copies of messages on multiple machines, but it also means that you'll have access to your e-mail no matter where you're checking it from. Keep in mind that occasionally you'll need to uncheck this box and check mail, just to clear out all the space that your e-mail is taking up on the server. You don't want to run out of space.

15. **If your ISP told you not to use POP3 extensions, then check the Disable Support For All POP3 Extensions check box.**

16. **Click Forward to proceed.**

    You're now finished setting up for incoming mail. In the Sending Email dialog box, shown in Figure 9-9, do the following:

17. **Change the Server Type entry if yours isn't SMTP.**

    I assume that you're sending e-mail with SMTP.

Figure 9-9:
The
Evolution
Sending
Email dialog
in Fedora
Core 5.

18. **Enter the full name of the SMTP mail server in the Host text box.**

    The name may be something like smtp.example.com.

19. **If you were told to use SSL for security, in the Use Secure Connection (SSL) drop-down list box, select either Always or Whenever Possible, depending on what your ISP has specified.**

20. **If you were told to use additional authentication for sending mail, check the Server Requires Authentication check box.**

    Typically, nothing is required here. If you don't check this box, skip to the next set of instructions. Otherwise, proceed to the next step.

21. **Under Authentication, select the appropriate Type as instructed by your ISP.**

    If you're not sure, click Check For Supported Types.

22. **Under Username, enter the login name you're supposed to use to authenticate with your outgoing mail server.**

    This name may be different from the one you use for incoming mail.

23. Check the Remember Password check box so that you don't have to enter your password each time you send mail.

Just make sure, again, to log out or use the Lock Screen option so that no one can send joke e-mails at your expense!

24. Click Forward to proceed.

You have now reached the wonderfully simple Account Management dialog box.

25. Either leave the Name entry as it is (your e-mail address) or change it to something descriptive so that you can tell which account you're looking at if you have a list of accounts you need to use.

It's common for your e-mail address to appear in this final box as something like `jane@computer5.example.com`. If this happens for you, you'll want to edit this entry so that it matches your real e-mail address, which in Jane's case is `jane@example.com`.

26. Click Forward to proceed to the Timezone dialog box.

Click the city closest to yours on the timezone map, or use the Select dropdown list bar to choose your proper timezone.

27. Click Forward to proceed to the Done dialog box.

Here you see just a quick message saying that you're finished.

28. Click Apply to save your settings.

The Evolution program opens, as shown in Figure 9-10.

Figure 9-10:
The Evolution application window in Fedora Core 5, with the Microsoft Exchange connector installed.

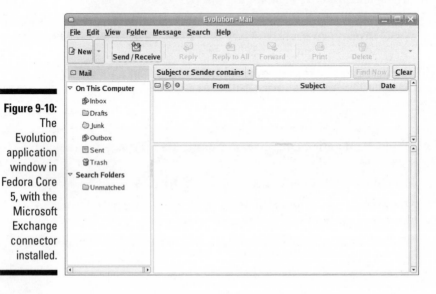

Sending and checking e-mail

The following steps outline how to create a new e-mail message and send it:

1. **Click New.**

   A Compose A Message window opens, as shown in Figure 9-11. If you want to open another new item such as a new contact list entry or a new calendar appointment, click the arrow next to New to open the list of options to choose from.

2. **Type the recipient's e-mail address (such as bob@example.net) or a list of addresses separated by commas (such as bob@example.net, tom@example.org) in the To text box.**

3. **If you need to add a CC (Carbon Copy) or BCC (Blind Carbon Copy) to the list of recipients, open the mail message's View menu and select the appropriate field(s) to appear and then enter the appropriate address(es) into those fields.**

4. **Type the topic of your e-mail into the Subject text box.**

5. **In the lower window, type the body of your e-mail.**

   Use the handy formatting buttons and the Format menu if you want to "pretty up" your e-mail. If you want to use the formatting buttons, set your Format type to HTML first.

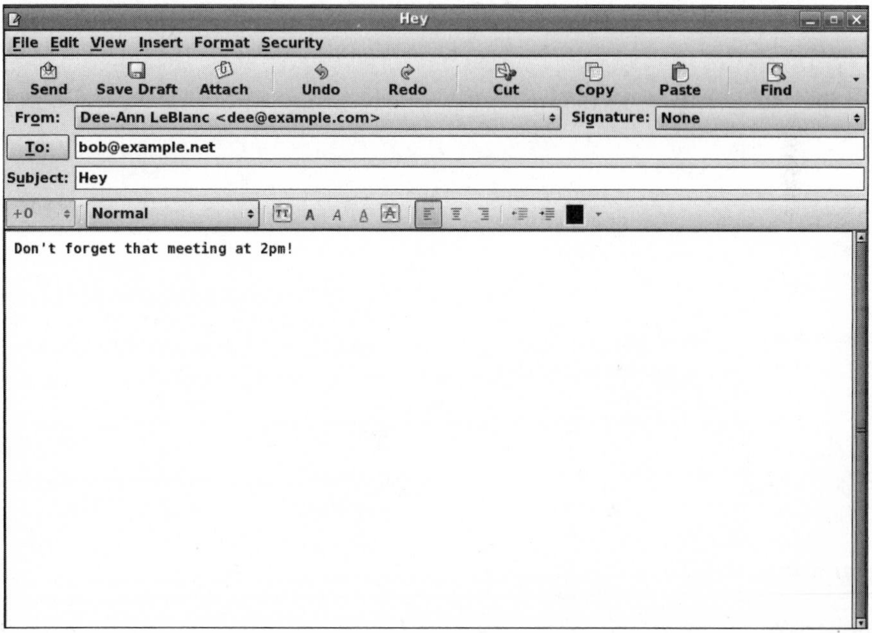

Figure 9-11: An Evolution Compose A Message window in Fedora Core 5.

6. **If you want to add a signature to the bottom of your e-mail, click the drop-down list box next to Signature and select Autogenerated.**

   To create custom signatures, go to the main Evolution window and choose Edit⇨Preferences to open the Evolution Settings dialog box (see Figure 9-12). Select the account you want to create the signature(s) for and then click the Edit button to open the Evolution Account Editor. In this dialog box, in the Identity tab, click Add New Signature. Here, you can create and format your new signature, and after you click the Save and Close button, you can choose which signature should be the default in the Identity tab's Signature drop-down list box. Get rid of the extra dialog boxes by clicking OK or Close on each one.

7. **When you finish typing your message, click the Send button.**

   The e-mail is now added to your Outbox, where you can edit it if you want.

8. **Click the Send/Receive button.**

   Your e-mail goes out, and Evolution checks for new incoming mail.

Take some time to really explore Evolution. As you can see just from the figures in this chapter, this program has many features, including the ability to filter junk mail.

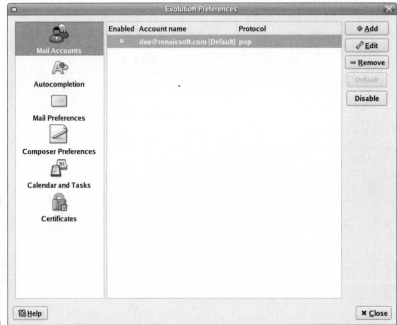

Figure 9-12:
The
Evolution
Settings
dialog box
in Fedora
Core 5.

Taking Advantage of Instant Messaging

Instant messaging (IM) between people is like using a telephone — except that you type your conversation rather than speak it. In addition, you can simultaneously hold multiple instant messaging conversations without the need for additional connections to the Internet. America Online (AOL) provides one popular instant messaging service, named AOL Instant Messenger, or AIM. Others are ICQ, MSN, Yahoo!, and Google. A wide variety of computer operating systems, including Linux, support these various services (and, in fact, GAIM runs on more than just Linux).

The distributions covered in this book use the following instant message programs by default:

- **Fedora:** GAIM (`http://gaim.sourceforge.net/`)
- **Knoppix:** GAIM
- **Linspire:** GAIM
- **Mandriva:** Kopete (`http://kopete.kde.org/`) and GAIM
- **SuSE:** GAIM and Kapote
- **Xandros:** Kopete
- **Ubuntu:** GAIM

Because GAIM is the default in Fedora, that's what I cover in detail. Kopete should work about the same.

Using the GAIM Instant Messenger

You launch GAIM with the following menu selections:

- **Fedora:** Choose Applications➪Internet➪Internet Messenger.
- **Knoppix:** From the Main Menu, choose Internet➪GAIM Instant Messenger.
- **Linspire:** Launch➪Run Programs➪Internet➪Instant Messenger.
- **Mandriva:** From the Main Menu, choose Internet➪Instant Messaging➪GAIM.
- **SuSE:** Applications➪Internet➪Chat➪GAIM Instant Messenger.
- **Ubuntu:** Applications➪Internet➪GAIM Instant Messenger.

After the application starts for the first time (see Figure 9-13), its main and account management dialog boxes both appear. To tell GAIM about one of your IM accounts:

1. **Click the Add button in the Accounts dialog box.**

   The Add Account dialog box, shown in Figure 9-13, appears.

2. **In the Protocol drop-down list box, select the IM network you want to use.**

   Your options are AIM/ICQ (if you need to use either AIM or ICQ, choose this option), Gadu-Gadu, GroupWise, IRC, Jabber, MSN, Napster, SILC, Yahoo, and Zephyr.

   If you want to use Google Instant Messenger, see the instructions at `www.google.com/support/talk/bin/answer.py?answer=24073`.

3. **In the Screen Name text box, enter the login name for your IM account.**

   If you're using ICQ, use your membership number.

4. **In the Password text box, enter your IM password for this account.**

5. **In the Alias text box, enter the name you actually want to show in people's IM clients, unless you want to use your screen name.**

6. **Click the Remember Password check box to put a check in it so that you don't have to enter your password every time you connect to this IM service.**

   Remember to log out or use the Lock Screen option if you walk away from your computer, just in case someone gets it in his head to go play a trick on you and send messages to people by using your IM client.

7. **Check the Auto-Login box if you want GAIM to automatically log this account on when you start it.**

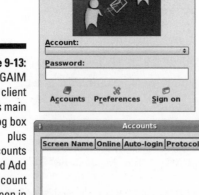

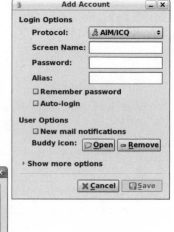

Figure 9-13: The GAIM IM client with its main dialog box plus Accounts and Add Account open in Fedora Core 5.

8. **If you get e-mail through this service and want to know when new mail has arrived, check the New Mail Notifications check box.**

9. **If you want to use a tiny picture as a *buddy icon* (of yourself, your dog, or whatever else you might want to use), click the Open button next to the Buddy Icon label and then navigate to the picture you want to use.**

10. **If you want access to the more advanced options for this IM service, click the Show More Options arrow to expand the Add Account dialog box.**

11. **When you finish entering your information, click Save to add this IM account to your accounts list.**

Go through this process for each account you want to use with GAIM. Then, in the main dialog box, click Sign On to log into all the accounts that you selected as Auto-Login. You can also open the Accounts dialog box by clicking Accounts from the main dialog box and then clicking the individual check boxes next to the accounts to log into them one by one. After you connect, you can alter your preferences in the Buddy List dialog box by choosing Tools⇨Preferences. Again, GAIM has more to it than this, so it's definitely worth playing around with this tool.

Troubleshooting your IM connections

If you've been using most of these IM clients with other operating systems, after your Linux system has successfully connected to the IM service, your existing buddy lists are automatically imported. If you haven't ever used AIM or MSN, you can now set up buddy lists. *Buddy lists* contain the usernames of people you want to communicate with through the instant messaging service. Your buddy list lets you know when your "buddies" are online and available to receive an instant message.

Sometimes, your Linux system is unable to connect properly to the IM service. When this problem happens, an error message pops up on your screen and indicates a failure to connect. You may be unable to connect to the IM service for several reasons:

- ✔ You may have entered the wrong password for your IM account or chosen the incorrect IM account name.

- ✔ Your computer may not be connected to the Internet. Try opening your Web browser to see whether you can get to a Web site, which tells you whether you're connected to the Internet.

- ✔ If you can open a Web site but can't get IM to work, the IM system may be unavailable. This problem occurs at times because of maintenance of the IM service or an excessive amount of traffic on the Internet or on the IM service.

✔ If you attempt to access the IM service from your computer at work, your company or organization may block the IM service for security or productivity reasons. If using IM at your work is permitted, check with your network administrator to see whether he can help you out.

✔ Often, companies use firewalls between the company's network and the Internet to keep out unwanted traffic on the company's network. If the firewall is configured to block IM traffic, you cannot use IM across the Internet.

Downloading with BitTorrent

Say what you want about file sharing, but it's popular. Networks such as BitTorrent (www.bittorrent.com) have actually found legitimate use among software companies and other content distributors, as a way of offering downloads for larger files without having to take the brunt of the bandwidth use themselves, so it's worth looking at how to use this software under Linux.

Typically a BitTorrent client is not installed by default, though this isn't always the case. You can use the information in Chapter 12 to install a client, using this guideline of what clients are available with which distribution:

✔ **Knoppix:** None, perhaps because this is a bootable distribution.

✔ **Fedora:** Use the tools discussed in Chapter 12 to install `bit torrent-gui`. When installed, you can run it by choosing Applications➪Internet➪BitTorrent File Transfer.

✔ **Linspire:** LTorrent is installed by default; go to Launch➪Run Programs➪Internet➪LTorrent.

✔ **Mandriva:** Use the package installation tool discussed in Chapter 12 and search on the term `bittorrent`. Install `bittorent` and `bittorrent-gui`.

✔ **SuSE:** KTorrent is installed by default; go to Applications➪Internet➪Data Exchange➪KTorrent.

✔ **Ubuntu:** A client is already installed; select Applications➪Internet➪ BitTorrent.

✔ **Xandros:** Use Xandros Networks to install BitTornado, which you'll find under Internet. After the package is installed, you will find it at Launch➪ Applications➪Internet➪Bittornado Client.

I cover the Fedora client, but the others work on the same principle. When you find out that a file is available over BitTorrent, you first download the .torrent file for the item. After you have this file downloaded:

1. **Start your BitTorrent client as discussed earlier.**

   The Fedora client is shown in Figure 9-14.

Figure 9-14:
The Bit-
Torrent
window
in Fedora
Core 5.

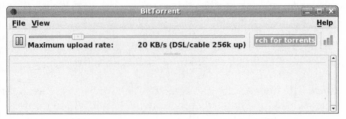

2. **Select File➪Open Torrent File.**

   A file browser window appears.

3. **Navigate to and select the .torrent file for the document you want to download, and then click OK.**

   The file appears in what looks a lot like a music player format, as shown in Figure 9-15. You can speed up the download by offering faster uploads to other BitTorrent users, using the Maximum Upload Rate slider. If you have broadband (see Chapter 8) then 40kbps works well.

   It can take a minute or so for the tool to fully synchronize, so expect the projected time to drastically change for a bit until it settles on a consistent value.

4. **Wait until the download is complete, and then choose File➪Quit to close the client.**

Figure 9-15:
The Bit-
Torrent
window in
Fedora Core
5 with a
file down-
loading.

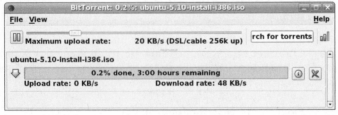

Talkin' on the Phone

The new craze these days is chatting on the phone over the Internet.
Whether you're just wanting to experiment or are a complete devotee, Linux

offers the software you need to take part. Think of the Internet phone networks like Instant Messenger networks. One of the most popular networks for this purpose is Skype (www.skype.com), so that is what I focus on here, along with SIP (Session Initiation Protocol), which is a popular default that you can use a wider variety of programs with. You first need the proper hardware, whether it's a phone you can actually plug into your computer (a SIP phone for example) or just a combination of a headset and a microphone — preferably not the lowest-end model so you'll get the best sound quality. When you have the hardware, it's time to get the software:

- **Fedora:** The default client (Ekiga, www.ekiga.org) is available through Applications➪Internet➪IP Telephony, VoIP and Video Conferencing. Two SIP clients are also included in the repositories, as discussed in Chapter 12, are KPhone (www.wirlab.net/kphone) and Linphone (www.linphone.org). Skype isn't included but you can download a Linux client from www.skype.com.

- **Knoppix:** Not included.

- **Linspire:** Go to the CNR as discussed in Chapter 12, to the Internet section, and install Skype. There is also PhoneGaim (GAIM with an embedded SIP phone client, www.phonegaim.com) for other types of Internet calling.

- **Mandriva:** In the commercial versions of Mandriva, you can choose the following from the Main Menu: Internet➪Instant Messaging➪Skype. Users of the free version can try Main Menu➪Internet➪Gnome Meeting (www.gnomemeeting.org), which is a combination video/audio client. This program also is available for other distributions, including Fedora.

- **SuSE:** Choose Applications➪Internet➪Telephone and then the program you want to use. Options include GnomeMeeting, KPhone, and Linphone.

- **Ubuntu:** Nothing, although Applications➪Internet➪GnomeMeeting is available by default. You can use the tools discussed in Chapter 12 to install Linphone for SIP calling.

- **Xandros:** Either Launch➪Applications➪Internet➪Voice Over IP Phone or Skype Internet Calling, depending on which version of Xandros you have. You can add the additional option by using the techniques discussed in Chapter 12.

To install Skype in Fedora, do the following:

1. **Point your Web browser to** www.skype.com.

2. **Click Download Skype.**

   You are taken to the Download Skype page.

3. **Click the penguin or the word Linux.**

   You are taken to the Download Skype for Linux page.

 4. **Right-click the Download the Public Key link and select Save Link As from the context menu.**

The Save As dialog box appears.

 5. **Click Save to save the file into your download directory (by default this is your Desktop).**

The dialog box closes, and the file appears on your desktop.

 6. **Select Applications⇨Accessories⇨Terminal.**

A terminal window appears, as discussed in Chapter 14.

 7. **Type** `su` **- to temporarily become the root user.**

 8. **Type** `rpm --import /home/`*user*`/Desktop/rpm-public-key.asc`**, where** *user* **is your user account, such as /home/dee/Desktop/rpm-public-key.asc.**

I am assuming that your downloads directory is Desktop. If it isn't, adjust the file path accordingly.

 9. **Click the X in the upper right corner of the terminal window to close it.**

10. **Click the RPM for Fedora entry, even if it isn't for Fedora 5.**

Notice that you can get Skype for SuSE and Mandriva here too. An Opening skype dialog box appears, with the full name of the file in the title.

11. **Leave Open with Install Software selected, and click OK.**

The Downloads window opens during the download, and then when the download is complete, the Password For root dialog box opens.

12. **Enter your root (administrator) password and click OK.**

The Installing Packages dialog box appears.

13. **Click Apply.**

The software installer adds the software to your system. When the installation is finished, an Information dialog box appears.

14. **Click OK to close the dialog box, and click the X in the upper right corner of the Downloads window.**

15. **If Skype (Figure 9-16) doesn't appear in your Applications⇨Internet menu, log out and back in (no need to reboot). It should show up after that.**

Before being able to make a call, you need to select Tools⇨Add a Contact — you can also select Tools⇨Search for Skype Users. Then (of course, your hardware has to be set up) you can click their name in the list and click the Phone button to give them a call!

Figure 9-16:
The Skype
Internet
telephony
client.

Working with Other Internet Tools

You may want to explore a variety of other types of tools, depending on your needs. This section covers some pointers to get you started, so if you go to Chapter 12 and want to add the appropriate software (or find yourself digging through menus and wondering what the program may be called), you aren't completely lost.

- ✔ **FTP programs:** If you want to FTP, a commonly used program in the Linux world is GFTP. This program is available for all five distributions discussed in this book, although it's only installed by default in Mandriva. The KDE equivalent is KBear.

- ✔ **IRC programs:** While the IM clients support IRC these days, you may prefer a program that's used only for IRC. Common programs for this purpose are X-Chat and KIRC.

- ✔ **File sharing:** LimeWire is a popular one if you want to use the Gnutella network.

- ✔ **RSS readers:** Firefox has a number of RSS extensions designed for it. In addition, Straw is a popular RSS program.

In general, if you're not sure what programs to use, do a Web search on the type of thing you want to do (like RSS) and the word Linux.

Part III
Getting Up to Speed with Linux

The 5th Wave
By Rich Tennant

"It's called Linux Poker. Everyone gets to see everyone else's cards, everything's wild, you can play off your opponents' hands, and everyone wins except Bill Gates, whose face appears on the jokers."

In this part . . .

In this part of the book, I expand my coverage of Linux beyond what's part and parcel of the operating system to include its many other facilities and capabilities. These components are critical to making Linux the raging monster of productivity that a well-constructed, properly configured system can represent.

Here you read about the Linux file system and how to manage its constituent files and directories, as well as how to control which users or groups are permitted to access these vital system resources. You also can read about using the Linux command-prompt environment, known as the *shell,* along with some key capabilities that should be part of any savvy Linux user's standard repertoire.

In addition, you find out how to keep your system current and install new software. You also get the inside scoop on all that security stuff that computer experts are always going on about. Those who like working without a net can dabble with working on the command line, while those who want nothing to do with (gasp) typing can leap straight to the fun of customizing the look and feel of your GUI.

Chapter 10

Manipulating Files and Directories

> *There is no need to do any housework at all. After the first four years, the dirt doesn't get any worse.*
>
> — Quentin Crisp

here's no avoiding it. At some point, you have to work with the files and directories in your system. Fortunately, after you get familiar with the rules and commands, you feel more comfortable (even if you find yourself being reminded from time to time of working in good old MS-DOS). Because many people find that working at the command line is easier when dealing with files, in this chapter I cover both the typed commands and the graphical tools you have at your disposal.

Working with Files in the GUI

People who prefer to stay graphical like to work with the GUI *file managers* offered in Linux instead of having to access a command prompt to work with files. A *file manager* is a program, such as Windows Explorer, that enables you to dig through and manipulate your files and directories with your mouse and sometimes just a bit of typing. In this section, I take you on a tour of the file managers that, by default, come with popular Linux distributions.

Sailin' with Nautilus

In the GNOME desktop environment (so in Fedora Core, SuSE, and Ubuntu if you're using your distribution's defaults), the file manager is *Nautilus*. Moving through the filesystem in Nautilus involves a couple of different skills. In the first place, you need to know where you want to begin. This decision isn't as difficult as it sounds. Use the Places menu as detailed in Chapter 6 if you don't want to start from your home folder, or do one of the following:

- ✔ **Fedora:** Double-click the Computer or Home icon on your desktop, choose anything from the Places menu, or choose Applications⇨System Tools⇨File Browser for the ability to see a tree on the left and folder contents on the right as you're probably used to from other operating systems.

- ✔ **SuSE:** Double-click the Computer or Home icon on your desktop, or choose anything from the Places menu. To see a tree view on the left as you would normally expect, select View⇨Side Pane.

- ✔ **Ubuntu:** Choose anywhere in the Places menu or Applications⇨ Accessories⇨File Browser. Two panes are enabled by default. Figure 10-1 shows an example of what you can see with Nautilus open in an example home directory.

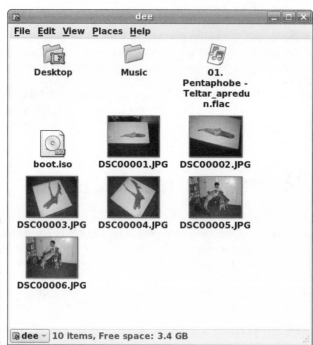

Figure 10-1:
Nautilus
displaying
Dee's home
directory
in Fedora
Core 5.

Double-click the Home item on your desktop if you're using a distribution that has one.

When you have the window open to where you want to start, you need to find out how to navigate. To use a file, just double-click it, and proceed to the section "Opening files and running programs," for Nautilus later in this chapter. You also double-click folders to open them and access their contents. When you open a folder and aren't in tree view, a separate window opens, leaving the window you were already working in open as well. You can close the original window if you want by choosing File⇨Close or clicking the X in the window's upper-right corner.

If you find that you've got way too many directories open, choose one of the following commands:

- **File⇨Close Parent Folders:** Closes all the folders used to get to this directory.

- **File⇨Close All Folders:** Closes all the file browser folders you have open.

- **File⇨Close:** Closes just this folder.

You can also easily return to a folder previously accessed, if you want. (For example, maybe you're in /home/jane/documents/invoices and want to go back to /home/jane without opening and closing multiple folders.) To do so, look at the bottom left of the folder window to find the name of the subdirectory you're in (such as invoices). Click that name, and you open a list that has all the parent directories plus the current one. The list might look like the following for the example:

```
home
jane
documents
invoices
```

To back up, you can select the spot in the directory tree (for example, jane to go to /home/jane) you want to move to.

Setting how much you see in a folder

Are you getting too much information about each file or not enough? Experiment with the View menu. The major listing options under the View menu include the following commands

- **View As Icons:** This default option shows all files as icons with names beneath them, refer to Figure 10-1.

- **View As List:** This command gives you a list of information about the file, as well as its icon and name (see Figure 10-2). Note that there are still small icons available along the left of the listing.

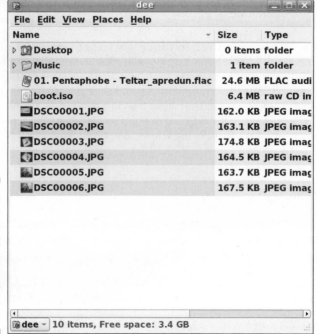

Figure 10-2:
Nautilus
with the
View As List
option in
dee's home
directory
in Fedora
Core 5.

Along with these View menu commands, you can also use

✔ **View⇨Reload:** If you just created a file and don't see it in the folder, select this option.

✔ **View⇨Show Hidden Files:** All files in Linux whose names start with a dot (for example, .profile) are *hidden files*, meaning that you have to explicitly tell Linux you want to see them.

Along with these commands, you can choose the View menu's Zoom In, Zoom Out, and Normal Size options if you need to change the visual size of the folder's contents.

Creating files and folders

To create a new file or folder in Nautilus:

1. **Browse to the folder you want to create the item in.**

   You need to open a window for that folder and work from within that window.

2. **Right-click on an empty spot inside that folder.**

   Make sure that you didn't highlight anything in the folder. A context menu appears.

3. **Depending on what you want to accomplish, choose either Create Folder or Create Document.**

   - **The Create Folder command** creates a new folder in this directory.

   - **The Create Document command** opens the submenu that lets you choose to create either a document from a Template (top section, if you already have templates created) or an Empty File.

   The folder or file appears, highlighted.

4. **Type the name you want to assign to this folder or file and then press Enter.**

   The name is assigned to the folder or file.

Opening files and running programs

To open a file or run a program in Nautilus, double-click it. That's it! Well, not entirely. You can also right-click a file to open the context menu and then choose one of the following from the context menu:

✔ **Open with *program*:** If the file is associated with a particular program already, choosing this option is the same as double-clicking the file. More than one of these options may be listed, if your system knows that you have more than one program installed that can do the job — the top item with the folder icon next to it is the default. Choose whichever option you prefer.

✔ **Open with Other Application:** Choosing this option opens a submenu that contains a list of installed programs the system is aware of. You can select one of these programs if you find what you need in there by clicking Use A Custom Command. From here, you can

   - Type in the full *path* to the application (the full directory path, like `/usr/bin/konqueror`).

   - Click the Browse button to open a file browser and surf to the program you want to use.

After you select the program to open the file with, click Open to proceed.

Copying and moving files

You can copy and move items by using two different methods in Nautilus. The first is by using the usual method you're probably familiar with from Windows or the Mac OS — clicking and grabbing a file or folder and then dragging it where you want to go. You can click and drag between folder windows and into folder icons. Following are some handy tips:

✔ Hold down the Ctrl key while you drag if you want to make a copy rather than just move the file.

✔ If you want to drag the file into a folder icon, make sure that the folder icon is highlighted before you release the mouse.

✔ If you want to drag the file into a folder window but not into one of the folder icons, make sure that the folder icons are *not* highlighted before you release the mouse.

The other method for copying and moving files and directories involves the following steps:

1. **Right-click the file or directory you want to copy or move.**

2. **From the context menu that appears, choose Cut if you want to move the file or Copy if you want to copy it.**

   The file doesn't disappear after you make your selection if you're trying to move it.

3. **Navigate into the folder you want to move the file into.**

   You are ready when you have that folder's window open.

4. **Do one of the following:**

   • If you want to move or copy the file into a folder window, right-click inside that window (just make sure that nothing is highlighted) and then choose Paste.

   • If you want to move or copy the file into a folder icon rather than an open folder window, right-click the icon and then choose Paste Into Folder.

Deleting files and folders

To use Nautilus to delete either a file or a directory from the filesystem, follow these steps:

1. **Browse to the file or directory's location.**

2. **Select the file(s) or folder(s).**

   You can select the file or folder by doing one of the following:

   • Clicking the file or folder to highlight it.

   • Clicking the first item, holding Shift down, and then clicking the last item in the group to choose them all. (These items all must be lined up straight.)

   • Clicking the first item, holding Ctrl down, and then clicking each individual item you want to select.

   • Clicking and dragging your mouse button so that you make a box that contains all the items you want to select.

3. **Press the Delete key or right-click and select Move To Trash.**

   The file or folder vanishes from view. Keep in mind that if you are deleting a folder and the folder contains other files or folders, they go to into the trash right along with it.

These deleted items are in fact sitting in the Trash can, so they aren't really deleted from your hard drive. You can move these files out of the trash and back into your filesystem if you want to.

Taking out the trash

You can permanently delete the contents of your Trash folder by following these steps:

1. **Right-click the Trash icon.**

   This action opens a shortcut menu with options listed.

2. **Choose Empty Trash from the shortcut menu.**

   A confirmation dialog box opens.

3. **Click Empty in the confirmation dialog box to delete the contents of the Trash folder.**

   Linux permanently removes the items in the Trash folder. You can tell whether the Trash folder is empty by looking at the Trash waste can. If it's empty, it contains no files. If you see papers in it, it contains trash.

Viewing and changing permissions

Every file in Linux (and other forms of Unix) has a set of *permissions* that govern who is allowed to view it, run it, delete it, and so on. These permissions are used to make sure that people can't mess with the system's or each other's files, so they're pretty important. In this section, I focus on how to work with files in the GUI. See the section "A permissions primer," later in this chapter, for a breakdown of how file permissions work.

To view and change a file or directory's permissions in Nautilus, you need to follow these steps:

1. **Browse to the file or directory's location.**

   Opening the folder window that contains this item is sufficient.

2. **Right-click the file or directory.**

   A context menu appears.

3. **Choose Properties from the context menu.**

   The Properties dialog box appears with the Basic tab open.

4. **Click the Permissions tab.**

   The Permissions portion of the Properties dialog box appears, as shown in Figure 10-3.

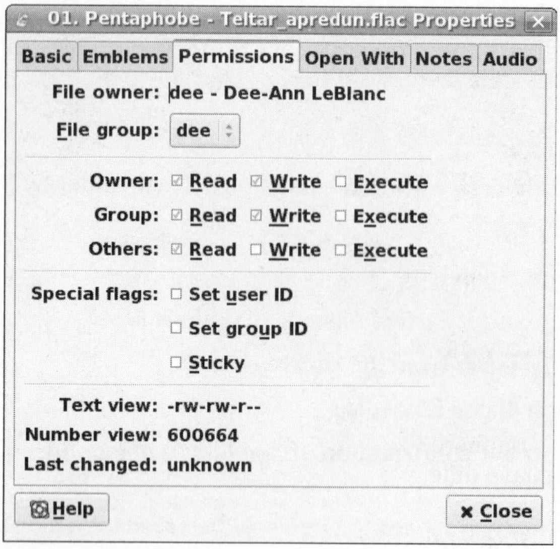

Figure 10-3:
The Nautilus
file
manager's
Properties
dialog box
with the
Permissions
tab
displayed, in
Fedora Core
5.

```
┌─────────────────────────────────────────────────────┐
│  01. Pentaphobe - Teltar_apredun.flac Properties  X   │
├─────────────────────────────────────────────────────┤
│ Basic  Emblems  Permissions  Open With  Notes  Audio  │
│                                                       │
│      File owner: dee - Dee-Ann LeBlanc                │
│      File group: [ dee  ⬍ ]                           │
│                                                       │
│       Owner:  ☑ Read  ☑ Write  ☐ Execute              │
│       Group:  ☑ Read  ☑ Write  ☐ Execute              │
│      Others:  ☑ Read  ☐ Write  ☐ Execute              │
│                                                       │
│  Special flags:  ☐ Set user ID                        │
│                  ☐ Set group ID                       │
│                  ☐ Sticky                             │
│                                                       │
│     Text view: -rw-rw-r--                             │
│   Number view: 600664                                 │
│   Last changed: unknown                               │
│                                                       │
│  ⊗ Help                              x Close          │
└─────────────────────────────────────────────────────┘
```

5. **Set the new permissions and ownerships.**

   See the section "A permissions primer," later in this chapter, for a break-down of what all this stuff means.

6. **Click Close to close the dialog box.**

   The file's permissions are now changed.

Rulin' with Konqueror

In KDE (and thus KNOPPIX, Linspire, Mandriva, and Xandros if you kept the defaults), the default file manager is Konqueror, as shown in Figure 10-4. You can access this program in these distributions by doing the following:

- **KNOPPIX:** Clicking the home icon on the panel at the bottom of the screen, or double-clicking one of the shortcut icons on the Desktop pointing to various parts of the filesystem or media.

- **Linspire:** Double-click the My Computer icon on the desktop or the File Manager icon on the panel.

- **Mandriva:** Double-click the Home or the Devices icon.

- **Xandros:** Has its own custom file manager, see the section "Excavating with the Xandros File Manager," later in this chapter for more.

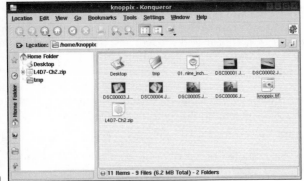

Figure 10-4:
The
Konqueror
file manager
open to
knoppix's
home
directory in
KNOPPIX
4.0.

Keep in mind that Konqueror looks slightly different from distribution to distribution and may have different default settings as well.

Navigating your filesystem

Moving through the filesystem in Konqueror mostly involves being familiar with the main row of icons beneath the top menu. These icons are, from left to right:

- **Left arrow:** Go back to the last directory you visited.

- **Right arrow:** If you went back previously, takes you to the directory you went back *from*.

- **Up arrow:** Go up a directory. For example, from /usr/bin to /usr.

- **Home:** Shows the contents of your home directory.

- **Reload:** Reloads the contents of the current directory.

- **Stop Loading:** Quits loading what it's trying to load.

- **Print:** Prints the selected document.

- **Zoom In:** Enlarges the icons.

- **Zoom Out:** Shrinks the icons.

- **View menus:** See the next section "Setting how much you see in a folder" for a discussion on the last three icons in the row.

Linspire's layout is slightly different; its version of Konqueror can use tabs to have multiple locations open at once so there are icons for opening and closing tabs, and its Go menu is slightly different as well.

To open a directory in Konqueror, locate it in the list and click (in KNOPPIX) or double-click (in Linspire and Mandriva), depending on how your system is set up to behave. The window changes to display that folder's contents.

Setting how much you see in a folder

If you want to see more or less information about each file, experiment by choosing View➪View Mode (or find the icons to the right of the Konqueror icon bar, below the menus). The major listing options in View➪View Mode may include, depending on the version of Konqueror you're using:

- ✔ **Icon View:** Shows all files as icons with names beneath them (refer to Figure 10-4). It's the default option.

- ✔ **MultiColumn View:** Lines your icons up in columns rather than rows.

- ✔ **Tree View:** Shows a list of information about the file, as well as its icon and name (see Figure 10-5). You can expand each folder in this list by clicking the plus sign next to it; to collapse the list, click the minus sign next to it.

- ✔ **Info List View:** Shows the icons and names in small list format.

- ✔ **Detailed List View:** Works like Tree View, but lacks the ability to expand and collapse directories.

- ✔ **Text View:** Works like Detailed List View, but without the pretty icons.

- ✔ **Image View:** Lets you use an image browser embedded in your file browser (Figure 10-6). If you choose this view option, use the left-hand tabs to click on the Home icon and browse to the folder you want to view. DVD version only.

- ✔ **Photobook:** Similar to Image View but laid out a bit differently.

- ✔ **File Size View:** Shows a funky graphical representation of your filesystem (Figure 10-7), with directories in blue, files in brown, and programs you can run in green. It's not available in all the distributions covered in this book, as this feature is pretty new. When you add new files, they don't show up unless you choose View➪Reload or click the Reload icon.

- ✔ **KfileReplace:** Opens a Search & Replace dialog box. DVD version only.

- ✔ **CVS FrontEnd:** Opens a dialog box capable of using a popular document management tool for programmers called CVS. DVD version only.

Figure 10-5:
Konqueror
with the
Tree View
option in
knoppix's
home
directory in
KNOPPIX
4.0.

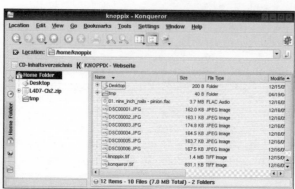

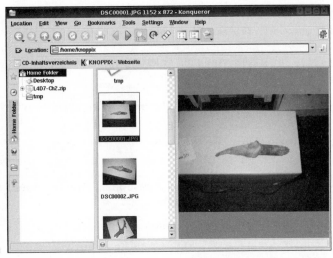

Figure 10-6:
Konqueror
with the
Image View
option in
knoppix's
home
directory in
KNOPPIX
4.0. Don't
worry, that's
not a knife;
it's a piece
of wood.

Figure 10-7:
Konqueror
with the File
Size View
option in
knoppix's
home
directory in
KNOPPIX
4.0.

Along with these View menu settings, you can also use

✔ **View➪Reload:** If you just created a file and don't see it in the folder, choose this option.

✔ **View➪Show Hidden Files:** All files in Linux whose names start with a dot (for example, `.profile`) are *hidden files*, meaning that you have to explicitly tell Linux you want to see them.

Creating files and folders

To create a new file or folder in Konqueror:

1. **Browse to the folder you want to create the item in.**

2. **Right-click inside that folder.**

   Make sure that you didn't highlight anything in there. A context menu appears.

3. **Choose Create New.**

   A submenu appears.

4. **Depending on what you want to accomplish, choose either Folder or one of the File or Document options.**

   These commands do the following:

   • **Folder:** Creates a new folder in this directory.

   • **Text File:** Creates a plain text file.

   • **HTML File:** A Web page.

5. **In the query dialog box, enter the name for the folder or file you're creating.**

6. **Click OK to finish the creation process.**

Opening files and running programs

To open a file or run a program in Konqueror, single (KNOPPIX) or double-click it (Linspire and Mandriva). That's it! Well, not entirely, Konqueror itself may not support the file format. You can also right-click a file to open the context menu and choose the Open With menu. From there, you can either choose one of the suggested options in the context submenu, or you can choose Other to access the Open With dialog box. To use this dialog box:

1. **Either browse in the lower section to select which program you want to use to open this file, or type the full path to the application (the full directory path, like /usr/bin/konqueror) in the text box.**

   If you need to browse the filesystem, click the little folder icon to the right of the text box to open the browser.

2. **If you want to always use this application to open files of this type, check the Remember application association for this type of file check box.**

3. **Click OK to open or run the file.**

Copying and moving files

You can copy and move items by using two different methods in Konqueror. The first is by using the usual method you're probably familiar with — clicking and grabbing a file or folder and then dragging it where you want to go. The Tree View is handy for this method because you can open up folders until you find the one you want to copy into and then click and drag the file or folder into it. When you do so, a little context menu pops up asking whether you want to move the file, copy it, link it (see the section "Understanding long format file listings" to find out more about links; they're basically shortcuts), or cancel and not do anything.

The other method for copying and moving files and directories involves the following steps:

1. **Right-click the file or directory you want to copy or move.**

2. **In the context menu that appears, choose Copy if you want to copy the file or Cut if you want to move it.**

3. **Select the folder you want to move the file into.**

4. **Right-click in an empty spot in the folder and select Paste.**

Deleting files and folders

To use Konqueror to delete either a file or a directory from the filesystem, follow these steps:

1. **Browse to the file or directory's location.**

2. **Choose the file(s) or folder(s) you want to delete.**

   You can do so by:

   - Holding Shift down and then clicking at the end of the row or column that you want to select. (These items all must be lined up straight.)

   - Holding Ctrl down and clicking each individual item you want to select.

   - Clicking and dragging your mouse button so that you make a box that contains all the items you want to select.

3. **Delete your file or folder.**

   To do so, either:

   - Press the Delete key and say that yes, you want to move this item or these items to the Trash.

   - Right-click over the item(s) and choose either Delete to permanently remove the file or Move To Trash to give yourself the option to back up and pull it back out of the Trash later.

Taking out the trash

You can permanently delete the contents of your Trash folder by following these steps:

1. **Right-click the Trash icon.**

   This action opens a shortcut menu.

2. **Choose Empty Trash Bin.**

   Linux permanently removes the items in the Trash folder. You can tell whether your waste can is empty by looking at it. If nothing's in there, it's empty; if you see papers in it, you have files in the Trash.

Viewing and changing permissions

Every file in Linux (and other forms of Unix) has a set of permissions that govern who is allowed to access it, run it, delete it, and so on. These permissions are used to make sure that people can't mess with the system's files, or each other's, so they're pretty important. See the section "A permissions primer," later in this chapter, for a breakdown of file permissions in general. I focus here on how to work with them in the GUI.

To view and change a file or directory's permissions in Konqueror, you need to follow these steps:

1. **Browse to the file or directory's location.**

   Opening the folder that contains this item is sufficient.

2. **Right-click the file or directory.**

   A context menu appears.

3. **Choose Properties from the context menu.**

   The Properties dialog box opens with the General tab open.

4. **Click the Permissions tab.**

   The Permissions portion of the Properties dialog box appears, as shown in Figure 10-8.

5. **Set the new permissions and ownerships.**

   If you want to know how file access permissions work in Linux, see the section "A permissions primer," later in this chapter.

6. **Click OK to close the dialog box.**

   The file's permissions are now changed.

Figure 10-8: Konqueror's Properties dialog box with the Permissions tab displayed, in KNOPPIX 4.0.

Figure 10-8: Konqueror's Properties dialog box with the Permissions tab displayed, in KNOPPIX 4.0.

Excavating with the Xandros File Manager

Xandros offers a custom file manager (see Figure 10-9) that looks to be based on Konqueror. One method of accessing this file manager is by double-clicking the Home directory on your desktop. This file manager works similarly to the other file managers in this chapter. Because I am limited on space, I'll leave it at that, reminding you that Xandros in particular is designed for Windows users, so you can expect its file manager to be laid out and function like Windows Explorer.

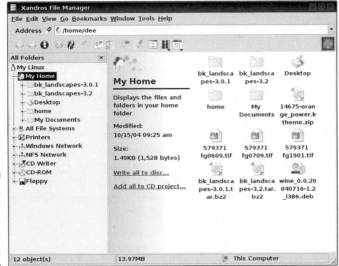

Figure 10-9: The Xandros file manager in Xandros 3.

Understanding Filesystem Mechanics

Chapter 11 focuses on how the filesystem is laid out, but this chapter covers what's happening under the hood as far as how to understand what you're seeing in file-system listings. These features are identical across Linux distributions, as the underpinning of working with Linux remains at least mostly the same no matter what version of Linux you're using.

Understanding long format file listings

Remember those detailed list views in the file managers? They typically contain information similar to this `ls -la` output here (see Appendix A for a list of commonly used commands in Linux):

```
drwx------ 2 dee   dee   4096 Jul 29 07:48 .
drwxr-xr-x 5 root  root  4096 Jul 27 11:57 ..
-rw-r--r-- 1 dee   dee     24 Jul 27 06:50 .bash_logout
-rw-r--r-- 1 dee   dee    230 Jul 27 06:50 .bash_profile
-rw-r--r-- 1 dee   dee    124 Jul 27 06:50 .bashrc
```

You may find some parts of this format easier to understand, at a glance, than others. The first item in each listing (the part with the letters and dashes — for example, the `drwx------` in the first line) is the *permission set* assigned to the item. Briefly, permissions define who can read the file, change it, or run it if it's a program. You can read more about permissions in "A permissions primer," later in this chapter. The second item in the first line (in this case, 2) is the number of hard links to the item.

A *link* is a fake file listing that points to another file, making a kind of shortcut. You use two kinds of links in Linux and Unix:

- ✔ **Soft link:** This link is like a Windows shortcut in that the link points back to the original file, and anything you do to the link happens to the original file. Erase the original file, and the link remains, but it becomes unusable. The link is broken without the original file.

- ✔ **Hard link:** This link doesn't have a counterpart in the Windows world. A hard link isn't just a shortcut; it's another instance of the file itself. The data in this file is saved in only one place, but you can edit either the original or the link, and the edit is saved for both instances of the file. Erase the original, and the file still exists as long as the link is there. It's like two doors to the same room!

The third item (dee) is the file's *owner,* and the fourth (dee) is the *group* —
depending on which version of Linux you're using, both these items may or
may not be identical. You can find out more about both of these in "A permissions primer," later in this chapter. The fifth item is the file's size in bytes. All
directories show up as 4,096 bytes. Everything else has its own size. You can
tell an empty file from the size of 0 bytes.

The sixth, seventh, and eighth entries are all related to the last time the file
was changed: the month (Jul), the date (29), and the time in 24-hour format
(07:48). Finally, the ninth item is the filename (for example, bash logout,
in the third row).

A permissions primer

If you find yourself scratching your head when looking at parts of that long
format file listing, don't worry. The "Comprehending file types" section, later
in this chapter, gives you a feeling for the first letter on each line, but nine
more characters are attached to that item before you get to the next column.
This group of nine is the set of *permissions* (also called a *permission set*) for
the file or directory. Linux, Unix, and even Mac OS X use permissions as a
way of providing file and directory security by giving you the means to specify exactly who can look at your files, who can change them, and even who
can run your programs. You need this capability when you have a bunch of
different users on the same machine, networked to the world.

Checking out the triads

Each permission set consists of three triads. Each of the triads has the same
basic structure but controls a different aspect of who can use what. Consider
the long format listing for /home/dee in the following code:

```
total 20
drwx------ 2 dee   dee   4096 Jul 29 07:48 .
drwxr-xr-x 5 root  root  4096 Jul 27 11:57 ..
-rw-r--r-- 1 dee   dee     24 Jul 27 06:50 .bash_logout
-rw-r--r-- 1 dee   dee    230 Jul 27 06:50 .bash_profile
-rw-r--r-- 1 dee   dee    124 Jul 27 06:50 .bashrc
-rw-rw-r-- 1 dee   dee      0 Jul 29 07:48 lsfile
```

The first character in the permission set refers to the type of file. For a directory, the character is shown as a d, as you see here for the first two items in
the preceding list; files are designated with a dash (-) instead. Each file or
directory's permission set is a group of nine characters — that is, the nine
characters that follow the first character (for a total of ten). But this group
of nine is really three groups of three, as shown in Figure 10-10.

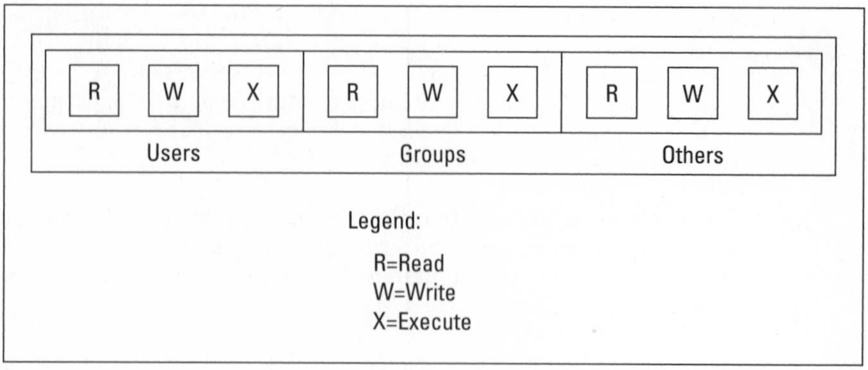

Figure 10-10:
Breakdown
of the nine
permission
characters.

The three triads are read as follows:

- The first triad consists of the second, third, and fourth characters in the long format file listing. This triad sets the permissions for the *user*, or *owner*, of the file. (Owners are discussed in the "Beware of owners" section, later in this chapter.)

- The second triad consists of the fifth, sixth, and seventh characters in the long format file listing. This triad sets the permissions for the *group* that is assigned to the file. (Groups are discussed in the "Hanging out in groups" section, later in this chapter.)

- The third triad consists of the eighth, ninth, and tenth characters in the long format file listing. This triad sets the permissions for *other*, or everyone who isn't the file's owner or a member of the owning group.

Although each triad is often different from the others, the internal structure of each one is made up in the same way. Focus specifically on how to read one triad before looking at the set of them together. Each triad includes three characters:

- The first character is either an r or a dash. The r stands for *read* permission. If r is set, the triad allows the entity it stands for (user, group, or other) to view the directory or file's contents.

- The second character is either a w or a dash. The w stands for *write* permission. If w is set, the triad allows the entity it stands for to add, delete, or edit items in this directory or file.

- The third character is either an x or a dash. The x stands for *execute* permission. If x is set, the triad allows the entity it stands for to access the files contained in this directory or to run the particular program in this file.

In all cases, if the dash sits in place of r, w, or x, the triad doesn't allow the entity the read, write, or execute permission.

The following sections describe owners and groups in more detail.

Beware of owners

You may have noticed by now that I talk a great deal about owners (users) and groups in Linux. Every file and directory has both of these components: a user from the /etc/passwd file that's assigned as its owner and a group from /etc/group assigned as the group.

Although an everyday user probably doesn't need to change file ownerships often, the root user does so regularly. If you add the file comments, for example, to /home/tom while you're logged on as the *superuser* (another term for the administrator, who is the person who owns the root account), root owns that file. The user tom can't do anything with it unless you have set the last triad's permissions to allow the *other* folks (those who aren't the file's owner or in the specified group) to read and write to the file. But this method is a pretty sloppy way of doing things because the whole idea of permissions is to reduce access, not to give everyone access. Instead, remember to change the file's owner to the user tom. You do this with the chown (*change own*er) command. For example, by typing chown tom comments, root changes the ownership over to tom. Then tom can work with this file and even change its permissions to something he prefers.

Hanging out in groups

Groups are more interesting to work with than owners. You use groups to allow the root user to assign to multiple users the ability to share certain filesystem areas. For example, in many versions of Linux, all users are added to a group named *users* (SuSE does this, for example). Then rather than a long format file listing such as the one shown in earlier in this chapter, you may see the following:

```
total 20
drwx------ 2 dee   users 4096 Jul 29 07:48 .
drwxr-xr-x 5 root  root  4096 Jul 27 11:57 ..
-rw-r--r-- 1 dee   users   24 Jul 27 06:50 .bash_logout
-rw-r--r-- 1 dee   users  230 Jul 27 06:50 .bash_profile
-rw-r--r-- 1 dee   users  124 Jul 27 06:50 .bashrc
-rw-rw-r-- 1 dee   users    0 Jul 29 07:48 lsfile
```

In other distributions (such as Fedora) a unique group is created for every user, which is why the earlier listings showed the owner and group items as identical (dee dee).

Comprehending file types

The first letter in any long format file listing tells you which type of file you're dealing with. In Table 10-1, I list the types you're likely to run into.

Table 10-1		Linux File Types
Label	*Type*	*Description*
-	Regular file	The item is an everyday file, such as a text file or program.
b	Block device	The item is a *driver* (control program) for a *storage medium,* such as a hard drive or CD-ROM drive.
c	Character device	The item is a *driver* (control program) for a piece of hardware that transmits data, such as a modem.
d	Directory	The item is a container for files, also referred to as a *folder* in some operating systems' lingo.

In addition to this, you find lots more different file types out there in the Linux world. By types, I'm not referring to extensions, such as .exe or .doc. Linux sees everything within its filesystem — even directories and hardware like your monitor — as "files." As a result, assigning a type to a file is merely a Linux machine's way of keeping track of what's what.

The main thing Windows users in particular want to know when they move to Linux is how to recognize programs. Instead of looking for files with particular extensions (like .exe) programs have (or need to have) an *executable permission* set so the system knows they are allowed to run. You can view or set this permission for a file by going to the Nautilus or Konqueror section and looking up how to do so.

On the command line, try out the file command, such as file Desktop, to find more about what a particular file contains.

Chapter 11

Checking Out the Linux Filesystem

. . . .

. . . .

> *I have an existential map. It has "You are here" written all over it.*
>
> — Steven Wright

*O*ne of the most frustrating things about mastering a new operating system can be figuring out where it keeps files. Instead of keeping all important system files in a single directory, such as the `C:\Windows` directory in Microsoft Windows, Linux follows the lead of its Unix cousins and spreads things out a bit more. Although the Linux and Windows setups involve different methods, they are both logical, although it may not feel that way until you understand where to look.

Another issue you come across is adding new *media* — hard drives, floppy disks, CD-ROMs, DVD-ROMs, zip disks, and more — to the existing filesystem. In this chapter, I focus on how the filesystem is organized and other handy topics, such as how to access data on a floppy disk. (In Chapter 10, you can find hints on how to do this when looking through the file managers.)

Introducing the Linux Filesystem

Linux may be all by itself on your hard drive, or maybe it's sharing your hard drive with another operating system, such as Microsoft Windows. All the hard drive space you allocated for Linux during the installation process is the majority of your Linux *filesystem.* Because you're running your own Linux machine, you need to be familiar with how it's put together — especially the sections that are dangerous to mess with!

Meet the root directory

Everything in the Linux filesystem is relative to the `root` *directory,* which is referred to as / and is the file-system base, a doorway into all your files — don't confuse this with the `root` user, which is the system administrator. The `root` directory contains a mostly predictable set of subdirectories. Each distribution varies slightly, but certain standards exist to which they all conform. The standards keep us all sane.

If you're interested in these standards, go to `www.pathname.com/fhs` and look at the latest version of the rules.

Rather than flooding you with everything at once, I start by talking about the *base directories,* meaning the items you find in /. Table 11-1 lists what you might find in this base location. (This list can vary some from distribution to distribution.) An asterisk (*) at the end of a description indicates that you shouldn't mess with this directory unless you have a *really good reason* because it contains files that are *very important* to the functioning of your system.

Table 11-1	Standard / Contents in Linux
Directory	*Contains*
/bin	Essential commands that everyone needs to use at any time*
/boot	The information that boots the machine, including your kernel*
/dev	The device drivers for all the hardware that your system needs to interface with*
/etc	The configuration files for your system*
/home	The home directories for each of your users
/lib	The *libraries,* or code that many programs (and the kernel) use*
/media	A spot where you add temporary media, such as floppy disks and CD-ROMs; not all distributions have this directory

Directory	Contains
/mnt	A spot where you add extra filesystem components such as networked drives, items you aren't permanently adding to your file system but that aren't as temporary as CD-ROMs and floppies
/opt	The location that some people decide to use (and some programs want to use) for installing new software packages, such as word processors and office suites
/proc	Current settings for your kernel (operating system)*
/root	The superuser's (root user's) home directory
/sbin	The commands the system administrator needs access to*
/srv	Data for your system's *services* (the programs that run in the background)*
/sys	Kernel information about your hardware*
/tmp	The place where everyone and everything stores temporary files
/usr	A complex hierarchy of additional programs and files
/var	The data that changes frequently, such as log files and your mail

Some of these directories have some equally important subdirectories, which I cover in the upcoming sections.

Meet the /etc subdirectories

Although the exact subdirectories that exist in /etc can change from distribution to distribution, the following two are fairly standard:

✔ The /etc/X11 directory contains configuration details for the X Window System (X), which runs your Graphical User Interface (GUI). See Chapter 14 for more on the GUI.

✔ The /etc/opt directory contains configuration files for the programs in the /opt directory, if you decide to use it.

An additional important location in Fedora is `/etc/sysconfig`, which contains configuration information for the *services* that start at boot time, including things like your networking. Each distribution tends to have its own way of handling networking information.

Meet the /mnt and /media subdirectories

You may or may not have any subdirectories in `/media` or `/mnt` by default (and you may not have both of these directories at the same time). Typically, however, you can look for the following:

- ✔ The `/mnt/floppy` or `/media/floppy` directory is used for adding a floppy disk to your filesystem — instead of the word `floppy`, you might see `fd0` or `floppy0`.

- ✔ The `/mnt/cdrom` or `/media/cdrom` (or `/media/dvd`, `/media/ cdrecorder`, and so on, depending on what type of hardware you have) directory is used for adding a CD-ROM, DVD-ROM, CD-Writer, and so on to your system.

In the "Finding CDs and More in Your GUI" section, later in this chapter, I show you how to add these items for each of the distributions. Fortunately you really don't need to know this information in the GUI because this is all taken care of for you. Still, it doesn't hurt!

Meet the /usr subdirectories

The `/usr` directory is often referred to as its own miniature filesystem hierarchy. This directory has lots of important or interesting subdirectories, as shown in Table 11-2. An asterisk (*) at the end of a description indicates that you need to leave that directory alone unless you have good reason to mess with it — *after* you gain lots of experience with Linux and know exactly what changes you need to make — so that you don't accidentally alter something your system needs in order to function correctly. An important thing to remember about this segment of the filesystem is that many advanced Linux users often use `/usr` to store programs that can be shared with other Linux machines.

Table 11-2	Standard /usr Subdirectories
Subdirectory	*Contents*
`/usr/X11R6`	The files that manage the X Window System (the wireframe underneath your GUI)*
`/usr/bin`	The commands that aren't essential for users but are useful*

Subdirectory	Contents
/usr/games	The games that you install on your system, except for those that you can choose to place in /opt
/usr/include	The files that the C programming language needs for the system and its programs*
/usr/lib	The shared code used by many of the programs in this /usr subhierarchy*
/usr/local	The programs and other items that you want to keep locally, even if you're sharing everything else in /usr
/usr/sbin	The commands that aren't essential for administrators but are useful*
/usr/share	The information that you can use on any Linux machine, even if it's running incredibly different hardware from what this one is running*
/usr/src	The source code that you use to build the programs on your system

Finding CDs and More in Your GUI

Chapter 10 covers how to use the file managers that come with the distributions covered with this book (and most other Linux desktop-based distributions, for that matter) — Nautilus and Konqueror. In this section, I take a look at how to use these tools to find your way around the filesystem. Some distributions make this process more intuitive than others, mostly due to tons of handy shortcuts that mean you can know less of what's happening under the hood — a pretty handy thing for desktop users.

Navigating the filesystem in Fedora

Fedora's filesystem navigation is all handled through Nautilus (see Chapter 10) if you're using its GNOME default. Some things are made pretty easy for you by default:

 ✔ When you insert a data CD-ROM or DVD-ROM, an icon appears along the left side of your desktop. Double-click this icon to open the item's contents. You can later remove it from the system by right-clicking the icon and choosing Eject from the subsequent shortcut menu.

✔ When you plug in a USB storage device such as a keychain, Fedora automatically adds an icon onto your desktop for that item, which you can double-click to open. After you're finished working with the USB device, close all the windows that were using it, right-click its icon on the desktop, and choose Unmount. Now it's safe to remove the keychain. It is vital that you unmount such a device before just removing it; you might lose data otherwise.

✔ When you insert a music CD, Fedora opens a music player and begins playing it.

✔ When you insert a video DVD, Fedora will attempt to load and play the DVD, but you may need to add more software to make this feature work due to legal reasons. See Chapter 18 for more information.

To change how Fedora handles all these items, choose System⇨ Preferences⇨Removable Drives and Media. If you shut off auto-loading for something, you can access a device's contents from any Nautilus window by choosing Places⇨Computer and double-clicking the appropriate icon in there. This action adds an icon onto your desktop as well.

✔ When you insert a blank CD or DVD writeable or rewriteable, Fedora opens Nautilus to the CD/DVD Creator window. (You can find out more about burning in Chapter 18.)

✔ When it comes to floppies, the computer can't reliably detect that a floppy was put into the drive. So, put the floppy into the drive, choose Places⇨ Computer, and then double-click Floppy Drive to access the disks's contents and add a floppy icon on your desktop. To remove the floppy, right-click the floppy icon on your desktop and then choose Unmount Volume. Wait until the floppy drive light is off before removing the floppy.

✔ If you want to access a network drive from Windows or that someone has set up on another Linux computer, and the ability to share has already been set up, choose Places⇨ Network Servers. This action lets you browse through your network to the computers that are offering files.

✔ If you want to access part of your Linux filesystem, choose Places⇨ Computer and then double-click the Filesystem icon.

✔ Access something on one of your hard drives that isn't part of your Linux installation (maybe a Windows drive).

For the last option listed, follow these steps:

1. **Open a command line terminal.**

   See Chapter 14 if you're not sure how to do so.

2. **Type su – and press Enter to become the root (administrative) user.**

   You will be asked to enter the root password. Do so when prompted and press Enter.

3. **Type `fdisk -l` to see all your hard drives and partitions.**

   If you're looking for a Windows partition, then you can find it right here. Ignore the items that have text similar to Windows 95 Ext'd; they're not really a data partition. Anything that has NTFS or FAT32 or VFAT is a Windows partition and is what you're interested in. If you're looking for a Linux partition (maybe you have more than one distribution installed on your system), then you want the ones that have the word *Linux* in their description and not the word *swap*.

4. **If you need to access an NTFS partition, see Chapter 12 for how to add NTFS support for your distribution (and how to check to see if it's installed).**

5. **When you think you know what partition you want to try, type `mount -t type /dev/partition /mnt` to add it to your filesystem, where *type* is the filesystem type, as shown in Table 11-3, and *partition* is the letter and number combination you saw in `fdisk` (such as `hde2`).**

   So, for example, after adding NTFS support, you might type `mount -t ntfs /dev/hde2 /mnt`. When you do so, you can find all of that partition's contents under the `/mnt` directory.

Table 11-3	Common Filesystem Types
Type	*Description*
ext2	"Older" Linux filesystem type
ext3	"Newer" Linux filesystem type, used by default in Fedora and Red Hat, among others
ntfs	"Newer" Windows filesystem type, started with Windows NT and commonly used in Windows XP
reiserfs	Another "newer" Linux filesystem type, used by default in Mandrake and SuSE, among others
vfat	"Older" Windows filesystem type, such as FAT32 and MS-DOS

6. **Browse as you need to.**

   You may find that you have read-only access to your NTFS partition and can't change anything on it.

7. **When you're finished, type `umount /mnt` to remove the partition's contents from your filesystem.**

The preceding steps work for all distributions.

Navigating the filesystem in Knoppix

Knoppix is another distribution that makes things as easy as possible, with a few little bumps along the way. When your system starts up, it automatically has icons along the left of your desktop for every drive and partition it finds. To help you find your way around:

- ✔ It's important to realize that because Knoppix is a bootable distribution, you already have a CD-ROM in use in the drive! If you only have one CD/DVD-ROM drive and you want to insert a CD or DVD to use with Knoppix, you're stuck. You can't eject Knoppix, because the CD is acting as your hard drive, containing all your programming. Here's where a portable or second installed drive can come in handy.

- ✔ To use a floppy, place the disk in your floppy drive and then click the floppy icon to access its content. When finished, close the window with the floppy's content and then remove the disk from the drive.

- ✔ To access drives on your network, click the Home icon on your panel, and then select Go➪Network Folders. From here, you can navigate among the files that are set up to share over the network. If you are told that "lisa" isn't installed or running:

  1. **Click the monitor icon on your panel to open a command line terminal window.**

  2. **In the terminal, type `su -`.**

     You are now in Knoppix as the root user. There's no password by default, but you can set one if you want.

  3. **Type `/etc/init.d/lisa start`.**

- ✔ To access your Linux filesystem, you can click the drive icons on your Desktop, or you can click the Home icon on your panel and then choose the Root Folder option along the left tabs (it looks like a red file folder).

- ✔ To access partitions and drives on your machine that aren't part of your Linux installation (like a Windows drive), click the various Hard Disk Partition icons until you find the one you're looking for.

Navigating the filesystem in Linspire

Because Linspire is designed for the absolute newcomer, you expect its filesystem navigation to be a point-and-click snap, and indeed they've made it pretty easy on you. To navigate your filesystem in this distribution:

- ✔ When you insert a data CD, CD-ROM, DVD, or DVD-ROM, Linspire opens a file browsing window with the item's contents. To remove the item from your system, close its window.

✔ When you insert a music CD, the CD player launches with the CD loaded.

✔ When you insert a video DVD, if you don't have the (commercial) DVD player installed, Linspire opens a CNR window where you can find out about the only fully legal DVD player for Linux. If you're a CNR member, the price is less than $5!

✔ When you insert a blank CD or DVD writeable or rewriteable, Linspire doesn't do anything automatically. See Chapter 18 for how to burn CDs and DVDs.

✔ When you insert a floppy, you need to click the Floppy icon to access its contents — this icon exists even if you don't have a floppy drive. When you're finished with the floppy, right-click the icon and choose Unmount before you remove the disk. Don't remove the disk until the drive light turns off, when you can be sure that all the data is saved properly.

✔ To access something on your network, double-click the Network Share Manager icon and browse away.

✔ To access something in your Linux filesystem, double-click the My Computer icon, click the arrow under Often-Used Folders, and select Top-Level Hard Drive.

✔ To access something on one of your other partitions (maybe a Windows partition), double-click the My Computer icon and then the appropriate Storage Device icon.

Navigating the filesystem in Mandriva

To find your way around in Mandriva:

✔ When you insert a data CD, CD-ROM, DVD, or DVD-ROM, Mandriva doesn't automatically add an icon to your desktop. To access them, double-click the Devices icon on your desktop. To remove the item from the drive, right-click the icon and choose Eject.

✔ When you insert a music CD, the CD player launches with the CD loaded.

✔ When you insert a video DVD, nothing happens. See Chapter 18 for more on viewing multimedia.

✔ When you insert a blank CD or DVD writeable or rewriteable, K3b burning software opens. See Chapter 18 for more details.

✔ When you insert a floppy, you need to double-click the Devices icon and then the Floppy icon to access its contents. To remove it, right-click the Floppy icon and choose Unmount.

✔ To access files on your network, double-click Devices and then one of Local Network, Network Services, or Samba Shares (Windows shares).

- To access something in your Linux filesystem, double-click the Home icon on your desktop and then click the Up arrow until you're in the root (/) directory.

- To access something on one of your other partitions (maybe a Windows partition), double-click your Home icon on your desktop, select Go⇨Storage Media. You can then double-click the Hard Disk icons to determine which of them you need to look within.

Navigating the filesystem in SuSE

SuSE is another distribution that offers some handy icons to make the browsing process more intuitive. To find your way around in SuSE:

✔ When you insert a data CD, CD-ROM, DVD, or DVD-ROM, a Konqueror window opens with the item's contents. You can remove the CD by closing the window and pressing the eject button on your computer.

✔ When you insert a music CD or a video DVD, SuSE recognizes it as such and asks whether it should open the item with a particular tool. Click Yes if you want it to do so, and No if not. If you want your choice to be your default answer, make sure to click the Do Not Ask Again check box to add the X. You may receive a message that DVD playback for all or particular DVDs is disabled due to legal reasons. If so, see Chapter 18.

✔ When you insert a blank CD or DVD writeable or rewriteable, an icon appears on the desktop for the media. See Chapter 18 for more on burning CDs and DVDs.

✔ When you insert a floppy, double-click the Floppy icon on your desktop to access its contents. When you're finished, close the window and press the ejection button on your computer to remove the floppy.

✔ To access something on your network, double-click the Computer icon on your desktop, and then double-click the Network icon in the Computer - File Browser window.

✔ To access something in your Linux filesystem, click the Computer icon on your desktop, and then double-click the Filesystem icon in the Computer - File Browser window.

✔ To access something on one of your other partitions (maybe a Windows partition), follow the instructions given in the Fedora section.

Navigating the filesystem in Ubuntu

Ubuntu doesn't offer desktop icons but it does have the Places menu on the upper panel. To find your way around in Ubuntu:

- ✔ When you insert a data CD, CD-ROM, DVD, or DVD-ROM, a Nautilus window opens with the item's contents. You can remove the item by right-clicking the icon and selecting Eject.

- ✔ When you insert a music CD or a video DVD, Ubuntu recognizes it as such and asks whether it should open the item with a particular tool. Click Yes if you want it to do so, and No if not. If you want your choice to be your default answer, make sure to click the Do Not Ask Again check box to add the X. You may receive a message that DVD playback for all or particular DVDs is disabled due to legal reasons. If so, see Chapter 18.

- ✔ When you insert a blank CD or DVD writeable or rewriteable, a dialog box appears asking what kind of CD you want to burn. Select the appropriate option. See Chapter 18 for more on burning CDs and DVDs.

- ✔ When you insert a floppy, select Places➪Computer and then double-click the Floppy icon to access its contents. When you're finished, right-click the Floppy icon and select Unmount Volume. Do not remove the floppy disk until the disk light turns off.

- ✔ To access something on your network, choose Places➪Network Servers. From here you can browse the network drives available.

- ✔ To access something in your Linux filesystem, choose Places➪Computer, and then double-click the Filesystem icon.

- ✔ To access something on one of your other partitions (maybe a Windows partition), follow the instructions given in the Fedora section.

Navigating the filesystem in Xandros

Because Xandros is another distribution aimed at newcomers, you expect it to be easy to navigate. Here's how to find your way around in this one:

- ✔ When you insert a data CD, CD-ROM, DVD, or DVD-ROM, the Xandros File Manager opens to its contents. You can remove this item by closing the window and pressing the eject button on your computer.

- ✔ When you insert a music CD, a music player opens.

- ✔ When you insert a video DVD, a video player may or may not open. See Chapter 18 for more on using multimedia.

✔ When you insert a blank CD or DVD writeable or rewriteable, the system does not react. See Chapter 18 for more on burning CDs and DVDs.

✔ When you insert a floppy, to access its contents, double-click the Home icon and then click the Floppy entry on the left. When you're finished, close the window and eject the floppy by using the button on the computer.

✔ To access something on your network, double-click the Home icon on your desktop and then choose either Windows network or NFS (Linux and other Unix) Network items on the left to browse the available entries.

✔ To access something in your Linux filesystem, double-click the Home icon on your desktop and choose Go⇨All File Systems.

✔ To access something on one of your other partitions (maybe a Windows partition), follow the instructions in the Fedora section.

Partitions Versus Directories

One very important (and geeky) thing to understand about the Linux filesystem is that it may not all be on one single hard drive or hard drive partition, and yet you don't have to keep track of what drive or partition it's on like you do in other operating systems. In the Microsoft Windows world, if you use separate hard drives or partitions, you have a specific letter designation for each one. The primary hard drive is C, the next is D, and so on. Under Linux, each of these drives and partitions quietly blends together.

If you partitioned your hard drives on your own, you know that you needed to specify a *mount point* for each partition — which is like an empty spot in a puzzle, where the outside partition or media can be plugged into the rest of the filesystem. In the case of a hard drive partition that's part of your primary filesystem and added at boot time, the mount point isn't in the /mnt or /media part of the filesystem. It's an item in the root directory — maybe /boot or / or /usr — or anywhere else in your directory hierarchy (like /usr/share). Later, when you're working on the computer, you don't need to know or care about whether the directories or files are all on one drive or are on multiple drives. You just do your thing.

The times you do need to know how Linux sees the hardware are when you're trying to add new hard drives, install the machine while not using automatic partitioning, or access temporary media. Table 11-4 lists a common breakdown of popular hardware designations. Note that these designations aren't in /mnt or /media; they're in /dev. They're the actual device driver shortcuts — which point to the real drivers. These names are typically used for convenience so that you don't have to remember exactly which driver to deal with.

Table 11-4	Common Drive Designations
Designation	*Description*
/dev/cdrom	CD-ROM drive; if you have more than one, then you may have /dev/cdrom1 and so on, and you also may see /dev/cdwriter, /dev/dvd, or even a hard drive designation such as /dev/hda
/dev/fd0	Floppy drive 1
/dev/fd1	Floppy drive 2
/dev/hda	First IDE hard drive
/dev/hda1	First IDE hard drive, first primary or extended partition
/dev/hda2	First IDE hard drive, second primary or extended partition
/dev/hdb	Second IDE hard drive
/dev/hdb1	Second IDE hard drive, first primary or extended partition
/dev/hdb2	Second IDE hard drive, second primary or extended partition
/dev/sda	First SCSI hard drive
/dev/sda1	First SCSI hard drive, first primary or extended partition, and often also a small USB drive like a thumbnail/keyring storage device

You probably see a pattern by now. A hard drive has a three-letter designation:

✔ An IDE drive's designation starts with /dev/*hd*; the first drive of this type is a, the second is b, and so on. The third IDE drive looks like this: /dev/hdc. If you're using something like a Promise controller that bypasses the main IDE controllers (I know, this is technical stuff), then your first IDE hard drive will, in fact, show up as /dev/hde. I know this one from personal experience!

✔ A SCSI drive's designation starts with /dev/*sd*; the first drive of this type is also a, the second is b, and so on. The fourth SCSI drive looks like this: /dev/sdd. USB drives are also seen as SCSI devices. A little item like a USB keychain is often seen as /dev/sda1 by your system if you don't have any permanent SCSI drives attached.

The number that follows the three-letter designation represents the partition you're referring to. I cover partitioning your hard drive in Chapter 2.

In Figure 11-1, I break down this concept, hopefully making it a bit more accessible. In this case, the user created three partitions for Linux. The first IDE drive is a single partition, allocated for the `root` partition. The second IDE drive is broken into two partitions. The first was given `/usr`; and the second, `/var`.

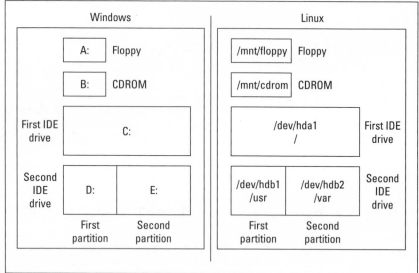

Figure 11-1: Linux versus Windows in handling partitions and hard drives.

If you move around the filesystem, you can't tell (and don't need to know) which of these directories is on which drive. The prompt, for example, doesn't change based on which drive each directory is on; the commands used for moving around the filesystem (see Appendix A) don't care about the underlying hard drive or drives.

Formatting Disks

A floppy disk, USB keychain, and any other small(ish) storage device often comes as a blank slate *or* formatted for Windows or Macintosh use (most often these days they come formatted for Windows). If the item is a blank slate, no computer can use it for anything. Many come by default formatted for Windows, which you can use in Linux with no problem — or you can change its formatting into a Linux setup. (The handy thing about leaving it as a Windows disk is that you can then use it to share things with Windows users.)

To format a floppy, place the floppy into your floppy drive and do the following:

- **Fedora:** Choose Places⇨Computer. In the Computer dialog box, right-click the Floppy Drive icon and choose Format from the context menu.

- **Knoppix:** Right-click the floppy icon on the desktop and choose Actions⇨Format Floppy Disk.

- **Linspire:** Choose Launch⇨Run Programs⇨Utilities⇨Floppy Formatter.

- **Mandriva:** From the Main Menu, choose System⇨Configuration⇨Hardware⇨Floppy Formatter or KFloppy.

- **SuSE:** Choose Applications⇨System⇨Filesystem⇨Floppy Formatter.

- **Ubuntu:** Choose Applications⇨System Tools⇨Floppy Formatter.

- **Xandros:** Double-click the Home icon on your desktop, right-click the Floppy entry in the left section, and choose Format.

Typically, the defaults are what you'll want to choose. If you want to format the disks for Linux, use the Linux Native (ext2) format. To share disks with Windows users, choose DOS (FAT). Another setting you may want to choose is Thorough rather than Quick.

Care and Feeding of Your Filesystem

Regardless of which operating system you're using, you need to keep your filesystem healthy and happy. Everything that you need to operate the machine and do your work (or play) on it exists in that filesystem. Keep it in good shape, and it's sure to treat you well in return. Fortunately, Linux does most of it automatically for you.

If your machine fails to reboot

If your machine didn't shut down cleanly (a nice euphemism meaning that it crashed or you shut the power off without properly shutting the machine down, as discussed in Chapter 5), the system checks the filesystem if necessary at boot time, taking the need to do this out of your hands. Usually the system is able to boot normally after such an event. If something went really wrong, you get this unnerving prompt that tells you to enter your password or press Control-D to continue. If this prompt appears, type your root (administrative) password, press Enter, and then follow these steps. Don't worry; more often than not, you can actually fix this problem.

Because it's a bit of an art at times trying to figure out which partition may be damaged, I walk you through a process where you check the most likely ones and then work through the rest in turn.

1. **Type df -h to see a list of all your partitions.**

    The df command lists the mounted partitions and media in addition to some statistics about them. You may, for example, see something like the following:

    ```
    Filesystem          Size  Used Avail Use% Mounted on
    /dev/hde2            54G   27G   24G  54% /
    /dev/hde1            99M  6.0M   88M   7% /boot
    none                506M     0  506M   0% /dev/shm
    /dev/hdf3            54G   39G   13G  76% /mnt/FC1
    ```

2. **Look for an item with /boot in the right column.**

    If you find one, great. Proceed to Step 3. Otherwise, skip to Step 10.

3. **On that same line, look on the left column to see what partition /boot is on.**

    In this example, /boot is on /dev/hde1.

4. **Type mount.**

    This command gives you something even more cryptic looking. In my example, it may be

    ```
    /dev/hde2 on / type ext3 (rw)
    none on /proc type proc (rw)
    none on /sys type sysfs (rw)
    none on /dev/pts type devpts (rw,gid=5,mode=620)
    usbdevfs on /proc/bus/usb type usbdevfs (rw)
    /dev/hde1 on /boot type ext3 (rw)
    none on /dev/shm type tmpfs (rw)
    /dev/hdf3 on /mnt/FC1 type ext3 (rw)
    sunrpc on /var/lib/nfs/rpc_pipefs type rpc_pipefs (rw)
    ```

5. **Locate the line with /boot on it once again and look at what "type" is being used.**

    In this case, **/boot on /dev/hde1** is formatted as type ext3. Keep this in mind. You'll need to use this information in Step 8.

6. **Type umount /boot.**

    This command should release the partition, if this is possible. If this command fails, type mount -o remount -o rw /dev/*device* /boot (for example, mount -o remount -o rw /dev/hde1 /boot).

    You never, never, never, never, never run the command I'm about to use on a partition you're using in read-write mode or you will mess it up badly! The remount command given above reloads the partition as read-only.

7. **Type df -h again to make sure that this partition is no longer listed.**

   In the example, you should now see:

   ```
   Filesystem          Size  Used Avail Use% Mounted on
   /dev/hde2           54G   27G   24G  54% /
   none                506M    0  506M   0% /dev/shm
   /dev/hdf3           54G   39G   13G  76% /mnt/FC1
   ```

   See, no /boot partition! If you used remount, instead type mount again to make sure it is listed as (ro) rather than (rw).

8. **What you type now depends on what type setting /boot had:**

   - **ext2 or ext3:** Type e2fsck -fy *partition*, such as e2fsck -fy /dev/hde1.

   - **reiserfs:** Type reiserfsck --fix-fixable *partition*, such as reiserfsck --fix-fixable /dev/hde1, and if this gives you more errors, follow with reiserfsck --rebuild-tree *partition*, such as reiserfsck -rebuild-tree /dev/hde1.

9. **Type exit and let the machine try to reboot.**

   If the machine can reboot, you're done, yay! If not, return to Step 6 and run through the process again. Sometimes, you actually need to try the fix more than once. If you reboot again at the end and it still fails, proceed.

10. **Repeat Steps 1 and 4, but this time look for the lines that correspond to the / directory.**

    In my example, / is mounted from /dev/hde2 and is formatted using ext3. Unfortunately, you can't remove the / filesystem since it's got all of your commands! But, there is still a safe way to do this.

11. **Type mount -o remount,ro /.**

    This command releases the root (/) partition and then adds it again, but this time as read-only so things won't be changing as you're working on it. That makes what you're about to do safe.

12. **Repeat Step 8 for the / partition.**

    So, for my example, the / partition is /dev/hde2, so you'd be starting with ext2fsck -fy /dev/hde2 or reiserfsck --fix-fixable /dev/hde2.

13. **Repeat Step 9.**

    Again, if it fails to reboot, repeat Steps 10 through 12 to see whether that fixes things.

Unfortunately, at this point, if the problem still occurs, it could be many, many things. Now is a good time to go to your local Linux Users' Group (see Chapter 4) or online help site.

Don't run out of room!

One of the most insidious problems that all computer users run into from time to time is a lack of disk space. The scope of this problem really depends on a number of things. The primary issue is that, if your `root` partition becomes 99 or 100 percent full, you need to use emergency rescue techniques (refer to Chapter 5) to boot the machine and clean it out. That's no fun, is it?

In the beginning, you're probably not in danger of filling the drives, unless you barely had enough room to install Linux in the first place. However, over time, you may forget about watching the drives for remaining space. Even experienced administrators run into this problem, so certainly you're forgiven if you do it too!

Really do try to make doing the following a habit:

1. **Open a command prompt window (see Chapter 14).**

2. **Type `df -h`.**

That's it! As you can see earlier in the section "If your machine fails to reboot," though you ignored it at the time, the columns include

- ✔ **Size:** How big the partition is

- ✔ **Used:** How much of the partition has been used already

- ✔ **Avail:** How much is left

- ✔ **Use%:** So we don't have to do mental math, a % of how much of the partition has been used up

When you start reaching 90 percent full, it's time to start doing some housecleaning!

Chapter 12

Adding Software to Linux

· ·

In This Chapter

▶ Recognizing tarballs, RPMs, and compressed files

▶ Creating tarballs and archives

▶ Compressing files

▶ Opening tarballs, archives, and compressed files

▶ Installing and removing RPMs

· ·

I will make you shorter by the head.

— Queen Elizabeth I

*W*hen you start using a new operating system, one of the most frustrating things is trying to figure out all the goofy file extensions. The Windows world has `.exe` and `.zip`. The Macintosh world has `.bin` and `.hqx`. What about the Linux world? It certainly has its fair share of bizarre extensions, but, really, they make a great deal of sense after you know the programs that make them. In this chapter, you find out all about `.tar`, `.gz`, `.tar.gz`, `.tgz`, `.bz2`, and `.rpm`. Anyone up for a game of Scrabble with alphabet soup?

After you have the letter jumble all figured out, you'll be happy to find that Linux offers a number of cool tools for working with these crazy files, updating your system, adding new software, and more.

Opening Downloaded Files

The Linux and Unix worlds are full of strange terms and acronyms. For example, if someone comes up to you out of the blue and starts talking about tarballs, you probably get a mental image of sticky, smelly balls of tar, maybe rolled in feathers. Yet a tarball is something you run into regularly in the Linux world, especially when you're looking for software or you need to save yourself some space. A *tarball* is a bunch of files (and possibly directories) packaged together in a `tar` file and then compressed by using the `gzip` utility.

WinZip can open tarballs with no problem on a Windows computer.

Fortunately, all you need to know is how to double-click a file in order to access the many formats listed in Table 12-1. When you double-click the file, your File Manager shows you what's inside.

While Table 12-1 mentions operating systems, it doesn't contain hard and fast rules. People tend to use whatever kind of programs they're comfortable with no matter what operating system they're on.

Table 12-1	Potential Formats for Downloaded Files	
Extension	*Meaning*	*Program(s) Involved*
`.bz`	Older form of .bz2.	bzip, bunzip
`.bz2`	Slower but more efficient compression for some types of files, like text files.	bzip2, bunzip2
`.deb`	Not a file to "open;" see the "Installing New Software" section, later in this chapter.	apt
`.gz`	Typical compressed file for Linux and Unix.	gzip, gunzip
`.iso`	A CD-ROM or DVD-ROM "image," which is a single file that contains a CD or DVD's entire contents. You have to tell your CD or DVD burner software that this file is an image so that it knows not to just place a copy of this file onto the media.	See Chapter 18.
`.rpm`	Not a file to "open;" ""see the "Installing New Software" section, later in this chapter.	rpm
`.tar`	A bunch of files bundled together.	tar
`.tar.bz2`	A *tarball*, which in this case is a .tar file inside a .bz2 file.	tar, bzip2, bunzip2

Extension	Meaning	Program(s) Involved
`.tar.gz`	A traditional *tarball*, which is a .tar file inside a .gz file.	tar, gunzip, gzip
`.tgz`	A traditional *tarball*, which is a .tar file inside a .gz file.	tar, gunzip, gzip
`.Z`	Old-style Unix compressed file.	compress, uncompress
`.zip`	Windows ZIP file.	zip, unzip

TIP

WinZip (`www.winzip.com`) can handle `.gz`, `.tgz`, and `.tar.gz` files (along with the `.bz2` versions) for Windows users.

Compressing and Packaging Files to Share

Life isn't all about "take, take, take" (or at least I should hope not!). Sometimes you've just gotta give. Creating care packages to share with other folks involves finding how to tell Nautilus (if you're a GNOME user) or Konqueror (if you're a KDE user) that you want to do so. However, because the overall process is so similar for both environments, I don't break these steps down into separate sections.

To package up and compress files for sending off to other people, navigate to the location where you've stored the file(s) — see Chapter 10 for how to move about in Nautilus and Konqueror — and then:

1. **Determine whether you want to compress or package a single file, a group of files, or a whole folder.**

   If the files and folders that you want to bundle together are flung all over the place in your filesystem, you may want to create a new folder and copy the items you want to bundle together into it — just for the sake of convenience. Chapter 10 shows you how to do so.

2. **Select the item(s) you want to package.**

   Chapter 10 explains how to do so. If you want to select a whole folder, navigate into its parent folder and just select the folder's icon instead of entering it.

3. **Right-click over the item(s) (or if you're using Nautilus, you can also choose the Edit menu).**

   The context menu appears if you right-clicked or, in Nautilus, the Edit menu opens.

4. **Create your archive.**

   How you create your archive depends on what distribution you're using:

   - **Fedora, SuSE, and Ubuntu:** In the context or Edit menu, choose Create Archive. In both cases, the Create Archive dialog box appears, suggesting a tarball (refer to Table 12-1) version of the file. If this is what you want, leave it alone, or change the file extensions (as discussed in Table 12-1) to match what you want. Then click Create, and Nautilus uses the end of the file's name to see what kind of compression to use.

   - **Knoppix:** In the context menu, select Compress. From this menu, choose the appropriate option as guided by Table 12-1: Gzipped tar Archive means to make a .tar.gz or .tgz file; the Compress As menu lets you select another alternative; the Add To menu lets you add the file to an existing archive in the current directory; and Add To Archive lets you specify the archive to add the file to.

   - **Linspire:** You cannot use the file browser in Linspire Five-0 to create an archive. Instead, you'll have to go to Launch⇨Run Programs⇨ Utilities⇨Archiving and Zip Tool to open the Ark program.

   - **Mandriva:** In the context menu, select Actions⇨Archive to create individual .zip files of each of the items you selected. For a more feature-rich alternative, from the main Mandriva menu choose System⇨Archiving⇨Compression and either the Ark or File-Roller program. You may only have one or the other. If so, it is likely placed directly in System⇨Archiving.

   - **Xandros:** In the context menu, choose Add to ZIP Archive if you're sharing with Windows users (this option can be used to make a brand new .zip archive), or Create TGZ Archive to make a tarball, as discussed in Table 12-1.

5. **If you want to rename the file or change where it should go in your filesystem, do so now.**

   Leave the `.tar.gz` or `.gz` part alone. Just change the first part. For example, if you're archiving the Files folder, then the suggested name might be `Files.tar.gz`. If you want to use `Files100305.tar.gz` for the actual name, you just add the date into the existing name.

6. **Click OK.**

   The archive is created.

Updating Your Software

In the last couple of years, updating your operating system and software in Linux has become easier and easier. Each Linux distribution has its own way of handling updates, so I cover how to update each one in its own section. The cool thing is that you're actually updating your operating system and its software all at once. Be sure you are connected to the Internet before you try to update!

I don't cover how to update Knoppix, however, because if you're using Knoppix, you didn't install anything to update!

Updating Fedora

To update your Fedora Core system:

1. **Select Applications⇨System Tools⇨Software Updater.**

   This action opens the Package Updater (pup) dialog box, as shown in Figure 12-1 — you may first be asked to enter your root (administrative password). You will likely have to wait while the tool reaches out to the Internet and loads update information. When this process is complete, the progress dialog box closes.

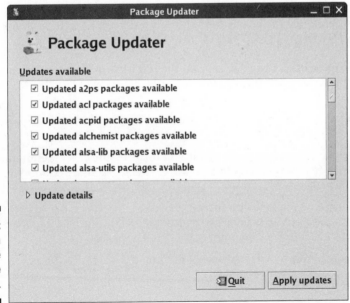

Figure 12-1:
The Fedora Core Package Updater.

2. **If you want information on any of the individual updates, click the item in the list and then click the arrow next to Update Details.**

   Information about the update will display beneath the list of available updates.

3. **Click Apply Updates to proceed.**

   The Resolving Dependencies for Updates dialog box appears with a progress bar — this progress can take a while the first time you update the machine. When the tool is sure that everything that each program needs is taken care of, this dialog box closes and another may appear telling you that *dependencies* were added — dependencies are packages that another package has to have in place in order to install and run properly. If so, click Continue to proceed. If you see a dialog box saying that there were errors resolving the dependencies, try again later. The server might not be properly synchronized.

   From here, you will see a Downloading dialog box. A progress bar shows you how much longer it will take for all the updates to be downloaded onto your computer. After downloading is complete, an Installing progress bar appears. When the updater finishes installing the packages, an Information dialog box appears, stating that the update is complete.

4. **Click OK to close the updater, if necessary.**

Updating Linspire

Here's where you get to meet Linspire's Click And Run Warehouse (CNR)! It's pretty cool stuff, especially for folks new to Linux. To update your system with CNR:

1. **Double-click the CNR icon on the left of your desktop, or single-click the icon on the left of your panel.**

   These two icons look identical — they're running men on a green background. When you activate this icon, the CNR-Client dialog box appears (see Figure 12-2).

2. **If you're using a free version of Linspire, click Get Membership and then Start Free Trial to sign up. If you're using a version you purchased, select Sign In.**

   I'm going to stick with the purchased instructions, because they're going to apply to free users as well after youhave your trial membership information. The My.Linspire Login screen appears.

3. **Enter your e-mail address in the Email Address text box.**

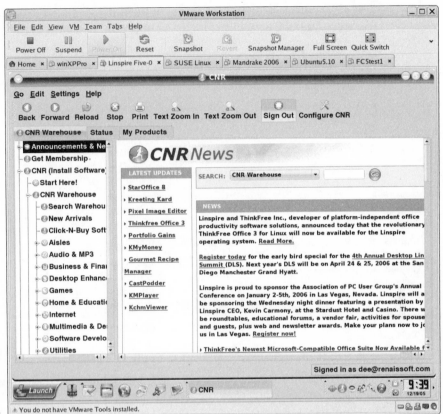

Figure 12-2:
The Linspire
CNR Client.

4. **If you haven't set up your CNR account yet, then click No, I Need To Create A New Account. Otherwise, click Yes, I Have An Account Password and enter that password in the text box.**

   I'm going to cover created accounts, because it's just an issue of filling out forms to set up for CNR otherwise.

5. **Click Go! to proceed.**

   Remember, I'm assuming that you've set up your account at this point. After you click Go, the CNR client returns to its default page.

6. **Click the My Products tab.**

   The My Products section appears (see Figure 12-3).

7. **Click Available Updates to see what software updates are available.**

   You may not have many at all, or you may have a lot.

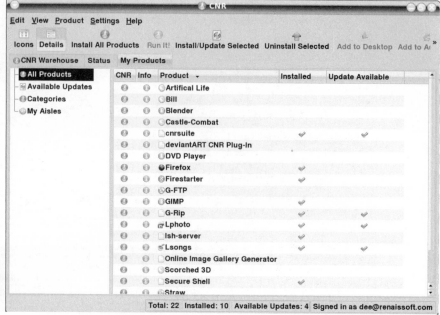

Figure 12-3:
The My
Products
tab of
Linspire
Five-0 CNR
Client.

8. **Select the update(s) you want to apply.**

   If you want to choose them all, click the topmost one, hold down the Shift key, and then click the bottommost one.

9. **Click Install/Update Selected to begin the update.**

   The Install/Update Products — CNR Client dialog box appears to let you know that the item(s) have been added to your download queue. If you don't want to receive this notice again, click the Do Not Show This Message Again check box. Click Close to get this dialog box out of the way.

10. **Click the X in the upper righthand corner to close the CNR Client.**

    To be safe, wait until the updates are finished.

Updating Mandriva

To update your Mandriva system, do the following:

1. **From the Main Menu, choose System➪Configuration➪Packaging➪ Mandriva Update.**

You may be asked for your root (administrative) password. The rpm-drake dialog box then appears to ask whether you really want to update your system.

2. **Click Yes when asked whether it's okay to continue.**

   Another question dialog box appears, asking whether you're connected to the Internet.

3. **When you're sure your Internet connection is on, click Yes to continue.**

   After rpmdrake finds the list of mirrors — sites you can use for updates — the Please Choose The Desired Mirror dialog box appears.

4. **Select the location closest to you and then click OK.**

   When the update server can be contacted, the Software Packages Update dialog box appears (see Figure 12-4).

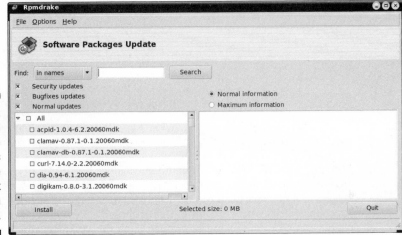

Figure 12-4:
The
Software
Packages
Update
dialog box
in Mandriva
2006.

5. **Click All to choose everything you can update.**

   You may be told that some packages can't be updated due to dependency issues. That's fine; just leave them for now.

6. **Click Install to proceed.**

   A progress dialog box shows you how far you are with each selected package during the download. While the packages are being installed, the graphical tool closes or becomes unavailable.

Updating SuSE

If you look on your upper SuSE panel, toward the middle, you find the SuSE Geek-O's head as an icon — or you may see a red circle if the Watcher has connected to the update servers in the past and knows there are updates available. This is the SuSE Watcher, which is your friend when it comes to system updates:

1. Click the SuSE Watcher icon.

The susewatcher dialog box, shown in Figure 12-5, appears.

Figure 12-5:
The suse-
watcher
system
updater
dialog box.

2. Click Start Online Update.

You may want to click the Automatically Check For Updates check box before you proceed so you can set up the system to always look for new releases. When you click the start button, you may be asked for your root (administrator) password; enter it and click OK if you are. After this, the YaST Online Update dialog box appears, as shown in Figure 12-6.

3. In the Installation Source drop-down list box, select the update server closest to you.

4. Click Manually Select Patches to remove the X from the box.

Otherwise you have to keep telling the updater Yes to various updates.

5. If you want to set up SuSE to automatically update itself (recommended if you're permanently connected to the Internet), click the Configure Fully Automatic Update button; otherwise, skip to Step 11.

The YOU Automatic Mode Setup dialog box appears.

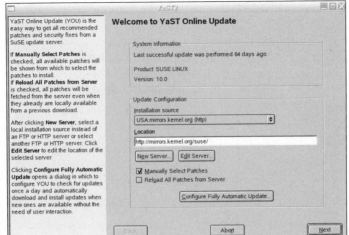

Figure 12-6:
SuSE's
YaST Online
Update
dialog box.

6. **Click Enable Automatic Update to add an X to its box.**

   The rest of the dialog box's settings become available.

7. **Change the hour (in 24 hour format) to the hour of the day you want to have this update run.**

   It's handy to run updates late at night when you're not using the computer.

8. **If you don't want the updater to install the updates, only download them so that you can add them yourself, click Only Download Patches.**

9. **Click OK to close the YOU Automatic Update Mode Setup dialog box.**

10. **Click Next to check for updates.**

    When the check begins, the Retrieving Information about New Updates dialog box shows you a progress bar. Then when all the information has been gathered, the Patch Download And Installation dialog box appears. You see two progress bars here, one labeled Patch Progress for the particular update being applied (which is described in the upper portion of the dialog) and the other for Total Progress so that you can see how long you have remaining. You may occasionally be asked about a particular patch. Typically you'll just want to say yes.

    If you want SuSE to erase the intermediate items it downloads during the update process, click Remove Source Packages After Update.

    When the update is complete, the Finish button becomes available.

11. **Click Finish to proceed to the Writing System Configuration dialog box.**

Here SuSE is just making sure that it knows where everything is. After this process is finished, the YaST Online Update dialog box closes. You can close the SuSE Watcher dialog box by clicking the Close Window button.

From now on, if you've automated updates, you won't have to do this by hand.

Updating Ubuntu

To update your Ubuntu system, use its built-in updating tool:

1. **Select System⇨Administration⇨Update Manager.**

You may be asked to enter your root (administrative) password. Do so if necessary. Then the Software Updates dialog box appears, as shown in Figure 12-7.

Figure 12-7:
The Ubuntu Software Updates dialog box.

2. **To install all the available updates, just click Install.**

If you want to know more about available updates, click Details and then the update in question. When you click Install, the Installing Updates dialog box appears with a progress bar displayed for the downloads, and then a new one for installations.

3. **When the update has finished, click Close to get rid of the dialog box.**

Updating Xandros

Xandros has added the Xandros Networks in order to help its users update their system and add new software with ease. To use this tool to update your operating system and software:

1. **Double-click the Xandros Networks icon on the left of your desktop.**

   The Xandros Networks dialog box opens (see Figure 12-8). You may be told that the tool needs to download package information. Click Yes to continue.

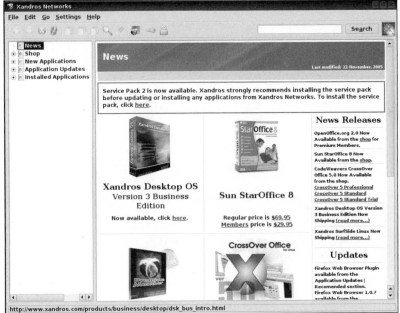

Figure 12-8: The Xandros Networks dialog box.

2. **When told the tool needs to download information, click OK.**

   After the download is complete, the Xandros Networks dialog box fills in.

3. **Choose File➪Install All Latest Updates From Xandros to install all available updates.**

   The Get Latest Updates dialog box appears.

4. **Click OK to proceed.**

   The password dialog box appears.

5. **Enter your Administrator/root password and press Enter.**

   The update begins. When it's complete, the Enter button goes away, and the animations stop.

6. **Click Close to close the Updater dialog box.**

7. **Choose File➪Quit to close the Xandros Networks client.**

Installing New Software

In many cases, installing new software isn't much harder than updating; it just depends on the distribution and what tools have been incorporated for this process. My focus in this section is on using these tools. Later, in the section "Finding More Software," I address how to add programs that aren't included in these tools. Within each distribution's section, I also tell you how to add many of the programs discussed throughout this book.

Again, Knoppix isn't included here, because you can't permanently install new software onto a CD!

Getting it Right with Fedora's Package Manager

Fedora offers a graphical software installation and removal tool. To make use of this tool to add programs, make sure that you are connected to the Internet and then do the following:

1. **Select Applications➪System Tools➪Add/Remove Software.**

   You may be asked to enter your root The Package Manager window appears (Figure 12-9). This window can take a minute or so to populate as the system looks to see what software it has installed, and what is available.

2. **Determine how you want to choose your software:**

   • **Search:** Click the Search button. Select Available Packages so you can search through only the packages you haven't installed. Then, type the text you want to look for in the text box, and click Search. The Search button changes to a Stop button, and as the Package Manager finds matches, they are displayed in the text area below, with the Stop button reverting to a Search button when the search is complete.

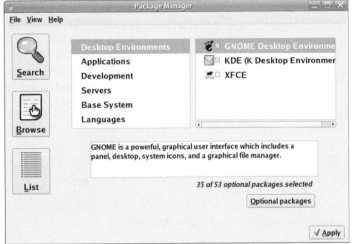

Figure 12-9:
Fedora Core
5's Package
Manager
with
Desktop
Environ-
ments
selected.

- **Browse through categories:** Click the Browse button to reveal a list of categories on the left. Select a category to reveal a list of package groups within that category on the right. If a group doesn't have a check in its box then that group is not selected, and its *base packages* won't be installed. Every group also has *optional packages*, which aren't selected by default but are available for installation. To see these, click the group on the right and then click the Optional Packages button to open the Packages dialog box (Figure 12-13) — the group must be checked in order for this button to become available. Click Close to get an Optional Packages window out of your way if necessary.

- **List packages:** Click the List button, and once the list of all possible packages is displayed, click the Available Packages radio button.

3. **Click empty boxes to check the software you want to install. If you want to remove software as well, then click checked boxes to empty them.**

4. **When you have marked all of the packages and groups you want to add, click Apply.**

   The Resolving Dependencies for Updates dialog box appears. This dialog box behaves exactly the same as the one in the Fedora updater, so you may be told that dependencies were added (click Continue) before the software downloads and installs. Eventually, the Information dialog box appears, telling you that the installation was completed.

5. **Click OK to close the dialog box and package management tool.**

Adding repositories

Fedora — along with other modern Linux distributions — uses *repositories* (sites that offer software to its automated tools) in order to track what's available and grab what it needs. By default, only the main Fedora and "updates" repositories are available for many reasons (some legal), so the first thing most people do is add a bunch of repositories to their list.

To add some cool repositories with the help of the official maintainer of the Fedora FAQ (www.fedroafaq.org), do the following:

1. **Open a terminal window as discussed in Chapter 14.**

2. **Type** su - **and press Enter to become the root user.**

   Your prompt changes to reflect your new identity.

3. **Type** cd /etc **and press Enter.**

   You are now in the /etc part of the filesystem.

4. **Type** mv -f yum.conf yum.conf.bak **and press Enter.**

   This command renames the file yum.conf to yum.conf.bck so you can easily back up to the original file.

5. **Type** wget http://www.fedorafaq.org/samples/yum.conf **and press Enter.**

   This command downloads the file yum.conf from http://www.fedorafaq.org/samples/ and saves it in /etc, creating a new /etc/yum.conf file for you.

6. **Type** rpm -Uvh http://www.fedorafaq.org/yum **and press Enter.**

   The command-line package manager downloads the program at this URL and installs it. This program changes the files in the directory /etc/yum.repos.d so that they contain a listing of some of the best repositories available.

7. **Close the terminal window by clicking the X in the corner.**

You now have access to a ton of software! You will be able to find these packages in the Package Manager's Search and List sections.

Adding the software in this book

I discuss a number of programs in this book, and you may want to give them a try. Some are already installed if you did a default Desktop installation of Fedora Core 5. Others you need to add. You can add many through the package manager:

✔ **Konqueror:** In Desktop Environments, activate the KDE (K Desktop Environment) group. This package will be added by default as part of KDE.

✔ **Kmail and/or Kontact:** In Desktop Environments, activate the KDE (K Desktop Environment) group. Click Optional Packages and select `kdepim` package. These programs are not added to the menus when they're installed, so see Chapter 6 for how to create a shortcut to put on your desktop or panel.

✔ **Amarok:** Choose Applications⇨Sound and Video, click the Optional Packages button, and check both the amarok and amarok-visualisation checkboxes

✔ **K3B:** Choose Applications⇨Sound and Video, click Optional Packages, and click the k3b checkbox

✔ **Mplayer and Mplayer-plugin:** Add the recommended repository and then add mplayer, mplayer-gui, and mplayerplug-in.

✔ **Thunderbird:** Choose Applications⇨Graphical Internet, click Optional Packages, and click the box next to `thunderbird`.

✔ **Macromedia Flash:** plugin to Fedora Core 5, first access a command line window as discussed in Chapter 14. Type `su -` to become the root user, and then type `yum --enablerepo=flash` to activate the Flash repository. Now you can close the Yum Extender and open it again (or open it if it wasn't already open) and find the `flash` package inside it to install.

Two major items you may want to add are not available through the yum repositories, but aren't too terrible to install either. The first of these is support for Java stuff you'll run into on the Web and elsewhere. To add Java support to Fedora Core 5:

1. **Point your Web browser to `www.java.com/en/download/index.jsp`.**

   The *Java Runtime Environment* download page appears.

2. **Click the Download Now button.**

3. **Click the Download button next to Linux RPM (self-extracting file).**

   An Opening dialog box appears.

4. **Choose Save To Disk and click OK.**

5. **Double-click your home directory icon to open your file browser.**

6. **Navigate to your default downloads directory, which is Desktop if you haven't set a new one in Firefox.**

7. **Right-click on the file that looks similar to jre-1_5_0_06-linux-i586-rpm.bin and choose Properties.**

   The file's Properties dialog box appears.

8. **Click the Permissions tab.**

   The Permissions section of the file Properties dialog box appears.

9. **Under Owner, select Execute and then click Close.**

   This file can now be run as a program.

10. **Right-click the file and select Rename from the context menu.**

11. **Add .sh to the end of the file's name and press Enter.**

12. **Double-click the file.**

   The Run Or Display dialog box appears.

13. **Click the Run In Terminal button.**

   You get Sun's Java license, or at least part of it, in a text window.

14. **At each screen that ends with MORE, press the space bar to proceed.**

   You eventually reach the text Do You Agree To The Above License Terms?

15. **Type yes and press Enter to proceed.**

   A file similar to jre-1_5_0_06-linux-i586.rpm now appears in the directory.

16. **Double-click the j2re RPM file.**

   The RPM is installed for you. You now have Java support.

17. **Open a terminal window as discussed in Chapter 14.**

18. **Type su - to become the root user.**

19. **Type ln -s /usr/java/jre1.5.0_06/plugin/i386/ns7/ libjavaplugin_oji.so /usr/lib/mozilla/plugins/ and press Enter.**

   You just created a shortcut to put the plugin in the right place.

Another item you may want to add support for is RealPlayer, which gives you MP3 support and can handle lots of different multimedia formats. To add this software:

1. **Point your Web browser to www.real.com/linux.**

   You see Real's Linux page.

2. **Click the Download RPM Package link beneath the big Download RealPlayer button.**

   The Opening RealPlayer dialog box appears.

3. **Make sure that the Open With Install Packages option is selected.**

4. **Click OK to download the file.**

   You're asked for your root password.

5. **Type your root password and click OK.**

   The Completed System Preparation dialog box appears.

6. **Click Continue to install the program.**

   When this process is complete, RealPlayer 10 appears in the Sound & Video menu.

Clicking and running with Linspire

Playing with Linspire's CNR Warehouse can be a lot of fun. To add new software with CNR, do the following:

1. **Double-click the CNR icon on the bottom left of your desktop or single-click the one on the left of your panel.**

   These two icons look identical; they're running men on a green background. When you activate it, the CNR-Client dialog box appears, as shown earlier in this chapter (see Figure 12-2).

2. **Look on the left for the section labeled Install Software By Category.**

3. **Click the + next to it, if you see one, to expand this menu.**

   The contents of the Warehouse appear, if they were hidden.

4. **Browse!**

   Browsing is the fun part! CNR actually allows you to download free software and to access commercial (pay for) software in the same interface, making it easy to install, which is pretty cool. So, find something you want to add.

5. **After you've located a program you want to add, click its name.**

   The listing looks something like what's shown in Figure 12-10.

6. **Install the program.**

   Click the green running man CNR icon to add this software with just one click.

What's this Aisle stuff you're seeing? You can create Aisles to group similar programs together in a menu and then let other Linspire users access them.

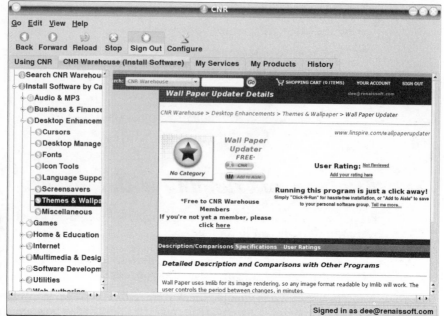

Figure 12-10:
The CNR
listing for
Wall Paper
Updater.

Believe it or not, that's it. If you followed these instructions, you probably just installed a program! Of course, if you chose something that you have to purchase, there's a bit more involved, but it's not bad.

Sometimes you can also actually add things by using the Programs menu and its submenus. If you know, for example, that you're looking for a Multimedia application, choose Launch⇨Run Programs⇨Multimedia & Design⇨CNR More. Then you can just select the application that you want to add to open the CNR tool directly to that program's page and then click the CNR button to install it.

Adding the software in this book

You can add most software for Linspire through the CNR Warehouse. To find the packages discussed in this book and add them, open your CNR client, click the CNR Membership Services tab, and look in the following CNR Warehouse sections:

✔ **Macromedia Flash support:** Search for `flash` to find the Flash 7 Plug-In.

✔ **Ximian Evolution:** Choose Business & Finance⇨Miscellaneous⇨Novell Evolution 2.

- ✔ **Kmail:** Choose Internet➪Email➪Kmail.

- ✔ **Amarok:** Choose Audio & MP3➪Amarok.

- ✔ **Mplayer:** Choose Multimedia & Design➪Video➪KKMplayer, which is a KDE-specific version of the Mplayer tool.

- ✔ **Thunderbird:** Choose Internet➪Email➪Thunderbird.

Making it happen with Mandriva

If you read the Fedora section earlier in this chapter, you're familiar with the idea of finding *software repositories* that contain handy prepackaged software just waiting to be added to your computer. Such repositories also exist for Mandriva, adding to this distribution's ease of use. First, you must locate these repositories, add them to your system so that it knows where to look, and then finally you can dig around for whatever software you're interested in.

Finding Mandriva repositories

To add repositories to Mandriva, you need to locate those that interest you most:

1. **Point your Web browser to** `http://easyurpmi.zarb.org/`.

2. **In section one, in the Mandriva Linux Version drop-down list box, choose 2006.**

3. **In Architecture, choose i586; under Package Manager, choose urpmi.**

4. **Click Proceed to Step 2.**

   You advance to the second portion of the Web page.

5. **Under Other Sources, check the available boxes. Then, in their corresponding drop-down list boxes, choose the locations closest to you.**

   See the legal concerns section in Chapter 18 to help you determine whether to check the boxes labeled plf. If you check these boxes, then choose a download location to use along with it. (In some cases, you won't be able to find one in North America.)

6. **Click Proceed to Step 3.**

Rather than typing the stuff listed in Step 3 at the command line, you're going to enter it into the GUI. Proceed to the next section to find out how. (However, you are welcome to just type the items as described on the page, if that's what you want to do.)

Adding Mandriva repositories to your system

After you have the list of repositories you want to add open in your browser (see the previous section for how to do so), go to the Main Menu and choose System➪Configuration➪Packaging➪Software Media Manager and then do the following:

1. **Enter your root password if asked, and then click OK.**

2. **In the rpmdrake dialog box, click Yes to continue.**

   The Configure Media dialog box appears (Figure 12-11).

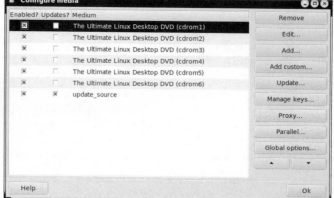

Figure 12-11: The Mandriva Software Media Manager.

3. **Click Add Custom.**

   The Add A Medium dialog box, shown in Figure 12-12, appears.

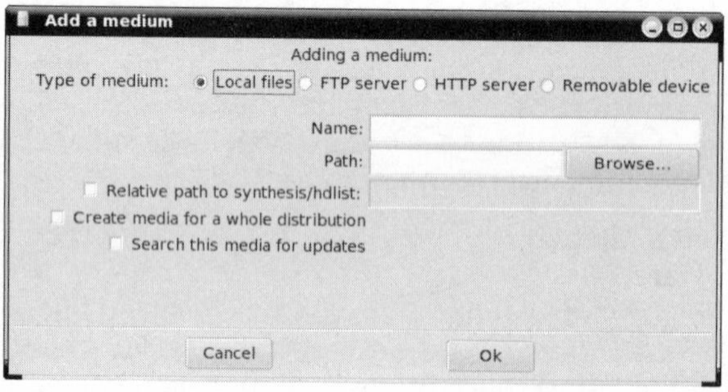

Figure 12-12: The Mandrake Software Media Manager's Add A Medium dialog box.

4. **Look at the beginning of the URLs you were given to determine what they start with.**

   For example, if you see the line:

   ```
   urpmi.addmedia main http://gulus.usherbrooke.ca/pub/
           distro/Mandrakelinux/official/2006.0/i586/
           media/main with media_info/hdlist.cz
   ```

   you're interested in the `http://` part.

5. **Select the appropriate radio button along the top.**

   Following the example, I would select HTTP server.

6. **In the Name text box, enter a short but descriptive name for this repository.**

   Typically, I stick with the short name shown in the listing, such as `jpackage` in the case of the example.

7. **In the URL text box, enter the URL you got from the Web site.**

   For example, type `http://gulus.usherbrooke.ca/pub/distro/Mandrakelinux/official/2006.0/i586/media/main`.

8. **Click the Relative path to synthesis/hdlist box.**

9. **Add the text that appears on the Web site's output for this entry, after the word "with."**

   Given the preceding example, I would add `media_info/hdlist.cz`.

10. **Click OK.**

    The tool downloads pertinent information from the site you just added.

11. **If you want to add more repositories, return to Step 1. Otherwise, click OK to close the tool.**

Installing software in Mandriva

After you've added your repositories (by following the instructions in the previous section), you can start adding new software by using the Mandriva GUI tools. To do so:

1. **From the Main Menu, choose System⇨Configuration⇨Packaging⇨ Install Software.**

   The Software Packages Installation dialog box appears (see Figure 12-13). You may be asked to enter your root password first.

2. **Type a keyword into the text box next to Find.**

   For example, you might type `mp3`.

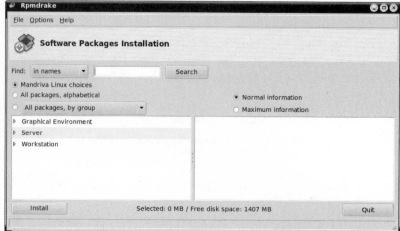

Figure 12-13:
The
Mandriva
Software
Packages
Installation
dialog box.

3. **Click Search.**

   The tool now searches through all the package descriptions and displays a list of those that contain the keyword.

4. **In the package listing, select a package you think you might be interested in.**

   More information about that package appears to the right.

5. **If you want to add the program, click in its box to add a check.**

   If it turns out that the program you select needs other programs, a dialog box pops up notifying you that they'll be added as well. Click OK to proceed if this happens. Then return to Step 2 if you want to look for more programs.

6. **When you're ready to add all the software you've selected, click Install.**

   If some of the software comes from your Mandrake CDs, you're asked to insert the appropriate CD when it's needed.

7. **When you're finished, click Quit.**

Adding the software in this book

To add the particular programs discussed in this book, add the following packages by using the Installation Manager:

- ✔ **Thunderbird:** mozilla-thunderbird (search on `thunderbird`)
- ✔ **Mplayer:** mplayer and mplayer-gui (search on `mplayer`)
- ✔ **Flash plug-in:** swfdec-mozilla (search on `mozilla`)

For RealPlayer and browser support for Java, however, see the Fedora section for how to add these items by hand.

Sassing with SuSE

OpenSuSE and SuSE's boxed sets come with an amazing amount of software. Just navigating the maze of what's included can be enough to make you tear your hair out if you don't know how to use the software management tools. Don't worry. I don't want to see any of you go bald (or more bald than you already are!). So, here's how you use it.

This section focuses on the installed versions of SuSE. Remember that the version included on the CD-ROM in the back of this book is a LiveCD and not an installed version.

As with most SuSE administration functions, start by choosing Desktop➪ YaST to pull up the SuSE administration tool. From there:

1. Choose Software➪Software Management.

The software management dialog box appears, as shown in Figure 12-14.

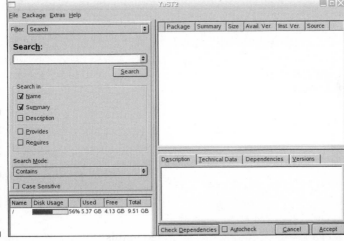

Figure 12-14: The SuSE YaST software management dialog box.

2. Under the Search In section, click Description to make sure that you're searching in program descriptions for your keywords.

3. **Enter your keyword in the Search text box.**

   For example, maybe you want to see what SuSE offers involving the `quicktime` movie format.

4. **Click Search.**

   A progress bar appears to let you know that SuSE is searching through all the program names and descriptions. When the search is complete, a list of possibilities appears in the top-right panel.

5. **Click a program to find out more about it.**

   More information appears on the lower-right portion of the window.

6. **For the programs you want to install, click the box next to the item to add a check mark.**

7. **Continue searching and selecting software.**

8. **When you're ready to proceed, click Accept.**

   If there are no dependencies, then the installation begins. If other programs need to be added in order to satisfy dependencies, the Automatic Changes dialog box appears. Click Continue to accept these additional packages.

9. **Insert the appropriate CDs or DVDs as they're requested.**

   After everything is installed, SuSE rebuilds the necessary configuration files, and then the software installation tool closes.

Prefer to use the DVDs? When you first enter YaST, choose Software⇨Change Source Of Installation. In the Software Source Media dialog box, choose Add⇨DVD to add the DVDs to the list. Then select the DVD entry in the listing and click Up so that it's in the list before the CDs. Click Finish, and you're ready to move on!

After you've added the software, because you're adding it from the installation media, you will probably want to update your system so that you get the latest versions of what you just added. If you want to add external repositories for SuSE software, enter YaST again and choose Software⇨Installation Source. From there, click Add and then add repositories from the official list (www.opensuse.org/Additional_YaST_Package_Repositories).

Adding the software in this book

To add the various programs discussed in this book, open up the YaST software management tool as discussed in the previous section, and then, in the Filter drop-down list box, choose Package Groups. Now you can see on the left a list of all the major package groups; and on the right are the contents of

the selected group. You can find the programs you're looking for in the following Package Groups locations:

- **Macromedia Flash plug-in:** Search for `flash-player`
- **Java support:** Search for java and look to find the package described as
  the Java(TM) 2 Runtime Environment.

Upscaling with Ubuntu

Ubuntu allows you to use their built-in software management tool to add new
software. To install software with this tool:

1. **Choose Applications⇨Add Applications.**

    You may be asked for your root password. If so, enter it. The Add
    Applications dialog box appears (Figure 12-15).

Figure 12-15:
Ubuntu's
Add
Applications
dialog box.

2. **Click the right-facing arrows to open various categories and browse,
   or type a keyword into the Search text box and then click the Search
   button.**

3. **When you see a program you want to try, select it to see more information in the right pane.**

4. **If you want to install this program, click the box to place a check in it.**

5. **Return to Step 2 as you select more software, and then click Apply to install the software you selected.**

   The Changes Pending dialog box appears, telling you what software will be added.

6. **Click Apply to proceed with the installation.**

   The software will be pulled from online. A Summary dialog box may appear. Read it and click Apply to continue if you see it. When the install finishes, the Changes Applied dialog box appears.

7. **Click Close to close the dialog box(es), and then when the initialization routine finishes, choose File⇨Quit to close the software addition tool.**

To add some of the applications mentioned in this book, look in the following sections of the Add Applications tool:

✔ **Amarok:** Choose Sound & Video⇨More Programs⇨Amarok

✔ **Mplayer and Mplayer-plugin:** Choose Sound & Video⇨More Programs⇨ Mplayer. You will be asked if you want to enable the repository that offers this program. Click Add.

✔ **K3b:** Choose Sound & Video⇨More Programs⇨K3b.

Xipping with Xandros Networks

Just as Linspire users can use the CNR Warehouse to add software, Xandros users can use Xandros Networks. To add software with this tool:

1. **Double-click the Xandros Networks icon on your desktop.**

   The Xandros Networks dialog box opens. If you are asked about downloading package information, click OK.

2. **Click the plus next to New Applications to expand that section of the menu.**

3. **Browse through the categories.**

4. **When you find a program you want to install, click the box next to it to add a check.**

5. **When you are ready to install the programs you want to add, select File⇨Install Selected Applications.**

   The Install Software dialog box appears. You can also, in the program description, click the Install Product link to immediately install a particular program.

6. **Click OK in the dialog box to download and install the program.**

   You may be asked to enter your root (Administrator's) password. Then, the software is downloaded and added to your machine. No muss, no fuss! When the update is complete, the Updating System dialog box stays open.

7. **Click Close to close the Updating System dialog box.**

8. **If you want to add more software, return to Step 3. If you're finished, choose File⇨Quit.**

Adding the software in this book

Many of the programs discussed in this book are either already installed (such as the Flash and Java plug-ins) or aren't offered through Xandros Networks. You can find Thunderbird by choosing Internet⇨Thunderbird Mail in the New Applications section. To add more software to your system, see the section "Finding More Software."

Finding More Software

What if you can't find what you're looking for through the official (and not so official) sources discussed in the previous section? Those aren't your only options. While I can't anticipate every situation you might find yourself in, I can at least give you some tips for how to find extra software and how to install much of it.

The general steps for finding new software involve:

1. **Check your distribution's manuals and forums for repositories that work well for other users, and add them to your software installation list.**

2. **If you don't know what you want, find out by opening your favorite Web search engine and searching on a feature and the word `linux`.**

   For example, maybe you want something comparable to the program irfanview from the Windows world, so you would search on `irfanview linux`.

3. **Sort through the search results and see whether a particular program is suggested. If not, then add the word `equivalent` to your search and search again.**

   So, to continue the example, you would search again but this time using `irfanview linux equivalent`. Now you start to see a program called `xnview` mentioned. It wouldn't hurt to turn around and look and see whether your distribution's software installation manager offers this program, before you bother installing it by hand.

4. **Do a Web search on the Linux program you're interested in.**

You more often than not find the program's home page.

5. **Click through to that program's home page.**

6. **Click through the Download link on that page.**

7. **Locate and download the most specific version matching your distribution.**

You may be offered, say, Windows, Unix, and Linux options. You would choose Linux in that case. If offered Linux x86 versus Linux ppc, choose x86 unless you're using Linux on an Apple Macintosh computer (which is not covered in this book). If you're offered an RPM or a tarball (see the beginning of this chapter for more information on these), then choose an RPM if you're using Fedora, SuSE, or Mandriva, and a tarball if you're using Linspire or Xandros — or if you tried the RPM on your Fedora, SuSE, or Mandrake system and it didn't work.

8. **After you have the program downloaded, install it as follows:**

   - If it's an RPM, open your file manager and double-click the download in order to install it.

   - If it's a tarball, open your file manager and double-click the file in order to open it up and look at its contents. There should be a file in there called README or INSTALL. This file contains instructions on what you need to do, and there may be more instructions available on the Web site itself. Working with tarballs just requires practice; it gets easier over time, so extract the file and get to it!

Upgrading Your OS

When a new version of your Linux distribution comes out, you may find that you want to upgrade to it. Typically, you can upgrade by downloading or purchasing the new version, starting it just as you would start a new installation but choosing Upgrade rather than Install. That's it!

Chapter 13

A Secure Linux Box Is a Happy Linux Box

I am Inspector Clouseau, and I am on official police business.

— Inspector Clouseau

You don't leave the front door of your house open when you go to work, do you? How about leaving it shut and locked but with a few nice, big windows open? The problem is that many people do this every day with their computers, and they don't even know it! In this chapter, I take a look at where your open doors and windows are and what you can do to secure them.

Every user's actions affect your overall system security. If your family members or officemates need access to your Linux machine, take the time to sit down and explain the facts of secure life to them. They can then apply this information to the other computers they use, because these issues aren't specific to Linux.

Choosing Secure Passwords

The first line of defense from intruders is the collection of passwords used on your system. For each account you have set up on your system, the passwords must be strong and difficult to figure out. If even one of the accounts has a weak password, you may be in for some trouble. Amazingly enough, in 70 percent of the cases where unauthorized individuals gained access to systems, the password for an account was the word *password* itself! When choosing good passwords, follow these rules:

- ✔ Don't use any part of your name.
- ✔ Don't use the names of friends, loved ones, or pets.
- ✔ Don't use birthdays, anniversaries, or other easily guessed dates.
- ✔ Don't use dictionary words.
- ✔ Don't keep your password written down near your computer, unless it's buried in something else, such as writing it into an address.
- ✔ Don't tell anyone your password. If someone needs to access specific files, give the person an account and set up permissions and groups properly so that they can do so.
- ✔ Do use a mix of lowercase letters, capital letters, and numbers.
- ✔ Do ensure that your password contains a minimum of eight characters.
- ✔ Do use acronyms made from sentences, such as having the password M8yodniT to stand for "My eight-year-old dog's name is Tabby."

Every person on your system needs to follow these rules, including you! Consider keeping a sheet of paper with these rules on it next to the machine.

I can't stress this advice enough: *Never* give out your password. Make sure that the people using your machine understand this rule. You can always find alternative methods to accomplish a task without giving out your password. If someone wants to use your machine, make an account for that person. Then they can have their own password!

Updating Software

All users can download and install new software. Of course, the programs they install are limited to the user's own permissions. The thing to be careful of here — as with any operating system — is that you don't get a version of a program that has been tampered with or is even an all-out fake trying to trick folks into installing it.

Most Linux applications and other Linux software programs are distributed by way of the Internet. In fact, the development cycle of new (and updates to) Linux software revolves around the Internet for file exchange, e-mail, and forum or newsgroup discussions. Make sure that you and other users of your

Linux system are comfortable with the Web sites that are used and visited. You need to develop a *list* of trusted sites that provide you with the information you need and are not misleading in their presentation. As a starting point, you can *trust* all the Web sites referenced in this book because I have accessed them all. If either you or a user of your Linux system is unsure whether you can trust a particular Web site, do some research and perhaps ask others for their opinions.

Chapter 12 details how to keep your distribution and its software up to date. Please, please, please, do so! After all, as the person in charge, your job is to make sure that this computer stays intruder-free. In addition to making sure that you do all the same things a user would do for both your user accounts and the superuser (root) account, no matter which Linux distribution you're running, you must keep up-to-date with security problems.

Network holes

On a Linux server or workstation — or any computer at all, using any operating system — you should not have any network services running that you don't intend to use. Think of each network program running as a glass window or sliding glass door in your house. Each network service is a weak spot, and many nasty folks are out there on the Internet who like to go up to all the houses and make note of how many windows and glass doors are on them, what kinds they are, and how easy they are to breach.

Controlling your services

The more flexible your distribution — as far as its ability to run desktops and many types of servers — the more services it may have running in the background by default. To open the network service management program for your distribution:

- **Fedora:** Choose System⇨Administration⇨Server Settings⇨Services (see Figure 13-1). The Services option may be directly in the Administration menu, it depends on the collection of software you currently have installed.

- **Knoppix:** From the Main Menu, choose Knoppix⇨Services. There is no central service control unit, but because this distribution is designed as a desktop, few services are available. This menu contains each service you have access to.

- **Linspire:** There is no central service configuration point, but this distribution is designed to be purely desktop, so there is little to do here anyway.

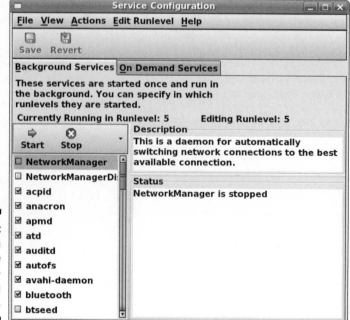

Figure 13-1:
The Fedora
Service
Configura-
tion dialog
box.

✔ **Mandriva:** From the menu, choose System➪Configuration➪Configure Your Computer. Enter your root password if asked, and then in the Mandriva Control Center dialog box, select System➪Enable or Disable The System Services.

✔ **SuSE:** Choose Desktop➪YaST. Inside the YaST Control Center, select System➪System Services.

✔ **Xandros:** Choose Launch➪Control Center➪System Administration➪ Services. There are few services here to deal with, however, because this system is designed strictly as a desktop.

✔ **Ubuntu:** Choose System➪Administration➪Services.

Services you may be interested in turning on or off include:

✔ **apmd:** This service may not be necessary in anything but a laptop. It's used for monitoring battery power.

✔ **iptables:** This service is your firewall (more on the firewall in the section "Controlling and adjusting your firewall," later in this chapter). If you need to momentarily shut it down, you can do so using the service control dialog box.

✔ **isdn:** This daemon is typically on by default in some distributions "just in case," but if you're not using ISDN networking (see Chapter 8) you don't need it.

✔ **kudzu:** If you're using Fedora and keep getting bugged about hardware stuff at boot time, shutting off this service will stop those messages. You can run it manually as root if you change hardware later.

✔ **lisa:** Discussed earlier in Chapter 11 in conjunction with network browsing in certain distributions.

✔ **mDNSresponder:** Shut this service off unless you're a Howl (www. porchdogsoft.com/products/howl) devotee. The nifd service should also be on or off (matching) with this one since it's related.

✔ **mdmonitor:** Shut this service off unless you implemented software RAID during your installation. (You had to go out of your way to do so, so if you don't know, you probably didn't!) If you change this service to on or off, make sure that mdmpd is also on or off (matching) as well.

✔ **pcmcia:** You only need this on laptops. It's for PCMCIA card support.

✔ **sendmail:** Even though you're probably not in need of a full-fledged mail server, shutting this service off can have unintended consequences because it's used to even handle internal mail on your system. Leave it on.

✔ **smartd:** If you're getting errors for this one at boot time, shut it off. It only works with certain IDE hard drives, so if you're not using that type of drive, it gives a (harmless) error.

✔ **spamassassin:** If you want to use this program in conjunction with your mail program, go for it! This program is used by default with Evolution in Fedora (see Chapter 9), so if you're using this combination of tools leave this service on.

✔ **yum:** On Fedora, lets you run a nightly automatic update for those whose machines are connected overnight.

In Fedora, when you check or uncheck a service, you need to make sure that it does or doesn't turn on when you reboot. You need to use the Start and Stop buttons to start or stop it immediately. Use the bottom-right part of the dialog to see whether Fedora is running right now.

Controlling and adjusting your firewall

Even better (but just as essential) than turning off unnecessary services is to make sure that you have a firewall in place. A firewall is like putting a big bunker around your house. It would then have openings that only fit people wanting to do certain kinds of things. Friends could fit in through one door, family another, and package deliveries to another.

In computer networks, each of the services discussed earlier always comes in through the same door (*port*, in computer-world lingo). You use firewalls to prevent anyone from being able to so much as touch a door, or port, unless you've explicitly set it up so that they can do so. This technique is especially important if you're on a cable network (see Chapter 8), where there's always some overactive jerk out there using his computer to knock on every other computer on the network's doors to see where it can get in.

You probably already did some basic firewall setup during installation. If you ever want to make changes, do the following (you may be asked to enter your root password along the way):

- ✔ **Fedora:** Choose System⇨Administration⇨Security Level and Firewall (see Figure 13-2).

- ✔ **Knoppix:** From the Main Menu, choose Knoppix⇨Services⇨Knoppix Firewall.

- ✔ **Linspire:** Click CNR on the desktop or panel as discussed in Chapter 12. When the CNR tool opens, choose Utilities⇨System Utilities⇨Firestarter. This tool helps you set up your firewall and is installed under Launch⇨Run Programs⇨Utilities.

- ✔ **Mandriva:** From the Main Menu, choose System⇨Configuration⇨Configure Your Computer⇨Security⇨Set Up A Personal Firewall In Order To Protect The Computer And The Network.

- ✔ **SuSE:** From the Main Menu, choose Applications⇨System⇨YaST⇨Security and Users⇨Firewall.

- ✔ **Xandros:** Choose Launch⇨Applications⇨Internet⇨Firewall Wizard. In the same menu is the Firewall Control application.

- ✔ **Ubuntu:** There is no firewall control tool installed by default. Instead, select Applications⇨Add Applications. Enter your root password if required, and in the Add Applications dialog box, use the text box in the lower left to run a search by typing `firewall` and clicking Search. Click the box next to Firestarter, and you may be told that the program is not installable unless you activate the `universe` repository — if this occurs, click Add, and when the list is refreshed, run the search again, and then select Firestarter again. Click Apply to tell the system you are ready to install the software, and then click Apply in the Changes Pending dialog box. Ubuntu installs the tool for you. Select Applications⇨System Tools⇨Firestarter to launch the firewall wizard.

Your options are typically something like Enable Firewall and Disable Firewall. If you have your computer directly connected to the Internet — and most computers are — make sure to use Enable Firewall. The only time that you should not have this firewall in place is when your machine(s) are behind a strong firewall already, or you have a critical application that won't work otherwise. For just one application, though, that's one huge risk! You can find out how to open up the proper doors in the firewall for that one program instead.

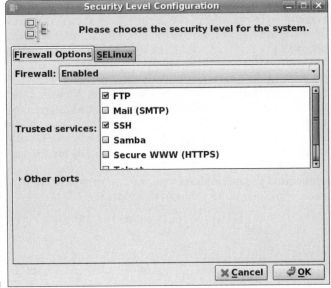

Figure 13-2:
The Fedora
Security
Level
Configura-
tion dialog
box.

Firewall lingo you may find handy includes:

- **eth0:** Your first Ethernet (network) card.

- **ppp0:** Your first modem.

- **HTTP and HTTPS:** Web stuff; only needed if you're running a Web server.

- **FTP and FTPS:** FTP server stuff; you don't need it if you're not running an FTP server.

- **SSH:** Select this one to keep open. I explain it in the next section.

Additional "security" products from Linspire include (in their Click And Run Warehouse under Services) SurfSafe parental controls and VirusSafe antivirus software.

The Secure Shell game (SSH)

One cool thing about Linux is that you can use the command line to connect to your account from anywhere, as long as you have the right software (and the machine you're connecting to isn't behind some kind of blocking software).

Some people tell you to use the `telnet` program to do this, but I beg you not to. Do not open the Telnet port in the security tool and do not use the `telnet` program. It sends information across the Internet in nice, raw text that anyone can snoop through.

First, you need to make sure that you have SSH installed, that you have an SSH server running, and that you enable SSH in your firewall. (See the section "Controlling and adjusting your firewall," earlier in this chapter, to handle the third concern). Some of the distributions already have the software in place for the first two issues. Others don't by default. Only those distributions that do not provide one or the other function automatically are discussed here:

- ✔ **Knoppix:** From the Main Menu, choose Knoppix➪Services➪Start SSH Server to allow people to SSH *into* this machine.

- ✔ **Linspire:** You can SSH *out of* this machine but there is no server to SSH *into* it.

- ✔ **Mandriva:** Use the software installer (see Chapter 12) to add the `openssh-server` program. Then, use the services control interface (see the section "Controlling your services," earlier in this chapter) to activate `sshd`.

- ✔ **Xandros:** Do the following to allow people to SSH *into* this machine:

    1. **Choose Control Center➪System Administration➪Services.**

    2. **Click the Administrator button and enter your root (administrator) password.**

    3. **Select ssh in the list.**

    4. **Click Properties.**

    5. **In Start Mode, select System Startup.**

    6. **Click OK.**

    7. **If in the Status column, the ssh row doesn't say Running, click Start to start the server.**

    8. **Choose File➪Quit.**

- ✔ **Ubuntu:** Allows you to SSH *out* but there is no software to SSH *in*.

Installing a Windows SSH program

If you want to connect to your SSH-enabled Linux box — or, actually, to any computer set up to accept SSH connections, not just a Linux one — from a Windows computer, go to www.siliconcircus.com/penguinet/ and get the PenguiNet telnet and SSH client for Windows (please don't use this for telnet, just SSH). A 30-day trial version is available, and if you like it, the full version is only around $25.

To install PenguiNet under Windows after downloading `PN2setup.exe`, just follow these steps:

1. **Open your file manager (such as Windows Explorer), browse to where you saved the download, and double-click the `PN2setup.exe` program.**

   This action opens the PenguiNet Setup Wizard. If you are given an Open File – Security Warning dialog box, click Run to reassure your machine that you want to run this program.

2. **Click Next to proceed.**

   The License Agreement dialog box opens.

3. **After you read the agreement (something you should always do), click I Accept The Agreement and then click Next to proceed.**

   The Select Destination Directory dialog box opens. I usually just stick with the defaults.

4. **After you select the directory in which to install PenguiNet, click Next.**

   The Select Start Menu Folder dialog box appears.

5. **After you select the proper folder, click Next.**

   The Select Additional Tasks dialog box appears. If you want to create a desktop icon or Quick Launch button, select the appropriate check boxes.

6. **After you have chosen your additional tasks, click Next.**

   The Ready To Install dialog box appears.

7. **Click Install to begin your PenguiNet installation.**

   An installation progress dialog box appears. When the installation is finished, the final installation screen appears.

8. **Select one or both of the final items.**

   I recommend that you check at least Run PenguiNet. You may also want to select View The PenguiNet Documentation if you like to get familiar with programs by reading their manuals.

9. **Click Finish.**

   The PenguiNet window appears (if you checked Run PenguiNet), as shown in Figure 13-3.

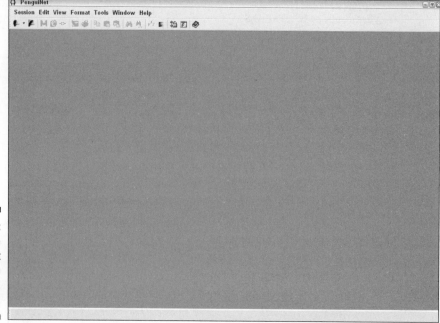

Figure 13-3:
The
PenguiNet
connection
program in
Windows.

Setting up and making your SSH connection in Windows

Either you have PenguiNet open from having installed it, or you need to open it now from your desktop shortcut or the Start menu. After you have done so, follow these steps:

1. **Choose Session⇨Connection Profiles.**

   The Connection Profiles dialog box opens, as shown in Figure 13-4.

2. **Click Add to open a new profile.**

3. **Enter the name for this profile in the Profile Name text box.**

4. **Enter your Linux box's IP address or full name (such as `computer.example.com`) in the Host text box.**

5. **In the Terminal Type drop-down list box, select Linux.**

6. **Enter your Linux login name in the Username text box.**

   You cannot use the root account here. Doing so is terribly bad for security.

7. **Enter your Linux login password in the Password text box.**

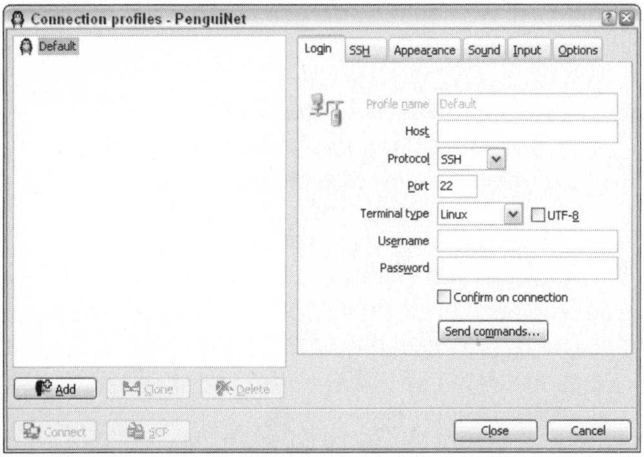

Figure 13-4:
The
PenguiNet
Connection
Profiles
dialog box.

8. **Click Connect to make the connection to your Linux machine.**

The Host Key Not Found dialog box opens the first time you connect this way. Click Connect and save the host key. You don't have to do this step again from this Windows machine. Check out Figure 13-5 to see a Linux command-line interface window on a Windows box! (I'm not sure why this default font is so "freehand"; you can change it for all your sessions by choosing Format⇨Change Font or per Connection Profile in the Preferences menu by selecting the profile and clicking the Appearance tab.)

Figure 13-5:
Your Linux
command
line in
Windows!

When you're finished, type **exit** at the command line, and your connection closes.

Connecting to your Linux box from another Linux box with SSH

Yes, you can connect from another Linux box, too. This task is a bit less complicated. Open a terminal window (see Chapter 14) and follow these steps:

1. **Type** `ssh` *username@ipaddress* or `ssh username@machinefull` name **to open the connection.**

   For example, type `ssh dee@192.168.1.6` or `ssh dee@computer.` `example.com` After you do this step, the following text appears:

   ```
   The authenticity of host '192.168.1.6 (192.168.1.6)'
        can't be established.
   RSA key fingerprint is
        ed:68:0f:e3:78:56:c9:b3:d6:6e:25:86:77:52:a7:6
        6.
   Are you sure you want to continue connecting (yes/no)?
   ```

2. **Type yes and press Enter.**

   You now see these lines:

   ```
   Warning: Permanently added '192.168.1.6' (RSA) to the
        list of known hosts.
   dee@192.168.1.6's password:
   ```

3. **Enter your login password and press Enter. Now you're in!**

Close the connection by logging out of the account (type **logout**).

Connecting to your Linux box from a Macintosh running OS X with SSH

The process from a Macintosh is similar to that under Linux. Go to Applications⇨Utilities⇨Terminal.app, which opens a command line window for you. Then type

```
ssh IPaddress
```

to access the same user account on the remote machine (again, you can use a computer's full name rather than the IP address), or type

```
ssh login@IPaddress
```

if you want to access the account *login* instead of the same account you're using on the Mac.

Software holes

When someone is already in your system — whether or not they're allowed to be there — you have additional security concerns to keep in mind. One of these involves what software you have on the machine. Believe it or not, each piece of software is a potential security hole. If someone can get a program to crash in just the right way, they can get greater access to your system than they should. That's a very bad thing!

One way to close software holes is to remove all programs you don't need. You can always add them later, if necessary. How exactly you do this task depends on the package-management scheme your distribution runs:

✔ **Fedora:** You can use the Add/Remove Software tool (see Chapter 12).

✔ **Knoppix:** You run it off CD, so it's hard to remove anything!

✔ **Linspire:** Open the CNR client (Chapter 12), click the My Products tab, select the program you want to remove from the list, and then click Uninstall Selected.

✔ **Mandriva:** From the Main Menu, choose System⇨Configuration⇨Packaging⇨Remove Software. In the dialog box, check the boxes for the programs you want to remove. When you're ready to proceed, click Remove.

✔ **SuSE:** Choose Applications⇨System⇨YaST⇨Software⇨Software Management. Locate the program you want to remove (see Chapter 12). Installed software has a check mark next to it. Click the mark until it becomes a trash can and then click Accept.

✔ **Xandros:** Open the Xandros Networks client as discussed in Chapter 12. Choose Installed Applications, browse to the program you want to remove, and click the Remove link in the program's description.

✔ **Ubuntu:** Choose Applications⇨Add Applications. Navigate to find the software you want to remove — all software that is installed has a check mark in the box next to it — and click the box to remove the check. Then click Apply. You may be told you cannot remove a program because others depend on it.

If it turns out that, as a result of dependencies, you lose other software that you want to keep, make sure to cancel the removal.

Keeping an Eye on Your Log Files with the System Log Viewer

One other security issue you may want to configure concerns *log files.* Your network programs, kernel, and other programs all run log files, which contain records of what has been happening on your system. You may be amazed at just how much information gets put in them! They're mostly in /var/log; take a look sometime.

Fortunately, tools are available that can help mere mortals sift through the wheat to look for the chaff of bugs and intruders.

To find your distribution's System Logs viewer:

- ✔ **Fedora:** Choose System⇨Administration⇨System Log (see Figure 13-6). You may have to manually open logs to view, which you can do by selecting File⇨Open, selecting the file whose contents you want to view, and then clicking Open.

- ✔ **Knoppix:** None.

- ✔ **Linspire:** From the CNR Warehouse (see Chapter 12), choose Utilities⇨ System Utilities⇨XWatch.

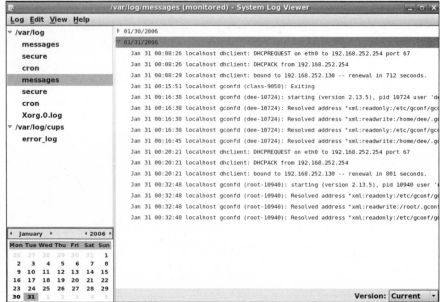

Figure 13-6:
The Fedora
System
Logs
watcher.

Sometimes the fastest way to find a program in the CNR Warehouse is to use the Search text box.

- ✓ **Mandriva:** From the Main Menu, choose System⇨Monitoring⇨ System Log.

- ✓ **SuSE:** Choose the Applications⇨System⇨Monitor⇨System Log.

- ✓ **Xandros:** None.

- ✓ **Ubuntu:** Choose Applications⇨System Tools⇨System Log.

Locating Security Resources

You can find a plethora of information on the Internet about desktop, network, and Linux security. Because of the massive volume of information available, I list some Web sites I like for security issues:

- ✓ **www.sans.org:** One of the major security-related sites on the Internet.

- ✓ **www.grc.com:** Provides some interesting tools, such as tools to test which ports are open on a system. Also, this site features many excellent articles dealing with system and network security. Click the Shields Up graphic.

- ✓ **www.tldp.org/HOWTO/Security-HOWTO/index.html:** *The Linux Security HOWTO*

- ✓ **www.linuxsecurity.com/:** Presents a plethora of information from Linux Security.com.

- ✓ **www.securityspace.com/:** Has lots of information about security issues and tools for different operating systems

Chapter 14

Working without the GUI

Whom computers would destroy, they must first drive mad.

— Anonymous

Many computing old-timers speak fondly of the command line. Others who developed their skills by pointing and clicking refer to the command line as some antiquated tool used by crusty old-timers. The truth is that most skilled computing professionals recognize the merits of both the graphical user interface (GUI) and the command-line interface (CLI). You must understand that the command line provides a powerful lever for operating your computer. If you ever watch over the shoulder of a skilled Linux geek, you notice that, after logging in, he doesn't take long to start tapping out seemingly cryptic instructions on a command line.

In this chapter, I explore the Linux program that provides the CLI, which is called the `bash` shell. Although many shells are available for Linux, `bash` is the most common, and for good reason. Basically, the creators of `bash` rolled many good features of other shells into one terrific package.

Each shell has its own way of handling commands and its own additional set of tools. I start by explaining what a shell really is, and when you understand that, you're ready to get down and dirty with `bash`. I cover specifically what you can do with some of the best features of the `bash` shell. Then I continue with working at the command prompt and get into `bash` shell interior decorating.

Shells come equipped to perform certain functions. Most of these features have evolved over time to assist the command-line jockey with myriad tasks. Although I only scratch the surface here, you're encouraged to read the man page for bash because it's likely one of the more complete and readable man pages in existence. You can read all about how to use man pages (the online Help system in Linux) in the "Help!" section, later in this chapter.

Playing the Shell Game

You need a way to tell the computer what you want it to do. In Linux, one of the ways to communicate with the computer is through something called the shell. A *shell* isn't a graphical thing; it's the sum total of the commands and syntax you have available to you to do your work.

The shell environment is rather dull and boring by graphical desktop standards. When you start the shell, all you see is a short prompt, such as a $, followed by a blinking cursor awaiting your keyboard entry. (Later in this section, I show you a couple of methods for accessing the shell.)

The default shell used in Linux is the bash shell. This work environment is based on the original Unix shell, which is called the Bourne shell and is also referred to as sh. The term bash stands for the *Bourne again sh*ell. The bash shell comes with most Linux distributions.

If you installed your Linux distribution to log in to a graphical desktop, such as GNOME or the KDE environment, you're likely not looking at a shell prompt. Rather, you interact with your computer via a mouse. You can start a bash session by:

- ✓ **Fedora:** Select Applications➪Accessories➪Terminal.
- ✓ **Knoppix:** Click the Konsole icon (looks like a computer monitor) on your panel.
- ✓ **Linspire:** Choose Launch➪Run Programs➪Utilities➪Terminal Program.
- ✓ **Mandriva:** Click the Konsole icon on yourpanel. (It looks like a computer monitor.)
- ✓ **SuSE:** Choose Applications➪System➪Terminal➪Gnome Terminal or Konsole, either will do.
- ✓ **Ubuntu:** Choose Applications➪Accessories➪Terminal.
- ✓ **Xandros:** Choose Launch➪Applications➪System➪Console.

Often, your shell prompt includes helpful information. For example, if you're logged in as dee on the machine catherine in Fedora Core 5, your prompt looks like this:

```
[dee@catherine ~]$
```

Before surveying a few of the shell capabilities, I need to tell you about another method for starting a shell session. First of all, notice that your shell prompt is merely inside a window that is part of your GUI desktop. Suppose that you want to start a shell session in a character-only or text environment.

To switch to a text environment, press Ctrl+Alt+F2. Don't be alarmed when your familiar graphical desktop disappears. It's still running in the background, and you can get back to where you left off in a moment. But first, a few words about the boring text screen you're looking at now (I hope).

You're looking at a virtual terminal, one of several available with your default installation. You probably see something like this:

```
catherine login:
```

Go ahead and type your username and password, which you're prompted for. You see a message indicating your last login date followed by the bash prompt:

```
[dee@catherine dee]$
```

Notice the similarity between this prompt and the open window you left behind in the GUI desktop. Both prompts are an indication that you have a bash session open. Note that, although it's accurate to say they're both the results of using the bash shell, they're distinct and separate *instances* of the same program. In other words, the environment you're working with here is exclusive of the bash environment you still have open in the GUI terminal window.

Are you wondering where your GUI desktop has gone? Just to settle your nerves a bit, do some jumping around. The GUI desktop is located at virtual terminal (VT) number 7 by default. You now have VT-2 open. Position your piano-playing fingers and strike the chord Ctrl+Alt+F7 (if this doesn't work, try Ctrl+Alt+F8). Within a second or two, your screen should flash and return you to your graphical desktop. Neat, huh? And guess what? The bash session you left open on VT-2 is still there; you never logged out. Go back again by pressing Ctrl+Alt+F2. Voilà! — right where you left it. Feel free to jump back and forth a few times and try some other VTs (F1 through F6). Whoopee! This virtual terminal stuff rocks.

Okay, when you have grown weary and bored with this little trick, exit (literally, type exit) to log out from each VT you may have opened and return to the graphical desktop and your bash prompt. Then you can explore what all the fuss is about with this *shell* doohickey.

Understanding bash Command Syntax and Structure

Many people happily skip through their Linux use without understanding the fundamentals of commands in the `bash` shell. Note that this approach makes you lose out on some cool capabilities available in `bash`. The more you know about how this shell's "language" works, the more interesting things you can do with it.

The basics of using `bash` at the command prompt often involve typing a command and any of its flags and values. For example, you enter the `ls -la ~` command to see a long-format listing of all files in your home directory, including those that start with a dot (.), which are *hidden files*. That other mysterious squiggle character is technically called a tilde. The *tilde* is a `bash` shortcut character that points to a user's home directory. For this example, I merely list the contents of my home directory.

You can break a command into three distinct components:

- ✔ The command name
- ✔ The options or flags
- ✔ The arguments

Consider this example.

Start with a simple command. The `du` command lists the contents of the directory you're now in, and its subdirectories, and how much hard drive space each item takes up, with a total at the end. Try typing just the `du` command by itself:

```
du
```

That's neat, but it probably raises more questions than it answers. The output gives you a long listing of data, but of what? Are those numbers in bytes, kilobytes, or messages from outer space? To clarify, try adding a simple option to your command:

```
du -h
```

You're still issuing the same command, but now you're providing additional direction on what you want displayed. The `-h` option tells `du` to show you the information in terms that humans can read more easily. Now *M*s, *K*s, and *G*s appear next to the numbers so that you can see how big these numbers actually are. But, wait — there's more. What if you just want to know the total amount of disk space this directory and its subdirectories are taking up? That calls for the -s flag:

```
du -s
```

What if you want the total for a different directory? Or just one of your subdirectories? In my case, I keep a Music subdirectory for the items I have copied from my CDs into Oggs (see Chapter 18). I can type the following command to see how much hard drive space that directory takes up in a human-readable way rather than have to count zeroes:

```
du -sh ~/Music
```

In this example, du is the command name, -sh indicates the flags (options), and ~/Music is an argument. The -sh flags can be accompanied by many more flags that provide various options applicable to the command.

Are you wondering where to find all the available options and arguments of a particular command? Most commands offer man pages, which are discussed in the "Help!" section, later in this chapter. Another good place to turn is the --help option, available with many commands. Note that --help displays a terse list of options, but it's nice and quick if you already know about an option but just can't remember exactly which one it is. Try it by entering the following command:

```
du --help
```

Cool, huh?

Starting Programs from the Shell

The most obvious, but perhaps not so apparent, use of the shell is to start other programs. Most utilities you use in Linux are separate and distinct executable programs. Users need a method to start these programs. In the GUI, you can associate an icon with a particular program, and the graphical environment contains the intelligence to start the program. Note that programs often require information drawn from environment variables, which are a part of the shell environment. (I discuss environment variables in more detail in the section "Working with Variables," later in this chapter.) For this reason, the GUI often calls the intended program via the bash shell. So you see, even the GUI finds the shell a necessity — although the GUI does its best to hide this detail from users.

For example, in the GUI after you have a terminal window open, type the following command at the prompt:

```
mahjongg
```

After a few seconds, the Mahjongg game is displayed. You can start any program at a command prompt that you can click from the GNOME menu if you know what the underlying program name is. Note that if you're in a virtual terminal (press Alt+F1) rather than the GUI, you may see an error message. Some programs require a graphical environment in which to run, which a character-based terminal obviously doesn't have.

Putting Wildcard Expansion to Good Use

Computing life would be tedious if you had to repeat the same command on multiple files. After all, aren't repetitive tasks what the computer was designed to do? *Wildcard expansion* refers to the ability of one command to be executed against many files. The asterisk (*) and the question mark (?) are two wildcard characters that are used to match any filename, or a portion of a filename. For example, you can use the following command to see a long directory listing that includes only files that end with a .doc filename extension:

```
ls -l *.doc
```

The files listed may include resume.doc, cover_letter.doc, and to_editor.doc, for example.

Working with Long Commands

As you become used to the command line, you should find some shortcuts to ease your typing chores. In this section, I show you some features of the bash shell designed to make your life on the command line as pleasant as possible. These features include command-line completion, editing, and using the history of previously entered commands.

Asking Linux to complete a command or filename for you

Considering that you do much more typing on the command line in Linux than you may normally do in a GUI environment, a feature that provides typing shortcuts wherever possible is great. Command completion is a function of the shell that completes filename and system commands.

The capability of the Linux file system to deal with practically unlimited sizes of filenames means that many filenames can become huge. Typing these long filenames can become cumbersome. Fortunately, with command completion, typing a command or a long filename is short work.

You may want to use command completion in two situations: to enter a command or to complete a filename.

Completing a command

Suppose that you want to type a command, but you can remember only that it begins with the letters up and is supposed to return the length of time that has passed since the system was rebooted. Type up at the command prompt and then press Tab:

```
[dee@catherine dee]$ up[TAB]
```

One of two things happens:

✔ If only one matching command is in the *search path* (directory locations for searching for programs; type echo $PATH to find out what yours is), your command line is completed with that command, and the system waits for you to press Enter to execute the command.

✔ If you hear a beep, it means that more than one command begins with up. Simply press Tab a second time, and all the possibilities are displayed. Locate the command on the list and continue typing it until the first letters are unique, at which point you can press the Tab key to complete the command.

Completing a filename

Command-line completion isn't only for commands; if you're typing a filename on your command line, you only need to type the first few characters and then press Tab. The shell usually searches the current working directory for filenames that match what you have typed and subsequently completes the filename on the command line. This feature behaves the same way as the command-completion feature in that, if more than one file contains the letters you type, you hear a beep and need to press Tab again to see a list of choices.

It takes a little getting used to, but after you have control of the Tab key and the shell command-line completion feature, you may wonder how you ever got along without it.

Accessing your command history

It's nice of the shell to remember what you have done, for better or worse. Having the shell keep track of the commands you enter makes it easy to

return to those gawd-awfully long commands you pecked at a while ago —
even days ago! Let me give you an example. Suppose that yesterday you man-
aged to issue a command to find all the *core dump* files in your system (core
dump files are massive files containing debugging data that only an expert
programmer or your computer can understand) and delete them. The command looked something like this:

```
find / -name core -exec rm {} \;
```

To reexecute the command, all you need to do is fish it out of your shell history and rerun it. The simplest way (if you're repeating the exact same version of the command you used last time, which in this case would be the
`find` command) is to type `!find` and press Enter. Doing so tells your system
to look through your history and rerun the last instance of `find` in the list.

On the other hand, if you have run the `find` command more than once and
want to make sure that you're reexecuting the right version, you need to read
through your command history. You can do so line by line by pressing the up-
arrow key repeatedly until you locate the command you want to reexecute.
Then just press the Enter key to run the command again.

The `history` command lists your last 20 commands (by default) when you
enter it at the prompt, in case you're curious about what they were.

Working with Variables

Variables in the `bash` shell are words or strings of text that computers use to
represent a piece of data. An example of using a variable is setting the variable `fruit` to contain the text `apple`. A number of standard variables contain information about your account and environment settings.

Variables versus environment variables

The first thing I need to make clear is that the `bash` shell has two classes of
variables:

- ✔ **Variables:** A variable can be referenced in a program or shell session,
  but it's visible and available to only that session or program.

- ✔ **Environment variables:** An environment variable can also be referenced
  by the shell or program. However, it has the added behavior of having
  its value copied to any other program or shell that is created from its
  environment.

You can usually tell at a glance the difference between a variable and an environment variable in `bash`. The normal convention is to name local variables in all lowercase or in mixed-case characters. An environment variable, however, is usually always in all uppercase letters.

Checking out commonly used environment variables

The bash shell has many environment variables. You may be amazed at the range of items these variables store. The handy thing is that, if something is stored in a variable, you can change it to suit your needs! In Table 14-1, I list the environment variables you're most likely to want to work with.

Table 14-1	Commonly Used bash Environment Variables	
Environment Variable	*Purpose*	*Value*
HISTSIZE	Determines the number of previously typed commands that are stored.	Number of commands
HOME	Sets the location of your home directory.	The path to your home directory
MAILCHECK	Sets how often the `bash` shell checks for new mail in your mailbox. If mail has arrived, you see a message similar to You have new mail the next time you do something at the command prompt.	Number of seconds to wait between checks
PATH	Sets the directories that `bash` looks in, and the order to look in them to find a program name you type at the command prompt.	Colon-separated directories
PS1	Sets your command prompt.	Command and formatting characters used to form the prompt

Most environment variables are established for you by the system administrator or perhaps by the shell itself. These variables are mostly read by programs to gather information, and you don't need to change their values.

However, you may want to alter the value of some environment variables. For example, in Table 14-1, the first entry, HISTSIZE, determines the number of lines of command-line history that are kept on file. You may have read the discussion, earlier in this chapter, of reexecuting a command from yesterday. (If not, refer to the section "Accessing your command history.") By setting a higher number for HISTSIZE, you can save an even longer list of previously executed commands.

Storing and retrieving variables' values

To assign a value to a variable, you just use the variable name followed by an equals sign (=) followed by the value to store:

```
MyVariable=MyValue
```

To retrieve the value represented by that variable, you need to precede the variable name with a dollar sign ($). Look at a variable, created by the shell, that determines what your prompt looks like. This variable is named PS1. First, you view the value being held by PS1:

```
echo $PS1
```

You likely see something like the following line:

```
[\u@\h \W]\$
```

Each of the characters preceded by a backslash represents a special instruction to the shell to return specific information when the shell prompt is referenced. See Table 14-2 for examples of special slash characters you can use in customizing your prompt.

Table 14-2	Pieces of the PS1 Puzzle
Component	**Result**
\!	Prints the position of the command in your history list.
\#	Prints the number of commands you have used during the current shell session.
\$	Prints a $ for user accounts or a # for the superuser.
\d	Prints the date in the following format: *day month date*.
\h	Prints the name of the machine you're logged in to.
\n	Moves down to the next line.
\s	Prints bash for the bash shell.

Component	Result
\t	Prints the time in 24-hour format.
\u	Prints your username.
\w	Prints the lowest current directory level.
\W	Prints the entire current directory.

Okay, on with the example; to change your shell prompt to something more amusing, enter the following line:

```
PS1='Hello \u, what can I do for you? => '
```

Note the single quotes. Immediately after pressing the Enter key, you see that your prompt has changed into something more inviting. Don't worry if you would rather have the original prompt: You can either reassign to the original prompt the value stored in PS1 or simply log out and log in again, and you're back to familiar territory.

Are you wondering which other variables your system has in store for you? You can view all environment variables at one time by typing **env**. Note that you may not have any reason to access variables on the command line as a casual use of Linux. However, after you get more proficient, you may want to journey into the shell programming capabilities of bash, in which case variable storage is quite handy, just as it is in any computer programming language.

What's with those single quotes? You have to be careful of some details when changing environment variables. If you're just assigning something to a number, you could just use, for example, HISTSIZE=250. However, if you want to use something with spaces in it, you need to use quotes. Which kind of quotes you use depends on what else you want to do.

If you want to display *exactly* what you have specified, use single quotes to create a *literal text string*. For example, type the following line at a command prompt:

```
echo 'Hello, my name is $USER'
```

Kinda goofy, huh? Take a look at a different kind of string that the shell interprets differently: an *interpolated string*. An *interpolated* value is one in which the shell interprets special characters before processing the value. Rather than use single quotes, this time you use the same example with double quotes:

```
echo "Hello, my name is $USER"
```

Notice what the output is this time. Rather than display the exact text you provided, the shell replaces the variable name, designated with a dollar sign, with the actual value stored in that variable.

Why did I use single quotes in the PS1 example? The items with the back-slashes (\) are *interpreted* one way or another. However, if you use double quotes with PS1, they're interpreted only once, so that item that lists what directory you're in changes only the first time. With a single quote, the variables are interpreted every time you do something. The double-quote example shows something like `Hello, my name is bob`. However, the single quote comes up with `Hello, my name is $USER`.

If you're going to play around with environment variables, I recommend that you start by using the methods I discuss in this section. After you have decided that you're comfortable with any changes you have made, you can make your changes permanent by opening the `~/.bash_profile` file and adding the same text there. The next time you log in, the changes go into effect. You can make changes for all your users' profiles in `/etc/profile` as well.

If you experiment heavily with these files, create a separate user account so that you can do whatever you want without messing up your own login. This advice especially goes for `/etc/profile`. You can damage everyone's logins with this one! To create a separate `/etc/profile`, you can make a backup by typing `cp /etc/profile /etc/profile.original`. Then edit `/etc/profile` knowing that you can always delete it with the `rm` command and use the `mv` command to rename `/etc/profile.original` to `/etc/profile`.

To create an environment variable from scratch, you will typically name it with all capital letters and then you have to "export" it. For example:

```
CUSTOMVAR="new variable"
export CUSTOMVAR
```

Don't be too discouraged if you don't understand all this variable stuff right now. As you become more proficient with Linux, you should explore *shell scripting.* Shell scripting is the art of creating computer programs with just the shell. Most Linux and Unix administrators speak shell script language like you and I speak our native tongues.

Using Redirection and Pipes

Redirection and pipes facilitate the flow of information. A *pipe* is exactly what it sounds like: It directs the output of one program to the input of another program. A pipeline may consist of several utilities plumbed together by pipes. At either end of this pipeline is, optionally, a redirection.

Almost all Linux utilities that require input and output have been plumbed with the following common interfaces: stdin (standard input), stdout (standard output), and stderr (standard error). By having a common method to feed input to a program or read data from the output of a program, you can glue utilities together into sophisticated solutions.

Redirecting command output

I discuss redirecting command output here because it's by far the most common form of information detouring. One example of *output redirection* involves telling a command to send its results to a file rather than to the screen, as you probably have been used to seeing. Start in some familiar territory by typing ls -la ~ and then pressing Enter, to produce something like the following:

```
total 20
drwx------ 2 sue   users 4096 Oct 30 07:48 .
drwxr-xr-x 5 root  root  4096 Oct 30 11:57 ..
-rw-r----- 1 sue   users   24 Oct 30 06:50 .bash_logout
-rw-r----- 1 sue   users  230 Oct 30 06:50 .bash_profile
-rw-r----- 1 sue   users  124 Oct 30 06:50 .bashrc
-rw-rw-r-- 1 sue   users    0 Jan 2  07:48 wishlist
```

Want to send this information to a file instead? You can use the > redirection operator to tell bash to send the data into a file rather than onto your screen. Enter the following command to send the information to a file named listing:

```
ls -la ~ > listing
```

Notice that nothing displays on the screen, as you normally would expect. That's because the shell has rerouted the output to a file named listing. To verify that the directory listing is there, enter the following command:

```
cat listing
```

The cat (and more) is explained Chapter 16.

Note that if you type ls -la ~ > listing again, the data is overwritten, meaning that the file's contents are wiped out and replaced with the new output. You can avoid this situation by using >> as your redirection operator, which tells bash to add the command's output to the end of the specified file.

If you type `ls -la ~ >> listing` in the same directory after making no changes, the contents of `listing` are as follows:

```
total 20
drwx------ 2 sue   users 4096 Oct 30 07:48 .
drwxr-xr-x 5 root  root  4096 Oct 30 11:57 ..
-rw-r----- 1 sue   users   24 Oct 30 06:50 .bash_logout
-rw-r----- 1 sue   users  230 Oct 30 06:50 .bash_profile
-rw-r----- 1 sue   users  124 Oct 30 06:50 .bashrc
-rw-rw-r-- 1 sue   users    0 Jan  2 07:48 wishlist
total 20
drwx------ 2 sue   users 4096 Oct 30 07:48 .
drwxr-xr-x 5 root  root  4096 Oct 30 11:57 ..
-rw-r----- 1 sue   users   24 Oct 30 06:50 .bash_logout
-rw-r----- 1 sue   users  230 Oct 30 06:50 .bash_profile
-rw-r----- 1 sue   users  124 Oct 30 06:50 .bashrc
-rw-rw-r-- 1 sue   users    0 Jan  2 07:48 wishlist
```

Laying pipes

Another `bash` shell feature enables you to connect commands so that the output of one becomes the input for the next one. This feature is referred to as a *pipe*. Suppose that you want to look over the details of all files in the `/etc` directory in long-listing format. If you type `ls -la /etc` to do so, a massive listing appears, and much of the information scrolls right past you. Although you can back up a bit by pressing Shift+PageUp, you may not be able to see everything.

To see all the information, you can do one of two things:

✔ Send the data to a file with redirection by typing something like `ls -la /etc > ~/etclisting` and then review the contents of `~/etclisting` with your favorite editor.

✔ Pipe the output to the `more` command(see Chapter 16).

To pipe the output to `more`, type `ls -la directory_path | more`, where `directory_path` is the directory for which you want to list the contents. The | symbol (which on the keyboard looks more like two vertical bars stacked on top of each other rather than just one solid line) tells `bash` that you want to use a pipe.

"Help!"

The *man page* system is the electronic manual for Linux (*man* is short for *man*ual), designed to provide users with a convenient reference to all the detailed command information. This information includes command prompt options, file formats, and program function usage.

The syntax for drawing a man page is man <command name>.

Don't know the command you're looking for or need basic information about using the man page system? Just type man man to get started. When you're finished reading the man page, press Q to exit.

Clearing the screen

The clear and reset commands are handy to know about when you're working in a shell. The clear command simply wipes the bash screen clean. Don't worry; it's not deleting any files or changing any settings — it's just tidying up so that you can start dumping new stuff to the screen again.

The reset command is a little more interesting. Suppose that you try listing a binary file to the screen with the cat command. After the computer finishes puking the result of executing the cat command on a binary file, you may get lucky and still be able to read your prompt. More likely, your prompt has been rendered into box characters of no special meaning, and typing on the keyboard gives you more of the same. To get back to normal, just type reset and press Enter. Note that it doesn't look like you're typing the word reset, but rest assured that the computer understands the series of characters and, after a couple seconds, should restore your shell environment to your native language.

Chapter 15

Gettin' Gooey with the GUIs

· ·

· ·

*T*he X Window System (or X) opens a world of possibilities. *X* is, in general, a set of applications that work together to provide a graphical interface. Think of these applications as the wireframe beneath your GUI, with GNOME and KDE (see Chapter 6) offering the pretty paper mâché coating. Some of these applications draw windows, some manage the look and feel, and others handle other aspects of the graphical world for you. All of them are configurable and even replaceable, which is enough to make the average user's eyes cross with way too many options!

GNOME and KDE are entirely creatures of convenience, offering integrated sets of window dressing so that you don't have to pick and choose your components. In this chapter, you get a chance to alter both KDE and GNOME's behavior to suit your own needs. For example, if you have a hard time reading text in those small command-prompt windows in the GUI, you can make both the windows and their fonts larger. You can change a wealth of other things, too, so read on and take a look.

If something goes terribly wrong in the GUI and you need to exit in a hurry, press Ctrl+Alt+Backspace. This key combination does one of two things. If you boot into the GUI, it collapses your GUI session and takes you to the GUI login prompt. However, if you boot to the command line, this key combination collapses the GUI immediately, taking you to the command line.

Press Ctrl+Alt+Backspace only in an emergency. This key combination doesn't cleanly stop the programs involved. You end up with all kinds of bits and pieces of programs, files, and other junk on your system.

Changing GNOME's Look and Feel

Change is inevitable, except from a vending machine.

— Anonymous

The GNOME desktop environment has an amazing set of features for you to explore. Some of these customization features are nice and practical, and others are just plain fun. I tried to group the types of changes into related topics so that you can peruse them easily. In GNOME-based distributions (Fedora, SuSE, and Ubuntu), you can typically find all the GNOME configuration options by going to the System or Desktop menu and then the Preferences submenu.

How do ya like them applets?

Applets are a collection of miniprograms that do anything from display the time to show system status — some can even show the depressing trickle of your battery power running out if you're using a laptop. Sure, some of these miniprograms are more useful than others. Then again, everybody needs a bit of entertainment too, right?

Adding an applet icon to the panel

You can have fun sifting through to see what kinds of applets are available to you. To look through your options and perhaps add an applet to the panel (remember that the panel is the bar along the top and/or bottom of your screen), follow these steps:

1. **Right-click any free space on your top or bottom panel and choose Add To Panel.**

   The Add To Panel dialog box appears, as shown in Figure 15-1. While the dialog box will look different in Ubuntu, it works the same.

   If you don't see an Add To Panel command, you're probably looking at the context menu for one of the applications on the panel. Try right-clicking elsewhere on the panel or closing some programs so that you can free up space amongst the minimized programs in the middle of your panel.

2. **Browse the available applets.**

3. **After you select the applet you want to add to your panel, click Add.**

   The applet is now on your panel.

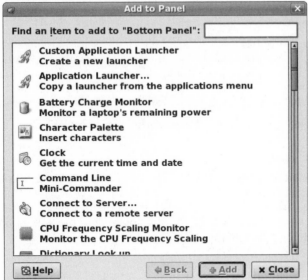

Figure 15-1:
The GNOME
and Fedora
5 Add
To Panel
dialog box.

If you then want to move the applet elsewhere on your panel, right-click it and choose Move from the shortcut menu. Then you can drag the applet around and click after you have it where you want to put it.

Configuring an applet

After you have an applet placed and running, you may be able to play with configuration options. Some of these options enable you to change what information is displayed. Others have a variety of look-and-feel settings.

To check for which configuration and other options are available for your applet, follow these steps:

1. **Right-click the applet and examine the shortcut menu that appears.**

   This shortcut menu is different from applet to applet. The bottom portion is always the same: Remove From Panel, Move, and Lock To Panel (prevent the icon from moving). Common entries for the top portion are Help and About. The rest of the items are either configuration options (see Step 2) or special applet features, such as the ability to copy the date from the Clock applet.

2. **Choose Preferences from the shortcut menu.**

   Not every applet has a Preferences dialog box. If this one does, the dialog box opens when you choose this option, and whichever configuration features this applet has are displayed.

3. **Alter the selections in the Preferences dialog box to customize this applet's behavior.**

Now you get to have some fun. Make changes so that you can see what this applet can do — as you make your changes, they appear in the applet on your panel. Each applet has its own set of features, so I can't do a general walkthrough here. Just remember that you can always go back and change the settings or remove the applet from your panel later.

4. **Click Close to save your changes and close the dialog box.**

Ditching an applet

You have room for only so many applets. And, if you're like me, you probably don't want to have every bit of free space cluttered with icons. To remove an applet from the panel, simply right-click the applet you want to remove and choose Remove From Panel from the shortcut menu that appears. With nary a whimper, the applet vanishes from the panel.

Don't forget the programs

You may be looking at your panel and wondering whether you can make any changes to the programs listed there, like you can with applets. The good news is that you *can* change the programs on the bar! They fit in the same empty spaces that applets do. You can also add a program to your desktop itself, if you want.

Adding a program to the panel or the Desktop

If you have a program you end up using often, you can add it to your panel by following these steps:

1. **Choose Applications and browse to the program you want to add to the bar.**

Don't open the program. Just point to the menu item with your mouse pointer.

2. **Right-click the program and choose Add This Launcher To Panel to add it to the panel, or Add This Launcher To Desktop to add it to the desktop.**

An icon for this program appears on your panel or Desktop.

After you have your program on the panel, you can run the program just by clicking its icon. If you added it to your Desktop, double-click the icon.

If you're not happy with where a desktop icon is placed, click it and then drag it to a new location. For a panel entry, right-click it and choose Move. This option allows you to drag the icon to where you want it. Click to fix it into place.

You can also add a *drawer* (menu button) to your panel for an entire menu. To do so:

1. **Click Applications and browse to the submenu you want to add.**

2. **Enter that submenu.**

   For example, if you want to add a button for the Graphics menu to your panel, open the Main Menu, move your mouse to the Graphics menu, and then move your mouse to the right into the contents of the Graphics menu.

3. **Right-click to open the context menu.**

4. **Choose Entire Menu, and then either Add This As Drawer To Panel or Add This As Menu To Panel.**

   A drawer shows you its contents in icons only, while a menu looks more like the actual submenu from the Main Menu.

Removing a program from the desktop or the panel

To get rid of an icon you have on your desktop, right-click the icon and choose Move To Trash from the shortcut menu that appears.

If you want to remove one of the programs on the panel, just right-click the icon you want to remove and choose Remove From Panel from the shortcut menu that appears. The icon vanishes from the panel. That's it!

Customizing KDE

Don't worry, you KDE users: You have plenty of options, too. You can customize your KDE setup in lots of ways, from the fun to the practical, so that you truly enjoy using it. As with GNOME, in fact, you can choose from far more features than I have room to cover in this chapter, so if you enjoy fiddling with the look and feel of your GUI, do some exploring on your own!

Applets keep fallin' on my head

Applets are miniprograms that do all sorts of things. An applet may display the time, show system status, or even offer a little frivolous fun. All kinds of applets are available out in the great big world of computer programming. A number of applets are included with your default KDE installation, although some of them are more useful than others.

Adding an applet icon to the panel

An interesting combination of applets is available in KDE, and you can easily add and remove these little gems from your KDE Panel as suits your needs. To add an applet to the panel (remember that the panel is the bar along the bottom of your screen) in KDE, follow these steps:

1. **Right-click a blank spot on the panel.**

   The panel's menu opens.

2. **Choose Add To Panel⇨Applet.**

   You find yourself looking at the Applet submenu's contents.

3. **Choose the applet you want to add to the Panel.**

On a particularly crowded panel bar, you may have to use the right and left arrow bars at the panel's ends to see the applet. You may need to delete from the panel, in fact, any items you don't use, to ensure that everything can show up. (See the section "Removing an applet," later in this chapter.)

Configuring an applet

Some applets have options that let you customize how they behave. Others are more boring and just do the same old thing no matter what you would prefer. To check which configuration and other options are available for your applet, follow these steps:

1. **Right-click the applet and examine the shortcut menu that appears.**

   This shortcut menu is different from applet to applet. In fact, there doesn't seem to be any real consistency in the menu options! (And not every applet even has a shortcut menu or a configuration option.) Look for entries such as Preferences, Settings, or the word *Configure.*

2. **Choose the appropriate command from the shortcut menu.**

   If you see a Configure or Preferences dialog box, make your changes and click Apply to see how that affects your applet without closing the dialog box. You may see more than one configuration dialog box or submenu, as is the case for the KNewsTicker applet.

3. **Alter the selections in the dialog box to customize this applet's behavior.**

   Experiment as much as you want. Just remember that you can always go back and change the settings or remove the applet from your panel later.

4. **Close the dialog box.**

   In a Preferences dialog box, click OK to close the window. Settings dialog boxes typically have a button, aptly named Defaults, that enables you to restore your defaults.

Removing an applet

You have room for only so many applets. And, if you're like me, you probably don't want to have every bit of free space cluttered with icons. To remove an applet from the panel, follow these steps:

1. **Right-click the panel on an empty spot.**

2. **Choose Remove From Panel⇨Applet.**

   The series of submenus opens, and you're finally looking at a list of the applets you now have on your panel.

3. **Choose the applet you want to remove from the panel.**

   The applet is no longer on your panel.

Adding programs to your panel

You can also add programs to your KDE Panel. To do so:

1. **Right-click on a blank spot on your panel.**

2. **From the shortcut menu, choose Add To Panel⇨Application Button.**

3. **From the Application Button submenu, browse to the program you want to add and select it.**

   The program appears on the left or right of your panel, depending on where you have room. (You remove programs from the panel the same way that you remove applets.)

Cluttering the desktop with icons

KDE allows you to alter which applets and programs appear on your panel, and on your desktop. Managing these shortcuts is a simple operation after you understand how it works.

Adding a program to the desktop

The panel has only so much room. Maybe you would rather have your program shortcuts lined up on the desktop as you do in Windows. To add one of these shortcuts, follow these steps:

1. **Click the Main Menu button to open the KDE Main Menu.**

2. **Open the submenu containing the program for which you want to make a shortcut.**

   For example, if you want to add The GIMP, open the Graphics submenu.

3. **Choose the program for which you want to make a shortcut.**

   Don't open the program. For example, to add The GIMP, you move your mouse to the program and then click and hold the mouse button.

4. **Drag the program to the desktop.**

   A little graphic follows your mouse pointer until you release the mouse button, at which point you're asked whether you want to add the shortcut to the desktop but not remove it from the menu (Copy Here); add the shortcut to the desktop and remove it from the menu (Move Here); or make an obvious shortcut that looks more like a Windows shortcut (Link Here). Typically, you choose Link Here.

If you're not happy with where a desktop icon is placed, click it and then drag it to a new location.

Removing a program from the desktop

If you want to remove one of the programs from the desktop, just right-click the icon you want to remove and choose Delete or Move To Trash, depending on which option is available — if you move items into the trash, remember to empty the trash later. The icon vanishes from the panel or desktop. That's it!

Prettying Up Your Desktop with Themes

You may be familiar with the ability to install desktop themes under Microsoft Windows. A *theme* in the desktop world refers to color schemes, images, and sounds applied to all portions of the desktop — window borders, fonts, icons, sound effects, and more — as part of a single, centralized entity. Many people are happy to find out that themes are available in the Linux world, too.

Many distributions offer collections of backgrounds you can download or that are already included. Chapter 12 includes pointers for the downloadable ones, and you can find the already installed ones usually by right-clicking on your desktop and choosing the option similar to Change Desktop Background.

Adding themes to GNOME

A large number of themes is available on the Internet for the GNOME desktop environment. To find and grab these themes for your own use, follow these steps:

1. **Point your Web browser to http://themes.freshmeat.net.**

   You're taken to the Themes Web site, where any number of GUI customization items is offered.

   If you're heavy into playing with customization, you can also check out http://art.gnome.org.

2. **On Freshmeat, click GTK, which is part of the GNOME desktop environment.**

   This action brings you to the appropriate section, to ensure that you choose themes that work with your system.

3. **Select the GTK 2.X Themes area.**

   Now you're in the section for the latest version of GNOME.

4. **Browse and choose the theme you want to try.**

   If you create an account and log in, you can use the Sort Order drop-down list box to change the order in which the items are displayed. When looking over a theme's information, keep your eye out for the requirements (sometimes called "dependencies") that go with the theme. Some themes require additional "engines" (software that runs behind the scenes), and you want to avoid them if you're uncomfortable with finding and adding software at this point. You're safe if you're looking for GTK themes.

5. **After you have chosen your theme, click its name to go to the theme-specific page.**

   There, you can find any comments someone has about the theme.

6. **Scroll down if necessary and click the link under Tar/GZ or Tar/BZ2, and then Save To Disk when asked what to do with the file.**

7. **Choose System⇨Preferences⇨Theme.**

   This action opens the GNOME Theme Preferences dialog box, as shown in Figure 15-2.

8. **Double-click your user's Home directory icon on your desktop.**

   The File Manager opens.

9. **Browse to where you stored the theme.**

   If you haven't changed the Firefox defaults, it will be in your Desktop directory.

10. **Make sure that the theme file is a .tar.gz file.**

    If not, you need to see Chapter 12 on how to convert this file to this format.

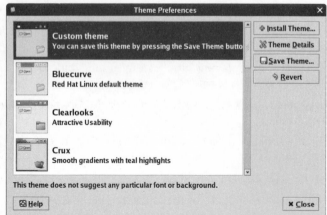

Figure 15-2:
The GNOME
Theme
Preferences
dialog box.

11. **Select the theme file and drag it into the left (Installer) pane of the Theme Preferences dialog box.**

An installer dialog box opens.

12. **Click Install.**

Your new theme is added to the themes list. Click OK when the Information dialog box informs you the install finished.

13. **Select your new theme in the listing.**

Your desktop changes to match the theme. If you do not see your theme in the list, select Custom Theme and then click Theme Details. You may find the theme listed in there.

14. **Click Close when you're happy with your desktop's look, and the Theme Preferences dialog box closes.**

Adding themes to KDE

Just as with GNOME, many themes are available for the KDE desktop. Most of the distributions covered in this book are using KDE version 3.4, so I am going to focus on this version.

To find and add themes for KDE:

1. **Point your Web browser to `www.kde-look.org`.**

2. **Click Themes/Styles, and then lKDE 3.2 - 3.5.**

Not sure what version of KDE you're running? Open the Configure Your Desktop/Control Center tool and you'll see a version number displayed.

3. **Among the tabs on the top, click the choice that will sort the themes in the method you prefer.**

   For example, you might click Highest Rated in order to see the themes people like the most.

4. **Browse and click the name of the theme you want to try.**

   This action takes you to the theme's page. Here, you find information about the theme, perhaps instructions on how to install it (unfortunately. there doesn't seem to be a lot of consistency here), and more. If you are nervous or have been having trouble getting themes to install, make sure to look for a theme that lists KDE 3.4 specifically. Folks feeling more adventurous might choose one for the 3.3 series. Reading the user comments can also be helpful in telling you if the theme is easy or difficult to install.

5. **Scroll down to the Download link and click it.**

   This link is usually at the base of the initial description information. When you click, a file browser dialog box appears.

6. **Browse to where you want to save the file and click Save.**

   The file is saved into the location you chose.

7. **If the file ends in `.gz`, `.zip`, `.tar.gzip`, or `.tar.bz2`, uncompress the file.**

   (If you're not sure how to uncompress the file, see Chapter 12.)

   The file may instead end in `.kth` or `.ktheme`. In this case, you don't need to open it up, so skip to Step 11.

8. **Open:**

   • **Knoppix:** From the Main Menu, choose Control Center. From inside the Control Center, choose Appearance & Themes⇨Theme Manager.

   • **Linspire:** There is no themes section in the Control Center, but you can install packages of themes through CNR as discussed in Chapter 12.

   • **Mandriva:** Uses a different setup than the others by default; if you have updated your installation, you may be able to follow these instructions but from a default install you will not.

   • **Xandros:** Launch⇨Control Center⇨Display⇨Theme⇨Theme Manager.

9. **Click Install New Theme.**

   The Select Theme File - Control Center dialog box appears.

10. **Click the name of the directory you created when you unpackaged the file.**

11. **Look for a file ending in .kth or .ktheme. If you find it, click it. Otherwise, you will need to find a new theme.**

12. **Click Open, and then look for the theme in the theme listing.**

13. **Click Apply to use this theme if you like the preview, and then you can close the dialog box at any time by clicking the X in the corner.**

    Feel free to surf through the other themes in the list to look at the preview. You may find that if your theme was only for a certain aspect of the desktop, it only appears under, say, the Icons button if it was an Icon theme.

You may find that you have to look in the various sections (Background, Colors, Window Decorations, Icons, and so on) to find all the pieces of the theme. If your Theme Manager has a theme customization section on the bottom with buttons, you may have to click in each of those to find parts of your new theme's information.

Tweaking the GUI's Innards

Behind GNOME and KDE lurks the X Window System, or "X." X provides the skeletal GUI structure and functionality. GNOME and KDE make use of this skeleton to provide you with a pleasant GUI environment. Whenever you configure hardware or other basic GUI features like resolution, you actually work with X, and not GNOME or KDE.

One of the /etc/X11/xorg.conf files contains your X configuration. (All three files look the same inside but you should only have one.) Although this file is just a normal text file, the format is complicated and confusing. Rather than make you work with this file by hand, the various Linux distributions provide a number of tools. (See Chapter 20 for which tool comes with which distribution.)

If you really enjoy experimenting with GUIs and fiddling with them, you can do a number of things. Go to www.linuxdoc.org and read the various X Window System and XFree86-related HOWTO files. Some are quite technical, but some are a bit more friendly, and you may be surprised by just how much you can tweak the Linux GUI. You can also find www.gnome.org and www.kde.org, as well as dozens of other useful sites out there.

Part IV
Getting Things Done

The 5th Wave   By Rich Tennant

"We're looking for applications that work well on a particularly open and distributed network."

In this part . . .

For many people, this part is the fun one! You find out how to edit files at the command line and in the GUI, including getting down and dirty with OpenOffice.org, the free office suite that rocks the Linux (and Windows, and OS X) world. You also get a bit crazy playing with multimedia. CDs, DVDs, audio files, movies, Internet radio . . . the sky's the limit when it comes to making your Linux machine a multimedia center.

Finally, for those who just can't leave Windows-only software and file formats behind, I cover how to add support for many of these items. I don't make the claim that everything Windows is supported under Linux, but you may be surprised at just how easy it is to find a way to use your Windows "stuff" (that's a high-level technical term, you know).

Chapter 16

Putting the X in Text

● ●

● ●

From text editors to word processors, Linux offers a wide variety of options for working with words. In this chapter, I take a look at different ways to view the contents of a text file, using some simple text editors in both the non-GUI and GUI environments. In Chapter 17, I take a look at office suites for those who would rather do word-processing.

Viewing the Contents of a Text File

Almost all configuration files in Linux are text files. In addition, many pseudo-programs (called *shell scripts*), all HTML documentation, and many other items in your system are text files. Fortunately, if you just want to see what's in a text file and don't want to do anything to its contents, you don't have to use an editor or word processor. You can use three command-line commands to view text files: `cat`, `less`, and `more`. I bet that you will grow to love them.

Yes, that first command is `cat`, and it's taken from the word *concatenate*, which means to bring together end to end — you can use the `cat` command on multiple-text files to have their text joined, one file's contents directly after another's. Typically you use this command in the Linux world in the format `cat filename`, where the contents of the file `filename` are displayed on the screen. For example, if you create the short text file `greetings` and then type `cat greetings`, you see the following:

```
$ cat greetings
These are the contents of the greetings file.
Meow!
$ _
```

Of course, if the file contains more than a screen's worth of information, `cat` spews it all out at one time like a big hairball, and all but the last screen of text scrolls off the screen. It's a good thing that you have some other choices. The one you're likely to choose is `less`, which displays the contents of a file a full screen at a time. Then you press the spacebar to continue to the next screen. You can also use the arrow keys to move up and down one line at a time, if you want.

An alternative to `less` is `more`. The main difference between the two is that with `more`, you can move only forward through the file and see only a screen's worth of information at a time. You can't back up.

To use either `less` or `more`, the format is similar to the format used with the `cat` command: `less` *filename* or `more` *filename*. When you finish reading the document, press Q to exit.

Editing Text Files with nano

If you aren't using (or can't use) the GUI, then you have numerous text editors available to you. The most powerful of these are `vi` and `emacs`, which you'll hear many people go on about. However, both these programs require a learning curve. For beginners who want to just edit the dang file and move on, I recommend `nano` and `pico`. These two editors are very similar, and one or the other is typically included with most Linux distribution (but, unfortunately, not all). The "friendly" text editors included with the distributions discussed in this book are

- ✔ **Fedora:** `nano`

- ✔ **Knoppix:** `nano` in the DVD version only — `joe` is included on the CD

- ✔ **Linspire:** None; see Chapter 12 to add `nano` through CNR

- ✔ **Mandriva:** None; see Chapter 12 to add one (`jed` and `joe` are both available)

- ✔ **SuSE:** `pico`

- ✔ **Ubuntu:** `nano` and `pico`

- ✔ **Xandros:** `editor`, which has a menu of function keys at the bottom of its screen

To open a file in nano, type **nano** *filename*, such as **nano file1**. This action opens the file in the `nano` editor, as shown in Figure 16-1.

You can then edit or type in that file as much as you need to.

Figure 16-1:
The file
`file1`
open in the
`nano` editor
in Fedora
Core.

Saving your work as you go

To save your file's contents without closing it (so that you can keep working on it):

1. **Press Ctrl-O to Write Out.**

   A prompt appears toward the bottom of the screen, asking for the name of the file and offering the current name as the default option.

2. **If you want to use the same name, press Enter. If you want to change the name, make your changes and then press Enter.**

   The lower part of your screen now displays that it wrote (saved) a certain number of lines

3. **Get back to work!**

Saving and moving on with your life

To save your file's contents and close it (because you're done working on it for now) — or to close the file and not save the changes — do the following:

1. **Press Ctrl-X to Exit.**

   A prompt appears toward the bottom of the screen, asking whether it should save the *modified buffer*. This question is a fancy way of asking whether you want to save your changes.

2. **Press Y to save your changes or press N to not save them.**

   If you press Y, you're asked for the name of the file and offered the current name as the default option. If you press N, nano closed and exited, so you're finished with these steps.

3. **If you want to use the same name, press Enter. If you want to change the name, make your changes and then press Enter.**

   The nano editor closes, and your file is saved.

Going with gedit

You're not stuck with just command-prompt-based text editors in Linux. Lots of graphical options are available. In this section, I cover gedit because it is the default GUI text editor for Fedora, which is on the DVD included with this book. The default GUI editors for the full range of distributions covered are as follows:

- ✔ **Fedora:** Access gedit by choosing Applications➪Accessories➪Text Editor (see Figure 16-2).

- ✔ **Knoppix:** Access KWrite or Kate by choosing Editors➪KWrite or Editors➪Kate.

- ✔ **Linspire:** Access KWrite by choosing Launch➪Run Programs➪Business & Finance➪Text Editor.

- ✔ **Mandriva:** Access Kate or KWrite from the Main Menu by choosing More Applications➪Editors➪Kate or More Applications➪Editors➪KWrite.

- ✔ **SuSE:** Access Kate, etc. by choosing Applications➪Utilities➪Editor and then either Kate, KEdit (not in all versions), or Text Editor

- ✔ **Ubuntu:** Access gedit by choosing Applications➪Accessories➪Text Editor.

- ✔ **Xandros:** Access KWrite (very similar to gedit and Kate) by choosing Launch➪Applications➪Accessories➪Text Editor.

Entering and editing text in gedit

gedit is strictly a *text editor,* in that you use it to generate raw text, whereas a *word processor* creates marked-up text that can be opened only by programs that can read that word processor's file formatting. If you want to add bold, italics, underlines, or any other special features to your document, proceed to Chapter 17.

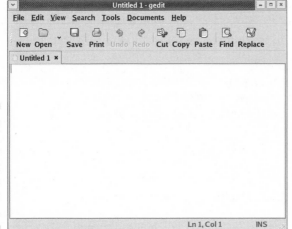

Figure 16-2:
The gedit
window
with a blank
file, in
Fedora
Core.

To enter text in gedit, just click within the big white space and start typing. You have access to the standard collection of editing tools, such as cut, paste, and copy. To use these, select the text you want to work with and then click the appropriate button on the gedit toolbar (or right-click and choose the appropriate command from the context menu).

The really interesting thing about this particular text editor is its plug-ins. To use these features, you need to follow these steps:

1. **Choose Edit⇨Preferences in gedit.**

   This action opens the Preferences dialog box.

2. **Click the Plug-Ins tab.**

   The Plug-Ins tab's contents appear.

3. **Click an item you're interested in within the Plug-Ins tab.**

4. **Click the About Plug-In button to get more information.**

   The information is contained within the small About window that appears.

5. **Click Close to get rid of the About window.**

6. **If you want to use this plug-in, click in its check box.**

   The plug-in is activated if a check appears in the check box.

7. **If the Configure Plug-In button becomes active for the plug-in you just selected, click the button to open the tool's plug-in configuration dialog box.**

   This dialog box will be different depending on which plug-in you're using.

8. **When you're finished with the individual plug-in's configuration, click OK to return to the Preferences dialog box.**

9. **If you want to examine more plug-ins, return to Step 3.**

10. **When you're finished selecting plug-ins, click Close to close the Preferences dialog box.**

You can now access the plug-ins from your `gedit` menus. Each one is placed in its appropriate location: for example, Change Case appears on the Edit menu.

Saving your work

As with most programs, you have two choices for saving your work. You can save your work and keep going or save it and then close the program. To just save the file and keep going, follow these steps:

1. **Click the Save button.**

   This button looks like a floppy disk. If you haven't ever saved this file, clicking it opens the Save As dialog box.

2. **Either choose one of the folders in the Save In Folder drop-down list box to save your file into, or click the right-facing arrow next to Browse For Other Folders to open the file browsing section.**

   The dialog box expands to allow you to browse to the location you want to use.

3. **If necessary, browse through the directories in the left or right pane until you're in the directory where you want to save the file.**

   Double-click the name of a directory to enter it or double-click the entry in the left pane to jump to its location first.

4. **Type the file's name in the Name text box.**

5. **Click Save to save the file.**

   The dialog box closes.

To close `gedit`, follow these steps:

1. **Choose File➪Quit.**

   If you haven't saved this file since the last time you changed it, the Question dialog box appears.

2. **If you see the dialog box, click Save to save your work or click Close Without Saving to abandon it.**

   The program closes, unless you have more than one file open, in which case you see the Question dialog box for each file you have altered but not saved.

Taking a Quick Look at Kate

Kate (see Figure 16-3) is the default editor in KDE and works much the same way as `gedit` does. However, Kate is actually a bit fancier than `gedit`, offering features such as exporting to HTML (choose File⇨Export), filtering various types of markup and coding to help spot errors (choose Tools⇨Highlighting), and more.

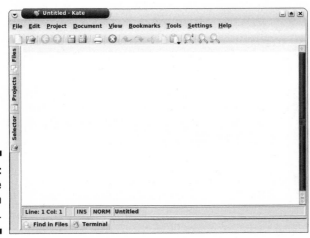

Figure 16-3:
The Kate editor in SuSE.

Chapter 17

Word Processing and More with OpenOffice.org

· ·

· ·

Words fly, writing remains.

— Spanish proverb, from *Dictionary of Proverbs,*
by Delfín Carbonell Basset

These days, just about everyone who has a computer has at least one office suite at their fingertips. If they're Microsoft Windows users, this suite is probably Microsoft Office, although it may be another worthy contender, such as Corel WordPerfect Office. In Linux, typically the suite is OpenOffice.org. This suite comes with Base (database), Calc (a spreadsheet), Draw (diagrams and figures), Impress (for presentations), Math (a word processor for writing mathematical formulas), and Writer (for word-processing).

After you figure out how to use one of the programs in this suite, you may be happy to find that the others are designed to look and work in very similar ways. You can even open and save files in Microsoft Office format, if you need to share them with people using it — and you can edit the Office files people send you, too.

That's enough *about* OpenOffice.org. In this chapter, you can *actually use* it!

Other office suites available for Linux users are the commercial OpenOffice.org relative StarOffice (www.sun.com/staroffice), Applixware Office (www.vistasource.com/products), KOffice (www.koffice.org), and GNOME Office (www.gnome.org/gnome-office/).

Word-Processing with OpenOffice.Org Writer

Word processors are almost required equipment these days. Kids use them to write letters to their grandparents. Grandparents use them to write letters to their grandkids. Whether you're working on the great American novel or a school book report, OpenOffice.org Writer has all the best features you expect to find these days in a word processor.

Starting it up

To start OpenOffice.org Writer in the distributions covered in this book, do the following:

- **Fedora Core:** Choose Applications⇨Office⇨Word Processor. Or you can click the Word Processor button on your upper panel.

- **Knoppix:** From the Main Menu, choose ⇨Office⇨OpenOffice.org⇨ OpenOffice.org Writer.

- **Linspire:** Choose Launch⇨Run Programs⇨Business & Finance⇨ OpenOffice⇨OpenOffice Word Processor.

- **Mandriva:** From the Main Menu, choose Office⇨Wordprocessors⇨ OpenOffice.org Writer.

- **SuSE:** From the Main Menu, choose Applications⇨Office⇨Word processor⇨OpenOffice.org Writer.

- **Xandros:** Choose Launch⇨Applications⇨OpenOffice.org⇨Word Processor. Xandros users who purchased the product also may have the option to install StarOffice through Xandros Networks (see Chapter 12), which is the commercial version of OpenOffice and contains additional fonts, templates, and more. Some purchasers also automatically have CrossOver Office (www.codeweavers.com) installed, which allows them to run Microsoft Windows applications such as Microsoft Word. See Chapter 19 for more.

✔ **Ubuntu:** Choose Applications➪Office➪OpenOffice.org2 Writer.

Taking a tour of OpenOffice.org Writer

Before you proceed, take a look at the GUI layout shown in Figure 17-1.

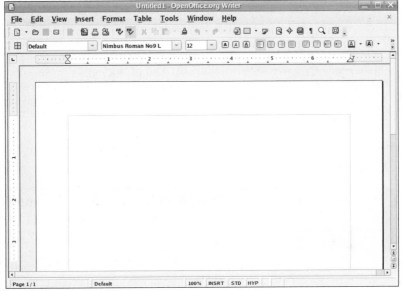

Figure 17-1: The OpenOffice.org Writer layout in Fedora Core 5.

Menu bar

Along the top of the window is the menu bar, something you should be used to if you typically work in Microsoft Windows. OpenOffice.org Writer has all the features you expect from a modern word processor. It has too many menu options to cover in depth, so I give you instead a (nonexhaustive) summary of what you find on each major menu:

✔ **File:** The usual Open, Save, Save As, Print, and Print Preview (under the term Page Preview) commands, along with a set of wizards (under the term AutoPilot) plus the ability to send documents through e-mail, create templates, create Web pages, and to access your database information

- ✔ **Edit:** The usual Select All and Find commands, along with change tracking, document merging, and document comparing

- ✔ **View:** The usual Zoom functions and toolbars, along with the abilities to show or hide formatting characters, and to see what the document would look like as a Web page

- ✔ **Insert:** The usual page breaks and special characters, along with indexes, tables, bookmarks, headers, footers, and cross-references

- ✔ **Format:** The usual character, paragraph, and page settings, along with styles, autoformatting capabilities, and columns

- ✔ **Table:** The usual table control options, including the ability to insert, delete, and select cells, convert between tables and text, and more.

- ✔ **Tools:** The usual spell-checking and thesaurus entries, in addition to hyphenation, autocorrection, an image gallery, and a bibliography database

These menus have more features than what is listed here. Go through and take a look; you may find a new favorite feature in there somewhere.

Standard toolbar

Beneath the menu bar is the standard toolbar. Each icon in this series represents a different functionality, which is detailed in Table 17-1.

Table 17-1	The OpenOffice.org Writer Standard Toolbar, from Left to Right
Button or Item	*What You Can Do*
New	Create new documents of various types. Click the downward arrow to select a particular type of document to create, from among any of the OOo types.
Open	Open an existing file for reading or editing.
Save	Save the current document. If you haven't saved this document before, the Save As dialog box opens.
Document as Email	Open a Compose email window in your preferred email program, and automatically attach this document.
Edit File	Edit the displayed Web page.

Button or Item	What You Can Do
Export Directly as PDF	Open a Save As dialog box with PDF selected as the file type.
Print File Directly	Send a file to the default printer.
Page Preview	Show this page as it would look if you printed it. To return from preview mode, click Close Preview.
Spellcheck	Run the spell checker on your entire document or the selected text.
AutoSpellcheck On/Off	Activate or turn off the automatic spell checker feature.
Cut	Remove the selected text from the document and save it in memory.
Copy	Make a copy of the selected document text and save it in memory.
Paste	Place the text from memory into the document at the cursor's current location. Click the down arrow to see options of how the text can be pasted.
Format Paintbrush	Pick up the formatting of the first text you click and apply it to the second text you click.
Undo	Undo the last change you made to the document. Click the down arrow to choose how far you want to back up to.
Redo	Reinstate the last change to the document after using Undo to cancel it. Click the down arrow to choose how far you want to redo.
Hyperlink	Open or close a dialog box that you can use to build complex hyperlinks.
Table	Insert a new table. Click the down arrow to drag and choose how many rows and columns the table should have.
Show Draw Functions	Access the many OpenOffice.org drawing utilities.
Find and Replace	Open or close the Find and Replace dialog box.
Navigator	Open or close the Navigator window, which allows you to jump to specific features within your document.

(continued)

Table 17-1 *(continued)*

Button or Item	What You Can Do
Gallery	Open or close a pane along the top of the document that provides access to clip art. Click this button again to close the pane.
Nonprinting Characters On/Off	Shows all spaces, return at the ends of paragraphs, and other characters that you don't normally see in your documents.
Zoom	Alter how large the document shows on your screen.
Help	Open the OpenOffice.org Help dialog box.

Formatting toolbar

The Formatting toolbar is directly below the standard toolbar in a default OpenOffice.org setup — though not on all distributions. As usual, you can remove the Formatting bar at any time by using the View menu. This series of icons allows you to click buttons and expand drop-down list boxes that represent standard word-processing functions, such as styles, fonts, font sizes, and formatting instructions. Most features on this bar are identical to what you see in most modern word processors. The button for paragraph background formatting is the only one that's particularly unusual.

This toolbar actually changes depending on what you're doing. If your cursor is within a table, for example, then the object bar contains useful buttons for working with tables.

Ruler

Directly below the Formatting toolbar in a default OpenOffice.org setup is the ruler. All modern word processors offer this item, which marks out the margins and tabs, for example, of your document in the measuring system of your choice. To change which system you want to use, right-click the ruler to open the Measurements pop-up dialog box.

Your document

Oh, yeah — that big, blocked-off white space that takes up most of the window. That's where you work on your documents! Just click in there and start typing. You can also access a Formatting shortcut menu by right-clicking in the document section.

OpenOffice.org Writer supports the following file formats (and more): its own OpenDocument (.ODT) format, StarWriter's format (.SXW), Microsoft Word 95, 6.0, 97, 2000, and XP (.DOC), Rich Text Format (.RTF), Text (.TXT), Web Page (.HTML), DocBook (.XML), and Microsoft Word 2003 XML (.XML).

Spreadsheets with OpenOffice.Org Calc

Some people like to balance their checkbooks by hand. When I first graduated from a university, I decided that it was time to get hold of my finances, and a spreadsheet was the way to do it. These days, I use spreadsheets to keep track of my "time card" when I'm doing consulting or contract work, help me manage project teams, and complete other tasks. I'm sure that you have your favorite uses for spreadsheets. The following sections take a look at OpenOffice.org Calc so that you can get to work.

Starting it up

To start OpenOffice.org Calc in the distributions I cover in this book, do the following:

- **Fedora Core:** Choose Applications⇨Office⇨Spreadsheet. Or you can click the Spreadsheet button in the upper panel.
- **Knoppix:** From the Main Menu, choose Office⇨OpenOffice.org⇨ OpenOffice.org Calc.
- **Linspire:** Choose Launch⇨Run Programs⇨Business & Finance⇨ OpenOffice⇨OpenOffice Spreadsheet.
- **Mandriva:** From the Main Menu, choose Office⇨OpenOffice.org Calc.
- **SuSE:** Choose Applications⇨Office⇨Spreadsheet⇨OpenOffice.org Calc.
- **Xandros:** Choose Launch⇨Applications⇨OpenOffice.org⇨ Spreadsheet.
- **Ubuntu:** Choose Applications⇨Office⇨OpenOffice.org2 Calc.

Taking a tour of OpenOffice.org Calc

Much of what you see in OpenOffice.org Calc should look familiar, between looking through OpenOffice.org Writer and other spreadsheet programs you have used. Take a look at the GUI layout shown in Figure 17-2.

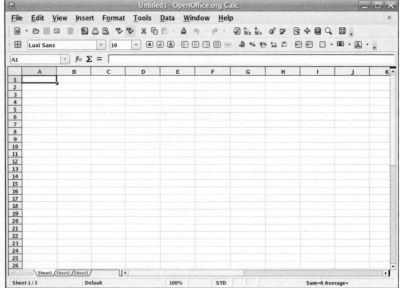

Figure 17-2:
The
OpenOffice.
org Calc
layout
in Fedora
Core 5.

Menu bar

Along the top of the window is the menu bar, a standard in the GUI world no matter which operating system you're using. OpenOffice.org Calc has all the features you expect from a modern spreadsheet system. It has too many menu options to cover in depth, so, instead, here's a (nonexhaustive) summary of what you find on each menu:

- **File:** The usual Open, Save, Save As, Print, and Print Preview (under the term Page Preview) commands, along with a set of Wizards plus the ability to send documents through e-mail, create templates, and create Web pages

- **Edit:** The usual Select All and Find commands, along with change tracking, headers and footers, and plug-in loading

- **View:** The usual Zoom functions and toolbars, along with the options for showing or hiding column and row headers

- **Insert:** The usual page breaks and special characters, along with cells, rows, functions, and external data

- **Format:** The usual cell and row formatting, cell merging, and page settings, along with conditional formatting

✔ **Tools:** The usual spell-checking and thesaurus entries, in addition to hyphenation, autocorrection features, an image gallery, and a macro creator and editor

✔ **Data:** The usual data selection, sorting, and grouping routines in one easy place for quick access.

These menus have more features than those listed here. Go through and take a look; you may find a new favorite feature in there somewhere.

Standard toolbar

Beneath the menu bar is the standard toolbar. Each icon in this series represents a different functionality, as shown in Table 17-2.

Table 17-2	The OpenOffice.org Calc Standard Toolbar, from Left to Right
Button or Item	*What You Can Do*
New	Open new documents of various types. Click the downward arrow to select a particular type of document to create, from among any of the OOo types.
Open	Open an existing file for reading or editing.
Save	Save the current document. If you haven't saved this document before, the Save As dialog box opens.
Document as Email	Open a Compose email window in your preferred email program, and automatically attach this document.
Edit File	Edit the displayed spreadsheet.
Export Directly as PDF	Open a Save As dialog box with PDF selected as the file type.
Print File Directly	Send a file to the default printer.
Page Preview	Show this page as it would look if you printed it. To return from preview mode, click Close Preview.
Spellcheck	Run the spell checker on your entire document or the selected text.
AutoSpellcheck	Activate or turn off the automatic spell checker feature.
Cut	Remove the selected text from the document and save it in memory.

(continued)

Table 17-2 *(continued)*

Button or Item	What You Can Do
Copy	Make a copy of the selected document text and save it in memory.
Paste	Place the text from memory into the document at the cursor's current location. Click the down arrow to see options of how the text can be pasted.
Format Paintbrush	Pick up the formatting of the first text you click and apply it to the second text you click.
Undo	Undo the last change you made to the document. Click the down arrow to choose how far you want to back up to.
Redo	Reinstate the last change to the document after using Undo to cancel it. Click the down arrow to choose how far you want to redo.
Hyperlink	Open or close a dialog box that you can use to build complex hyperlinks.
Sort Ascending	Re-order the selected data in ascending order.
Sort Descending	Re-order the selected data in descending order.
Insert Chart	Create a chart based on the selected data.
Show Draw Functions	Access the many OpenOffice.org drawing utilities.
Find and Replace	Open or close the Find and Replace dialog box.
Navigator	Open or close the Navigator window, which allows you to jump to specific features within your document.
Gallery	Open or close a dialog box that provides access to clip art.
Zoom	Alter how large the document shows on your screen.
Help	Open the OpenOffice.org Help dialog box.

Formatting bar

The object bar is directly below the function bar in a default OpenOffice.org setup. As usual, you can remove the object bar at any time by using the View menu. This series of icons allows you to click buttons and expand drop-down list boxes that represent standard spreadsheet functions, such as styles, fonts, font sizes, and number formatting instructions. Most features on this bar are identical to what you see in most modern spreadsheets.

Formula bar

Directly below the object bar in a default OpenOffice.org Calc setup is the Formula bar. Table 17-3 lays out what you find in this short collection of entries. This bar actually changes depending on what you're doing, offering you buttons for particular tasks, so don't panic if you look here and this table doesn't match what you see on your own Formula bar.

Table 17-3	The OpenOffice.org Calc Formula Bar, from Left to Right
Button or Item	**What You Can Do**
Function Wizard	Click to open the Function Wizard dialog box and browse to find the particular spreadsheet function you're looking for.
Sum	Click to start a SUM (addition) function in the Input Line.
Function	Click to place an = in the Input Line to signal that you're about to enter a function.
Input Line	Assign values or enter functions to fill a spreadsheet cell.

Your document

The document area is where you work on your spreadsheet. Just pick a cell and start typing. You can also access a Formatting shortcut menu by right-clicking in the document section.

OpenOffice.org Calc supports the following file formats (and more): its own OpenDocument spreadsheet format (.ODS), the StarOffice Calc format (.SXC); Data Interchange Format (.DIF); dBASE (.DBF); Microsoft Excel 95, 5.0, 97, 2000, and XP (.DOC); text-based comma-separated values (.CSV), Symbolic Link (SYLK), Web Page (.HTML), and Microsoft 2003 XML (.xml).

Presentations with OpenOffice.Org Impress

Most people would rather eat glass than speak in front of a group. Still, if you have to, you may as well have some cool presentation software to back you up. This program is what I use when I speak at conferences. (I use it even when my clients want me to send in my presentation in Microsoft PowerPoint format. Shh! Don't tell — they don't know the difference!) Give OpenOffice.org Impress a chance to impress you.

Starting it up

To start OpenOffice.org Impress in the distributions I cover in this book, do
the following:

- ✔ **Fedora Core:** Choose Applications➪Office➪Presentation. Or, you can
  click the Presentation button on your upper panel.

- ✔ **Knoppix:** From the Main Menu, choose Office➪OpenOffice.org➪
  OpenOffice.org Impress.

- ✔ **Linspire:** Choose Launch➪Run Programs➪Business & Finance➪
  OpenOffice➪OpenOffice Presentations.

- ✔ **Mandriva:** From the Main Menu, choose Office➪OpenOffice.org Impress.

- ✔ **SuSE:** Choose Applications➪Office➪Presentation➪OpenOffice.org
  Impress.

- ✔ **Xandros:** Choose Launch➪Applications➪OpenOffice.org➪Presentation.

- ✔ **Ubuntu:** Choose Applications➪Office➪OpenOffice.org2 Impress.

Using the Presentation Wizard

When you open OpenOffice.org Impress, the first thing that launches is the
Presentation wizard (see Figure 17-3), which you can also open later manually
by choosing File➪Wizards➪Presentation. If you don't want this wizard to
show up the next time you open OpenOffice.org Impress, then click the Do
Not Show This Dialog Again box.

Figure 17-3:
The
OpenOffice.
org
AutoPilot
Presentation
wizard
in Fedora
Core 5.

To use this wizard, follow these steps:

1. **Leave the Empty Presentation option selected (unless you have a template you need to work from) and click Next.**

   Dialog 2 appears.

2. **If you want to select one of the default slide backgrounds that come with OpenOffice.org Impress, you can do so by looking to the Select a Slide Design drop-down list box, choosing Presentation Backgrounds, and then clicking the various options to see what they look like to the right of the dialog box.**

   By default, there aren't many background templates. This is one area where Sun's StarOffice offers added value.

3. **If you want to select a presentation (content) layout template that was designed specifically for the template you chose in this dialog box's screen 1, you can do so by looking to the Select A Slide Design drop-down list box, choosing Presentation(s), and then selecting the presentation type you want to use.**

   Again, you find limited options here by default.

4. **If you want your presentation ultimately to appear on something other than a computer screen, adjust the Select An Output medium to match its intended setting.**

   Your choices are Screen, Overhead Sheet, Slide, and Paper.

5. **Click Next to proceed.**

   Dialog 3 appears.

6. **Under Select a Slide Transition, experiment with the various options in the Effect and Speed drop-down list boxes to narrow down how you want to move from one slide to another.**

   OpenOffice.org Impress animates these transitions for you as long as the Preview box is checked.

7. **If you want to navigate manually from one slide to the next (the Default option) while you give your presentation, skip to Step 10. If you want to have your presentation advance automatically, click the Automatic option.**

8. **In Duration Of Page, set how long you want each slide to stay up.**

9. **In Duration Of Pause, set how long of a blank gap you want to have between slides.**

   If you have Show Logo checked, the OpenOffice.org logo appears during the blank pauses.

10. **After you have your settings selected, click Create to proceed.**

    OpenOffice.org Impress opens, as shown in Figure 17-4. You may find it useful to click the X in the upper right of the Slides pane to clear up the window some.

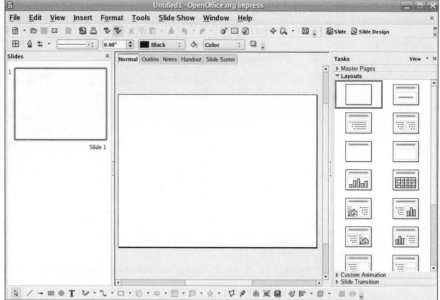

Figure 17-4:
The
OpenOffice.
org Impress
default look
in Fedora
Core 5.

Taking a tour of OpenOffice.org Impress

Before you proceed, take a look at the GUI layout shown in Figure 17-4. The Slides view on the left and the Tasks view on the right might look like clutter to some; if you don't need it, just click the X in the upper-right corner of each pane. You can bring them back at any time by choosing View⇨Slide Pane and/or View⇨Task Pane.

Menu bar

Along the top of the window is the menu bar. OpenOffice.org Impress has the many features you expect from a modern presentation package. It has too many menu options to cover in depth, so I give you instead a (nonexhaustive) summary of what you find on each menu:

✔ **File:** The usual Open, Save, Save As, and Print commands, along with a set of Wizards, plus the ability to send documents through e-mail and create templates

✔ **Edit:** The usual Select All and Find commands, along with the ability to quickly duplicate a slide

✔ **View:** The usual Zoom functions and toolbars, along with the ability to select whether you're looking at just slides, notes, or another section

✔ **Insert:** The usual new slide, along with charts, frames, graphics, and spreadsheets

✔ **Format:** The usual text-formatting features, along with layout, graphics, and style formatting

✔ **Tools:** The usual spell-checking feature, in addition to hyphenation, auto-correction, and an image gallery

✔ **Slide Show:** The usual slide show controller menu

These menus have more features than those listed here. Don't forget to do some exploring on your own.

Standard toolbar

Along the top of the window is the standard toolbar, which you can remove at any time by choosing View⇨Toolbars⇨Standard. Each icon in this series represents a different functionality and is described in Table 17-4.

Table 17-4	The OpenOffice.org Impress Standard Toolbar, from Left to Right
Button or Item	**What You Can Do**
New	Open new documents of various types. Click the downward arrow to select a particular type of document to create, from among any of the OOo types.
Open	Open an existing file for reading or editing.
Save	Save the current document. If you haven't saved this document before, the Save As dialog box opens.
Document as Email	Open a Compose email window in your preferred email program, and automatically attach this document.
Edit File	Edit the displayed file.

(continued)

Table 17-4 *(continued)*

Button or Item	*What You Can Do*
Export Directly as PDF	Open a Save As dialog box with PDF selected as the file type.
Print File Directly	Send a file to the default printer.
Spellcheck	Run the spell checker on your entire document or the selected text.
AutoSpellcheck	Activate or turn off the automatic spell checker feature.
Cut	Remove the selected text from the document and save it in memory.
Copy	Make a copy of the selected document text and save it in memory.
Paste	Place the text from memory into the document at the cursor's current location. Click the down arrow to see options of how the text can be pasted.
Format Paintbrush	Pick up the formatting of the first text you click and apply it to the second text you click.
Undo	Undo the last change you made to the document. Click the down arrow to choose how far you want to back up to.
Restore	Reinstate the last change to the document after using Undo to cancel it. Click the down arrow to choose how far you want to redo.
Chart	Insert a chart into the presentation by using the selected data.
Spreadsheet	Insert a spreadsheet into the presentation.
Hyperlink	Open or close a dialog box that you can use to build complex hyperlinks.
Display Grid	Display or remove the line-up grid from the slide.
Navigator	Open or close the Navigator window, which allows you to jump to specific features within your document.
Zoom	Alter how large the document shows on your screen.
Help	Open the OpenOffice.org Help dialog box.
Slide	Insert a new slide after the current one.

Button or Item	What You Can Do
Slide Design	Open the Slide Design dialog box.
Slide Show	Start a slide show.

Line and filling bar

The line and filling toolbar is directly below the standard toolbar in a default OpenOffice.org setup. As usual, you can remove the object bar at any time by using the View menu. This series of icons allows you to click buttons and expand drop-down list boxes that represent standard presentation-software functions, such as arrow styles, colors, line styles, and other formatting instructions. Most features on this bar are identical to what you see in most modern presentation programs.

View switchers

Just above your document you see a series of tabs, each of which takes you to a particular way of viewing your slide(s). Table 17-5 outlines the available views and what you find in them.

Table 17-5	Available OpenOffice.org Impress Views, in Alphabetical Order
View	**What you find**
Normal	Individual slide view in which you can add art to your slide.
Handout	Six slides per page, as you might print it for handouts.
Master	Individual slide view in which you can apply master formatting that will apply to all slides. Access this view by selecting View➪Master. You have the option in the Master submenu of choosing either Slide Master to view the master slide, Notes Master to view the master note page, or Master Elements to assign the information that is made available in the Master views.
Notes	Individual slide view in which you can see a small version of the slide plus your notes about that slide.
Outline	All-slides view with the slides listed in order for easy stepping through. Along the side, the slides are shown in thumbnail mode in a separate window as you navigate.
Slide Sorter	All-slides view with as many slides packed in as possible in columns and rows. Re-ordering slides is as simple as dragging them where you want to go and then dropping them.

Your document

The tabbed window contains your document. In Normal view, that document is your slide. You will need to click one of the tools in the Drawing Bar (discussed in the next section) in order to be able to enter any content. To add more slides before or after this one, right-click over the document area and select Slide⇨New Slide. For each slide, you can use the layouts in the Tasks pane on the right to change their setup.

OpenOffice.org Impress supports the following file formats (and more): its own OpenDocument presentation format (.ODP), StarOffice Impress's format (.SXI), Microsoft PowerPoint 97, 2000, and XP (.PPT or .PPS).

Drawing bar

Beneath the document window is a drawing toolbar, which allows you to select lines, arrows, shapes, and more for your presentation creation needs. Most of these buttons have downward-pointing arrows, which allow you to see the full range of features they offer.

Fine Art with OpenOffice.Org Draw

Whether you're an aspiring graphic artist or just need a tool that lets you generate simple graphics for use on their own, in a presentation, or elsewhere, OpenOffice.org Draw provides a host of drawing functions. If nothing else, it's a whole lot of fun to play with! Not everything in life has to be practical.

Starting it up

To start OpenOffice.org Draw in the distributions I cover in this book, do the following:

- ✔ **Fedora Core:** There is no direct menu access to the Draw program in Fedora Core 5. Instead, open one of the other OpenOffice.org tools and then select File⇨New⇨Drawing if you want to create a new drawing. You can open an existing OOo Draw document by double-clicking it in your file manager or choosing File⇨Open in another OOo tool and selecting that drawing..

- ✔ **Knoppix:** From the Main Menu, choose Office⇨OpenOffice.org⇨ OpenOffice.org Draw.

- ✔ **Linspire:** Choose Launch⇨Run Programs⇨Business & Finance⇨ OpenOffice⇨OpenOffice Drawings.

- ✔ **Mandriva:** From the Main Menu, choose Office➪OpenOffice.org Draw.

- ✔ **SuSE:** Choose Applications➪Graphics➪Vector Drawing➪OpenOffice.org Draw.

- ✔ **Xandros:** Choose Launch➪Applications➪OpenOffice.org➪Tools➪ Drawing Editor.

- ✔ **Ubuntu:** Choose Applications➪Office➪OpenOffice.org2 Draw.

Taking a tour of OpenOffice.org Draw

Before you proceed, take a look at the GUI layout shown in Figure 17-5. If you find the Pages pane on the left too much clutter, click the X in its upper right to get rid of it. You can bring it back at any time by selecting View➪Page Pane.

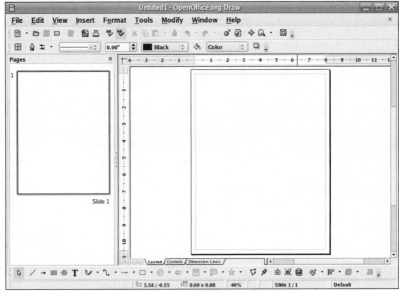

Figure 17-5: The OpenOffice.org Draw layout in Fedora Core 5.

Menu bar

Along the top of the window is the usual menu bar. OpenOffice.org Draw is a typical "vector" graphics program, meaning that it relies on lines rather than dots or other techniques. See Chapter 18 for discussion of the software used for editing photographs and other heavy-detail work.

OpenOffice.org Draw has too many menu options to cover in depth, so I give you instead a (nonexhaustive) summary of what you find on each menu:

- **File:** The usual Open, Save, Save As, Print, and Export commands, along with a set of Wizards (under the term AutoPilot) plus the ability to send documents through e-mail and create templates

- **Edit:** The usual Find, Replace, and other commands, and the not so usual Image Map

- **View:** The usual Zoom functions and toolbars, along with the ability to select the display quality

- **Insert:** The usual charts, frames, graphics, and spreadsheets, along with scanning functions

- **Format:** The usual line and graphics formatting, along with layers and style formatting

- **Tools:** The usual spell-checking, as well as hyphenation, autocorrection, an image gallery, and an eyedropper for grabbing colors

- **Modify:** Various options for altering the appearance of an object

These menus have more features those listed here. Go through and take a look; you may find a new favorite feature in there somewhere.

Standard toolbar

Beneath the menu bar is the standard toolbar, which you can remove at any time by choosing View➪Toolbars➪Standard. Each icon in this series represents a different functionality, as described in Table 17-6. As you can see, this main toolbar is more similar to that in OpenOffice.org Impress than to the one in OpenOffice.org Writer.

Table 17-6	The OpenOffice.org Draw Main Toolbar, from Left to Right
Button or Item	**What You Can Do**
New	Open new documents of various types. Click the downward arrow to select a particular type of document to create, from among any of the OOo types.
Open	Open an existing file for reading or editing.
Save	Save the current document. If you haven't saved this document before, the Save As dialog box opens.
Document as Email	Open a Compose email window in your preferred email program, and automatically attach this document.

Button or Item	What You Can Do
Edit File	Edit the document.
Export Directly as PDF	Open a Save As dialog box with PDF selected as the file type.
Print File Directly	Send a file to the default printer.
Spellcheck	Run the spell checker on your entire document or the selected text.
AutoSpellcheck	Activate or turn off the automatic spell checker feature.
Cut	Remove the selected text from the document and save it in memory.
Copy	Make a copy of the selected document text and save it in memory.
Paste	Place the text from memory into the document at the cursor's current location. Click the down arrow to see options of how the text can be pasted.
Format Paintbrush	Pick up the formatting of the first item you click and apply it to the second item you click.
Undo	Undo the last change you made to the document. Click the down arrow to choose how far you want to back up to.
Restore	Reinstate the last change to the document after using Undo to cancel it. Click the down arrow to choose how far you want to redo.
Chart	Insert a chart using the selected data.
Hyperlink	Open or close a dialog box that you can use to build complex hyperlinks.
Navigator	Open or close the Navigator window, which allows you to jump to specific features within your document.
Zoom	Alter how large the document shows on your screen.
Help	Open the OpenOffice.org Help dialog box.

Line and filling bar

The line and filling bar is directly below the standard bar in a default OpenOffice.org setup. As usual, you can remove the line and filling bar at any time by using the View menu. This series of icons allows you to click buttons and expand drop-down list boxes that represent standard presentation software functions, such as arrow styles, colors, line styles, and other formatting instructions.

Ruler

Directly below the line and filling bar in a default OpenOffice.org setup are the rulers. These items mark out the margins and tabs, for example, of your document in the measuring system of your choice. To change which system you want to use, right-click the ruler and change the Measurements to your preferences.

Your document

Click in that big white space and start doodling. You can also access a formatting pop-up menu by right-clicking in the document section.

OpenOffice.org Draw appears at first glance to have the most limited file type support for saving when you use the Save As dialog box, but in fact, it supports a wide range of graphics formats. You can save images to a format other than the OpenOffice.org Draw format (.ODG) by choosing File⇨Export.

Supported graphics formats are BMP, EMF, EPS, GIF, JPEG, MET, PBM, PCT, PGM, PNG, PPM, RAS, SVG, SWF (Flash), TIFF, WMF, and XPM.

Drawing bar

Beneath the document window is a drawing toolbar, which allows you to select lines, arrows, shapes, and more for your drawing creation needs. Most of these buttons have downward-pointing arrows, which allow you to see the full range of features they offer.

Managing Data with OpenOffice.org Base

Those who are used to using Microsoft Access, or who have to interact with a variety of database products, have in the past been left scratching their heads and wondering how best to handle these needs under Linux. Well, wonder no more! OpenOffice.org Base provides an interface to both Microsoft Access files and to other databases. This software is only available with those distributions that include OpenOffice.org 2 either as updates or by default at installation time.

Starting it up

To start OpenOffice.org Base in the distributions I cover in this book that include OpenOffice.org 2, do the following:

- ✓ **Fedora Core:** OpenOffice.org Base isn't installed by default in Fedora with the rest of OpenOffice.org. Use Chapter 12 to add OpenOffice.org Base from the Applications⇨Office/Productivity section's optional packages. After you have it installed, open it by selecting Applications⇨Office⇨Database Development.

- ✓ **Knoppix:** From the Main Menu, choose Office⇨OpenOffice.org⇨ OpenOffice.org Base.

- ✓ **SuSE:** Choose Applications⇨Office⇨Database⇨OpenOffice.org Base.

- ✓ **Ubuntu:** Choose Applications⇨Office⇨OpenOffice.org2 Base.

There are many different ways you can use this program. The essentials involve creating a database from scratch in a file on your system, working with Microsoft Access files, and working with databases that were created to use with many of the major database servers — even over the network. Since there are so many approaches and my space is limited, I will focus on two of the more common choices: creating new database files, and opening existing files, which includes Microsoft Access files.

The first interface you encounter when opening anything but a document you already worked with from the File⇨Recent Documents menu option is the Database Wizard (Figure 17-6).

Figure 17-6: The OpenOffice. org Base Database Wizard, used to open existing databases and create new ones.

Creating a new database file in the Database Wizard

In the Database Wizard dialog box, do the following to create a brand new database file:

1. **Select the Create A New Database radio button.**

2. **Click Next.**

   The Decide How To Proceed After Saving The Database dialog box appears, as shown in Figure 17-7.

Figure 17-7:
The
OpenOffice.
org Base
Database
Wizard's
Decide
How To
Proceed
After
Saving The
Database
dialog box.

3. **If you want to register this database as a data source in OpenOffice.org, leave Yes, Register The Database For Me selected; otherwise, select the No, Do Not Register The Database radio button.**

   A registered database is accessible by all of your OpenOffice.org applications, rather than just OpenOffice.org Base.

4. **If you immediately want to open this file for editing, leave the Open The Database For Editing check box checked; otherwise, click this option to uncheck the box.**

5. **If you want to immediately create a new table in the database by using the Table Wizard (using the wizard is recommended), click the Create Tables Using The Table Wizard check box to place a check in it.**

   For now, it's best to leave it off, so you can explore one step at a time.

6. **Click Finish.**

   The Save dialog box opens.

7. **Enter the name for your document in the Name text box.**

8. **Either select the directory you want to save the document to in the Save In Folder drop-down list box, or click the right-facing arrow next to Browse For Other Folders to navigate to where you want to save the document.**

9. **Click the Save button.**

   Whatever you specified should happen, happens. If you chose to immediately open the database, you will see something equivalent to Figure 17-8.

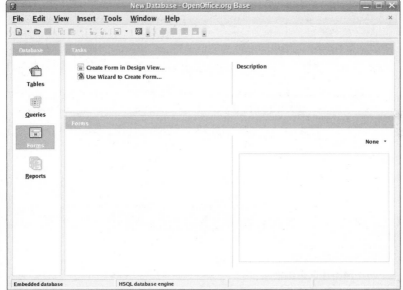

Figure 17-8:
A database
open in
OpenOffice.
org Base.

Opening an existing file in the Database Wizard

If you have an already existing Microsoft Access file that you want to open in OpenOffice.org Base, do the following from the initial Database Wizard dialog box:

1. **Select Open An Existing File.**

2. **If the file is in the Recently Used drop-down list box, select the file there. Otherwise, click the Open button.**

   If you clicked the Open button, the Open dialog box appears. Those who selected an item from Recently Used can click Finish and are done opening the file.

3. **Navigate to the file you want to open, and select the file.**

4. **Click Open.**

The file is opened into a window similar to that shown in Figure 17-8.

Taking A Tour of OpenOffice.org Base

Before you proceed, refer to the layout shown in Figure 17-8. This is your main OpenOffice.org Base window after you have a database open to work with. Let's take a look at what you'll find there.

Menu bar

Along the top of the window is the menu bar. OpenOffice.org Base gives you access to many of the features you may expect in a database interface:

- ✔ **File:** The usual Open, Save, and Save As commands, along with a set of wizards and the ability to send documents through e-mail

- ✔ **Edit:** The usual Copy and Paste commands, along with access to database properties, advanced settings, and the Form and Report wizards

- ✔ **View:** Access to toolbars and database objects, along with preview and sort features

- ✔ **Insert:** The ability to create forms, queries, and more

- ✔ **Tools:** The ability to assign relationships between tables, filter tables, run SQL queries, create macros, and more

Standard toolbar

Beneath the menu bar is the standard toolbar, which you can remove at any time by choosing View➪Toolbars➪Standard. Each icon in this series represents a different functionality, as described in Table 17-7. As you can see, this main toolbar is more similar to that in OpenOffice.org Impress than to the one in OpenOffice.org Writer.

Table 17-7	The OpenOffice.org Base Standard Toolbar, from Left to Right
Button or Item	*What You Can Do*
New	Open new documents of various types. Click the downward arrow to select a particular type of document to create, from among any of the OOo types.
Open	Open an existing file for reading or editing.

Button or Item	What You Can Do
Save	Save the current document. If you haven't saved this document before, the Save As dialog box opens.
Copy	Make a copy of the selected document text and save it in memory.
Paste	Place the text from memory into the document at the cursor's current location. Click the down arrow to see options of how the text can be pasted.
Sort Ascending	Sort the entries in the lower-right pane in alphabetical order.
Sort Descending	Sort the entries in the lower-right pane in reverse alphabetical order.
Form	Create a form.
Help	Open the OpenOffice.org Help dialog box.
Open Database Object	Open the selected item in the lower-right pane.
Edit	Open the design view for the selected item in the lower-right pane.
Delete	Delete the selected item in the lower-right pane.
Rename	Rename the selected item in the lower-right pane.

The Database pane

To the left of the main window is the Database pane. In this pane you see four icons: Tables, Queries, Forms, and Reports. Select these icons to determine what appears in the two rightmost panes — for example, to work with your tables, select the Tables icon.

A *query* allows you to ask complex questions regarding your database.

The Tasks pane

The upper-right pane is the Tasks pane. In here, you see what types of things you can do for a particular selection in the Database pane. Use the Description to the right to decrypt any of the terms that make your eyes cross.

The Tables/Queries/Forms/Reports pane

The lower-right pane shows the tables, queries, forms, or reports that already exist. You can open any of these to work in by double-clicking them in this pane.

Layout with OpenOffice.Org Math

There's nothing like trying to type a math or science report and having to either use multiple lines to show your equations (which never looks right!) or write them by hand. OpenOffice.org Math is a great solution to this problem. You can lay out your equations and more in this program and then insert them into any of your OpenOffice.org documents. Whether you're a middle school student or a professional engineer, OpenOffice.org Math just may thrill you.

Many OpenOffice.org Math functions are different from what you're used to if you have looked at all the other OpenOffice.org programs. However, in many ways this program is less complex than some, thanks to its special-purpose nature. Keep in mind that it's not a calculation program. It's for laying out complex formulas on paper or the screen.

Starting it up

To start OpenOffice.org Math in the distributions I cover in this book, do the following:

- **Fedora Core:** There is no menu option for OpenOffice.org Math in Fedora Core 5. Instead, open another OpenOffice.org application and choose File⇨New⇨Formula.

- **Knoppix:** From the Main Menu, choose Office⇨OpenOffice.org⇨ OpenOffice.org Math.

- **Linspire:** Choose Launch⇨Run Programs⇨Business & Finance⇨ OpenOffice⇨Additional Programs⇨OpenOffice Math.

- **Mandriva:** From the Main Menu, choose Office⇨Wordprocessors⇨ OpenOffice.org Math.

- **SuSE:** There is no menu option for this program, so follow the same instructions given in the Fedora section.

- **Xandros:** Choose Launch⇨Applications⇨OpenOffice.org⇨Formula Editor. This editor may be under an additional Tools submenu.

- **Ubuntu:** Choose Applications⇨Office⇨OpenOffice.org2 Math.

Taking a tour of OpenOffice.org Math

Before you proceed, take a look at the GUI layout shown in Figure 17-9.

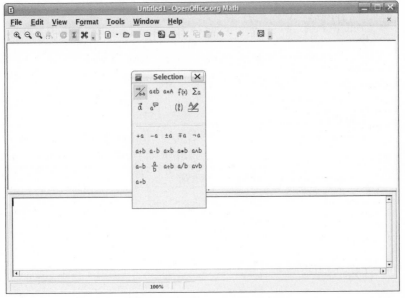

Figure 17-9:
The
OpenOffice.
org Math
layout.

Close the Selection dialog box by clicking the small X in the upper-right corner of its window for now, to keep things as uncluttered as possible. You can get it back at any time by choosing View⇨Selection.

Menu bar

Along the top of the window is the menu bar, a standard in the GUI world no matter which operating system you're using. OpenOffice.org Math may be unlike any program you may have used already, so I don't say anything about what you may expect to find there. I just give you a (nonexhaustive) summary of what you find on each menu:

- ✔ **File:** The usual Open, Save, Save As, and Print commands that you find in most GUI programs, along with a set of Wizards and the ability to send documents through e-mail

- ✔ **Edit:** The usual Select All, Copy, and Paste commands, along with specialized commands for moving within the formula

- ✔ **View:** The usual Zoom functions and toolbars, along with screen update features and more

- ✔ **Format:** The usual font type, font size, spacing, and alignment features and more

- ✔ **Tools:** The usual Customize and Options entries for customizing the program's setup and behaviors, in addition to formula importing and access to the symbol catalog

Standard toolbar

Along the top of the window is the standard toolbar, which you can remove at any time by choosing View⇨Toolbars⇨Standard. Each icon in this series represents a different functionality. You're likely to find this main toolbar quite different from those in the other OpenOffice.org programs. Mostly, it's just smaller. Each icon is described in Table 17-8.

Table 17-8	The OpenOffice.org Math Standard Toolbar, from Left to Right
Button or Item	*What You Can Do*
Zoom In	Show the image larger.
Zoom Out	Shrink the image.
1	Show the image at its actual size.
Show All	Show the whole formula in the largest size that will fit on the screen.
New	Open new documents of various types. Click the downward arrow to select a particular type of document to create, from among any of the OOo types.
Open	Open an existing file for reading or editing.
Save	Save the current document. If you haven't saved this document before, the Save As dialog box opens.
Document as Email	Open a Compose email window in your preferred email program, and automatically attach this document.
Export Directly as PDF	Open a Save As dialog box with PDF selected as the file type.
Print File Directly	Send a file to the default printer.
Cut	Remove the selected text from the document and save it in memory.
Copy	Make a copy of the selected document text and save it in memory.
Paste	Place the text from memory into the document at the cursor's current location.

Button or Item	What You Can Do
Undo	Undo the last change you made to the document. Click the down arrow to choose how far you want to back up to.
Restore	Reinstate the last change to the document after using Undo to cancel it. Click the down arrow to choose how far you want to redo.
Help	Open the OpenOffice.org Help dialog box.
Update	Update the formula shown in the document window.
Formula Cursor	Turn on or shut off the formula cursor.
Catalog	Open the Symbols dialog box.

Document section

Things get tricky here if you've never used formula-editing software. You can't type anything in the main (upper) document window in OpenOffice.org Math. Instead, you type in the Commands (lower) window. Right-clicking in the Commands window opens a shortcut menu. To help you get used to working with the formulas, I suggest that you play around with this tool. For example, if you have never used software like this, you might follow these steps:

1. **Right-click in the Commands window.**

   The main shortcut menu opens.

2. **Select a submenu to open.**

   For example, `Formats`.

3. **Select a formula component within this submenu.**

   I'm a geek, and I fondly remember taking a class on matrices, so I chose matrix {...} as an example. Immediately, the code that's needed in order to add a matrix to my formula appears in the Commands dialog box. A moment later, because I'm letting the program refresh the rest of the screen as I work, I see what the matrix looks like in the document window. The combination is shown in Figure 17-10.

4. **Replace each of the `<?>` entries with the proper letters and numbers for your formula.**

   When I change `matrix{<?> # <?> ## <?> # <?>}` to **matrix{A # B ## C # D}**, I see the result shown in Figure 17-11.

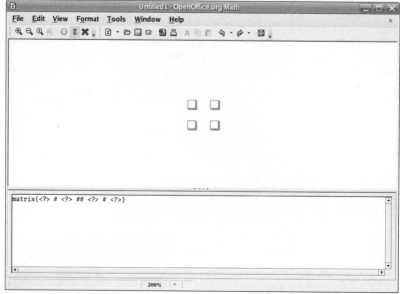

Figure 17-10:
Starting
to add a
matrix in
OpenOffice.
org Math.

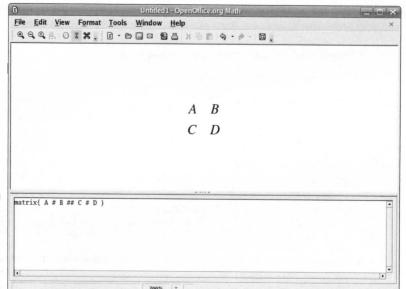

Figure 17-11:
A 4-x-4
matrix in
OpenOffice.
org Math.

5. Continue adding components to the formula until you're finished.

Suppose that you want to multiply the matrix by 3. To find out how, press Enter to go down to the next line in the Commands window (to use as "scratch paper"), right-click to display the pop-up menu, and choose Unary/Binary Operators⇨a Times b. This choice adds the phrase `<?> times <?>` beneath the matrix code. Now you know how to format a multiplication, so erase this phrase and use it as a guideline to change your formula to:

```
3 times matrix{A # B ## C # D}
```

This line gives the result shown in Figure 17-12. I could go on, but I hope by now that you're eager to start with your own explorations!

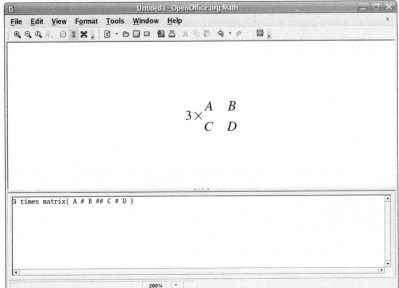

Figure 17-12:
A complete
formula in
OpenOffice.
org Math.

OpenOffice.org Math supports (among others) its own OpenDocument format (.ODF), the equivalent StarOffice format (.SXM) and MathML 1.01 (.MML), which isn't a program. *MathML* is a standard, similar to HTML for working on the Web, and 1.01 is a specific version of this standard. For this particular version of MathML, see `www.w3.org/TR/REC-MathML`. The main standard page is available at `www.w3.org/Math/`. If you need to add formulas to Web pages, this site can be quite an interesting read!

Configuring Printing for OpenOffice.org

Before you can print from OpenOffice.org, you may need to set up printing for this suite. If you already set up your printing in Chapter 7, try printing a page from any of the OpenOffice.org applications and see whether it works. For those that are unable to print from OpenOffice.org but can print from other applications, open the OpenOffice.org print tool from:

- ✔ **Fedora, Mandriva, SuSE, and Ubuntu:** Integrated with the main print manager, so you don't need to do anything.

- ✔ **Knoppix:** From the Main Menu, choose Office⇨OpenOffice.org⇨ OpenOffice.org Printer Administration.

- ✔ **Linspire:** Choose Launch⇨Run Programs⇨Business & Finance⇨ OpenOffice⇨Additional Programs⇨OpenOffice Printer Administration.

- ✔ **Xandros:** Choose Launch⇨Applications⇨OpenOffice.org⇨Printer Administration. The option may be under an additional submenu called Tools.

Then do the following:

1. **Click New Printer.**

   The Choose A Device Type dialog box appears.

2. **Make sure that Add A Printer is selected and then click Next.**

   The Choose A Driver dialog box appears.

3. **Scroll through this screen and locate the make and model of your printer or choose Generic Printer.**

4. **After you make your selection, click Next.**

   The Choose A Command Line dialog box appears.

5. **Click Next to skip this item.**

   The Choose A Name dialog box appears.

6. **Change the name for this printer if you want.**

7. **If you want to use this printer as your default, click the Use As Default Printer box.**

8. **Click Finish to add this printer to your list and then Close to close the printing tool.**

   Before you close the tool, you may want to click Test Page to see whether you can print a test page.

Chapter 18

Multimedia Wow!

The price of freedom is responsibility, but it's a bargain, because freedom is priceless.

— Hugh Downs

In these days of computing in noisy Technicolor, it just doesn't feel like a computer unless you can make it sing and dance. This used to be a weak point for Linux, but these days there's little that I can't do on my Linux desktop machine. From listening to CDs to watching QuickTime movies, you can do just about anything. Sometimes it just takes a bit of elbow grease to get things working.

Time to take a trip on the wild side and get your Linux box doing the Macarena.

Because legal complications surround a number of multimedia programs and their use in countries like the United States of America, some multimedia capabilities had to be removed from some Linux distributions. However, these capabilities are still available if you know where to look — and if you're in a legal jurisdiction that allows listening to MP3s, watching DVDs, or other touchy subjects under patent laws and the Digital Millennium Copyright Act (DCMA). Chapter 12 shows you how to add many of the features discussed throughout this chapter.

Checking Your Sound Card

Before you can listen to tunes, you have to make sure that your sound card is working properly. After the configuration issues are dealt with, you can move on to the fun stuff like listening to CDs and Internet radio and downloading tunes.

Many distributions ask you to test your sound as part of the installation or immediate post-installation routine. Just in case you skipped this step, the first thing to do here is locate the sound-testing program (if one exists) to see whether yours is working:

- **Fedora:** Choose System⇨Administration⇨Soundcard Detection to see whether the card is correctly detected and plays test sounds.

- **Knoppix:** From the Main Menu, choose KNOPPIX⇨Configure⇨ Soundcard Configuration to start the sound configuration utility.

- **Linspire:** Choose Launch⇨Settings⇨Control Center⇨System Administration⇨Information⇨Sound to see whether the card is correctly detected. If you are a daring and savvy hardware person then you can make alterations by starting in the main Control Center panel and selecting Sound & Multimedia⇨JACK Sound Server⇨Advanced⇨ Advanced Settings.

- **Mandriva:** From the Main Menu, choose System⇨Configuration⇨ Configure Your Computer⇨Hardware⇨Look At And Configure Hardware and then click the actual name of your sound card under Soundcard, rather than its label, to see whether the card is correctly detected.

- **SuSE:** Choose Desktop⇨YaST⇨Hardware⇨Hardware Information⇨ Sound, and then click the plus next to the specific sound card to make sure it is properly listed.

- **Xandros:** Choose Launch⇨Control Center⇨Hardware Information⇨ Sound to see what sound card the operating system found (you may find yours under an additional System menu). To make changes, follow the same instructions given for Linspire.

- **Ubuntu:** Choose System⇨Preferences⇨Sound to make sure your card was found correctly.

Looking into Your Mixer

If the card seems to be detected properly, then a look at your mixer is the next important step. Sometimes cards are picked up right, and yet the mixer for some reason by default has things muted, or other strange things are set. To find the mixer:

- ✔ **Fedora:** Choose System➪Preferences➪Volume Control.
- ✔ **Knoppix:** From the Main Menu, choose Multimedia➪KMix.
- ✔ **Linspire:** Choose Launch➪Run Programs➪Audio & MP3➪Volume Control.
- ✔ **Mandriva:** From the Main Menu, choose Multimedia➪Sound➪KMix.
- ✔ **SuSE:** Choose Applications➪Multimedia➪Volume Control (there may be another menu layer with another Volume Control component in your version). You may find other programs useful in this menu as well.
- ✔ **Xandros:** Choose Launch➪Applications➪Multimedia➪Sound Mixer.
- ✔ **Ubuntu:** Choose Applications➪Sound & Video➪Volume Control.

Mixer terms of interest include the following:

- ✔ **Lock:** When two slider bars appear for a setting, this option just makes sure that they're always level with one another.
- ✔ **Mute:** No sound comes from this section.
- ✔ **PCM:** Control the volume for audio files as opposed to, say, CDs.
- ✔ **Volume:** Control the overall volume.

Finally, many of the distributions have a little volume control icon on the panel. If everything else looks right in the mixer but you get no sound, click it and make sure that it hasn't been pulled down to the bottom.

Investigating Troublesome Sound Issues

If your sound isn't working, your card may not be supported. The following strategies can help you to track down a potential solution:

- ✔ Proceed to the manufacturer's Web site and locate the page for the specific card that you have. This page often has a link to technical support, drivers, and downloads. If it does, follow these links and see whether a *driver* (the piece of software that tells your operating system how to talk to each piece of hardware) is available for your card in Linux. If drivers are listed by *kernel version* — the version of the Linux core that you're using — type uname -r to see your version number and then choose the closest driver that you can. You also might have to try the central tech support page on that site if there isn't one dedicated to the hardware in question.

✔ Search on www.google.com for the make and model of your card, plus the word *Linux*. For example, I might search for

```
Yamaha YMF-744B Linux
```

You may be lucky enough to find a nice, simple solution to your problem. Or, you may find one that requires you to have a degree in Geekspeak. If so, see the Web sites that I mention in Chapter 1 for where to go for help that you can understand.

✔ Two special sound-related projects in Linux also might be able to help you. One is Advanced Linux Sound Architecture (ALSA), which you can find at www.alsa-project.org. The other is Open Sound System (OSS) at www.opensound.com. There's also the Linux Sound & MIDI site at http://linux-sound.org/.

Listening to CDs

Most of the distributions automatically open up CD players when you place a music CD into the drive. You can, of course, also open the CD player manually if you choose, from:

✔ **Fedora:** The default CD player in Fedora is actually the Totem Movie Player, but there is a simpler and yet more feature-rich tool for this purpose, so that is what I focus on here. Choose Applications⇨Sound & Video⇨CD Player (see Figure 18-1) to start the GNOME CD Player.

✔ **Knoppix:** DVD only. From the Main Menu, choose Multimedia⇨CD Player, with the minor caveat that you need to have a second CD drive to use it because the main CD drive has Knoppix in it!

✔ **Linspire:** Choose Launch⇨Run Programs⇨Audio & MP3⇨Lsongs (see Figure 18-2).

✔ **Mandriva:** From the Main Menu, choose Multimedia⇨Sound⇨KsCD (see Figure 18-3).

Figure 18-1:
The plain-
Jane
CD Player
in Fedora
with a CD
playing.

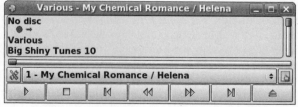

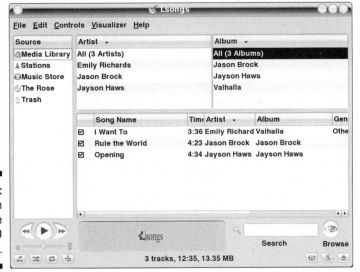

Figure 18-2:
Lsongs in
Linspire
with a CD
inserted.

Figure 18-3:
The KsCD in
Mandriva
with a CD
playing.

✔ **SuSE:** Choose Applications⇨Multimedia⇨CD Player⇨CD Player or KsCD.

✔ **Xandros:** Choose Launch⇨Applications⇨Multimedia⇨CD Player.

✔ **Ubuntu:** Choose Applications⇨Sound & Video ⇨CD Player.

If CDDB doesn't recognize your CD, you can add it to the database by:

✔ **Fedora, Knoppix, SuSE, and Ubuntu:** In the row above the bottom, click the Open Track Editor button to open the CDDB Track Editor on the right (see Figure 18-4), type the pertinent information, and then click Save. You can click the right-facing arrows to expand this dialog box to enter even more information.

✔ **Mandriva and Xandros:** Click the CDDB button, type the pertinent information, and then click Upload.

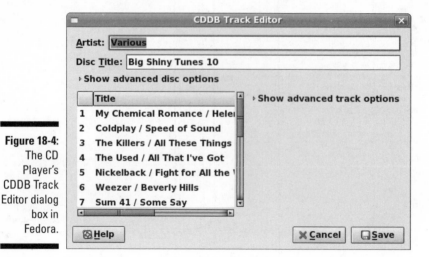

Other menus are available in these players as well. Take a moment to explore and set up their default behavior so that it matches what you like — in most cases you can tell the system to not automatically play CDs when inserted. See Chapter 11 for how the various distributions react when CDs are inserted.

Listening to Internet Radio

Listening to Internet radio stations in Linux is not always the simplest thing in the world, depending on your distribution. Because of various laws, patents, and licensing problems, some formats like MP3 are not always supported out of the box. The best way to see what you're set up to support right now is to simply try and listen. After you're sure that your sound is set up properly, you can try many Web sites with your default browser:

- ✔ **SHOUTcast** for finding links to thousands of online stations, at www.shoutcast.com
- ✔ **Radio-Locator** for finding "regular" radio stations offering online versions, at www.radio-locator.com

In Linspire's Lsongs, SHOUTcast stations are already available by default.

The first place to try is SHOUTcast. When you find a station that you want to listen to:

1. **Click the Tune In! button.**

   If you already have your software set up, you can listen automatically. However, you probably don't if you haven't listened to online radio before. If you've never listened to this program's format before, you will be asked what program to use to open the content.

2. **If a program is suggested, click OK to proceed. Otherwise, you will need to navigate through your filesystem to manually choose the program.**

   If you have never used this program before, it probably has a setup routine it will want you to go through before you continue.

3. **If required, walk through the program's setup routine.**

   Even after all of this, you might be told that the file format isn't supported. Fortunately, you are told here what format this is (for example, mpeg).

4. **If your software doesn't support the file's format, install a program that does.**

   For any formats that won't play, first turn to Chapter 12 and find how to add RealPlayer and the tools mentioned below. If these tools cannot play what you're trying to listen to, see Chapter 19 for products that let you run Windows software under Linux.

Software you're likely to encounter as you experiment with Internet radio includes:

- ✔ **Amarok:** A full-featured audio player that's got some really cool features, like the ability to load images of your album covers. This is my preferred audio tool, and it can be added to most of the distributions discussed in this book. See the section "Using Amarok" later in this chapter for more.

- ✔ **Rhythmbox Music Player:** Adding MP3 support to this program is a legally-tricky matter since MP3 is a patented format requiring proper licenses to use legitimately. The FedoraFAQ site at www.fedorafaq. org has more. Aside from the MP3 issue, this tool can play CDs, Internet (streaming) radio, and downloaded music.

- ✔ **RealPlayer:** The all-too-familiar program from other operating systems. It can play Internet (streaming) radio and downloaded music.

- ✔ **HelixPlayer:** A version of RealPlayer without the pieces that have to be handed with pay licenses (like MP3s). It can play Internet (streaming) radio and downloaded music.

- ✔ **MPlayer-Plugin:** A browser plug-in that you can use at times to listen to formats that other players may not support, including Windows formats. Least likely to be legal if you're in the United States.

✔ **XMMS:** A Winamp clone that can play Internet (streaming) radio and downloaded music. Sometimes comes with MP3 support and sometimes doesn't, but typically you can add MP3 support regardless through your distribution's extra repositories (see Chapter 12).

✔ **Kaffeine:** A full-featured audio/video media player for Internet (streaming) radio, downloaded files, CDs, DVDs, and so on. Again, this program is of questionable legality in the United States. In SuSE, if you get a complaint about "demux" not being included, install the oggmtools package (see Chapter 4).

✔ **Xine:** A full-featured audio/video media player for Internet (streaming) radio, downloaded files, CDs, DVDs, and so on. Again, this program is of questionable legality in the United States. In SuSE, if you get a complaint about "demux" not being included, install the oggmtools package (see Chapter 4).

Listening to Downloaded Music

Downloading music from the Internet is a fun activity. A lot of people like to pretend that it's both legal and ethical, when in fact, it's often theft, depending on where you grabbed the music. I leave that ethical issue between you and your belief system, but because my own ethics say that it's theft, I'm going to focus on showing you music that you're *welcome* to download — legally and ethically! Take a look at strategies for finding such music, along with how to listen to it.

One place to find such material is on a band's own Web site. Many groups today realize that offering free downloads of their work is a great PR move — if people love the sample songs, they're more likely to go out and buy the album. For an example, I use one of my own favorite bands, Evanescence (www.evanescence.com).

Evanescence, like many other bands, has its page done mostly with Macromedia's Flash tool. (See Chapter 12 for how to add this functionality to your distribution.) To listen to music files in general, I personally recommend Amarok, which (again) you can get by using the tools discussed in Chapter 12 as well — see the section "Using Amarok" later in this chapter for more — but here are the defaults for each distribution:

✔ **Fedora:** Choose Applications⇨Sound & Video⇨Rhythmbox Music Player.

✔ **Knoppix:** From the Main Menu, choose Multimedia⇨Sound⇨XMMS.

✔ **Linspire:** Choose Launch⇨Run Programs⇨Audio & MP3⇨Lsongs.

- ✔ **Mandriva:** From the Main Menu, choose Multimedia⇨Sound⇨Amarok. See the section "Using Amarok" later in this chapter for more.

- ✔ **SuSE:** Choose Applications⇨Multimedia⇨Audio Player⇨Amarok. See the section "Using Amarok" later in this chapter for more.

- ✔ **Xandros:** Choose Launch⇨Applications⇨Multimedia⇨Media Player.

- ✔ **Ubuntu:** Choose Applications⇨Sound & Video⇨Rhythmbox Music Player.

Using Amarok

Amarok (http://amarok.kde.org/) might just be the best music player available in Linux. This feature-rich and professional-looking tool lets Linux desktop users feel like they're actually in the modern age. I don't have room to cover every option in exhaustive detail, but I'll give you the nickel tour at least.

To begin, if Amarok isn't already installed you need to add it to your distribution if possible. See Chapter 12 for how to do this. If you have installed the application or it's already there, you can then launch it by going to:

- ✔ **Fedora:** Applications⇨Sound & Video⇨amaroK

- ✔ **Linspire:** Launch⇨Run Programs⇨Audio & MP3⇨Audio Player (amaroK)

- ✔ **Mandriva:** From the main menu, choose Multimedia⇨Sound⇨Amarok

- ✔ **SuSE:** Applications⇨Multimedia⇨Audio Player⇨amaroK

- ✔ **Ubuntu:** Applications⇨Sound & Video⇨amaroK

What you see by default may look a little different, I'm focusing on how Amarok is presented in Fedora, so adjust accordingly if needed. The first time you start Amarok in Fedora, The First-Run Wizard launches and displays the Welcome screen. Click Next to proceed to the Interface screen. Here, you can choose whether to have Amarok in one big piece of two different ones. I will assume you chose the former.

Clicking Next again takes you to the Collection screen. Here, you can expand (click the + symbols) and retract (click the - symbols) parts of the filesystem until you find the sections that contain your music. When you expose these folders (for example, /home/dee/Music), click in their box to add a checkmark. Leave the Scan Folders Recursively (look in subfolders), Watch Folders For Changes (pick up new files automatically), and Import Playlists (look for existing playlists and load them) boxes checked, or check them if they aren't. In this way, you let Amarok do most of the work.

Once you're done marking the necessary folders, click Next to continue to the Database screen. If you're not a database guru, just click Next and then Finish. Otherwise, take a moment to configure the database setup, and then click Next and Finish. Either way, when you're done you are taken to a screen similar to what's shown in Figure 18-5.

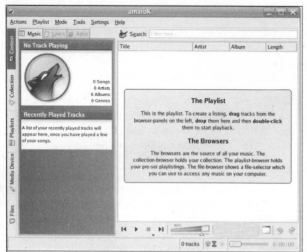

Figure 18-5: The Amarok audio player in Fedora Core 5.

From here, you need to add music to the right-hand side in order to play it. You can individually drag and drop but there are lots of other ways to do this. Let me take you on a tour of the interface to point some of them out.

Along the left of the Amarok window is a collection of tabs. What you see and what I see might be different, depending on your version. Each tab offers a certain segment of functionality, and may change the interface to the left of the playlist. The tabs displayed in Fedora from top to bottom are:

✔ **Context:** Allows you to access information about your music (Figure 18-6). This tab actually has another three tabs inside it, along the top. The left-most tab, Music, shows you collated information about the music you have listened to up to this point. The Lyrics tab, in the middle, does its best to load the lyrics for the song you're listening to and gives you click-able options if it can't decide exactly which song it might be — the first time you click this tab you may be offered a Run Script Manager button, if so, click it, select one of the two Lyrics options, and click Run. The right-most tab, Artist, looks on Wikipedia (www.wikipedia.org) for information about the group or artist associated with the song. Lyrics and Artist both have controls along the top for you to explore.

Figure 18-6:
The Amarok
Context tab,
Music
subtab, with
covers
loaded
using the
Cover
Manager.

The Context tab is much cooler if you go to Tools⇨Cover Manager and
click Fetch Missing Covers. When the proper cover is found, click Save.
Or, if it wasn't found, click Next Cover to cycle through other possibilities until you feel the right one.

✔ **Collection:** Shows you your music collection. Above the listing, click the
Group By button in order to choose features such as whether the collection is organized by group, album, and so on. In the Filter Here text box,
you can type in keywords to determine what songs are displayed. Or, in
the Entire collection dropdown-list box, you can specify if you want to
have only the most newly-added songs listed.

✔ **Playlists:** Here is where you create new playlists and access those that
are already available. The Smart Playlists section offers you a variety of
pre-built playlists, such as All Collection for those who want to listen to
everything they have, 50 Random Tracks to let the player pick them for
you, Genres if you took the time to assign genre information when ripping your CDs, and more. Dynamic Playlists are different from Smart
Playlists in that they're constantly changing. The Random Mix dynamic
playlist, for example, chooses music randomly from your collection and
then keeps choosing it as you continue listening. For Suggested Songs,
you put a few key songs in your playlist and then Last.fm (www.last.fm)
builds you a personalized online radio station with music that it consid-
ers similar. If you're a big fan of online radio or are curious about it, then

check out the Radio Streams section's Cool-Streams folder. Here you'll find lots of radio stations to choose from.

✔ **Media Device Browser:** Click this tab and then Connect to open the Configure Media Device dialog box. Here, you can choose from various portable storage device types if you have one (VFAT refers to Windows-based devices), so Amarok can load music from them.

✔ **Files:** Browse through your filesystem to find individual songs you want to click and drag into the playlist.

No matter how you get music over into the playlist on the right, once it's there you can click the Play button at the bottom of the pane to play the selected track. You can also double-click a track to play it. Below the volume slider you will find a set of controls (hover your mouse over the icon to see what it's currently set to), the most important of which are:

✔ Random Mode: Lets you turn playlist randomization on or off.

✔ Repeat: Lets you set whether to stop playing music when the whole playlist has been played (no repeats), repeat a specific track, or repeat the whole playlist.

There is much more to Amarok. Take the time to explore this tool and really customize it to your satisfaction. When you close this program, the Docking In System Tray dialog box appears. It warns you that Amarok will continue to run and appear as a system tray icon on your panel. You can avoid this by choosing Actions⇨Quit instead of clicking the X in the corner of the application to close the program. If you leave the program on your panel, you can open it at any time by clicking the little wolf icon in your panel.

Ripping Music Tracks from CDs

This is another topic that's impossible to cover without at least acknowledging that both ethics and legal issues are involved. I'm not going to get into legalities here, but my personal ethics are that it's fine to rip (copy) music off my own CDs for my own use. If I want to pull my favorite songs off CDs that I purchased and set them up so I can listen to them collectively in a random playlist off my computer's hard drive, I don't see a problem with this. However, doing this and then taking the CD back for a refund is theft, in my opinion.

So, with that said, a number of music ripping programs are available in Linux:

✔ **Fedora:** Choose Applications⇨Sound & Video⇨Sound Juicer CD Extractor (see Figure 18-7).

✔ **Knoppix:** None, although you'd need a second CD drive anyway!

Figure 18-7:
The Sound
Juicer CD
Extractor in
Fedora.

- **Linspire:** As discussed in Chapter 12, go to the CNR Warehouse and go to the section Audio & MP3➪Rippers & Encoders to download G-Rip. After this program is installed, choose Launch➪Run Programs➪Audio & MP3➪G-Rip to run it.

- **Mandriva:** From the Main Menu, choose Multimedia➪Sound➪aSound Juicer CD Ripper.

- **SuSE:** Choose Applications➪Multimedia➪CD/DVD Tools➪Grip.

- **Xandros:** None, though you can use the Xandros File Manager to burn CDs. (See the section "Burning Data CDs and DVDs," later in this chapter.)

- **Ubuntu:** Choose Applications➪Sound & Video➪Sound Juicer CD Ripper.

To rip songs with the Sound Juicer, from a CD that you've already inserted:

1. **For each song that you don't want to rip, uncheck the check box next to the song.**

   The check mark disappears for each song that you don't want to digitize.

2. **Choose Edit➪Preferences.**

   The Preferences dialog box appears, as shown in Figure 18-6.

3. **Select your preferred sound format.**

   If you're limited on space, I highly suggest Ogg Vorbis because this format is easily handled on Linux machines without any inherent legal problems and is also better compressed than MP3 for equivalent sound. However, if you want to go for higher quality for a home sound system, then chose FLAC, which is another open format but without any loss in sound quality.

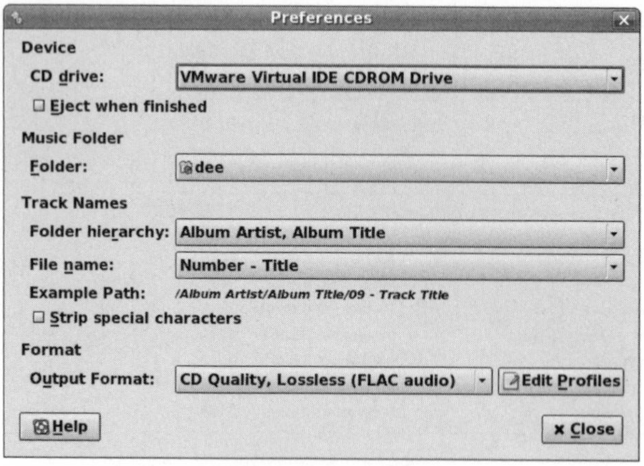

Figure 18-8:
The Sound
Juicer
Preferences
dialog box.

4. **Click the Folder drop-down list box to choose where you want to save your music files.**

   If the location you want to use isn't listed, select Other and then browse to the folder you want to use.

5. **In the Track Names section, select how you want Sound Juicer to name and arrange the files in subdirectories.**

6. **Make any other configuration changes you want to make.**

7. **When finished making changes, click Close.**

   The dialog box closes.

8. **Click Extract.**

   The Sound Juicer window shows you a progress bar along the bottom, and highlights the track it's currently working on. A dialog box appears when the extraction is complete.

9. **Choose Eject in the dialog box.**

   The CD tray opens.

10. **Remove the CD and close the tray.**

11. **Close Sound Juicer.**

Burning Data CDs and DVDs

A CD and DVD burner is a great way to make data backups (especially if it's a rewriteable), save and share your digital photos, put together multimedia memento scrapbooks, and more. Many tools are available that allow you to burn CDs under Linux, but you can also burn CDs and DVDs by using the filesystem navigation tools discussed in Chapter 10, right-clicking the file you want to burn, and choosing the proper options from the context menu.

Tools specifically written for burning CDs and DVDs that come with your distribution or can be installed are:

- **Fedora:** Choose Applications⇨Sound & Video⇨K3b if you have KDE installed (even if you're using GNOME), or add Grip (see Chapter 12).

- **Knoppix:** From the Main Menu, choose Multimedia⇨K3b, though remember you will need a second CD or DVD drive for this.

- **Linspire:** Choose Run Programs⇨Audio & MP3⇨CD and DVD Burning (K3b).

- **Mandriva:** None installed by default. Using Chapter 12, look for the programs arson and xcdroast.

- **SuSE:** Choose Applications⇨Multimedia⇨CD/DVD Burning⇨K3b or the other available option(s); any will do.

- **Xandros:** Choose Launch⇨Applications⇨Multimedia⇨DVD Writer (which can also write CDs).

- **Ubuntu:** Use the tools from Chapter 12 to install K3b.

Here I will focus on K3b. To add this program to the distributions where it is not available by default, but it is available, see Chapter 12. When you launch this tool in Fedora Core 5, you see the window shown in Figure 18-9.

Figure 18-9:
The K3b CD and DVD burner in Fedora Core 5.

If all you want to do is create a CD or DVD out of an ISO file you downloaded, do the following:

1. **Select either Tools⇨Burn CD Image if this is an ISO file for a CD-ROM, or Tools⇨Burn DVD ISO Image if this is a file for a DVD-ROM.**

   Both actions open the Burn CD Image dialog box (Figure 18-10).

2. **In the Image to Burn section, click the folder button and navigate to the file you want to burn onto CD or DVD.**

3. **When you find it, select it and click OK.**

   The file name and information now appears in the dialog box.

4. **If you have more than one burner for some reason, make sure that the proper one appears in Burning Device, and change the selection if necessary.**

5. **In Speed, if you are burning a CD or DVD of a Linux distribution, lower it to at least 4x. Otherwise, you are usually safe to leave it as is.**

   If you find that when you burn CDs or DVDs they often seem to end up "coasters" (burns that didn't work), lower the speed you usually use.

6. **Click Save User Defaults if you want to use most of these settings for every burn.**

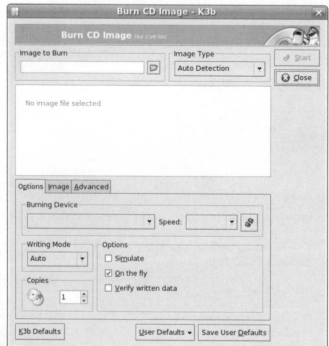

Figure 18-10:
The K3b
Burn CD
Image
dialog box.

7. **Click Start to begin your burn.**

   A dialog box appears with two progress bars. The first shows you the write preparation progress, and then the second shows you the total progress, including burn time.

8. **If this is a re-writable media, then you'll be asked if you want to erase its contents so it can be written over. Answer appropriately.**

   If you tell K3b to erase the media, then the Erasing dialog box appears during that part of the process. When the erasure finishes, the tray opens, ejecting the media, and then automatically closes again. This moment is when the actual burning session starts. The next time the disk ejects, the process is complete.

9. **Remove your new CD or DVD from the drive and then click Close to close the burn information dialog box, and Close again to close the main burn dialog box.**

10. **Select File⇨Quit to close K3b.**

Notice that this program has some other interesting features down in the bottom portion of the main window. Clicking one of the Project buttons will help you create a music (audio) CD, a data DVD, or a data CD from scratch.

Creating and Modifying Graphics

The GIMP is a graphics program that's considered in many ways equivalent to Adobe Photoshop. Many don't consider The GIMP the friendliest program on the planet, but at the very least, it has enough features to keep you busy experimenting for weeks! To open The GIMP:

The GIMP may not already be installed. In Linspire and Xandros in particular, you might need to use what you discovered in Chapter 12 to add this software before you can use it.

- ✔ **Fedora:** Choose Applications⇨Graphics⇨The GIMP.

- ✔ **Knoppix:** From the Main Menu, choose Graphics⇨GIMP Image Editor.

- ✔ **Linspire:** Use the tools in Chapter 12 to open CNR to the Multimedia & Design section and install GIMP. When installed, you can find this program by choosing Launch⇨Run Programs⇨Multimedia & Design⇨ Image Editor (The GIMP).

- ✔ **Mandriva:** From the Main Menu, choose Multimedia⇨Graphics⇨The GIMP v2.

- ✔ **SuSE:** Choose Applications⇨Graphics⇨Image Editing⇨The GIMP.

✔ **Xandros:** Use the tools in Chapter 12 to open Xandros Networks, go to the Graphics section, and install GIMP Image Editor. When installed, choose Launch⇨Applications⇨Graphics⇨GIMP Image Editor to run the program.

✔ **Ubuntu:** Choose Applications⇨Graphics⇨Gimp Image Editor.

When you start The GIMP for the first time, you have to walk through its user setup routine. Fortunately, you can just click Continue each time, unless you're a graphics guru who has a particular reason to want to do things in a different way. After you've clicked past all these dialog boxes, a collection of one or more dialog boxes pops up containing the GIMP main dialog box (see Figure 18-11) plus additional tool dialog boxes. I recommend closing all but the main one for now, just to keep your screen and brain uncluttered.

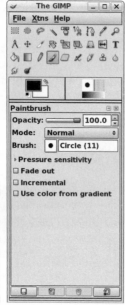
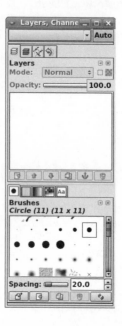

Figure 18-11:
The GIMP's
main dialog
box
in Fedora
Core 5.

The GIMP is an incredibly complex program, with entire books written for the people who really want to use it heavily. Great starter links for working with The GIMP are

✔ **GIMP Tutorials Pointer Page:** http://empyrean.lib.ndsu.nodak.edu/~nem/gimp/tuts

✔ **RRU GIMP Tutorial:** www.rru.com/~meo/gimp/Tutorial

✔ **The official GIMP.org site's tutorials page:** www.gimp.org/tutorials

✔ **The GIMP Savvy Web site (with a full book available for reading online):** http://gimp-savvy.com/

Watchin' Movies

These days, you can watch many kinds of movies on your computer. Whether it's a Flash animation, a DVD, or a movie trailer, you've got the tools that you need right at your fingertips (or just a click away). You may have even installed some already, while trying to access other multimedia features. Here are some of the tools of the trade.

Watching a DVD in Linux is a bit of a legal quagmire if you live in the United States. The Digital Millennium Copyright Act (DMCA) and other issues make it tricky for any open source program to navigate the licensing maze when it comes to movies that are encoded or protected in various fashions. However, not all DVDs have such countermeasures enabled: There are DVDs that Americans can watch under Linux with no trouble. (Note that I say *watch*, and not *copy* or *pirate*.)

For more on the DMCA and the problems it causes, see `anti-dmca.org`.

To watch a DVD in Linux, first check Chapter 11 to see what your distribution will do if you just pop a DVD into your drive — you may not need to do anything but put the DVD into the drive and let the system do its thing. You can also start a player by hand, although you may have to download it first:

- ✔ **Fedora:** Choose Applications⇨Sound & Video⇨Movie Player. Use Chapter 12 to add more.

- ✔ **Knoppix:** From the Main Menu, choose Multimedia⇨Video⇨xine media player.

- ✔ **Linspire:** Choose Launch⇨Run Programs⇨Multimedia & Design⇨Media Player (Kplayer). If this program can't play all of your DVDs, purchase a legal, full-featured DVD player from the Click And Run Warehouse by using the tools discussed in Chapter 12.

- ✔ **Mandriva:** From the Main Menu, choose Multimedia⇨Video⇨Kaffeine.

- ✔ **SuSE:** Choose Applications⇨Multimedia⇨Video Player⇨Totem or one of the others

- ✔ **Xandros:** Launch⇨Applications⇨Multimedia⇨Video Player.

- ✔ **Ubuntu:** Choose Applications⇨Sound & Video⇨Totem Movie Player.

The version of Totem that comes with Fedora and some other distributions is stripped-down in terms of formats it can support — again, this is a legal issue more than anything else. Often it is possible to replace this version with the full one by uninstalling Totem, adding software repositories that contain multimedia tools, and then installing the full version of Totem from the repositories (all of these skills are discussed in Chapter 12). This is the solution I recommend for watching DVDs.

The section "Listening to Internet Radio" earlier in this chapter mentioned some additional tools you may want. Typically, it's a good idea to have as many of these installed as you can manage, in case one works better with a particular file with another. Also, there is mplayer, which I recommend along with its associated plugin for watching content from your hard drive. I will spend a moment getting you acquainted with mplayer (see Chapter 12 for how to install it).

When you launch Mplayer, the tool shown in Figure 18-12 appears.

Figure 18-12:
The
Mplayer
media
player.

The player may load automatically when you double-click the file or insert the media you want to watch, or it may not. If it doesn't load automatically, right-click the main window and select Open. Within, select Play File to play a file on your hard drive, navigate to the file you want to play in the file browser, and then click OK. The controls on the "media player panel" work as you might expect as far as stop, pause, play, and so on go.

Enjoy!

Chapter 19

Windows-Only Media Formats and Programs

A gentleman is a man who can play the accordion, but doesn't.

— Unknown

There is little that is more maddening than to find a file online or have someone send a file, just to discover that you can't use it. While this issue is less of a problem for Linux users as each day passes, things do sometimes still crop up that have to be worked around, particularly if you switch to Linux and then realize you have certain programs you can't live without and can't seem to replace.

Fortunately, you have a number of options available whether you need to use files or run Windows programs. If you're looking for software to try with existing files or a Linux equivalent to a beloved Windows program, then a good place to start (aside from Chapter 12) is www.linuxrsp.ru/win-lin-soft/table-eng.html. Here, you can see why today it's surprising if you can't find a program under Linux to do what you need. Some of this software is "commercial" in that it's for sale, and other programs are free.

If you do find that you actually need to run a Windows program under Linux, you have both commercial and free options available, although you have far more commercial options. This chapter looks at both possibilities so you can choose what meets your needs.

Commercial Software

A growing number of commercially available tools let you work with anything from Microsoft Office to your Windows games under Linux. Mind you, ultimately the Linux user's goal is to not have to use any of these extra program layers — but in the meantime, it's nice not to be inconvenienced. I've reviewed, or at least used, every one of these products (often more than once over the years), so I'm not just going by their Web sites.

Many of these vendors offer server, as well as desktop products. I'm focusing on the desktop. For more about their server products, check out their Web sites.

CodeWeavers

CodeWeavers (www.codeweavers.com) provides an excellent product that I use from time to time: CrossOver Office. This program allows you to use Microsoft Office (along with a growing number of office applications) directly under Linux. It also comes with a hefty number of plug-ins (see Figure 19-1) that you might miss when it comes to Web surfing. It's a bit jarring to run Microsoft Word and Windows Media Player under Linux at first — because there's no *native* (without special software) way to do this otherwise — but it's certainly handy. You can even use the iPod's iTunes through CrossOver Office!

What I most appreciate about CodeWeavers (and all these companies, really) is that they are very upfront about what works really well, what works except for a few features, and what doesn't work. All you have to do is check their Web site. For those who always seem to want to scream "piracy" when it comes to Linux, you actually do have to own the programs you want to run (say, Microsoft Office) and install them through CrossOver Office off their original CDs or DVDs. However, you don't have to own the version of Microsoft Windows the software would run under. CodeWeavers has built a reimplementation of the necessary Windows functionality under the hood instead.

Figure 19-1:
The
CrossOver
Office Install
Software
dialog box,
in Fedora
Core 5.

Are you an iPod and iTunes junkie? There's no Linux version of iTunes available, but CrossOver Office lets you run iTunes for Windows under Linux.

A plus to CodeWeavers CrossOver Office is that the applications run in individual windows just like every other program on your machine. A minus is that not all Windows software is supported, because hooks have to be built under the hood for each new program.

CrossOver Office comes with the Xandros Deluxe and Business desktops (available for installation through the Xandros Networks; see Chapter 12) and is available for purchase from the Xandros Networks store for other Xandros users. Those using other distributions can purchase this product directly from the company's Web site.

Win4Lin

Another option is Win4Lin (www.win4lin.com). Win4Lin actually offers you a platform within which you install Microsoft Windows (so have those CDs handy) and then run programs on top of it. At this writing, Win4Lin supports Windows 95, 98, ME, 2000, and XP (see Figure 19-2).

A plus for Win4Lin is that it supports a more full range of Windows software. By default, this program makes you run all of your Windows applications within a single windowframe. See the Win4Lin Administration Guide for information on how to change this behavior.

Figure 19-2:
Windows
XP under
Win4Lin
in Fedora
Core 5.

Cedega

More interested in games than office tools? There's also TransGaming's Cedega (`www.transgaming.com`), which was once called WineX. This version of the free Wine project (see the upcoming section "Installing and Using Wine") is specifically designed to support Direct X, which is used in Windows to make programming for multimedia and games easier. Subscribers have access to regular updates, allowing them to make use of their favorite games and also add any games they like to the growing list of games that are being tested with the system.

Go to `www.transgaming.com/searchgame.php` to find a listing of the games, in order, that users have tried with Cedega (Figure 19-3) and what success they have had with these games.

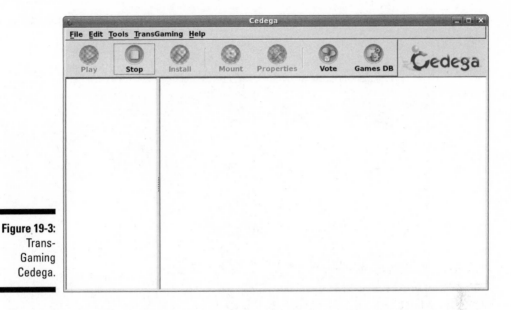

Figure 19-3:
Trans-
Gaming
Cedega.

A plus to Cedega is, again, that you don't need to keep those Windows (OS) CDs lying around. However, its support for individual games can be spotty, so be sure to check the Web site before you invest in this product. Also, be sure to make use of the help forums!

VMware

If you absolutely *have* to do something under Windows itself but only have one computer and it's running Linux (or vice versa, for that matter), there's also VMware (www.vmware.com). This is a popular tool in technical support offices where people need access to many different kinds of machines to test things. It's also popular with authors, like myself, because it allows us to grab those tricky screenshots of the boot process and installer screens.

In VMware, you run a full session of another operating system (or even an extra session of the same one you're running on the main machine) within your desktop — see Figure 19-4. If your machine is powerful enough, you could have five different operating systems all running in their own windows on a single computer.

Figure 19-4:
A VMware window containing Windows XP, but running in Linux.

A minus to VMWare is that it requires a bit of extra oomph in your system. Check out its requirements and then try to go as far *above* them as you can. It also runs in a self-contained window. A plus, though, is that this program really is the next best thing to buying another computer.

Installing and Using Wine

And then there's Wine (www.winehq.org), a complete rebuild of Microsoft Windows functionality that runs under Linux. Wine is in many ways the mother of everything in the previous section. However, because it's a free and very complicated project, it's not quite as friendly as the commercial versions. It's kind of like the others but with all the makeup and hairspray removed.

Some Linux distributions offer Wine RPMs directly on their installation CDs or through their packaging schemes. For the distributions covered in this book, do the following to install WINE for the distributions that don't have it already installed, or to start it for the distributions that do have it. (See Chapter 12 for more details on installing software.)

- ✔ **Fedora Core:** Available through the Package Manager as the wine package, depending on what repositories you've added (see Chapter 12).

- ✔ **Knoppix:** Available through the command line, not the Main Menu.

- ✔ **Linspire:** Available through the CNR Warehouse in the base section (see Chapter 12).

- ✔ **Mandriva:** Available through the package installation program (Chapter 12). Search for wine.

- ✔ **SuSE:** Available through YaST's software installation routine (see Chapter 12). You can find it in Software➪Software Management. Search for the wine package.

- ✔ **Xandros:** Not available. The truly adventurous are welcome to go to www.winehq.org, click the Download link, and try to build this program from source code (see Chapter 12).

- ✔ **Ubuntu:** Not available. See the Xandros entry for more.

You can find the Wine documentation at www.winehq.org/site/docs/wineusr-guide/index. Start in the "Configuring Wine" section.

Now comes the fun part — trying to run your old Windows software. You don't really run Wine, per se. Instead, you invoke Wine whenever you need to use something from the Windows world. To install a Windows program through Wine, insert the CD-ROM or floppy into the appropriate drive. Your distribution might open the File Manager for you, or you may need to open the File Manager manually. Regardless, your goal is to run the installation routine, which is typically SETUP.EXE. You can double-click this icon in the File Manager and, when asked what program you want to use to open this file, answer wine.

As I write this, I'm trying some old home-design program I bought back when I was silly enough to think I'd be able to afford to build a house before I was ninety. Because it's difficult to describe a standard Wine session, I thought I'd walk you through how this goes for me.

The installer loads and runs just fine. I stick with the defaults (because Wine is still a work-in-progress and it's best not to taunt it with getting too fancy) and then wait while the installer adds all the files to my SuSE system. Now, to run my new-old software. To run a Wine program, I first need to know what the path is to that program. I can find it by looking in the ~/.wine directory. In this case, the program was installed into /home/dee/.wine/fake_windows/ Program Files/HOUSE. The file house.exe looks like the one for launching the program.

If you're trying to find the .wine directory in the GUI and can't see it, you probably have to go to the View menu and choose Show Hidden Files. So, to run the program, I double-click it and, when asked what program to run it with, enter wine. That's it (see Figure 19-5). Now pull out those old Windows 95 and 98 CDs and give them a try! Not all of them will work, but some probably will. The cool thing is that you can keep trying them on and off over time as newer versions of Wine come out.

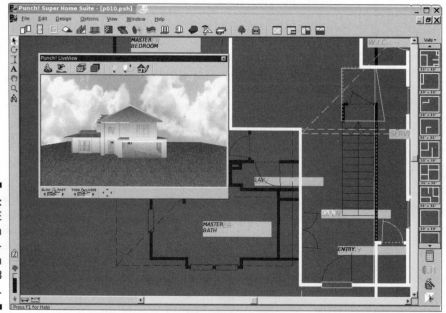

Figure 19-5:
WINE
running an
old home-
design
Windows 98
program.

Part V
The Part of Tens

The 5th Wave

By Rich Tennant

"Think of our relationship as the latest
version of Red Hat Linux – I will not
share a directory on the love-branch
of your life."

In this part . . .

In this part of the book, I cover answers to the questions most frequently asked about Linux. I explain some key Linux installation and setup points, as well as share more routine troubleshooting tips and tricks. This is where to turn if you are having some trouble and need a helping hand, or if there's something bugging you about your setup. I also give you two cool uses for that Knoppix part of the book's DVD.

Chapter 20

Ten Troubleshooting Tips

- -

In This Chapter

▶ Dealing with frozen installations

▶ Changing your boot environment

▶ Recovering when you see some black-and-white text screen!

▶ Escaping a hung GUI

▶ Using multiple resolutions

- -

*T*roubleshooting is like reading a mystery novel. You have some facts, symptoms, and details, but you don't know whodunit. You have to take whatever information you have, work with that data, weigh the various possibilities, and then narrow them to a single suspect. Finally, you need to test your theory and prove that your suspect is the guilty party.

Troubleshooting problems in Linux (or any operating system) can encompass many hardware and software issues. Whether the problem is the operating system, the hardware, or a service giving you fits, you can use some basic troubleshooting techniques to start your investigations:

✔ **Document the problem.** Write down any and all symptoms that the system is showing, including actions you can and can't do. Jot down any information you see in error messages.

✔ **Examine the Linux log files.** You can find most of these in the /var/log directory. Look for the word "error."

✔ **Compare your problem system with a working system running the same distribution and version.** Sometimes, comparing configuration files and settings may uncover the problem or narrow the possibilities.

✔ **Check connections.** Check to make sure that all the hardware is connected properly and powered on. Verify that all cables and connections are attached properly. There's always someone, somewhere, accidentally kicking a cable out from a wall connection.

✔ **Remove new hardware.** Remove any hardware that you have changed or added recently (before the problem started) and see whether the problem disappears. If so, you can probably conclude that the new or changed hardware (or its driver) is the culprit and start researching solutions.

✔ **Reduce the number of active programs.** Stop running unnecessary services and applications that aren't related to the problem at hand. You may more easily figure out what's happening if other services and applications aren't getting in the way.

✔ **Check to see whether the problem is reproducible.** Does the same sequence of events produce the same problem? Suppose that when you try to print to a color printer, nothing happens. If nothing happens *every* time you attempt to print, the problem is reproducible. If, instead, sometimes your information is printed and at other times it isn't, the problem pattern isn't the same and isn't reproducible — or it's caused by something more complicated than just clicking one button. Unfortunately, problems that are nonreproducible are more difficult to resolve because it seems that no set pattern of events re-creates those problems.

After you've come up with a solution, take a few moments to document the situation. Note the symptoms of the problem, its cause, and the solution you implement. The next time you encounter the same problem, you can call on your notes for a solution rather than reinvent the wheel.

If you don't have any problems to troubleshoot (yet), document your environment *before* you do. Making a backup of your /etc directory and your /boot directory is a great place to start.

"The Linux Installer Froze"

When you're installing Linux, the installation may just freeze. If it does, wait a bit and make sure that the installation program really froze. (Sometimes, the software just takes a while to process information.) If the software looks like it has frozen, there's no harm in rebooting your computer and starting over — just as you would do with any operating system installation. Sometimes, you can reboot and never have that problem again. At other times, the problem may happen twice in a row and then be fine the third time. Be sure to try several times before giving up.

If the installation still freezes in the same spot or close to the same spot, go to the distribution's support pages (see Chapter 2). These pages may talk about some known problems and solutions that can help you and should show you how to join discussion lists in order to get more assistance.

Otherwise, diagnosing the problem can be tricky and may seem more like voodoo than science. Here are some tips:

✔ **If this problem happens repeatedly at exactly the same spot, you may have a bad installation disk.** If you're a Fedora Core or Red Hat Enterprise Linux user, see the next section, "For Fedora Core Users," and then return here if that technique doesn't solve your problem. Otherwise, try the disk in another machine if possible and see whether the installation fails in the same place there. If you purchased this disk with a Linux distribution, contact the distribution's technical support team. If you got the disk with a book, contact the publisher's technical support team. If you burned the disk yourself, try burning a new copy at a slower speed.

✔ **If this problem happens repeatedly at exactly the same spot and you don't have a bad installation disk, the trouble may be with one of your machine's hardware components.** If you can, try trading hardware between machines. If not, you may need to choose a different machine on which to install Linux or try another distribution.

✔ **If the problem seems to happen randomly, your particular Linux distribution may not be compatible with that particular machine.** Again, you can try trading some hardware around, installing Linux on another machine, or using another distribution.

 If you're not sure whether your installer has frozen, try pressing various combinations of Alt+F#, where # corresponds to one of the function keys. Depending on the distribution, the installer has not completely frozen if you can see different screens when you try this technique.

For Fedora Core Users

When installing Red Hat Linux 7.3 or later (Fedora Core 5 is considered "later"), a special solution is available to people who run into problems that seem to have absolutely no explanation, such as the installer freezing. This solution doesn't work with the DVD provided with this book, because it contains more than just the Fedora software, so continue with this section only if you downloaded your own DVD or purchased it from a third party, or if you downloaded or otherwise acquired the Fedora CDs.

If your installation keeps dying while Anaconda (the Red Hat installer program) is placing packages on your hard drive, follow these steps to try to fix it:

1. **Place the DVD-ROM or the first Fedora Core CD-ROM into your drive.**

2. **Reboot the machine.**

3. **Wait until you reach the black-and-white screen where you usually press Enter to start the installation.**

   If you reach a graphical installation screen, you missed the screen you're looking for. You need to reboot, repeat this step, and then proceed.

4. **At the prompt, type linux mediacheck and then press Enter.**

   Text scrolls by, and then you see a screen with a bright blue background. Then the CD Found dialog box appears.

5. **Tab to the OK button and press Enter to proceed to the media examination.**

   This step opens the Media Check dialog box. If you've changed your mind and just want to start the installation, use the Tab or arrow keys to select Skip and then press Enter.

6. **If you want to test the first CD-ROM or the DVD-ROM, tab to the Test button and press Enter. If you want to test another installation CD-ROM, tab to the Eject CD button and press Enter.**

   If you chose the second option, remove the first CD-ROM from the CD-ROM drive and replace it with the CD-ROM you want to test. Close the CD-ROM drive and make sure that Test is selected.

7. **Press Enter to begin the media check.**

   The Media Check status box opens and shows you the name assigned to the DVD-ROM or CD-ROM and how much progress has been made. At the end of the inspection, the Media Check Result dialog box opens.

8. **Look at the text after and the result is.**

   If the result is PASS, nothing is wrong with the DVD-ROM or CD-ROM itself. Your installation woes are caused by something else. Return to the section "The Linux Installer Froze," earlier in this chapter.

   If the result is FAIL, the DVD-ROM or CD-ROM you just tested is flawed. If you purchased this CD-ROM or DVD-ROM, you need to talk to the company you purchased it from to see whether you can get a replacement. On the other hand, if you burned your own DVD-ROM or CD-ROM, I recommend doing one of the following:

   - Burn the DVD-ROM or CD-ROM again, at a speed of 4x or lower.

   - Burn the DVD-ROM or CD-ROM again on a newer drive with BurnProof technology (www.digital-sanyo.com/BURN-Proof) or something similar.

If the DVD-ROM that came with this book is defective, contact the technical support address listed in this book, not Red Hat. However, remember that the media-checking routine does not give you a reliable PASS or FAIL for this particular DVD-ROM.

"I Told the Installer to Test My Graphics, and They Failed"

The installer may have misguessed what hardware you have. Double-check the settings as best you can. If they look right, try choosing a lower resolution for now and testing again, and if that fails try a lower number of colors and test again. You can then try setting things back the way you want them after the machine is fully installed and updated, when it hopefully will have a fix for whatever the problem might be.

"The Installer Tested My Graphics Fine, but My GUI Won't Start"

If your Linux installation program showed you a GUI test screen saying that you were ready to proceed with the rest of the installation, you probably expected that the GUI would start with no problem. Unfortunately, that doesn't always happen.

Each distribution has its own set of graphics configuration tools. If you boot your machine for the first time and see error messages when you're trying to enter the GUI automatically or when you type `startx` to start the GUI manually, use the following tools to fix the problem:

- ✔ In Fedora Core, use `system-config-display`.

- ✔ In Knoppix, you don't install. Use the options available when you boot it in order to tell it specifics about your display.

- ✔ In Linspire, use `xorgconfig`.

- ✔ In Mandriva, use `drakconf` and select Hardware⇨Configure Your Monitor.

- ✔ In SuSE, use `sax2`.

- ✔ In Ubuntu, none of these tools is included.

- ✔ In Xandros, use `xorgconfig`.

- ✔ Your last resort is `xorgconfig`. This fully text-based tool *should* be available with most distributions.

"I Think I'm in Linux, but I Don't Know What to Do!"

Two different screens tend to cause panic to folks new to Linux. The first of these screens, shown in Figure 20-1, is in fact a sign that you installed the software and booted the machine successfully. Jump for joy! It's just that you're booting into the command-line environment rather than the GUI environment. If you reach a screen similar to the one shown in Figure 20-1, the computer is asking you to log in with the username for an account and a password that you created during the installation process.

Figure 20-1:
A Linux command-line login prompt.

If you created only the root account, you can log in there as `root`.

After you enter the username and password, you find yourself at the screen shown in Figure 20-2, which just happens to be the second spot where people get worried. If you see this screen, you have not only booted properly into Linux, but you're also logged in and using the machine! Give yourself a good pat on the back.

Figure 20-2:
Logged in at the Linux command line.

What do you do from here? Anything you want. Surf through this book for commands you want to run. Type startx to start up the GUI. If you didn't install any GUI (which means you selected a minimal install option with no graphical interface, or you actually unselected graphics), you may want to reinstall, or you' have to add all the tools by hand (which is not a quick job!)

"I Don't Want to Boot into This!"

Are you booting into the command-line environment when you want to use only the GUI? Or are you finding that you're already booting into the GUI and you would rather boot to that nice, clean, black-and-white command-line screen? You're not stuck with either of these options. You can change them at any time.

You can press Ctrl-Alt-F# to change out of the GUI to a command line terminal at any time and then Alt-F7 or Alt-F8 to switch back.

Changing your boot environment "permanently"

The word *permanently* is in quotes in the heading because you can, of course, go back and change this setting later, if you want. *Permanently* just refers to the fact that after you have made this change, every time you boot the system, it automatically goes into the preferred environment until you change it.

You can't make this change in Linspire, Ubuntu, or Xandros unless you want to boot into *single-user mode*, which is basically "safe mode" and not much use. Well, okay, you can, but you would need a techie friend to set up a bunch of stuff for you. Linspire and Xandros assume that you don't want to do this. You can't do this in Knoppix either, but then it's a LiveCD so you won't be doing anything permanent to it.

To make this change in Fedora, Mandriva, or SuSE, you need to edit what's called a *runlevel*. Fortunately, all three of these distributions use the same runlevel settings, so the instructions are the same for all of them:

    1. In the GUI, open a command line terminal.

        If you're not sure how to do so, see Chapter 14. If you're not in the GUI and you're already logged in, type su - to become the root user.

2. **Type** `cp /etc/inittab /etc/inittab.old` **to make a backup.**

   Now, if something happens while you're editing the `inittab` file, you can always restart fresh with the old version.

3. **Open the inittab file in your preferred text editor.**

   Some Linux text editors are covered in Chapter 16.

4. **Scroll down until you find a line similar to the following:**

   ```
   id:5:initdefault:
   ```

   This line appears near the top of the file. What you're interested in here is the number. In most mainstream Linux distributions, the number 5 tells Linux to boot into the GUI, and the number 3 tells Linux to boot into the command line. In the preceding example, therefore, I boot into the GUI.

5. **Change the number in this line.**

   If it's a 5, change it to 3, and vice versa. Make sure that all colons and other items are left properly in place, or else your machine will have problems booting later.

6. **Save and exit the file.**

   The changes go into effect the next time you reboot the system.

If you do end up having problems booting the system, in many current Linux distributions (including the one that comes with this book) your installation disk can be used as an emergency boot disk. Check your documentation for information about the distribution you're using if it's not Red Hat 10.

Changing your boot environment just for now

At any time, you can have your Linux box switch between full command-line mode and full GUI mode. The instructions I give here assume that you're using Fedora, Mandriva, or SuSE. (Knoppix, Linspire, Ubuntu, and Xandros don't give you this option.)

To switch between modes, do the following:

- ✔ To change from the GUI login to the command-line login, open a terminal window and type (as root) `init 3`.

- ✔ To change from the command line login to the GUI login, type (as root) `init 5`.

"I Want to Change Screen Resolutions"

Do you want or need to swap between resolutions in the GUI on the fly? Suppose that you want to use 1,024 x 768, but you work on Web pages and want to be able to see how they look in a browser at 800 x 600 or even 640 x 480. Your machine is very likely already set up to do this, but you just need to know how!

If your machine is set up for it, you can change resolutions by pressing the key combination Ctrl+Alt+Plus, where Plus is the big plus (+) sign on your number pad — you can't use the plus sign on the main keyboard for this one.

If you're using a keyboard without a number pad — as you will be if you're using a laptop — or your machine isn't set up to be able to change on the fly, you need to change your resolution through your display configuration program. You can find this option at:

- ✔ **Fedora:** Choose System➪Administration➪Display.
- ✔ **Knoppix and Linspire:** From the Main Menu, choose Control Center➪ Peripherals➪Display.
- ✔ **Mandriva:** From the Main Menu, choose System➪Configuration➪ Configure Your Desktop➪Peripherals➪Display.
- ✔ **SuSE:** Choose Desktop➪YaST➪Hardware➪Graphics Card And Monitor➪ Monitor.
- ✔ **Ubuntu:** Choose System➪Preferences➪Screen Resolution.
- ✔ **Xandros:** Choose Launch➪Control Center➪Display➪Settings.

"My GUI Is Hung, and I'm Stuck!"

One quick solution to this problem is the key combination Ctrl+Alt+Backspace. If this doesn't do the trick, your system is in really bad shape! Try to switch to a virtual terminal by using Ctrl+Alt+F5. If this key combination also does nothing, you need to reboot the machine.

"Help, My Machine Hangs During Boot!"

When configuring a Linux machine, you may encounter problems with the `/etc/grub.conf` file. This file indicates the operating system or systems to which your system can boot, and the file also contains Linux start-up settings. Linux can boot from any of your hard drives — not just the master IDE drive on the primary IDE channel. Consider this list of potential solutions if the `/etc/grub.conf` file makes trouble:

- ✔ If you have altered or added hard drives, you may need to change the `boot` line in the `/etc/grub.conf` file.

- ✔ If you haven't made hardware changes, check to make sure that your `/etc/grub.conf` file is referring to the correct location of the Linux image. (The program code that loads and executes at runtime and is located in the `/boot` directory.)

- ✔ If the location under the `/boot` directory or the device for the root entry is incorrect, your system can't boot to Linux. In this situation, a rescue or emergency disk is helpful. Refer to Chapter 5 for instructions on using a rescue disk.

- ✔ If you're working with a multiboot operating system environment, be sure that your `/etc/grub.conf` file contains entries for each of your operating systems. Each operating system or Linux installation needs to be in separate entries.

- ✔ If your file contains entries to switch to a higher-resolution display and you have boot problems, try reducing the video setting to simple VGA.

Linux allows you to use spaces and other characters in filenames that you may or may not be able to use in filenames on other operating systems. However, some Linux applications may stumble when they encounter file or directory names containing spaces. Usually, a safe bet is to stick with alphanumeric characters and avoid spaces and odd characters, such as question marks and exclamation points.

"Aaargh! I Forgot My Root Password! What Do I Do?"

Fear not. You have a way around this problem! You need to boot into *single user mode,* which you can accomplish by rebooting your machine and then doing the following:

- ✔ **Fedora:** When you see the blue screen with the words "Press any key to enter the menu," press a key. At the GRUB boot screen, press **E**, which takes you to a configuration file. Use the arrow keys to go to the line starting with `kernel`, and press **E** again to edit that line. At the end of the line, add the word `single`, press Enter to put the change into place, and then press **B** to boot the machine.

✔ **Knoppix:** You can just reboot the machine and start over.

✔ **Linspire, SuSE, and Xandros:** Even in single user/failsafe mode, you need the root password for these distributions. See your user documentation or contact technical support for how to recover your root password.

✔ **Mandriva:** Reboot the computer and at the boot menu, select the Failsafe option.

✔ **Ubuntu:** When you see the words "Loading GRUB menu, please wait," press Esc. Then choose the topmost recovery mode option.

No matter what distribution you're using, now's your chance to change the root password to one you can remember. Type passwd and then enter the new password twice as directed. When you're done, type exit and then boot the machine normally.

Chapter 21

Two Knoppix Ten-Steps

Until you walk a mile in another man's moccasins you can't imagine the smell.

— Robert Byrne

LiveCDs are a great way to experiment with Linux in general, or a particular distribution of Linux, because many of them offer a live version for download or purchase. Because Knoppix is recommended as the LiveCD to use for preinstallation tasks in this book, I thought I would make sure to give you some more fun things you can do with this CD-ROM so that you don't feel like you wasted your time burning it! I won't even do what my husband suggested and make one of the ten entries be to use the disk as a Frisbee, because I'd hate for you to feel cheated out of something truly cool.

Rescuing Files off a Machine That Won't Boot

One cool use for Knoppix is to recover the important files that might be left on a messed-up computer that otherwise won't boot. You can use Knoppix for this task whether those files are in Linux or Windows (even on an NTFS partition!). Then you can either e-mail the files to yourself — you can find a simple e-mail program in the Main Menu where you choose Internet⇨KMail — or attach a USB storage device to the machine and copy the data onto it.

To access a USB storage device, plug it in, and Knoppix automatically adds an icon on your desktop for it! However, there's a caveat here. It mounts all filesystems as read-only so that you're going to have to change the USB drive to read-write first:

1. Click the terminal with the black screen icon on your panel.

A terminal window appears.

2. Type `su -` to become the root (administrative) user.

You're not prompted for a password.

3. Look at the new icon and see what was put in the brackets.

For example, [sda1], which is the typical label for a USB drive.

4. Type `mount -o remount,rw /mnt/`*`drive`* to remount the drive as read-write.

So, for example, `mount -o remount,rw /mnt/sda1`.

5. Find where the files are that you want to copy off your hard drive(s), using the GUI.

If you have lots in lots of places, focus on one group for now and come back and do another later.

6. Look in the Location bar for the folder the files are in.

So, for example, if it says file:/mnt/hda1/web, the folder is /mnt/hda1/web.

7. Use the `cd` command to change to this directory in the command line terminal.

For example, `cd /mnt/hda1/web`.

8. Type `ls` to see the directory's contents.

There they are!

9. Use the `cp` command to copy the file(s) you want to copy over.

Some hints:

- To copy all files in this directory and all its subdirectories to /dev/sda1, type `cp -r * /dev/sda1`

- To copy all the files in this directory but no subdirectories, type `cp * /dev/sda1`

- To copy all files whose names begin with an a, type `cp a* /dev/sda1`

- You may want to bundle and compress the files first. In that case, use the program found in the Main Menu by choosing Utilities⇨Ark to do so and tell it to create the archive directly on the USB drive, which shows up on your desktop as Hard Disk Partition [sda1] (which refers to /dev/sda1 and /mnt/sda1).

10. **Right-click the USB device on your desktop and select Unmount.**

This action makes sure that all your data was saved properly.

Recovering a Root Password with Knoppix

If you're using SuSE, Linspire, Xandros, or another distribution that requires you to enter a root password even to enter single user mode, you need external tools to help you recover when you forget what your root password is. This problem is another major reason that many system administrators keep Knoppix on hand. To recover your root password, do the following:

1. **Place the Knoppix CD into your CD-ROM drive and reboot the computer. After the computer successfully boots into Knoppix, determine which partition refers to your main Linux installation. If you currently don't have a file browser window open anywhere within that partition (see Chapter 11 for discussions of partitions), click the partition icon to open the browser.**

   You're looking for your root (/) partition. Chapter 11 details what you find there if that helps. Basically, open each of the partition icons on your desktop and figure out which one looks like the right section of your filesystem. For example, if the root partition is /dev/hda3, click the Hard Disk Partition [hda3] icon.

2. **Click the Terminal Program icon on your panel and then type su - to access the root user's account. Make sure to close the file browsing window that's accessing your root partition, and then type mount -o remount -o rw /dev/partition to remove the partition and read it as a full read-write filesystem.**

   You're not prompted for a password when switching to root. For an example of what to type, if your root partition was on /dev/hda3, you type cd /mnt/hda3.

3. **Type cd /mnt/partition/etc to change to the /etc directory inside the mounted root partition's base directory.**

4. Type `cp passwd passwd-orig` to make a backup copy of your main user and password file, and then type `joe passwd` to open the `/etc/passwd` file in the joe text editor.

   Don't skip the copying step. It lets you revert to the original file if you mess something up! When inside joe, you can press Ctrl-K and then the H key to display the Help menu at the top of the screen at any time. To get rid of that menu, press the same key combination again.

5. Look for the line similar to `root:x:0:0:root:/root:/bin/bash` and delete the x (or anything else) from between the first two colons so that the line looks more like the following:

   ```
   root::0:0:root:/root:/bin/bash
   ```

6. Press Ctrl-K and then the X key to save the file and exit the program. When asked for the name of the file to save, just press Enter to accept the default.

7. Type `reboot` to reboot the machine. When the CD-ROM ejects, remove it from the drive and press Enter to continue rebooting.

8. After you reboot into your system, log into a regular user account. Open a terminal window and type `su` - before pressing Enter to become the root user.

   When you deleted that *x* in Step 5, you actually erased any password from the root user. If you're prompted for a password, just press Enter without typing anything.

9. Open the /etc/passwd file in your preferred text editor. Find the line you edited before and add the x back into place between the two colons.

   It should look something like this initially:

   ```
   root::0:0:root:/root:/bin/bash
   ```

   Remember, this is a lowercase x you are adding. It should look like the following when you're done:

   ```
   root:x:0:0:root:/root:/bin/bash
   ```

10. Save and exit the file. Then type `passwd` and press Enter.

    You're prompted for a new root password.

Problem fixed!

Part VI
Appendixes

The 5th Wave   By Rich Tennant

"When we started the company, we weren't going to call it Red Hat. But eventually we decided it sounded better than Beard of Bees Linux."

In this part . . .

This part adds some extra material to support the rest of this book. Starting with the ever-popular and useful Appendix A, you find a reasonably comprehensive and friendly compendium of common Linux commands, ready for use as a desktop reference. Appendix B provides an overview of and information about the DVD included with this book (and how to get a set of CDs if you don't have a DVD-ROM drive), including basic booting instructions when installing Fedora Core Linux and a list of what's on the DVD.

Appendix A

Common Linux Commands

Computing novices often marvel at the keyboard dance Linux experts typically perform. Sure, these experts know about modern advances like the mouse and graphical interface, but these keyboard musicians prefer the home keys and find that they can work faster that way. It takes some time to reach this level of proficiency, but every expert was a novice at one time, and any novice can become an expert with plenty of practice.

In this appendix, you find the commands listed by themes, according to what they can actually do for you.

So, read on — and dazzle your friends with your command-prompt finesse. When they ask you how and where you figured out all those commands, just smile and mumble something about the voices in your head — and, of course, keep this section dog-eared and within reach of your computer.

Linux Commands by Function

Because every command serves a specific purpose, organizing these tools into groups according to their individual functions isn't difficult. If you know what you need to do but don't know which command does the job, flip through this section to start your search. From here, you can dig further by referencing man pages and other help information (online sites and reference books, for example) or by looking in this book's index for further coverage.

To access a man page, type **man *command*** at a command prompt. For example, man ls shows you the help information for the file listing command.

Getting Help

When you're digging around for help on a command, you can call on an interesting range of shell commands for assistance, as shown in Table A-1.

Table A-1	Shell Help Commands
Command	*Purpose*
apropos	Looks for commands that contain a keyword in their man page descriptions.
info	One way of finding help information. You can find instructions for this tool at www.gnu.org/software/texinfo/manual/info/, or you can use the built-in tutorial by starting the info tool and pressing the H key when inside it.
man	The primary way of getting help in Linux and Unix.
whatis	Gets a one-line description of a command.

Locating details about the command-prompt options of a command is a never-ending pursuit. The man page system provides some helpful guides at your fingertips for rapidly finding this detailed information.

Archiving and compressing

Although disk space isn't as much of a premium as it once was, bandwidth and backup media still are. Subsequently, this group provides a potpourri of tools for compacting and organizing data for storage, as shown in Table A-2.

Table A-2	Archiving and Compressing Tools
Command	*Purpose*
bzip2	Compresses files into .bz2 format. Used mostly for incredibly large sets of text files (which is what source code actually is).
bunzip2	Uncompresses .bz2 files.

Command	*Purpose*
compress	Compresses files into `.Z` format. Pretty old and not used much in the Linux world.
gunzip	Uncompresses `.gz` files and `.tgz` files.
gzip	Compresses files into `.gz` format.
tar	Packages files together in a group. The most common way of using this command is `tar xvf filename`, such as `tar xvf download.tar`.
uncompress	Uncompresses files from `.Z` format.
unzip	Uncompresses files from `.zip` format.
zip	Compresses files into `.zip` format.

Built-in bash commands

Some commands don't even seem to exist if you try to look up their help information in the man pages, and the commands don't show up as files on your system. Remember, as you type commands at the prompt, that you're communicating with a type of program called a *shell*. (In my case, it's bash, the default Linux shell.) The shell has a set of commands, included in the following list, that you can use to communicate with it, as shown in Table A-3.

Table A-3	Shell Commands
Command	*Purpose*
alias	Creates or lists command shortcuts.
env	Lists your current environment variables and their settings.
export	Whenever you're told to set an environment variable, create the variable and then use this command so that the variable will be remembered properly.
history	Lists off the last 1,000 commands you've typed.
unalias	Removes command shortcuts.

If you try to view the man page entry for some of these commands, you find instead the help information for BASH BUILTINS loads. To search through this manual, press the forward slash (/) key to open the man search interface and then type the name of the command you want to search for. Press Enter to start the search. The interface stops in the first spot where the term is found. If you want to try again, press the N key to proceed to the next occurrence of the word.

For example, you might be reading the massive bash man page (type man bash to access this page), but perhaps you're only interested in items related to *prompts,* which are the bits of text that appear to the left of your cursor in a text window. An example prompt is

```
[dee@catherine dee]$
```

So, you might type /prompt and press Enter to jump down to the first instance of this word. If the text around the word doesn't reflect what you're looking for, you press the N key to jump to the next one, and so on.

Files and file system

No matter which operating system you're using, it's hard to do anything without being able to find your way through and work with the file system. The following utilities help you find your way:

File organization

Boxing, packing, sorting, shipping — I'm always shuffling files around on my system. File organization commands provide tools for moving files and file system units around, as shown in Table A-4.

Table A-4	File Organization Tools
Command	*Purpose*
cd	Changes directories.
cp	Copies a file.
df	Shows partitions and how much space they have.
du	Shows how much disk is being used in the current directory and below.
ln	Creates a shortcut.

Command	Purpose
ls	Lists the contents of a directory or information about a file.
mkdir	Creates a directory.
mv	Moves or renames a file.
pwd	Shows the path for the directory you're currently in.
rm	Deletes a file.
rmdir	Deletes an empty directory.

File attributes

Files are much like candy bars. The wrappers provide information about the ingredients, size, and package date — all descriptive of the tasty nugget inside. (Perhaps the wrapper is even childproof.) Files keep all this wrapper information in an *inode.* Along with the capability to change file inode information, these commands can return data about the content of the file, as shown in Table A-5.

Table A-5	File Attributes Commands
Command	**Purpose**
chgrp	Changes the group associated with a file.
chmod	Changes a file's permissions.
chown	Changes who owns a file.
file	Shows what type of file you're dealing with.
stat	Shows some statistics about the file.
touch	Creates an empty file of this name.
wc	Shows how many words, lines, and so on are in this file.

File locators

Where, oh, where can my file be? These commands, shown in Table A-6, help you locate files in Linux's monster tree-structure file system:

Table A-6	File Locators Commands
Command	**Purpose**
find	Hard-core filesystem search tool.
locate	Lighter-weight filesystem search tool.
which	Tells you the path for the program that would be run if you typed this command.

File viewers

Text file browsing is a favorite pastime of many a system user. These tools provide a variety of utilities for viewing the contents of readable text files of all sizes. Unlike using a full-screen editor, you cannot damage the contents of a file with these commands, shown in Table A-7, because they're just viewers, not editors:

Table A-7	File Viewers
Command	**Purpose**
cat	Dumps the contents of the file to your screen.
head	Shows the first ten lines of a file.
less	Shows the file a screen at a time.
more	Shows the file a screen at a time.
tail	Shows the last ten lines of a file.

File system commands

These commands, listed in Table A-8, provide information or perform actions on the entire file system, from creation and tuning to repair and recovery. Some of these commands return data only, whereas others also provide you with surgical instruments for serious file-system hacking:

Table A-8	File System Commands
Command	**Purpose**
badblocks	Searches a partition for bad blocks.
e2fsck	Checks and repairs an ext2 or ext3 filesystem.
e2label	Applies a filesystem label to an ext2 or ext3 partition.

Command	Purpose
eject	Ejects a CD or DVD.
fsck	Can check and repair many types of filesystems.
mkfs	Creates a filesystem (format a partition).
mount	Loads a partition into your filesystem.
sync	Saves all information out of buffers onto disks.
tune2fs	Adjusts ext2 and ext3 filesystem parameters.
umount	Removes a partition from the filesystem.

mtools

The mtools suite of utilities provides a nice way to transfer information to your Microsoft friends. Although Linux has native support for Microsoft Windows and DOS file systems, your Microsoft cohorts don't have access to Linux (ext2 and ext3) file systems. To keep everyone happy, you can buy preformatted MS-DOS disks and use them with the mtools commands (see Table A-9) so that you can swap them back and forth with your friends who are using Windows:

Table A-9	mTools Commands
Command	**Purpose**
mcd	Changes directory in DOS format on a DOS disk.
mcopy	Copies DOS files to and from Linux.
mdel	Deletes a DOS file.
mdeltree	Deletes a DOS directory and its contents.
mdir	Lists a DOS directory's contents.
mdu	Shows how much space is taken and available for a DOS partition.
mformat	Formats a partition for DOS.
mlabel	Applies a DOS volume label.
mmd	Creates a DOS directory.
mmount	Mounts a DOS disk or partition.
mmove	Moves or renames a DOS file or directory.

System control

These commands provide system-wide information and control. Normal users can run many commands to obtain system information; however, commands that actively change the configuration of the system need to run while you're logged in as root — or have utilized the su command to temporarily become the superuser.

Administration

Some administration commands, shown in Table A-10, don't fall neatly into a category.

Table A-10	Administration Commands
Command	*Purpose*
passwd	Change a particular user's password. Any user can run this command to change their own password. Only root can use it to change someone else's.
su	Switch to another user account without logging out of this one. The best way to use this command is su – so your filesystem path and other information is loaded.

Kernel module handling

You may sometimes need to add kernel support for an additional device (software or hardware). If this need arises, you have a limited number of choices: You can either rebuild the kernel or install a loadable kernel module. Although rebuilding a kernel doesn't exactly require a PhD in nuclear science, consider it a time-consuming nuisance that's best to avoid. The commands in Table A-11 enable you to include the kernel support you need while the system is running, without having to rebuild the entire thing from scratch.

Table A-11	Kernel Support Commands
Command	*Purpose*
depmod	Regenerates your module dependencies.
insmod	Loads a module by hand.
lsmod	Lists the modules your kernel has loaded.
modprobe	Loads a module by hand along with its dependencies and settings.
rmmod	Unloads a module by hand.

Processes

Most of your system activity requires processes. Even when your system appears idle, a dozen or so processes (programs) are running in the background. These commands, shown in Table A-12, enable you to check under the hood to make sure that everything that needs to be running is running and that you're not overheating or overtaxing resources:

Table A-12	Process Commands
Command	**Purpose**
crontab	Sets up commands to run at regular intervals.
kill	Stops a process by its number. Often used as kill -9 for a harsh stop for something that won't die.
killall	Stops a process by name rather than number.
nice	Assigns a CPU use priority to a process.
pidof	Gets a program's ID number.
ps	Gets a lot of programs' ID numbers, usually used as ps aux.
pstree	Shows the relationships between programs.
renice	Changes a program's CPU use priority.
top	Shows resource use over time.

Appendix B

About the DVD-ROM

he DVD-ROM included with this book contains everything you need to install and run Fedora Core 5. This is the equivalent of the four CD-ROMs you would have to download from the Fedora Project's Web site and includes the following:

- **Fedora Core 5:** A complete copy of the software for the latest and greatest version of the Red Hat—sponsored free version of Linux, for your computing pleasure. If you are interested in the source code, you can download it directly from Red Hat's Fedora Project site at `http://fedora.redhat.com`. We thought that you might not mind us using the space that would have gone to multiple CD's worth of source code to include lots and lots of other software instead!

- **RPM (Red Hat Package Manager):** The Red Hat software distribution and installation management environment, wherein Linux updates and new facilities are packaged for easy installation on your Linux machine.

- **KDE (the K Desktop Environment) and GNOME (GNU Network Object Model Environment):** The two leading graphical user interfaces for Linux. You can pick the one you like best!

- **Mozilla Firefox:** The best-of-breed Web browser for your Linux machine, just waiting for your surfing pleasure.

- **Samba:** The best way to integrate Linux servers with Windows users. Samba lets your Linux machine masquerade as a Windows server so that Windows users can grab files and print documents hassle free.

- **Apache Web Server:** The world's most popular (or at least, most frequently used) Web server software.

- **Games!:** Tons of games; enough to help you procrastinate for weeks!

- **OpenOffice.org:** A full-featured and popular office suite.

If you don't have a DVD-ROM drive, send in the coupon in the back of this book to Wiley Publishing, Inc. to receive the complete CD set. (See coupon for details.)

But that's not all. This DVD also contains the ISO images (the files you can use to make your own CDs) for:

- ✔ The popular Knoppix 4.02 LiveCD
- ✔ The full version of Linspire Five-0, which you would normally have to buy
- ✔ A LiveDVD (see Chapter 4 for an explanation of a LiveDVD) version of the popular SuSE Linux 10 distribution
- ✔ The "open circulation" (free) version of Xandros 3
- ✔ The full, free version of Mandriva 2006; another popular distribution

(See Chapters 1 and 4 for more information on these distributions.)

Both the Xandros and Mandriva ISO images are zipped, meaning that they are in files that end in .zip. Zip files are compressed, and you can open them in Windows by double-clicking them and using the built-in compression tool, or by downloading WinZip (www.winzip.com) to do the work for you. Once you have these files unzipped, you can handle them just as you would any other ISO.

For Fedora and Knoppix, you can use these directly off the DVD-ROM. The others can use your own CD burning software and (legally) use it to write the ISO images to CDs. While Ubuntu is covered in this book, there was no room for it on the DVD-ROM. Chapter 4 explains where to download this distribution.

Make sure that you tell your CD burner you're working with ISO images (usually the option has something to do with the word "image"). If you burn the CD and find that it contains just one big file (the ISO file), it will not work. The ISO image actually contains all the files that would be on the CD, so if you put the CD in and find that it contains many files, the CD was created properly.

System Requirements

Make sure that your computer meets the following minimum system requirements. If your computer doesn't match up to most of these requirements, you may have problems when using the contents of the DVD-ROMs:

- ✔ **A PC with an Intel-compatible Pentium-class processor:** I recommend a 400 MHz Pentium IV or better for using Graphical mode, although for a heavy-use desktop system, "more is better."
- ✔ **At least 256MB of RAM:** You need at least 192MB of RAM for Graphical mode. (Linux can handle as much RAM as you can fit into a typical PC, and more is almost always better than less.)

✔ **At least 1GB of hard drive space:** I recommend 10GB if you want to install all the software from the DVD-ROM. You need less space if you don't install every program, but you should go ahead and make more than 10GB of space available, to give yourself more options and room for file storage. Again, more is better.

✔ **A DVD-ROM drive — double-speed (2x) or faster:** The faster the DVD-ROM drive, the faster your installation experience. A coupon is offered in this book if you need to order CDs to replace the DVD.

✔ **Just about any VGA monitor:** Just about any monitor does the trick, but you want one that's capable of displaying at least 256 colors or grayscale.

✔ **A keyboard and a mouse:** You need both items so that you have a way to communicate with your Linux system and tell it what to do!

✔ **Some kind of network connection:** Again, the faster your Internet connection, the less time it takes to update your installation to the most recent versions. I use a cable modem for my Internet connection, and I like the increased speed when it comes to dealing with the many and varied sources of Linux software and updates online. See Chapter 8 on the various ways to connect to the Internet.

If you need more information on PC basics, check out *PCs For Dummies* by Dan Gookin (published by Wiley Publishing, Inc.).

Using the DVD-ROM

You can take either of two basic approaches to using the Fedora Core installation DVD-ROM. I cover each one in separate step-by-step lists. I tell you in this section how to pick which set of instructions to follow. The two ways to use this DVD-ROM are shown in this list:

✔ If you can boot from your DVD-ROM drive (which probably means that you have a newer PC), follow the instructions in the following section.

✔ If you can't boot from your DVD-ROM drive, for whatever reason, you may want to use the coupons included in this book to obtain CD-ROMs, or to download and burn CD-ROMs yourself as discussed in Chapters 3 and 4.

Booting from the DVD-ROM

To install items from the DVD-ROM to your hard drive, follow these steps:

1. **Insert the DVD-ROM into your computer's DVD-ROM drive.**

2. **Reboot your PC.**

As long as your PC is configured to boot from the DVD-ROM, this step starts the Linux installation process for you automatically.

3. **To install Fedora type** `linux` **and press Enter, or to boot into Knoppix without having to install anything, just press Enter.**

Congratulations! The Linux installation process is now underway. For the rest of the gory details on this fascinating task, please consult Chapter 3. If you had to order the CD-ROMs, then boot with the first CD for the same effect as booting with the DVD.

And some people say that installing Linux is hard! What could be easier than this? On the other hand, if all you want to do is investigate the contents of the Linux installation DVD-ROM, simply insert it into your machine's DVD-ROM drive. After that, you can browse through the DVD-ROM's contents right there in Windows. The contents are described in the following section.

What You Find in Fedora Core 5

Here's a summary of the software on the DVD-ROM, arranged by directory organization. If you use Windows, the DVD-ROM interface helps you navigate the DVD-ROM easily; you can use most of its contents only if you already have Linux installed.

The contents of the DVD consist of all four installation CD-ROMs' worth of material for Fedora Core 5, plus the ISO files discussed earlier in this chapter. Not all the software is installed automatically. You find out in Chapters 3 and 12 how to customize what's added. Aside from that, the DVD has useful install utilities and a handy-dandy README file that explains precisely what you find. The directory structure may look similar to the following (except for lacking my handy annotations, of course):

```
/media/cdrom
    |----> Fedora
    |           |----> RPMS       -- binary packages, incl:
    |           |                      OS, GUIs, Apache, etc.
    |           |----> base       -- info on release 5
    |                                  used by install process
    |----> images                 -- boot & driver disk
    |                                  images
    |----> isolinux               -- boot files
    |----> repodata               -- software repository
              information
                                  used for the install
    |----> README                 -- general read me file
    |----> RELEASE-NOTES          -- current info about this
              release
    |----> RPM-GPG-KEY            -- GPG sigs for Red Hat pkgs
```

Both CDs include *GPG signatures,* allowing the installer to check the contents of the files against the stored security data to make sure that the files haven't been changed. (The assumption is that all changes would be for the worse, such as Trojan horses or viruses.) Thus, signatures provide a way to make sure that everything is safe and wholesome for your computer!

If You've Got Problems (Of the DVD-ROM Kind)

I tried my best to locate programs that work on most computers with the minimum system requirements, as the Fedora team did for its operating system. Alas, your computer may differ, and some programs may not work properly for some reason.

The two likeliest problems are that you don't have enough memory (RAM) for the programs you want to use or that you have other programs running that are affecting the installation or running of a program. If you see error messages like `Not enough memory` or `Setup cannot continue,` try one or more of the following methods and then try using the software again:

- ✔ **Close all running programs.** The more programs you're running, the less memory is available to other programs. Installers also typically update files and programs; if you keep other programs running, the installation may not work properly.

- ✔ **In Linux, close your GUI environment and run demos or installations directly from a command line.** The interface itself can tie up system memory or even conflict with certain kinds of interactive demos. Use the command prompt to browse files on the DVD-ROM and launch installers or demos.

- ✔ **Have your local computer store add more RAM to your computer.** This step is, admittedly, a drastic and potentially expensive one, depending on the price of RAM at the time. If you have a modern PC with less than 64MB of RAM, however, adding more memory can really help the speed of your computer and enable more programs to run at the same time.

If you still have trouble with the DVD-ROM, please call the Wiley Product Technical Support phone number at 1-800-762-2974. Outside the United States, call 1-317-572-3994. You can also contact Wiley Product Technical Support through the Internet at `www.wiley.com/techsupport`. Wiley Publishing provides technical support only for installation and other general quality control items; for technical support on the applications themselves, consult the program's vendor or author.

To place additional orders or to request information about other Wiley products, please call 1-800-225-5945.

Index

Notes

Notes

Notes

Notes

Wiley Publishing, Inc.
End-User License Agreement

READ THIS. You should carefully read these terms and conditions before opening the software packet(s) included with this book "Book". This is a license agreement "Agreement" between you and Wiley Publishing, Inc. "WPI". By opening the accompanying software packet(s), you acknowledge that you have read and accept the following terms and conditions. If you do not agree and do not want to be bound by such terms and conditions, promptly return the Book and the unopened software packet(s) to the place you obtained them for a full refund.

1. **License Grant.** WPI grants to you (either an individual or entity) a nonexclusive license to use one copy of the enclosed software program(s) (collectively, the "Software") solely for your own personal or business purposes on a single computer (whether a standard computer or a workstation component of a multi-user network). The Software is in use on a computer when it is loaded into temporary memory (RAM) or installed into permanent memory (hard disk, CD-ROM, or other storage device). WPI reserves all rights not expressly granted herein.

2. **Ownership.** WPI is the owner of all right, title, and interest, including copyright, in and to the compilation of the Software recorded on the disk(s), CD-ROM or DVD "Software Media". Copyright to the individual programs recorded on the Software Media is owned by the author or other authorized copyright owner of each program. Ownership of the Software and all proprietary rights relating thereto remain with WPI and its licensers.

3. **Restrictions on Use and Transfer.**

   (a) You may only (i) make one copy of the Software for backup or archival purposes, or (ii) transfer the Software to a single hard disk, provided that you keep the original for backup or archival purposes. You may not (i) rent or lease the Software, (ii) copy or reproduce the Software through a LAN or other network system or through any computer subscriber system or bulletin-board system, or (iii) modify, adapt, or create derivative works based on the Software.

   (b) You may not reverse engineer, decompile, or disassemble the Software. You may transfer the Software and user documentation on a permanent basis, provided that the transferee agrees to accept the terms and conditions of this Agreement and you retain no copies. If the Software is an update or has been updated, any transfer must include the most recent update and all prior versions.

4. **Restrictions on Use of Individual Programs.** You must follow the individual requirements and restrictions detailed for each individual program in the About the DVD appendix of this Book. These limitations are also contained in the individual license agreements recorded on the Software Media. These limitations may include a requirement that after using the program for a specified period of time, the user must pay a registration fee or discontinue use. By opening the Software packet(s), you will be agreeing to abide by the licenses and restrictions for these individual programs that are detailed in the About the DVD appendix and on the Software Media. None of the material on this Software Media or listed in this Book may ever be redistributed, in original or modified form, for commercial purposes.

5. Limited Warranty.

(a) WPI warrants that the Software and Software Media are free from defects in materials and workmanship under normal use for a period of sixty (60) days from the date of purchase of this Book. If WPI receives notification within the warranty period of defects in materials or workmanship, WPI will replace the defective Software Media.

(b) WPI AND THE AUTHOR(S) OF THE BOOK DISCLAIM ALL OTHER WARRANTIES, EXPRESS OR IMPLIED, INCLUDING WITHOUT LIMITATION IMPLIED WARRANTIES OF MER-CHANTABILITY AND FITNESS FOR A PARTICULAR PURPOSE, WITH RESPECT TO THE SOFTWARE, THE PROGRAMS, THE SOURCE CODE CONTAINED THEREIN, AND/OR THE TECHNIQUES DESCRIBED IN THIS BOOK. WPI DOES NOT WARRANT THAT THE FUNC-TIONS CONTAINED IN THE SOFTWARE WILL MEET YOUR REQUIREMENTS OR THAT THE OPERATION OF THE SOFTWARE WILL BE ERROR FREE.

(c) This limited warranty gives you specific legal rights, and you may have other rights that vary from jurisdiction to jurisdiction.

6. Remedies.

(a) WPI's entire liability and your exclusive remedy for defects in materials and workman-ship shall be limited to replacement of the Software Media, which may be returned to WPI with a copy of your receipt at the following address: Software Media Fulfillment Department, Attn.: *Linux For Dummies,* 7th Edition, Wiley Publishing, Inc., 10475 Crosspoint Blvd., Indianapolis, IN 46256, or call 1-800-762-2974. Please allow four to six weeks for delivery. This Limited Warranty is void if failure of the Software Media has resulted from accident, abuse, or misapplication. Any replacement Software Media will be warranted for the remainder of the original warranty period or thirty (30) days, whichever is longer.

(b) In no event shall WPI or the author be liable for any damages whatsoever (including without limitation damages for loss of business profits, business interruption, loss of business information, or any other pecuniary loss) arising from the use of or inability to use the Book or the Software, even if WPI has been advised of the possibility of such damages.

(c) Because some jurisdictions do not allow the exclusion or limitation of liability for conse-quential or incidental damages, the above limitation or exclusion may not apply to you.

7. U.S. Government Restricted Rights.
Use, duplication, or disclosure of the Software for or on behalf of the United States of America, its agencies and/or instrumentalities "U.S. Government" is subject to restrictions as stated in paragraph (c)(1)(ii) of the Rights in Technical Data and Computer Software clause of DFARS 252.227-7013, or subparagraphs (c) (1) and (2) of the Commercial Computer Software - Restricted Rights clause at FAR 52.227-19, and in similar clauses in the NASA FAR supplement, as applicable.

8. General.
This Agreement constitutes the entire understanding of the parties and revokes and supersedes all prior agreements, oral or written, between them and may not be modified or amended except in a writing signed by both parties hereto that specifically refers to this Agreement. This Agreement shall take precedence over any other documents that may be in conflict herewith. If any one or more provisions contained in this Agreement are held by any court or tribunal to be invalid, illegal, or otherwise unenforceable, each and every other pro-vision shall remain in full force and effect.

GNU General Public License

Version 2, June 1991
Copyright (C) 1989, 1991 Free Software Foundation, Inc.
59 Temple Place - Suite 330, Boston, MA 02111-1307, USA

Preamble

The licenses for most software are designed to take away your freedom to share and change it. By contrast, the GNU General Public License is intended to guarantee your freedom to share and change free software–to make sure the software is free for all its users. This General Public License applies to most of the Free Software Foundation's software and to any other program whose authors commit to using it. (Some other Free Software Foundation software is covered by the GNU Library General Public License instead.) You can apply it to your programs, too.

When we speak of free software, we are referring to freedom, not price. Our General Public Licenses are designed to make sure that you have the freedom to distribute copies of free software (and charge for this service if you wish), that you receive source code or can get it if you want it, that you can change the software or use pieces of it in new free programs; and that you know you can do these things.

To protect your rights, we need to make restrictions that forbid anyone to deny you these rights or to ask you to surrender the rights. These restrictions translate to certain responsibilities for you if you distribute copies of the software, or if you modify it.

For example, if you distribute copies of such a program, whether gratis or for a fee, you must give the recipients all the rights that you have. You must make sure that they, too, receive or can get the source code. And you must show them these terms so they know their rights.

We protect your rights with two steps: (1) copyright the software, and (2) offer you this license which gives you legal permission to copy, distribute and/or modify the software.

Also, for each author's protection and ours, we want to make certain that everyone understands that there is no warranty for this free software. If the software is modified by someone else and passed on, we want its recipients to know that what they have is not the original, so that any problems introduced by others will not reflect on the original authors' reputations.

Finally, any free program is threatened constantly by software patents. We wish to avoid the danger that redistributors of a free program will individually obtain patent licenses, in effect making the program proprietary. To prevent this, we have made it clear that any patent must be licensed for everyone's free use or not licensed at all.

The precise terms and conditions for copying, distribution and modification follow.

Terms and Conditions for Copying, Distribution and Modification

0. This License applies to any program or other work which contains a notice placed by the copyright holder saying it may be distributed under the terms of this General Public License. The "Program", below, refers to any such program or work, and a "work based on the Program" means either the Program or any derivative work under copyright law: that is to

say, a work containing the Program or a portion of it, either verbatim or with modifications and/or translated into another language. (Hereinafter, translation is included without limitation in the term "modification".) Each licensee is addressed as "you".

Activities other than copying, distribution and modification are not covered by this License; they are outside its scope. The act of running the Program is not restricted, and the output from the Program is covered only if its contents constitute a work based on the Program (independent of having been made by running the Program). Whether that is true depends on what the Program does.

1. You may copy and distribute verbatim copies of the Program's source code as you receive it, in any medium, provided that you conspicuously and appropriately publish on each copy an appropriate copyright notice and disclaimer of warranty; keep intact all the notices that refer to this License and to the absence of any warranty; and give any other recipients of the Program a copy of this License along with the Program.

   You may charge a fee for the physical act of transferring a copy, and you may at your option offer warranty protection in exchange for a fee.

2. You may modify your copy or copies of the Program or any portion of it, thus forming a work based on the Program, and copy and distribute such modifications or work under the terms of Section 1 above, provided that you also meet all of these conditions:

   a) You must cause the modified files to carry prominent notices stating that you changed the files and the date of any change.

   b) You must cause any work that you distribute or publish, that in whole or in part contains or is derived from the Program or any part thereof, to be licensed as a whole at no charge to all third parties under the terms of this License.

   c) If the modified program normally reads commands interactively when run, you must cause it, when started running for such interactive use in the most ordinary way, to print or display an announcement including an appropriate copyright notice and a notice that there is no warranty (or else, saying that you provide a warranty) and that users may redistribute the program under these conditions, and telling the user how to view a copy of this License. (Exception: if the Program itself is interactive but does not normally print such an announcement, your work based on the Program is not required to print an announcement.)

   These requirements apply to the modified work as a whole. If identifiable sections of that work are not derived from the Program, and can be reasonably considered independent and separate works in themselves, then this License, and its terms, do not apply to those sections when you distribute them as separate works. But when you distribute the same sections as part of a whole which is a work based on the Program, the distribution of the whole must be on the terms of this License, whose permissions for other licensees extend to the entire whole, and thus to each and every part regardless of who wrote it.

   Thus, it is not the intent of this section to claim rights or contest your rights to work written entirely by you; rather, the intent is to exercise the right to control the distribution of derivative or collective works based on the Program.

   In addition, mere aggregation of another work not based on the Program with the Program (or with a work based on the Program) on a volume of a storage or distribution medium does not bring the other work under the scope of this License.

3. You may copy and distribute the Program (or a work based on it, under Section 2) in object code or executable form under the terms of Sections 1 and 2 above provided that you also do one of the following:

a) Accompany it with the complete corresponding machine-readable source code, which must be distributed under the terms of Sections 1 and 2 above on a medium customarily used for software interchange; or,

b) Accompany it with a written offer, valid for at least three years, to give any third party, for a charge no more than your cost of physically performing source distribution, a complete machine-readable copy of the corresponding source code, to be distributed under the terms of Sections 1 and 2 above on a medium customarily used for software interchange; or,

c) Accompany it with the information you received as to the offer to distribute corresponding source code. (This alternative is allowed only for noncommercial distribution and only if you received the program in object code or executable form with such an offer, in accord with Subsection b above.)

The source code for a work means the preferred form of the work for making modifications to it. For an executable work, complete source code means all the source code for all modules it contains, plus any associated interface definition files, plus the scripts used to control compilation and installation of the executable. However, as a special exception, the source code distributed need not include anything that is normally distributed (in either source or binary form) with the major components (compiler, kernel, and so on) of the operating system on which the executable runs, unless that component itself accompanies the executable.

If distribution of executable or object code is made by offering access to copy from a designated place, then offering equivalent access to copy the source code from the same place counts as distribution of the source code, even though third parties are not compelled to copy the source along with the object code.

4. You may not copy, modify, sublicense, or distribute the Program except as expressly provided under this License. Any attempt otherwise to copy, modify, sublicense or distribute the Program is void, and will automatically terminate your rights under this License. However, parties who have received copies, or rights, from you under this License will not have their licenses terminated so long as such parties remain in full compliance.

5. You are not required to accept this License, since you have not signed it. However, nothing else grants you permission to modify or distribute the Program or its derivative works. These actions are prohibited by law if you do not accept this License. Therefore, by modifying or distributing the Program (or any work based on the Program), you indicate your acceptance of this License to do so, and all its terms and conditions for copying, distributing or modifying the Program or works based on it.

6. Each time you redistribute the Program (or any work based on the Program), the recipient automatically receives a license from the original licensor to copy, distribute or modify the Program subject to these terms and conditions. You may not impose any further restrictions on the recipients' exercise of the rights granted herein. You are not responsible for enforcing compliance by third parties to this License.

7. If, as a consequence of a court judgment or allegation of patent infringement or for any other reason (not limited to patent issues), conditions are imposed on you (whether by court order, agreement or otherwise) that contradict the conditions of this License, they do not excuse you from the conditions of this License. If you cannot distribute so as to satisfy simultaneously your obligations under this License and any other pertinent obligations, then as a consequence you may not distribute the Program at all. For example, if a patent license would not permit royalty-free redistribution of the Program by all those who receive copies directly or indirectly through you, then the only way you could satisfy both it and this License would be to refrain entirely from distribution of the Program.

If any portion of this section is held invalid or unenforceable under any particular circumstance, the balance of the section is intended to apply and the section as a whole is intended to apply in other circumstances.

It is not the purpose of this section to induce you to infringe any patents or other property right claims or to contest validity of any such claims; this section has the sole purpose of protecting the integrity of the free software distribution system, which is implemented by public license practices. Many people have made generous contributions to the wide range of software distributed through that system in reliance on consistent application of that system; it is up to the author/donor to decide if he or she is willing to distribute software through any other system and a licensee cannot impose that choice.

This section is intended to make thoroughly clear what is believed to be a consequence of the rest of this License.

8. If the distribution and/or use of the Program is restricted in certain countries either by patents or by copyrighted interfaces, the original copyright holder who places the Program under this License may add an explicit geographical distribution limitation excluding those countries, so that distribution is permitted only in or among countries not thus excluded. In such case, this License incorporates the limitation as if written in the body of this License.

9. The Free Software Foundation may publish revised and/or new versions of the General Public License from time to time. Such new versions will be similar in spirit to the present version, but may differ in detail to address new problems or concerns.

Each version is given a distinguishing version number. If the Program specifies a version number of this License which applies to it and "any later version", you have the option of following the terms and conditions either of that version or of any later version published by the Free Software Foundation. If the Program does not specify a version number of this License, you may choose any version ever published by the Free Software Foundation.

10. If you wish to incorporate parts of the Program into other free programs whose distribution conditions are different, write to the author to ask for permission. For software which is copyrighted by the Free Software Foundation, write to the Free Software Foundation; we sometimes make exceptions for this. Our decision will be guided by the two goals of preserving the free status of all derivatives of our free software and of promoting the sharing and reuse of software generally.

NO WARRANTY

11. BECAUSE THE PROGRAM IS LICENSED FREE OF CHARGE, THERE IS NO WARRANTY FOR THE PROGRAM, TO THE EXTENT PERMITTED BY APPLICABLE LAW. EXCEPT WHEN OTHERWISE STATED IN WRITING THE COPYRIGHT HOLDERS AND/OR OTHER PARTIES PROVIDE THE PROGRAM "AS IS" WITHOUT WARRANTY OF ANY KIND, EITHER EXPRESSED OR IMPLIED, INCLUDING, BUT NOT LIMITED TO, THE IMPLIED WARRANTIES OF MERCHANTABILITY AND FITNESS FOR A PARTICULAR PURPOSE. THE ENTIRE RISK AS TO THE QUALITY AND PERFORMANCE OF THE PROGRAM IS WITH YOU. SHOULD THE PROGRAM PROVE DEFECTIVE, YOU ASSUME THE COST OF ALL NECESSARY SERVICING, REPAIR OR CORRECTION.

12. IN NO EVENT UNLESS REQUIRED BY APPLICABLE LAW OR AGREED TO IN WRITING WILL ANY COPYRIGHT HOLDER, OR ANY OTHER PARTY WHO MAY MODIFY AND/OR REDISTRIBUTE THE PROGRAM AS PERMITTED ABOVE, BE LIABLE TO YOU FOR DAMAGES, INCLUDING ANY GENERAL, SPECIAL, INCIDENTAL OR CONSEQUENTIAL DAMAGES ARISING OUT OF THE USE OR INABILITY TO USE THE PROGRAM (INCLUDING BUT NOT LIMITED TO LOSS OF DATA OR DATA BEING RENDERED INACCURATE OR LOSSES SUSTAINED BY YOU OR THIRD PARTIES OR A FAILURE OF THE PROGRAM TO OPERATE WITH ANY OTHER PROGRAMS), EVEN IF SUCH HOLDER OR OTHER PARTY HAS BEEN ADVISED OF THE POSSIBILITY OF SUCH DAMAGES.

END OF TERMS AND CONDITIONS

nt Writing

7645-5307-0

Home Buying

0-7645-5331-3 *†

Also available:

- Accounting For Dummies †
  0-7645-5314-3
- Business Plans Kit For Dummies †
  0-7645-5365-8
- Cover Letters For Dummies
  0-7645-5224-4
- Frugal Living For Dummies
  0-7645-5403-4
- Leadership For Dummies
  0-7645-5176-0
- Managing For Dummies
  0-7645-1771-6

- Marketing For Dummies
  0-7645-5600-2
- Personal Finance For Dummies *
  0-7645-2590-5
- Project Management For Dummies
  0-7645-5283-X
- Resumes For Dummies †
  0-7645-5471-9
- Selling For Dummies
  0-7645-5363-1
- Small Business Kit For Dummies *†
  0-7645-5093-4

ndows XP / **Excel 2003**

7645-4074-2

0-7645-3758-X

Also available:

- ACT! 6 For Dummies
  0-7645-2645-6
- iLife '04 All-in-One Desk Reference
  For Dummies
  0-7645-7347-0
- iPAQ For Dummies
  0-7645-6769-1
- Mac OS X Panther Timesaving
  Techniques For Dummies
  0-7645-5812-9
- Macs For Dummies
  0-7645-5656-8

- Microsoft Money 2004 For Dummies
  0-7645-4195-1
- Office 2003 All-in-One Desk Reference
  For Dummies
  0-7645-3883-7
- Outlook 2003 For Dummies
  0-7645-3759-8
- PCs For Dummies
  0-7645-4074-2
- TiVo For Dummies
  0-7645-6923-6
- Upgrading and Fixing PCs For Dummies
  0-7645-1665-5
- Windows XP Timesaving Techniques
  For Dummies
  0-7645-3748-2

ng Shui

7645-5295-3

Poker

0-7645-5232-5

Also available:

- Bass Guitar For Dummies
  0-7645-2487-9
- Diabetes Cookbook For Dummies
  0-7645-5230-9
- Gardening For Dummies *
  0-7645-5130-2
- Guitar For Dummies
  0-7645-5106-X
- Holiday Decorating For Dummies
  0-7645-2570-0
- Home Improvement All-in-One
  For Dummies
  0-7645-5680-0

- Knitting For Dummies
  0-7645-5395-X
- Piano For Dummies
  0-7645-5105-1
- Puppies For Dummies
  0-7645-5255-4
- Scrapbooking For Dummies
  0-7645-7208-3
- Senior Dogs For Dummies
  0-7645-5818-8
- Singing For Dummies
  0-7645-2475-5
- 30-Minute Meals For Dummies
  0-7645-2589-1

Digital otography

7645-1664-7

Starting an eBay Business

0-7645-6924-4

Also available:

- 2005 Online Shopping Directory
  For Dummies
  0-7645-7495-7
- CD & DVD Recording For Dummies
  0-7645-5956-7
- eBay For Dummies
  0-7645-5654-1
- Fighting Spam For Dummies
  0-7645-5965-6
- Genealogy Online For Dummies
  0-7645-5964-8
- Google For Dummies
  0-7645-4420-9

- Home Recording For Musicians
  For Dummies
  0-7645-1634-5
- The Internet For Dummies
  0-7645-4173-0
- iPod & iTunes For Dummies
  0-7645-7772-7
- Preventing Identity Theft For Dummies
  0-7645-7336-5
- Pro Tools All-in-One Desk Reference
  For Dummies
  0-7645-5714-9
- Roxio Easy Media Creator For Dummies
  0-7645-7131-1

*e Canadian edition also available

*e U.K. edition also available

wherever books are sold. For more information or to order direct: U.S. customers visit www.dummies.com or call 1-877-762-2974.
mers visit www.wileyeurope.com or call 0800 243407. Canadian customers visit www.wiley.ca or call 1-800-567-4797.

WILEY

SPORTS, FITNESS, PARENTING, RELIGION & SPIRITUALITY

0-7645-5146-9

0-7645-5418-2

Also available:

Adoption For Dummies
0-7645-5488-3

Basketball For Dummies
0-7645-5248-1

The Bible For Dummies
0-7645-5296-1

Buddhism For Dummies
0-7645-5359-3

Catholicism For Dummies
0-7645-5391-7

Hockey For Dummies
0-7645-5228-7

Judaism For Dummies
0-7645-5299-6

Martial Arts For Dummies
0-7645-5358-5

Pilates For Dummies
0-7645-5397-6

Religion For Dummies
0-7645-5264-3

Teaching Kids to Read For Dun
0-7645-4043-2

Weight Training For Dummies
0-7645-5168-X

Yoga For Dummies
0-7645-5117-5

TRAVEL

0-7645-5438-7

0-7645-5453-0

Also available:

Alaska For Dummies
0-7645-1761-9

Arizona For Dummies
0-7645-6938-4

Cancún and the Yucatán For Dummies
0-7645-2437-2

Cruise Vacations For Dummies
0-7645-6941-4

Europe For Dummies
0-7645-5456-5

Ireland For Dummies
0-7645-5455-7

Las Vegas For Dummies
0-7645-5448-4

London For Dummies
0-7645-4277-X

New York City For Dummies
0-7645-6945-7

Paris For Dummies
0-7645-5494-8

RV Vacations For Dummies
0-7645-5443-3

Walt Disney World & Orlando For D
0-7645-6943-0

GRAPHICS, DESIGN & WEB DEVELOPMENT

0-7645-4345-8

0-7645-5589-8

Also available:

Adobe Acrobat 6 PDF For Dummies
0-7645-3760-1

Building a Web Site For Dummies
0-7645-7144-3

Dreamweaver MX 2004 For Dummies
0-7645-4342-3

FrontPage 2003 For Dummies
0-7645-3882-9

HTML 4 For Dummies
0-7645-1995-6

Illustrator CS For Dummies
0-7645-4084-X

Macromedia Flash MX 2004 For D
0-7645-4358-X

Photoshop 7 All-in-One Desk
Reference For Dummies
0-7645-1667-1

Photoshop CS Timesaving Tech
For Dummies
0-7645-6782-9

PHP 5 For Dummies
0-7645-4166-8

PowerPoint 2003 For Dummies
0-7645-3908-6

QuarkXPress 6 For Dummies
0-7645-2593-X

NETWORKING, SECURITY, PROGRAMMING & DATABASES

0-7645-6852-3

0-7645-5784-X

Also available:

A+ Certification For Dummies
0-7645-4187-0

Access 2003 All-in-One Desk
Reference For Dummies
0-7645-3988-4

Beginning Programming For Dummies
0-7645-4997-9

C For Dummies
0-7645-7068-4

Firewalls For Dummies
0-7645-4048-3

Home Networking For Dummies
0-7645-42796

Network Security For Dummies
0-7645-1679-5

Networking For Dummies
0-7645-1677-9

TCP/IP For Dummies
0-7645-1760-0

VBA For Dummies
0-7645-3989-2

Wireless All In-One Desk Refere
For Dummies
0-7645-7496-5

Wireless Home Networking For D
0-7645-3910-8

& SELF-HELP

5-6820-5 *†   0-7645-2566-2

Also available:

- Alzheimer's For Dummies
  0-7645-3899-3
- Asthma For Dummies
  0-7645-4233-8
- Controlling Cholesterol For Dummies
  0-7645-5440-9
- Depression For Dummies
  0-7645-3900-0
- Dieting For Dummies
  0-7645-4149-8
- Fertility For Dummies
  0-7645-2549-2

- Fibromyalgia For Dummies
  0-7645-5441-7
- Improving Your Memory For Dummies
  0-7645-5435-2
- Pregnancy For Dummies †
  0-7645-4483-7
- Quitting Smoking For Dummies
  0-7645-2629-4
- Relationships For Dummies
  0-7645-5384-4
- Thyroid For Dummies
  0-7645-5385-2

TION, HISTORY, REFERENCE & TEST PREPARATION

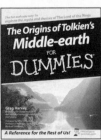

45-5194-9   0-7645-4186-2

Also available:

- Algebra For Dummies
  0-7645-5325-9
- British History For Dummies
  0-7645-7021-8
- Calculus For Dummies
  0-7645-2498-4
- English Grammar For Dummies
  0-7645-5322-4
- Forensics For Dummies
  0-7645-5580-4
- The GMAT For Dummies
  0-7645-5251-1
- Inglés Para Dummies
  0-7645-5427-1

- Italian For Dummies
  0-7645-5196-5
- Latin For Dummies
  0-7645-5431-X
- Lewis & Clark For Dummies
  0-7645-2545-X
- Research Papers For Dummies
  0-7645-5426-3
- The SAT I For Dummies
  0-7645-7193-1
- Science Fair Projects For Dummies
  0-7645-5460-3
- U.S. History For Dummies
  0-7645-5249-X

Get smart @ dummies.com®

- **Find a full list of Dummies titles**
- **Look into loads of FREE on-site articles**
- **Sign up for FREE eTips e-mailed to you weekly**
- **See what other products carry the Dummies name**
- **Shop directly from the Dummies bookstore**
- **Enter to win new prizes every month!**

* Canadian edition also available
* U.K. edition also available

herever books are sold. For more information or to order direct: U.S. customers visit www.dummies.com or call 1-877-762-2974.
ers visit www.wileyeurope.com or call 0800 243407. Canadian customers visit www.wiley.ca or call 1-800-567-4797.

Linux® For Dummies®, 7th Edition
Source Code Offer

To comply with the GNU GPL, we provide separately the Linux source code. Anyone may use this fulfillment offer to receive the source code on DVD. If you'd like the source code sent to you, please follow the instructions below to order by phone, online, or coupon.

For each ordering method, please use ISBN: 0470049871 when prompted. The cost is $2.04 (USD) plus shipping.

Terms: Void where prohibited or restricted by law. Allow 2-4 weeks for delivery.

To order by phone:

Call toll free in the United States: 1-877-762-2974. International customers, dial 1-317-572-3994. Give the operator the appropriate ISBN. Please have your credit card ready.

To order online:

Go to http://www.wiley.com/
Use the Product Search feature to search for Linux For Dummies 7E Source Code or 0470049871. Place the item in the shopping cart.

To order by coupon:

Complete the coupon below.

Include a check or money order for $2.04 (USD) plus shipping. To find out the shipping costs, call 1-877-762-2974 in the US or 1-317-572-3994 for international customers.

Send it to us at the address listed at the bottom of the coupon.

Name _____

Company _____

Address _____

City _____ **State** _____ **Postal Code** _____ **Country** _____

E-mail _____ **Telephone** _____

Place where book was purchased _____

☐ Check here to find out what we're up to by joining our email list — a convenient way to receive news about our products and events as well as about special discount offers.

Return this coupon with the appropriate US funds to:

Wiley Publishing, Inc.
Customer Care
Linux For Dummies, 7th Edition - Source Code [0470049871]
10475 Crosspoint Blvd.
Indianapolis, IN 46256

Terms: Wiley is not responsible for lost, stolen, late, or illegible orders. For questions regarding this fulfillment offer, please call us at 1-877-762-2974 or 1-317-572-3994.